Khubilai Khan

Portrait of Khubilai Khan. National Palace Museum, Taipei.

Khubilai Khan

His Life and Times

Morris Rossabi

UNIVERSITY OF CALIFORNIA PRESS
Berkeley · Los Angeles · London

950.2
Ros

University of California Press
Berkeley and Los Angeles, California

University of California Press, Ltd.
London, England

© 1988 by
The Regents of the University of California

The University of California Press gratefully acknowledges
support from the China Publication Subventions program.

Library of Congress Cataloging-in-Publication Data

Rossabi, Morris.
    Khubilai Khan: his life and times.

    Includes bibliographies and index.
    1. Khubilai Khan, 1215-1294.   2. Mongols—History.
3. China—Kings and rulers—Biography.   I. Title.
DS452.6.K83R67   1987   950'.2'0924 [B]   86-25031
ISBN 0-520-05913-1 (alk. paper)

Printed in the United States of America

1   2   3   4   5   6   7   8   9

*To the memory of my father, Joseph
Rossabi, and my friend and colleague
Professor Joseph F. Fletcher, Jr.*

Contents

Illustrations

Preface

Khubilai Khan was a real person. Though Samuel Taylor Coleridge's poem "Kubla Khan" persuaded many readers that Khubilai was a mythical or legendary figure, he was most assuredly an actor on the historical stage, who not only influenced China and much of Asia but also affected the course of European history. Many of his contemporaries throughout the world had heard of him, and he is mentioned in thirteenth- and fourteenth-century books written in a variety of languages. Similarly, artists from different lands painted his portrait. He is represented as a Mongol in formal Chinese paintings; as a typical Muslim potentate, with the dress and physical features of a caliph, in Persian miniatures; and as a European king, with a Caucasian appearance, in manuscripts of Marco Polo's account of his travels. Each civilization depicted Khubilai in its own light. As a result his fame spread throughout the world.

His life and career spanned the rise and decline of the Mongol empire. He was born in 1215, the year in which his grandfather Chinggis Khan seized Peking, and his death in 1294 coincided with the deterioration and dismemberment of the Mongol empire that had been gradually created from the early thirteenth century on. He was significant because he was the first of the Mongol rulers to make the transition from a nomadic conqueror from the steppes to effective ruler of a sedentary society. His reign in China witnessed the construction of a capital city, the development of a legal code and a new written script for all the languages in the Mongol domains, and court patronage of the theater, the arts and crafts, and science and medicine.

Despite Khubilai's role in Asian, if not world, history, he has not been accorded a serious biography. Walker Chapman has written a charming children's book about him, but it is based exclusively on English-language sources. The two Japanese biographies, by Otagi Matsuo and Katsufuji Takeshi, and the Chinese biography, by Li T'ang, have relied principally on the Chinese accounts and have hardly consulted the Middle Eastern and European sources. I have found all four works useful and do not wish to detract from the authors' contributions. Yet there is room for a new scholarly biography of the Great Khan.

After I had completed the manuscript for this book, I came across a 1986 biography of Khubilai Khan by Chou Liang-hsiao. Although it is based only on Chinese sources, Chou's biography merely confirms the themes I present in this book.

One of the difficulties that previous biographers and I have faced lies in the sources. The majority of the official Chinese histories, the most voluminous of the sources, portrayed Khubilai as a typical Confucian ruler, not as a real human being. Anecdotes and personal information and vignettes were scarce. The prospects for a study of the life of Khubilai Khan thus appeared to be discouraging. Some years ago when I first conceived of a biography of the Great Khan, I initially read and translated the annals (*pen-chi*) of his thirty-four-year reign in the Chinese dynastic history (*Yüan shih*). The annals consisted of an almost day-by-day description of official events at court—the visits of foreign envoys, the promotion of officials, and the announcement of domestic policies, for example. But they yielded few clues about Khubilai's personality and his ideas and programs. They emphasized Khubilai's bureaucratic role and offered but a glimpse of him as a person. A biography based merely on the Chinese records could not be written. Moreover, since the Mongol written language had just developed at the time of Khubilai's birth and no real tradition of historical writing existed, few if any contemporary native sources were at hand. Fortunately, other sources were available. Since the Mongol empire encompassed much of Asia, historians and travelers representing other cultures wrote about the Great Khan. The Persian historian Rashīd al-Dīn, the Korean officials who compiled their own court chronicle, the *Koryŏ-sa*, and Russian, Arab, Armenian, and Syriac writers provided interesting and useful vignettes concerning Khubilai that supplemented the Chinese accounts. Similarly, the Venetian traveler Marco Polo wrote at great length and with abundant detail about Khubilai's court. This combination of sources offered sufficient details for a study of Khubilai's life and times. When there are gaps in our knowledge, I have so indicated. But I think the main features and themes of his life and career are discernible in the available sources.

Historical research and writing are, for the most part, solitary enterprises. A scholar spends much of his time alone in libraries or at home. Yet numerous organizations and individuals enable the scholar to pursue his research and facilitate his work. I have been fortunate enough to receive assistance and support that have proved invaluable in the completion of this book. I should like to take this opportunity to thank those who most directly influenced or helped me.

I am grateful to the National Endowment for the Humanities and the American Council of Learned Societies for awarding me fellowships to undertake the research and writing of this book. Their support permitted me the time and opportunity to travel to libraries and to the sites associated with Khubilai. The Harvard-Yenching Library at Harvard University, the East Asiatic Library at Columbia University, and the Library of Congress were the main repositories at which I worked. The librarians at all three of these great research centers were helpful and invaluable guides to the Oriental sources in their collections. Similarly, librarians at the Royal Library in Copenhagen, the Tōyō Bunko in Tokyo, and the National Palace Museum in Taipei facilitated my research, and I should like to thank them for their assistance and their courtesy. A number of museum curators offered vital leads for my studies. Dr. Thomas Lawton of the Freer Gallery of Art, Dr. Stan Czuma and Mr. Wai-kam Ho of the Cleveland Museum of Art, as well as curators at the Uzbek State Historical Museum in Tashkent, the State Historical Museum in Ulan Bator, the Kansu Provincial Museum in Lan-chou, and the British Museum, have provided encouragement and assistance at various critical stages, and I am grateful to them all.

Some of the ideas expressed in this book were first presented as speeches or lectures to a variety of scholars and laymen, and I want to thank these audiences for permitting me to test my hypotheses on them. The Columbia University Seminar on Traditional China, the Program in East Asian Studies at Princeton University, the Oriental Studies Program at the University of Pennsylvania, the East Asian Studies Program at the University of Toronto, the Harvard University

Seminar on Inner Asia, the Middle Eastern Program at Ohio State University, the International Conference on Islam at the Hebrew University in Jerusalem, the East Asian programs at Oberlin College and at the University of Kansas, the Middle Eastern Center at the University of Chicago, and the Chinese Studies Program at the University of Ghent offered congenial forums for the discussion of Khubilai and his times. I should like to thank the participants at these meetings for their questions and comments, and I am particularly grateful to those scholars who invited me to attend and to address these sessions: Professor Hans Bielenstein of Columbia, Professor Frederick Mote of Princeton, Professor Susan Naquin of the University of Pennsylvania, Professor Wayne Schlepp at Toronto, the late Professor Joseph Fletcher, Jr., at Harvard, Professor Stephen Dale at Ohio State, Professor Rafi Israeli at the Hebrew University, Professor Dale Johnson at Oberlin, Professor Wallace Johnson at Kansas, Professor John Woods at the University of Chicago, and Professor Charles Willemen at Ghent. Dr. John Langlois, formerly of Bowdoin College, invited me to present a paper on Khubilai Khan and Islam at a scholarly conference on China under Mongol Rule, sponsored by the American Council of Learned Societies, and I convened a conference on International Relations in East Asia, Tenth through Fourteenth Centuries, also funded by the ACLS. The discussions at these sessions helped me clarify my ideas about Khubilai and his era. Speeches in front of general audiences at the Asia Society in New York City, Iona College, the Wilton Public Library in Wilton, Connecticut, the Cosmopolitan Club, the Brearley School, the Cathedral School, and the Fieldston School in New York were not only enjoyable but also stimulating. The questions at the end of these presentations compelled me to rethink some ill-founded assumptions.

Doris Tomburello typed this book with the same dispatch and accuracy that she has my previous writings. I am deeply grateful for her care in detecting a number of careless errors. Other friends or colleagues who have helped me include Professor Charles Peterson of Cornell, Professor Herbert Franke of the University of Munich, Mr. and Mrs. Gordon Derzon, Mrs. Debora Kramer, Mr. George Moulton, Dr. and Mrs. Stan Czuma, Dr. Andrew Nemeth of the University of Pennsylvania, Professor Hok-lam Chan of the University of Washington, Mr. Peter Stern, Mr. William Frost, Ms. Gretchen Dykstra, Joseph and Françoise Shein, Jane and Thomas Martin, and Drs. Dennis and Catherine Niewoehner. I am also grateful to Sheila Levine,

Sally Serafim, and Susan Stone of the University of California Press for their valuable contributions to the book.

The members of my family helped to expedite the completion of this book. My parents, Mr. and Mrs. Joseph Rossabi, my brother and sister-in-law Mayer and Naomi Rossabi, my uncle, Clement Hakim, my mother-in-law, Mrs. John Herrmann, Sr., and my brother-in-law and sister-in-law, Mr. and Mrs. John Herrmann, Jr., provided shelter for my wife, my children, and me in New York in the early days of my research, and they assisted in numerous other ways as well. My daughter Amy and my son Tony helped in many ways—from offering words when I was stumped in my writing to baking cookies when I needed sustenance to playing ball when they decided I was too sedentary. My wife Mary deserves much of the credit for this book. She was its first reader and editor and its best critic. Like Khubilai's wife Chabi, she has proved to be an indispensable helpmate. For all this and much more, I am very grateful.

I should point out that the original manuscript of this book was over twice the present size. For additional details, the reader may consult it at the East Asiatic Library of Columbia University.

Note on Transliteration

The following standard systems have been adopted for the transliteration of Oriental names and terms: Wade-Giles for Chinese, Hepburn for Japanese, and McCune-Reischauer for Korean. The only exceptions are for names and terms (e.g., Peking, Canton,) that have become commonly accepted in English. I use Hangchow instead of the contemporary term Lin-an. The Royal Asiatic Society system has been used for the transliteration of Persian. Again, certain generally accepted terms and names employed in English have been retained.

Antoine Mostaert's scheme for the transliteration of Mongolian, as modified by Francis W. Cleaves, has been used except for these deviations:

č is ch,
š is sh,
γ is gh,
q is kh, and ǰ is j.

CHAPTER ONE

The Early Mongols

Khubilai Khan lived during the height of Mongol power. He was born at the beginning of the Mongol expansion and grew up as Mongol armies spread far to the north and west. Khubilai and his grandfather Chinggis were the most renowned of the Mongols in this glorious period of their and indeed Eurasian history. Eurasian history begins with the Mongols. Within a few decades in the thirteenth century, they had carved out the most sizable empire in world history, stretching from Korea to Western Russia in the north and from Burma to Iraq in the south. Their armies reached all the way to Poland and to Hungary. In the process, they destroyed some of the most powerful dynasties of their age: the ʿAbbāsid rulers of the Middle East and Persia, the Chin and Southern Sung dynasties of China, the Khwāraz-mian khanate of Central Asia. For a generation, the Mongols were masters of much of Eurasia and terrorized the rest.

Though their empire lasted less than a century, it inextricably linked Europe to Asia,[1] ushering in an era of frequent and extended contacts between East and West. And, once the Mongols had achieved relative stability and order in their newly acquired domains, they neither discouraged nor impeded relations with foreigners. Though they never abandoned their claims of universal rule, they were hospitable to foreign travelers, even those whose monarchs had not submitted to them. They expedited and encouraged travel in the sizable section of Asia that was under Mongol rule,[2] permitting European merchants, craftsmen, and envoys, for the first time, to journey as far as China. Asian goods reached Europe along the caravan trails, and the ensuing European demand for these products eventually inspired the search for a sea route to Asia. Thus, the Mongol era indirectly led to the European age of exploration of the fifteenth century, which culminated in the discovery of the sea route around the Cape of Good Hope to Asia and in Christopher Columbus's unsuccessful effort to find a western route to the Indies.

The Mongols accomplished much more than simply linking Europe and Asia. They governed many of the territories they had seized. With the indispensable help of Chinese, Persian, and Turkic advisers and administrators, they progressed from plunderers to rulers. They set up governments and bureaucracies, devised systems of taxation, and promoted the interests of farmers, herdsmen, and merchants. Since most of the Khans were either tolerant of or indifferent to foreign religions, active persecution of any sect in the Mongol realm was rare. Some of the Mongol leaders encouraged the various native cultures, patronizing artists, writers, and historians. Chinese drama, Persian historical writing, and Tibetan Buddhist art and architecture all flourished during the Mongol occupation.

Yet the dark side of Mongol rule ought not to be ignored. Their armies so devastated some of the regions they conquered that recovery took years, even decades. Toward those who dared to resist them, they showed no mercy. A thirteenth-century Persian historian writes of their "massacring, plundering, and ravaging" and adds that in one of their campaigns, "with one stroke a world which billowed with fertility was laid desolate, and the regions thereof became a desert, and the greater part of the living dead, and their skin and bones crumbling dust; and the mighty were humbled and immersed in the calamities of perdition."[3] Modern writers have often been equally harsh in assessing the Mongols, one implying that the Mongols increased the brutality of Chinese court life, that they "brought violence and destruction to all aspects of China's civilization," and that they were "insensitive to Chinese cultural values, distrustful of Chinese influences, and inept heads of Chinese government."[4]

The victorious Mongols have scarcely left us their own versions of their campaigns and of the rule and administration of their empire, unfortunately, since they did not develop a written language until the time of Chinggis. Thus the Mongol written sources of the thirteenth century are meager, and most of our knowledge of them derives from the chronicles of the peoples they subjugated: the Chinese, the Persians, the Koreans, the Armenians, the Arabs, and various others. It is only natural, then, that they were often depicted as brutal and tyrannical. Certainly some of the more outlandish tales of Mongol cruelty, even monstrousness, must be discounted.

THE BIRTH OF A MONGOL EMPIRE

Mongolia, the homeland of Khubilai Khan and his ancestors, is a land of striking contrasts, of "lofty mountains with snowtopped peaks and rich, wooded areas with rivers, streams, and lakes."[5] It is hemmed in by mountains in the east, the west, and the north that block precipitation, and in the south, the Gobi Desert offers a formidable obstacle. Most of the Gobi is suitable for neither a pastoral nor an agricultural economy. Though it is not entirely lifeless, its almost unbearable heat in summer and chilling winds and patches of snow in winter make it most inhospitable. Only the sturdiest of humans and animals can survive in this bleak and hostile environment.

Most of the population lives in the central or steppe regions of Mongolia, where water and grass, the two staples of a pastoral economy, are available in sufficient quantities. The steppelands lack enough water to support intensive agriculture, but they are ideally suited for animal husbandry. The traditional economy relied upon five principal animals—sheep, goats, and yaks for food, clothing, shelter, and fuel; camels for transport, thus facilitating trade particularly through the deserts; and horses for mobility. Horses were used in cavalries in warfare and provided the mainstays of the justly renowned Mongol postal system, which enabled them to transmit official messages and reports throughout their domains.[6]

Like other pastoral nomads, the inhabitants of the steppe had a fragile economy, constantly threatened by drought, severe winters, and the spread of disease among their animals. Thus trade with the agricultural civilizations, particularly with the Chinese, was a necessity. In times of great distress, the steppe dwellers sought and sometimes received grain from the Chinese. They also obtained craft articles from them, in return offering animals and animal products. When the Chinese refused to trade, they organized raids to obtain by plunder the goods they could not secure through peaceful means.

In the late eleventh and early twelfth centuries, a new group known as the Mongols emerged in the steppe lands. Originally organized around clans (Mong.: *obogh*), they began at this time to develop into tribes (*aimagh*). Tribal chieftains, who initially may have been religious leaders, now were selected for their military prowess and with the support of the nobles (*noyad*) who controlled the common herders. The loyalty that nobles owed to their tribal leaders rested on an individual and personal relationship, for the Mongols had no abstract concept of loyalty to the office of tribal chieftain. The chieftains, who were responsible for the military training of the tribe, organized hunts designed, at least in part, as military exercises. The emphasis on military training for all Mongols offered the chieftains the advantage of virtually total mobilization in case of war.

By the late twelfth century, the Mongols dominated this land. Some Mongol tribes had united peacefully; still others had been subjugated by the strongest chieftains. There was no centralized leadership, however, and independent Turkish tribes, including the Uighurs, the Naimans, the Kereyid, and the Onguts, continued to reside in the same territory.

Under the leadership of Chinggis Khan (ca. 1162–1227), the Mongols burst upon the rest of Asia.[7] Chinggis united the diverse Mongol tribes and organized them into a powerful military machine. He was undoubtedly a military genius and a brilliant political tactician. Yet as Owen Lattimore has observed, "all his natural talent would not have got him very far ... if he had not been born ... at a propitious time and in just the right geographical region."[8]

Chinggis capitalized on developments among the Mongol tribes. Their movement toward unity, their growing ethnic consciousness and identification, and their developing military strength helped him to organize the tribes under his banner and then challenge the sedentary civilizations. In part, the uncertainties inherent in the Mongol economy and their need for foreign trade, which was on occasion denied to them by their neighbors, prompted his military campaigns. In addition, a sharp decline in the mean annual temperature of Mongolia, which translated into a reduction in the height and in the amount of grass in the steppes, adversely affected the Mongols.[9] Their animals were endangered, and their own survival dictated either trade with China or raids and attacks on their southern neighbor. Thus Chinggis, who believed that the Sky God Möngke Tenggeri had charged him with the responsibility of unifying the Mongols and perhaps ruling the world, had both the conditions and the opportunity to lead them out of their traditional homeland to conquer other territories.

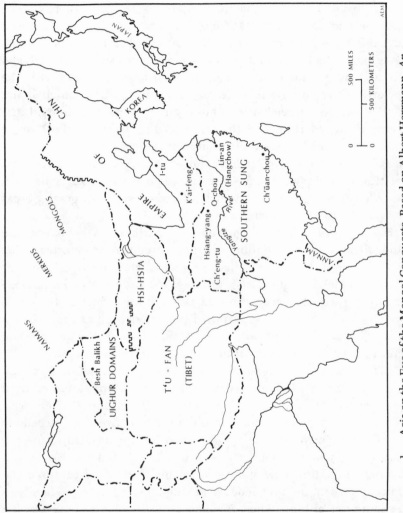

1. Asia on the Eve of the Mongol Conquests. Based on Albert Herrmann, *An Historical Atlas of China*, 38–39.

In the 1190s and early 1200s, Chinggis (or Temüjin, as he was
known before he was accepted as leader of all the Mongols) prepared
himself to assume a prominent role in the world.[10] He assembled a
private army (nököd), composed of loyal and trustworthy friends and
allies and divided into groups of a thousand, each constituting a
chiliarchy and led by a chiliarch, who superseded the authority of the
old tribal and clan leaders.[11] He imposed tight discipline on his troops,
developed an intelligence network, established an excellent cavalry,
devised new tactics and adapted traditional ones such as the feigned
retreat, and planned his campaigns thoroughly. Then, with the
powerful force that he had created, and through the judicious use
of alliances, he succeeded in subduing the Tatars, the Kereyid, the
Naimans, the Merkid, and the other leading tribes in the Mongol
territories.[12] In 1206, the most prominent Mongol nobles gathered at
an assembly (khuriltai) to endorse him as their ruler and to award him
the title of Chinggis Khan. To consolidate his authority, he then
provided appanages or fiefs, which offered control over grazing areas
and people, to his own family and relatives.[13]

Having pacified the Mongols and other tribes in what is now the
Mongolian People's Republic, Chinggis sought to bring other lands
under his control. Before an attack on another state, he invariably sent
envoys to the foreign ruler with so-called orders of submission,[14]
demanding acquiescence to his rule. Often, if the foreign state agreed,
he would allow its leaders to retain power, so long as they offered
taxes and performed the services he required, but if the foreign state
refused to submit, he was ruthless in overcoming its resistance.

His military campaigns were remarkably successful. First, he
compelled the Hsi Hsia dynasty of Northwest China, founded by a
nomadic people known as the Tanguts, to offer tribute.[15] Then, with
control of China's trade routes through the Northwest, he turned his
attention to North China, then governed by the Jurchens, a people
from what is now Manchuria who had conquered the North and
founded the Chin dynasty.[16] By 1215, his troops had captured the
Chin capital of Yen-ching (modern Peking), forcing the royal family to
flee south to K'ai-feng, where for almost two decades they staved off a
final defeat.[17] In 1219, turning westward, Chinggis led two hundred
thousand troops on a punitive expedition in Central Asia against the
Khwārazmian shah, 'Alā' al-Dīn Muḥammad, who had executed several of the khan's merchants and envoys.[18] By February of 1220,
Chinggis's troops had sacked the Central Asian town of Bukhara, and

1. Mongols in Battle. From a Rashīd al-Dīn manuscript.

within a month they occupied and looted Samarkand, massacring many of its inhabitants but not harming thirty thousand of its artisans and engineers, whom they sent to the Mongol lands.[19] By 1221, Chinggis had conquered Central Asia and modern Afghanistan, and two of his generals, Jebe and Subötei, had reached all the way to the Crimea before rejoining the other Mongol troops.[20] At his death in August of 1227, Chinggis was campaigning against the rebellious Tanguts in Northwest China. His body was transported to northeast Mongolia, where he was buried, and forty young women and at least forty horses were sacrificed at his tomb.[21]

Chinggis bequeathed more than a vast territory to his descendants. In 1204, he ordered a captive called T'a-t'a T'ung-a in the Chinese sources (Tatar Tonga?) to adapt the Uighur Turkic script to provide the Mongols with a written language.[22] He cultivated the religious leaders of the conquered areas, believing that good relations with the clergy would translate into good relations with the people whom they led, and to gain their support, sometimes even exempted the clergy from taxation. One of his more enduring legacies was the use of foreigners as scribes, interpreters, tutors, advisers, merchants, and even soldiers—a policy pursued by his successors, and particularly by Khubilai Khan. Finally, he issued the *Jasagh*, a set of rules often called the first Mongol law code.[23] Since it reflected the mores and customs of a nomadic society, it required considerable modification when the Mongols sought to rule sedentary civilizations, but it indicated the need for written laws and regulations with the growth of the Mongol empire.

CHINGGIS KHAN'S SUCCESSORS

In spite of his many accomplishments, Chinggis failed to delineate a precise and orderly succession to the khanate. By one Mongol tradition, the youngest son would inherit the father's flocks, grazing areas, and other forms of wealth. Another tradition gave the oldest son leadership of the clan or tribe, with the youngest son inheriting the property. Still another stressed seniority, giving the younger brother of a dead leader precedence over the leader's sons. These principles of succession, however, do not seem to have applied to the khanate. The procedure was to convene a *khuriltai* of the most prominent Mongol nobles to elect the new khan on the basis of tanistry—a collective judgment that the candidate was the most talented or competent.[24] Thus, succession to the khanate was unpredictable. When a *khuriltai* could not agree, violent and bloody struggles for power occasionally ensued.

After Chinggis's death, two full years elapsed before a new khan assumed power. In 1229, the four Chinggisid lines effected a compromise, which eventually resulted in the first territorial division of the Mongol domains. Under this scheme, Chinggis's grandson Batu became the Khan of the Golden Horde, which included the Mongols' westernmost lands and eventually encompassed Russia. Chinggis's second son, Chaghadai (ca. 1185–1242), received jurisdiction over Central Asia, while his youngest son (and Khubilai's father), Tolui (ca. 1190–1231/1232), a rough-and-tumble military man addicted to alcohol, was granted lands in North China and in the Mongol homeland. Partly because of his flexibility, his abilities as a conciliator, and his toleration of foreigners and foreign ideas, Ögödei (1186–1241), Chinggis's third son, became the Khaghan, or Khan of Khans, the overall ruler of the Mongol domains.

Ögödei continued his father's expansionist policies. In 1234, his

2. Chinggis Khan and His Four Sons. From a Rashīd al-Dīn manuscript.

troops crushed the Chin dynasty and occupied all of North China.[25] A few months earlier, the state of Tung Hsia in Liao-yang, or modern southern Manchuria, was defeated. By 1238, the king of Korea had been compelled to submit and to present tribute to the court.[26] To the west, one of Ögödei's armies seized Georgia and Greater Armenia, and another reached the frontier of Tibet.[27] By far the most spectacular, however, were the Mongol campaigns against Russia, starting in 1237. Representatives of all four Chinggisid lines, together with one hundred fifty thousand Mongol, Turkic, and Persian troops, took part in the campaigns.[28] Despite dissension and hostilities between Batu and Tolui's son Möngke, on the one hand, and Ögödei's son Güyüg and Chaghadai's son Büri, on the other hand, the expeditions were remarkably successful. Mongol armies defeated the Bulghars, the Bashkirs, and the Comans, tribal peoples residing along the Russian frontiers. Batu's forces crossed the Volga and occupied the towns of Riazan, Moscow, and Vladimir-Suzdal by March of 1238, and the town of Kiev by December of that year. Having swept across Russia, the Mongols next targeted Eastern Europe. In the spring of 1241, they struck at Poland; on April 9, after a savage battle in the town of Liegnitz, they sliced off an ear from each of their victims, collecting nine full bags.[29] In short order they vanquished Poland, and then turned south toward Hungary. By the end of the year, Batu had seized Pesth and Buda, but early in 1242 he withdrew his troops back to Russia, prompted by the death of Ögödei on December 11, 1241. To elect the new Khaghan, Batu and the other Mongol nobles needed to meet in the Mongol homeland. Ögödei's death, then, had probably saved Europe.

Like his father, Ögödei did not limit himself to territorial expansion. He recruited a sinicized non-Chinese official, whose name in the Chinese records is given as Yeh-lü Ch'u-ts'ai, to help him govern his newly subjugated lands in China. Yeh-lü knew that some Mongols wished to convert Chinese farmland into grazing areas, but argued that the tax revenues derived from agriculture would exceed any income from pastoralism on land unsuited for animal husbandry.[30] He devised a regular, orderly system of taxation to replace the extraordinary, irregular levies of the Mongols, and organized ten bureaus to collect these taxes.[31] Yeh-lü's Mongol and Turkish opponents sought to convince Ögödei that Yeh-lü's scheme was less lucrative than their own plan, by which Central Asian Muslims would be granted licenses to collect taxes. Since the merchants would receive a share of the taxes they garnered, it was in their interest to squeeze as much as they could from the Chinese.[32] Eager for additional income, Ögödei in 1239 generally sided with Yeh-lü's opponents, though he did not totally dispense with Yeh-lü's tax program.

Yeh-lü was more successful in persuading Ögödei to construct a capital. The Khaghan recognized the need for an administrative center for his growing domain. He chose, however, to build his capital in Khara Khorum in the heart of the traditional Mongol homeland.[33] To build and maintain this new town required importing vast quantities of supplies, for it was an artificially created capital and could not sustain a large population on its own resources. It lay far from the trade routes, outside the agricultural heartland, and far from sources of raw materials. A contemporary visitor revealed that every day five hundred carts laden with merchandise reached Khara Khorum.[34] The maintenance of elaborate buildings like the Khaghan's palace, known to the Chinese as the Wan-an kung, imposed an even heavier burden. To guarantee provisions for the town, Ögödei initiated a policy of favoring merchants and supporting commerce that would be pursued by his successors, including Khubilai Khan.[35]

KHUBILAI AND HIS MOTHER

After the death of Ögödei in 1241, Khubilai began to emerge on the historical stage. Khubilai's father had been passed over as the successor to Chinggis, and it appeared that Khubilai too would play a subsidiary role in Mongol history. Few could have foreseen that he would eventually become the most powerful figure in the Mongol domains.

One of those who did was his remarkably competent and intelligent mother, Sorghaghtani Beki.[36] She had lofty ambitions for her four sons, and she dedicated herself to their careers. All four eventually became prominent in the Mongol lands. Möngke, the oldest, was the Khaghan from 1251 until his death in 1259; Khubilai succeeded his older brother and ruled from 1260 to 1294; Hülegü destroyed the 'Abbāsid dynasty, which had governed much of the Middle East and Persia since 749, and established his own dynasty in Persia; and Arigh Böke, as the youngest son, would rule the Mongol homeland.

Sorghaghtani Beki's contemporaries throughout the known world considered her to be the most remarkable woman of her age. The European missionary John of Plano Carpini, who visited Mongolia before her sons became the Khaghans, noticed that "among the Tartars this lady is the most renowned, with the exception of the Emperor's Mother...."[37] The Persian historian Rashīd al-Dīn wrote that she was "extremely intelligent and able and towered above all the women in the world."[38] And a Hebrew physician named Bar Hebraeus, who lived in the Middle East, praised her as "a queen [who] trained her sons so well that all the princes marvelled at her power of administration.... And it was in respect of her that a certain poet said 'If I were to see among the race of women another woman like this, I should say that the race of women was far superior to that of men!'"[39] It is rare to find such unanimity among these thirteenth-century observers and historians. Without the political involvement and adroit manipulation of this remarkable woman, the descendants of Tolui might never have replaced those of Ögödei as the main Mongol royal line in East Asia.

Sorghaghtani Beki was the niece of Ong Khan, ruler of the Kereyid tribe. When Chinggis conquered the Kereyid, he offered Sorghaghtani in marriage to his own son Tolui. Little is known about the relationship between Sorghaghtani Beki and Tolui.[40] We may surmise that husband and wife were often separated. He almost always accompanied his father on military campaigns. Rashīd al-Dīn reports that "no prince conquered as many countries as he,"[41] certainly the supreme compliment for a Mongol of that generation. Tolui distinguished himself in Chinggis's campaigns against the Chin dynasty in the 1210s, and from 1219 through the early 1220s he commanded one of the main detachments in his father's assaults on the cities of Central Asia. After Chinggis's death in 1227, Tolui served on military expeditions, principally against the Chin, for his brother Ögödei. In 1231/1232, two years before the final destruction of the Chin dynasty,[42] Tolui died.

There are several contradictory versions of the circumstances of his death. One of the least plausible portrays him as a great martyr. According to this account, when Ögödei was near death, and the shamans had brewed a concoction to alleviate his discomfort, Tolui appeared and rushed into the shamans' yurt. He swallowed the medicine, and appealed to the gods, exclaiming, "Take me instead of Ögetei [Ögödei] and cure him of his sickness, and lay his sickness upon me."[43] Shortly thereafter, Tolui died, and the Khan miraculously recovered. A more likely scenario, however, which is supported by contemporary historians is that Tolui, like many other Mongols, drank himself to death.[44]

When Ögödei sought to arrange a marriage for the widow Sorghaghtani, she politely demurred. Ögödei proposed a marriage with his son Güyüg—a union of aunt and nephew. This union would have linked the two main princely families in East Asia and ensured an orderly succession to the position of Khaghan, avoiding the disputes, even wars, that erupted between the sons of Ögödei and the sons of Tolui. Sorghaghtani Beki courteously but firmly spurned Ögödei's offer, however, explaining that her responsibility to her four sons outweighed her desire to marry the Khaghan's son.[45]

Her political genius is perhaps best demonstrated by her religious toleration. Though she was herself a Nestorian Christian, she did not discriminate against the other religions in the Mongol realm, and even patronized Buddhism and Taoism to win favor with her Chinese subjects.[46] Nor did she neglect Islam.[47] She offered alms to poor Muslims, rewarded the *shaikhs* (religious leaders), and contributed funds to build mosques and theological schools, including the Khaniyya *madrasa* (religious academy) in the Central Asian city of Bukhara.[48] She never denied her Nestorian faith, however, and even Marco Polo, who visited China twenty years after her death, knew that she was a Christian.[49] Yet she thought that the cultivation of the various religions in her land was well worth her efforts, and the writings of contemporary historians throughout Eurasia attest to her success.

Khubilai was born on September 23, 1215, the year that Chinggis Khan seized Peking. The sources on Khubilai's childhood, his education, and his early travels are limited. Khubilai was, until 1251, merely a member of a collateral branch of the royal family. Barring a catastrophe or untoward event, he would remain part of the nobility but not play a decisive role in the affairs of the realm, so his career did not need to be richly documented. It seems clear, however, that his upbringing was left to his mother, for his father was often away on military campaigns with his own father, Chinggis.[50] She ensured that the young Khubilai learned to ride and to shoot with bows and arrows. Like all other Mongols, he also took an active part in hunts, which he continued to enjoy even in old age, as attested to by one of the few extant paintings of Khubilai.[51] Sorghaghtani was also determined that he be literate and recruited a Uighur named Tolochu to teach him to read and write Mongol.[52]

His exposure to Chinese ways also stemmed from his mother's assertiveness. After her husband's death, Ögödei had reluctantly granted her request of an appanage, in 1236 turning over to her the area of Chen-ting (in North China in present-day Hopei province). As the ruler of a population of Chinese farmers rather than Mongol pastoral nomads, she recognized that policies which exploited the peasants and plundered the resources of the area were short-sighted, if not disastrous. Tax revenues would be greater, she believed, if she fostered the native agrarian economy instead of imposing a Mongol-style pastoral economy.[53]

Khubilai eventually followed his mother's example. In the same year, 1236, Ögödei also offered Khubilai the appanage of Hsing-chou, a region in Hopei with a population of ten thousand households.[54] At first, he adopted a laissez-faire policy toward his appanage, which he governed from Mongolia as an absentee ruler. Though he did not condone the exploitation of the Chinese inhabitants, Khubilai's absence kept him from scrutinizing the actions of his officials and retainers. He was unaware of and unable to prevent them from burdening the population. Tax merchants imposed heavy taxes, and local officials demanded excessive labor service,[55] and in protest, the farmers abandoned their homes and land, resettling in areas not under Mongol control. By the time Khubilai realized what had happened, many of the original ten thousand households had fled from his domain. To halt this exodus, he replaced the Mongol retainers and the tax merchants who had earlier governed the area with regular officials, the so-called Pacification Commissioners (Chin.: *an-ch'a shih*), who were primarily Chinese (though they are not specifically identified in the sources). Regular taxes were assessed, the extraordinary levies were lifted, and a number of Chinese were recruited to help manage the economy.[56] Khubilai's new policies, to regain the confidence of the local inhabitants and to coax defectors into returning, succeeded, and by the late 1240s, those who had fled were beginning to return to their homes and the region was once again stable.

KHUBILAI AND HIS ADVISERS

Even at this early stage in his career, Khubilai was already relying on Chinese advisers. Throughout his life and career, he would also consult Nestorian Christians, Tibetan Buddhists, and Central Asian Muslims.

His earliest advisers were an eclectic lot. In 1242, Khubilai summoned to his domain the Buddhist monk Hai-yün (1202–57).[57] Hai-yün, whom Ögödei had appointed as the abbot of an important monastery in North China, introduced Khubilai to the precepts and practices of Chinese Buddhism,[58] and the two men developed a close relationship. The Buddhist cleric even bestowed a Chinese name, Chen-chin (True Gold), on Khubilai's second son.[59] Chao Pi (1220–76) and Tou Mo (1196–1280), two other counselors who joined Khubilai in the early 1240s, lectured the young Mongol nobleman on Confucianism, emphasizing the virtues and duties of the ruler.[60]

Why were these Chinese willing to serve as advisers to a conqueror who was not ethnically Chinese?[61] North China had a three-century-old tradition of non-Chinese rulers, as both the Liao (907–1125) and Chin (1115–1234) dynasties, which were governed by non-Chinese, had employed Chinese advisers and officials to help them rule their territories. Even so, the men who served under Khubilai left themselves open to charges of disloyalty or even treason. Some joined for the monetary rewards and perquisites. Others wanted to promote the sinicization of Khubilai and the Mongols in order to improve the lot of the Chinese people, hoping, through their advice and assistance, to shape Khubilai's views and actions.[62]

Though they clearly influenced his attitudes as a young Mongol noble, Khubilai was hardly a puppet to be easily manipulated by them. Caution marked his dealings with the Confucians, and he had misgivings about over-reliance on them. In a conversation with Chang Te-hui, one of his early counselors, Khubilai wondered out loud whether the Buddhist counselors to the Liao and the Confucian advisers to the Chin had contributed to the decline and fall of the two dynasties.[63] Chang responded ingenuously that he knew little about Liao, but was well informed about conditions at the end of Chin. At that time only one or two advisers to the Chin were Confucian scholars; the rest were military men, who resorted to arms to resolve disputes. Since only about one in thirty advisers were Confucians, how could they be blamed for the collapse of the Chin? This response satisfied Khubilai, and he permitted Chang to recruit twenty or so Confucian scholars to his advisory group.[64] Nonetheless, his questions reveal his doubts about the Confucian scholars.

His rudimentary knowledge of spoken Chinese and ignorance of written Chinese, moreover, limited his relations with Confucian scholars. He was not proficient enough to carry on sophisticated dialogues about Confucian doctrines. When his Chinese advisers lectured him on the Confucian classics, he needed to wait for a Mongol translation of the Chinese.[65] His inability to read Chinese further reduced his exposure to Confucian writings.[66] He could read the Uighur script of Mongolian, but his limitations in spoken and written Chinese gave him an incomplete view of what his Chinese advisers said or wrote.

In addition, Khubilai also recruited non-Chinese as advisers, for he welcomed any capable men with practical suggestions for ruling his domain in Hsing-chou. Like his grandfather, he relied on Uighur Turkish advisers and officials, whom he employed as military advisers, translators, and interpreters.[67] The Nestorian Christian Shiban, a senior secretary to Khubilai, and Mungsuz (Chin.: Meng-su-ssu), one of his most influential advisers and later his brother-in-law, were two of his most prominent Uighur counselors.[68] Mongol military men and Central Asian Muslims were also attracted to his domains.[69] By the 1240s, therefore, he had about forty advisers whom he could consult about the political and financial administration of his domain.[70]

One other influential adviser was his remarkable second wife, Chabi. Her early life remains a mystery: the Persian accounts scarcely mention her, and only a few Chinese texts yield much information about her.[71] We know that she and Khubilai were married just before 1240, because her first son was born in that year, but nothing is known of her life between 1240 and the eve of Khubilai's accession as Great Khan in 1260. Contemporary sources hardly mention Khubilai's first wife, Tegülün (Chin.: T'ieh-ku-lun), or his two other principal wives, Tarakhan and Bayaghuchin.[72] He had four households (Mong.: ordo), each supervised by a main wife under whom were a number of subordinate wives and concubines. The only ordo that is accorded much attention in accounts of the period is Chabi's, the second.

The attention to Chabi is warranted, for she had a great impact on Khubilai, influencing, for example, his views on religion. She was an ardent Buddhist and was, in particular, attracted by Tibetan Buddhism. She gave her first-born son a Tibetan name (Dorji, b. 1240, from Tibetan rDorje).[73] There is no specific evidence that she induced Khubilai to invite Buddhist monks to his territory before he became the Great Khan, but she certainly did not dampen his enthusiasm for conversations about Buddhism with Hai-yün, and she may have encouraged Khubilai in his desire to unravel the complexities of Buddhist doctrine. She herself donated some of her jewelry to Buddhist monasteries.[74]

In sum, by the 1240s, Khubilai had no shortage of advisers in his

3.   Khubilai and Chabi on a Cookout. From *Livre des merveilles*. Manuscript from the Bibliothèque Nationale, Paris.

entourage, from a variety of philosophies and ethnic groups. Though he was not the first Mongol to seek counsel and assistance from the peoples he had subjugated, Khubilai was unique in having such a large coterie of advisers, which eventually encompassed Chinese Confucian scholars, Tibetan lamas, Central Asian Muslims, and Uighur Turks. But his role in making state policies was still minor, if not nonexistent. This would change with the change in the fortunes of the house of Tolui.

THE RISE OF THE HOUSE OF TOLUI

Ögödei's death in 1241 was the first step in the decline of his house and offered opportunities for the descendants of Tolui. Ögödei had favored his grandson Shiremün as his successor, but Ögödei's assertive wife Töregene was determined to place her own son Güyüg on the throne.[75] Ignoring her late husband's wishes, Töregene maneuvered to have herself appointed as regent until the Mongol notables met to elect a new ruler, and she remained the regent for four years while Güyüg was on military campaigns in the West. The irregularity of the succession tarnished the reputation of the house of Ögödei. Töregene's policies, too, harmed the interests of Ögödei's descendants, and she was accused of treachery, corruption, and exploitation of her subjects by the Chinese and the Persian historians.[76] These characterizations are perhaps overdrawn because they were written after the line of Tolui had displaced that of Ögödei as the Mongol rulers. Töregene's actions, however, aroused much opposition in North China. Two Muslims, ʿAbd al-Rahmān and Fāṭima, whom she appointed as tax collectors and advisers, imposed high tax quotas on the Mongols' territories there.[77] The institutions that she devised were ill suited for governing a sedentary population. At the same time, Sorghaghtani was gaining allies by providing generous gifts to the Mongol notables and by successfully ruling her domain, but she was unable to challenge Töregene.

Thus, Töregene had her way: her son Güyüg was enthroned as the Khaghan in 1246. Though he eliminated the two Muslim tax collectors and advisers, he intended to maintain the same policies as his mother and to rule as other nomadic chieftains traditionally had—that is, with the goals of increasing revenue and seizing additional territory, but with scant concern for his sedentary subjects.[78] His troops expanded into Tibet, and the Mongols gained the services of a Tibetan monk with the title ʿPhags-pa (1235–80) at this point.[79] Güyüg's armies also captured more land in Georgia and Armenia. They even appeared to threaten Western Europe, and the pope and the Holy Roman Emperor, Frederick II (1194–1250), responded to the threat by dispatching John of Plano Carpini to seek an agreement with the Mongols and to urge them to convert to Christianity.[80] Since Güyüg flatly rejected any agreement and demanded instead that Europe submit to him, the only benefit of John's mission was his fine report on his travels entitled *Ystoria Mongolarum* (History of the Mongols).[81]

Güyüg's success in expanding the empire did not lessen the tensions among the descendants of Chinggis Khan. Sorghaghtani Beki continued covertly to seek allies among the Mongol nobility, and her closest and most influential ally turned out to be Batu, the ruler of the Golden Horde. A deep enmity had developed between Batu and Güyüg during the Russian campaign, in which they had both taken

Chinggis Khan and His Descendants

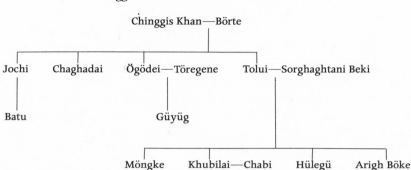

part. In 1247, determined to settle accounts with his adversary, Güyüg gathered his troops for a planned surprise attack. Sorghaghtani learned of his plan and warned Batu, placing herself in great danger should Güyüg ever discover her treachery. Her gamble paid off, because, fortunately for her, Güyüg died en route to Batu's encampment.[82] By promptly warning Batu, she had affirmed her alliance with him, and he, as the oldest member of the third generation of Chinggis Khan's descendants, would vastly influence the choice of the new Khaghan.

Allied with Batu and supported by her sons, Sorghaghtani was now ensured that the new Khaghan would be from the house of Tolui. In 1251, Batu and Sorghaghtani convened a *khuriltai* in Central Asia, close to Batu's domain, and had her eldest son, Möngke, elected as the Khaghan.[83] Möngke's brothers, Khubilai, Hülegü, and Arigh Böke, must have played a role in rallying support for their sibling, but the sources offer few details about their participation. Their mother had achieved her objective, for one of her sons was now the ruler of the vast Mongol domains. She lived just long enough to enjoy her victory, and died in the first month of 1252 (February 12–March 11). To demonstrate their gratitude and reverence, her sons and their descendants erected tablets in her honor in both Ta-tu (as Peking was known in Mongol times) and Chen-ting fu, the seat of her appanage. A portrait of her was hung in a Nestorian church in the North Chinese town of Kan-chou in 1335, but since it is no longer extant, we have no conception of the appearance of this remarkable woman.[84]

Though her son Möngke took power in 1251, his opponents had not simply renounced their claims. The descendants of Chinggis's sons Ögödei and Chaghadai insisted that because the *khuriltai* had been held in Central Asia and not in the Mongols' traditional homeland, Möngke's accession was illegitimate. A conflict ensued, marking the first violent struggle for the throne. Güyüg's widow Oghul Ghaimish joined Chaghadai's son Büri in seeking to overthrow Möngke and to replace him with Ögödei's grandson Shiremün. Within a few months, however, Möngke, with the help of much of the Mongol nobility, crushed his opponents and exacted swift and horrible reprisals. Seventy-seven commanders who had assisted the houses of Ögödei and Chaghadai were executed, and several of them had their mouths "stuffed with stone until they died." [85] Oghul Ghaimish was also executed. Shiremün was turned over to Khubilai for punishment, and accompanied him on several journeys until Khubilai, suspicious of Shiremün's intentions, had him executed.

With his rivals safely out of the way, Möngke was now the acknowledged ruler of the Mongol world. He continued his mother's policy of religious toleration and subsidized mosques and Buddhist monasteries. A Persian historian noted, for example, that Möngke "showed most honor and respect to the Muslims and bestowed the largest amount of gifts and alms upon them." [86] Möngke also conducted a census and devised a tax system that was less onerous on the Mongols' peasant subjects than the ones imposed by Töregene and Güyüg. Under his scheme, state agencies, not the Mongol nobility, would collect taxes, in the hope of minimizing the exploitation of the subject peoples. [87]

Like his predecessors, Möngke sought to increase the territory under Mongol domination. Like his grandfather Chinggis and his father Tolui, he recruited non-Mongol troops who offered expertise otherwise unavailable to the Mongols. [88] His commanders were instructed to refrain from wanton destruction of conquered lands. Moreover, they were directed to dispatch orders of submission to rulers of territories before actually attacking; only if these demands were rebuffed should they use force. [89]

Möngke made his younger brother Hülegü commander of the forces heading westward to "pacify" the Islamic states and lands. Starting in 1256, Hülegü led his troops toward the stronghold of the powerful Ismāʿīlī order of Islam, popularly and perhaps misleadingly known as the Order of the Assassins. [90] At their fortress of Alamūt, high in the Elburz mountains south of the Caspian Sea, the Ismāʿīlīs had "strengthened the fortifications and built up a great store of provisions." [91] Confident of their ability to withstand a Mongol onslaught and siege, the Ismaʿīlīs rejected Hülegü's order to submit. In response, Hülegü bombarded Alamūt with stone missiles, and by early 1257 the Ismaʿīlīs were compelled to surrender. Because they had resisted him, Hülegü showed no mercy, permitting his troops to massacre most of them. The ʿAbbāsid caliph in Baghdad, who also resisted Hülegü's demand for submission, also suffered the Mongols' wrath. In 1258, Hülegü defeated the ʿAbbāsids, sacked Baghdad, and executed the caliph.[92]

The Western campaign was a resounding success. But in the East, Möngke and his younger brother Khubilai faced even greater opposition. It was during these expeditions, however, that Khubilai established his reputation and became sufficiently prominent to lay claim to leadership of the Mongol world.

CHAPTER TWO

Khubilai Emerges

While Hülegü was expanding Mongol power in the West, Möngke continued to plan for the conquest of the Southern Sung dynasty of China. His eagerness for conquest was, in part, due to Sung incursions on Mongol-controlled territory. Just before he took power Sung troops had, for example, attacked the town of Yung-ning in the modern-day province of Honan. Möngke and his military advisers decided, therefore, on a strategy of opening several fronts in any invasions of the Sung. A direct north-south assault was insufficient and probably doomed to fail. One way of threatening the Chinese dynasty was through an attack from the west, but the Kingdom of Ta-li in the province of modern Yünnan was an obstacle. The Mongols needed first to pacify that region in order to use it as a base for a foray against the Sung. In 1252, Möngke selected his brother Khubilai to lead an expedition into the remote province of Yünnan, which was traditionally not part of the Middle Kingdom.

THE TA-LI CAMPAIGN

Until this time, Khubilai had been busily consolidating his power in North China. In the early months of his brother's reign, Khubilai had extended his authority to much of North China. He had, of course, requested and received Möngke's permission to enlarge the territory under his administration, which was distinct from his own appanage in Hsing-chou. His request had been reasonable. The Mongol armies had successfully overrun the Central Plain in North China, but they found it difficult to obtain a steady supply of grain and other food. Transporting such supplies was an arduous, burdensome task. Under prodding from his adviser Yao Shu, Khubilai suggested that he be permitted to establish military farms, given the Chinese name of *t'un-t'ien*, in Honan and Shensi.[1] The Chinese soldiers among his forces would be stationed throughout this region and would serve not merely as occupiers but also as self-sufficient farmers. This scheme would enable the troops to grow their own food as well as to impose greater surveillance and controls over the population. A specific bureau, known in Chinese as the Ching-lüeh ssu, was organized in Pien-ching (around K'ai-feng, the capital of the Chin dynasty) to supervise these military farms.[2] The military colonies sustained themselves, and the region prospered, facilitating Khubilai's efforts to maintain a strong base in China.

Meanwhile Möngke invited Khubilai to choose between Nan-ching (the area around K'ai-feng) and Ching-chao (in Sian, one of the oldest capitals in China) as his newly granted appanage in addition to Hsing-chou. Having scant knowledge of these terrains, Khubilai consulted his Chinese advisers, particularly Yao Shu. They explained to him that the irrigation and soil of Nan-ching were inferior to those of Ching-chao. The Yellow River occasionally flooded the Nan-ching area, and some of the soil was excessively salty and unsuitable for farming. On the other hand, Ching-chao, which dominated the Kuan-chung region, was much more fertile and less populous.[3] Khubilai was persuaded by these arguments and selected Ching-chao. Möngke, apparently impressed that his brother had chosen the territory with the smaller population, rewarded him with another appanage in Huai-meng in Honan. In his new appanages, Khubilai established among other offices a Pacification Bureau (Chin.: Hsüan-fu ssu) to maintain the peace and an agency to print paper money, which promoted trade.[4]

Thus, Khubilai became ever more concerned with China as his economic and political prosperity grew to depend upon his Chinese territories. At the same time he grew more and more separated from the ways, institutions, and values of his Mongol forebears. Even so, he was still and would always remain a Mongol, despite the need to accommodate to some Chinese views and practices in order to rule successfully.

Late in 1252, Khubilai became even more involved in Chinese

affairs after the Great Khan commanded him to bring the Kingdom of Ta-li under Mongol jurisdiction. Ta-li was composed of a variety of non-Chinese peoples, but Chinese had gradually been moving in that direction for centuries. It was the logical next step for Chinese expansion, as control of this territory would enable them to trade unhindered with Burma and South Asia. The conquest of Ta-li was thus not simply a Mongol objective. It would surely have been a principal goal of any Chinese dynasty as well.

Though Khubilai received Möngke's orders in July of 1252, he did not move toward Ta-li until September of 1253. Khubilai characteristically made minute, even exhaustive, preparations for his military campaigns, leaving nothing to chance. He believed that his troops must be ready for any obstacle they encountered and that supplies should be plentiful and readily available. The preparations for his campaign against Ta-li were particularly important, for it was his first major assignment. Finally, at the age of thirty-six, he was being granted responsibility for a vital military objective. His father and his older brother Möngke had assumed leadership of expeditions while still in their teens or early twenties. Since Khubilai's opportunity to demonstrate his own leadership had not come until a more mature age, he did not wish to lose this opportunity.

Two of the most talented figures in the Mongol territories accompanied him to Ta-li. Uriyangkhadai, the son of Subötei, one of Chinggis Khan's great generals, was assigned to lead one of the armies campaigning in the southwest, while the Confucian teacher Yao Shu traveled with his protector and employer Khubilai to Ta-li, an area inhabited by peoples whom the Chinese believed represented an inferior culture.[5] Uriyangkhadai had had much more front-line experience than Khubilai and proved invaluable in battle. The Chinese sources credit Yao Shu with reducing the bloodshed in the expedition and with helping to bring about the surrender of Ta-li with relative ease. But even though his advice probably contributed to the success of the campaign, the Chinese historians may well have exaggerated his role and the efficacy of his suggestions.

In the late summer of 1253 Khubilai felt prepared to undertake his assigned mission. Gathering his troops at Lin-t'ao in the northwestern province of Shensi, he began his long march to the south. To reach the Yünnan plateau, he and his army had to traverse rugged mountainous terrain. They needed to travel through Szechwan to arrive at the valley of the Ta-li kingdom, which was bounded and nourished by three great rivers: the Salween (known to the Chinese as the Nu-chiang), the upper streams of the Mekong (the Lan-ts'ang chiang), and the Yangtze (Chin-sha chiang). While in Lin-t'ao, Khubilai sent an embassy led by three envoys to demand that the King of Ta-li submit. Known to the Chinese as Tuan Hsing-chih, the king was actually a figurehead, and real power was held by his leading minister, Kao T'ai-hsiang. It was up to Kao to respond to Khubilai's overture. Kao's response proved unfortunate for him and for Ta-li: he executed all three envoys.[6]

Under the circumstances, Khubilai had no choice but to take punitive action against Ta-li. The deaths of his emissaries offered him an additional incentive for punishing the peoples of the Southwest. His strategy for the conquest of Ta-li was deceptively simple: Uriyang-khadai would lead his forces from the west toward Ta-li, Khubilai would engage the enemy directly, and a group of princes and their forces would attack from the east. This three-pronged assault began in late October of 1253, and Khubilai assumed that it would take a bloody war to compel Ta-li to capitulate. Kao T'ai-hsiang, adamantly refusing to surrender to the Mongol armies, instead massed his forces on the banks of the Chin-sha chiang and awaited the enemy. Khubilai's troops reached the opposite bank in November, and, unde-terred by the seemingly formidable force on the other side, Khubilai ordered his soldiers to fashion rafts out of sheepskin bags in order to cross the river.[7] Supervising construction of the rafts was Bayan, one of the generals who accompanied him. This was the first time that Khubilai and Bayan, who would become one of Khubilai's most trusted and capable military aides, ever collaborated on an enterprise. At this juncture, Bayan led his troops in a daring night-time fording of the river, and the Mongols rapidly defeated the surprised enemy, forcing Kao T'ai-hsiang to return at a rapid pace to the capital and killing much of Kao's army. His most formidable opposition now in disarray, Khubilai could concentrate on a final assault on the town of Ta-li.

According to the Chinese sources, the real hero of the campaign was Yao Shu. As a good Confucian, he wished to avoid a Mongol massacre of the inhabitants. In typical Confucian fashion, he used a historical par-allel to persuade Khubilai of the value of a nonviolent tactic. Yao told Khubilai of Ts'ao Pin (930–99), a renowned general at the time when the newly founded Sung dynasty sought to consolidate its control over China. In 975, the Sung emperor dispatched Ts'ao to pacify the area around modern Nanking. En route, Ts'ao feigned illness. When his underlings gathered around to determine the cause of his ailment, he informed them that he would get well only if they pledged not to plunder Nanking or massacre its inhabitants. They acquiesced, and the conquest of Nanking was accomplished peacefully.[8] Yao, urging Khubilai to follow Ts'ao Pin's example, proposed that the Mongols send an advance force to Ta-li with banners proclaiming that they would not wantonly kill and loot and that all that they desired was simple acceptance of Mongol overlordship. According to Yao, this non-violent tactic would inevitably lead Ta-li to submit without a fight.

However, this account smacks of Chinese myth-making after the fact. The Mongols had for decades used the very tactic Yao proposed, pledging not to harm or destroy a town if its inhabitants peacefully surrendered. Khubilai surely did not need instructions in the peaceful subjugation of a hostile or at least unpacified population. His grandfather before him had repeatedly employed the tactic of terrorizing foreigners into submission. By defeating any unyielding opponents in a most brutal manner, Chinggis hoped in this way to intimidate others on his line of march into surrendering. Now Khubilai was employing precisely the same technique. He had decisively defeated Ta-li's most important army, obviating the need for either a massacre of its remaining defenders or a loss of Mongol troops in an all-out attack on the capital city.

Again, the surrender of Ta-li is shrouded in Chinese myth-making. The Chinese sources report that Khubilai, adhering to Yao Shu's principle of seeking the peaceful submission of Ta-li, ordered his men to fashion a silk banner with a message assuring the inhabitants of the capital that their lives would be spared if they capitulated. With these guarantees in hand, Ta-li opted for surrender, and Khubilai kept his word, executing only the officials who were responsible for killing his envoys and leaving the rest of the population unharmed.[9] But this version of events gives rise to a number of questions. If the message on the banner was written in Chinese, could Ta-li's population read the language? Even if they could, would the Mongols use this Chinese tactic when they had their own traditional, tested, and successful policy of "orders of submission"? That Mongol policy was in effect similar to the strategy credited to Yao Shu. Therefore, the Mongols did not need Yao's strategy. Khubilai would simply send envoys with the orders of submission directly to the king of Ta-li. This is a more likely scenario than the one presented in the Chinese sources.

In any case, Khubilai's troops occupied the capital without much opposition. In the dead of night, Kao T'ai-hsiang tried to escape but did not get far. Two of Khubilai's military commanders pursued and apprehended him, but Kao would not give his captors the satisfaction of seeing him humble himself before them. Miffed by Kao's arrogance, Khubilai had him decapitated at the tower of the southern gate leading to Ta-li.[10] He then executed those involved in the killing of his envoys. The bodies of the three envoys were given a proper burial, and Khubilai ordered Yao Shu to compose a eulogy for the martyred ambassadors.[11] Though he put Kao T'ai-hsiang to death, he spared Kao's family. Kao's children were later given a Chinese education and were not discriminated against, in fact.[12]

Nor was the system of government enjoyed by Ta-li totally altered. Yao Shu gathered all the seals and books in the Ta-li archives and presumably took them back to the Mongol court,[13] but Khubilai did not overturn its ruling dynasty. Instead, the Tuan family shared power over Ta-li with Khubilai's appointee Liu Shih-chung, who was granted the title of Hsüan-fu shih (Pacification Commissioner).[14] Khubilai also offered oxen and seeds to the inhabitants before heading back toward North China.

The illustrious general Uriyangkhadai remained behind to continue the campaigns in the southwest, and his campaigns were so successful that soon most of the southwest was under Mongol control. Uriyangkhadai pacified numerous tribes in the southwest, even venturing into Tibet. By 1257, he had turned eastward and sought the submission of Annam. But the heat, the jungle, and the insects and mosquitoes all took their toll on his troops, and their battles with the Annamese were inconclusive. Though he briefly occupied Hanoi, Uriyangkhadai was not victorious here, as he had been in the southwest. Nevertheless, the ruler of Annam promised to send tribute to the Mongol court, no doubt to get the foreign troops off his land.[15]

Thus, with the help of Uriyangkhadai, Khubilai's first military foray was a smashing triumph. He had accomplished what Möngke had requested. Though his troops had not suffered heavy casualties, he had extended Mongol control into a critical region—a base from which to launch an invasion of South China and a thoroughfare for an expansion of trade with Burma and India. He had earned his spurs in the traditional Mongol way, through a military campaign. His older brother Möngke had had his initiation in the Western campaigns of the 1230s. Khubilai's expedition, although not as wide-ranging, was no less successful. To be accepted as a leader, a Mongol needed to show his abilities as a military administrator, and thus Khubilai had now taken a long stride toward gaining the respect of the Mongol nobility.

KHUBILAI'S ADMINISTRATION OF HIS APPANAGE

Having shown his mettle in combat, Khubilai could now refocus his attention on his administration in North China. As a by-product of the Ta-li campaign, he had enlarged his lands to encompass much of the present provinces of Shensi and Honan. A stable administration was essential for such an expanded territory. Khubilai appointed Lien Hsi-hsien, a Uighur and only twenty years old at the time, as Pacification Commissioner of the Kuan-hsi circuit (in Ching-chao), one of the more important regions in his domains, to create an orderly system of government. Ching-chao embraced parts of Szechwan, which included numerous non-Chinese peoples and was thus difficult to govern, and Shensi. In the words of the stereotyped terminology of the Chinese dynastic histories, Lien's task was "to curb the violent and support the weak." [16] As a typical Confucian, he first looked to education as a means to achieve his objectives. He invited a Confucian luminary named Hsü Heng, later a prominent figure in Khubilai's government, to take charge of the schools and to recruit able scholars into the official class. But Lien went even further to protect the interests of scholars. Regulations initiated by Ögödei and carried on by Khubilai prevented Mongol nobles from employing Confucian scholars as slaves. Influential Mongol leaders had, however, evaded these rules and compelled scholars to perform demeaning tasks. Lien ordered the local authorities to register scholars so as to prevent them from being abused.[17] Moreover, diviners, who were also exploiting the populace, were to be punished and more carefully regulated. He appointed literate and educated administrators who promoted agriculture, issued paper money to encourage commerce, and collected taxes for Khubilai's needs. In short, he stabilized Khubilai's domains and contributed to their prosperity.

Now assured that his domains were capably governed, Khubilai could concern himself with long-range plans. Here he sought guidance from an astute Buddhist monk named Liu Ping-chung, whom he apparently consulted frequently from this time on. Their relationship is described and idealized in the Chinese accounts. According to a recent biographer of Liu, it is difficult

> to discern the reality until one has torn down the dual barriers of traditional stereotypes and popular legends. . . . In the official history of the Yüan period, Liu Ping-chung is given the full attributes of an ideal imperial adviser. The close rapport between the ruler and his ministers is a main theme in the Confucian political philosophy. While the sovereign who receives the Mandate of Heaven rules by virtue of his sage qualities, he is dependent on his wise ministers for counsel and assistance. . . . This is the dual concept "sage ruler" and "virtuous minister." Virtuous ministers, like sage rulers, become heroes. They are exalted and idolized. . . . It is only after having dispelled the traditional stereotypes and popular legends that we can arrive at an objective appraisal of Liu Ping-chung.[18]

Even discounting the exaggeration in the Chinese texts, Liu clearly influenced Khubilai's early career and policies. The Great Khan must surely have been impressed with Liu's many talents. Liu was a fine calligrapher and painter, a passable poet, and an outstanding mathematician and astronomer. In fact, he collaborated with several other Chinese experts to devise a new, more precise calendar for the Mongols. This calendar, known as the Shou-shih li, was promulgated after his death and was valued as exceedingly accurate. He was also well versed in the doctrines and rituals of Taoism, Buddhism, and Confucianism, a knowledge that served him well first when he participated in an official court debate between Buddhists and Taoists in 1258 and then when he revised the music and other ritual ceremonies for his Mongol sponsors. It is easy to see why Khubilai would recruit this Renaissance man for his corps of advisers.

Liu was first brought to Khubilai's attention in 1242, by the Buddhist monk Hai-yün, whose career we have described earlier. Liu was only about a year younger than the Mongol khan, and they appear to have developed a close rapport from the start. Only twenty-six years old at the time, Liu had already served as a minor functionary in government, studied mathematics and astronomy, explored Taoist rituals and magic, and been initiated as a monk in the Ch'an (in Japanese, Zen) order of Buddhism. His wealth of experience, along with a practical, political bent, attracted Khubilai's notice, and his mixture of high-minded moral principles and concrete, practical proposals captivated Khubilai.

Liu strove to convey this ideal mixture in a ten-thousand word memorandum he presented to Khubilai.[19] In the time-honored Confucian manner, he began by referring to the legendary Chinese emperors of the era before written history. This invocation of the heroes of the past was part of the rhetoric meant to persuade a traditional Chinese ruler of the efficacy of the policies proposed by the author. If the ruler wished to attain the kind of golden age represented by the sage emperors, Liu stated, he needed to follow the advice that he was about to offer. Liu's advice consisted of a number of specific recommendations. Through all of these ran the familiar theme of the nurturing and protection of the scholar-officials, who were perceived as national treasures. Liu advocated that Khubilai rely on them to implement his program and build schools throughout his domain to prepare young men for the civil service examinations that would qualify them to join the scholar-official class. Not only did Liu advocate the reintroduction of the traditional Chinese examinations; simultaneously, he sought to restore the ancient Chinese rituals and musical ceremonies. In addition, Liu also proposed fixed tax and legal systems that would not overburden Khubilai's Chinese subjects. In the manner of a typical Chinese scholar, he concluded with an appeal to Khubilai to instruct scholars to prepare a history of the defeated Jurchen Chin dynasty.

In fact, Khubilai approved of nearly all of these proposals, with but two exceptions. He opposed the revival of the civil service examinations, because such a move would imply a commitment to the use of Chinese or at least Chinese-speaking officials and advisers. Khubilai wanted greater flexibility and did not intend to be dependent on the Chinese. He also temporarily shelved the proposal to compile a history of the previous dynasty.[20] Khubilai was, after all, still neither the ruler of the Mongol domains nor the emperor of China. It was not up to him to order the writing of a dynastic history. The authority to promote such a scholarly enterprise belonged to Möngke, if anyone. Liu surely understood that Khubilai had no authority to implement this proposal, and his motives in making it are difficult to fathom. Did he think that he could influence Möngke through his younger brother? Did he believe that Khubilai would become the Great Khan?

After accompanying Khubilai on his campaign to Ta-li, Liu devoted his attention to long-range plans. The Chinese sources give Liu, along with Yao Shu, some credit for preventing the indiscriminate killing of Ta-li's inhabitants and the plunder of their lands. I have already questioned this version of events. In any case, now Khubilai and his advisers had several years' respite from warfare, and they had the time to initiate a large-scale project that would demonstrate Khubilai's growing attachment to and concern for his Chinese subjects: the establishment of a capital within Khubilai's new domains in the sedentary world. Some Chinese sources attribute this idea to Liu while others make no mention of his involvement in this decision. Khubilai's contribution ought not to be discounted. He needed little, if any, persuasion to recognize the symbolism of the construction of such a center, at any rate. Perhaps Khubilai and Liu ought to share the credit.

The location they selected was north of the Luan River and thirty-six miles west of the Ch'ing dynasty (1644–1911) town of Dolōn-Nūr (Seven Lakes).[21] It lay about a ten-day journey by horse from Peking along the edges of both the Chinese agrarian frontier and the Mongol pasturelands. Traditional Mongols could not quite accuse Khubilai of abandoning his heritage and siding with the Chinese, for several Mongol princes had in fact built towns in the steppes. Yet Khubilai had signaled a change in focus to his Chinese subjects when in 1256 he ordered that Liu Ping-chung choose a site for the town on the basis of the principles of "wind and water" or geomancy, a traditional Chinese practice.[22] It is not clear whether Khubilai viewed this new town as a capital or simply as a summer residence. He originally named it K'ai-p'ing, but in 1263 he changed its name to Shang-tu (Upper Capital), in contrast to Chung-tu (Central Capital), the contemporary name for Peking.[23]

Still another signal for Khubilai's sedentary subjects was that K'ai-p'ing was modeled on Chinese capitals of the past. Apart from a sizable hunting preserve, in the Mongol manner, the placement of some of its buildings reflects Chinese influence.[24] The town was divided into three sections. The outer city, the first of these sections, was in the shape of a square surrounded by an earthen wall twelve to eighteen feet in height.[25] Each side of the square encompassed 4,500 feet, and six gates, two each on the west and east walls and one each on the south and north walls, permitted entry into this part of the city. Six watchtowers or turrets were constructed on each wall to offer a special measure of protection. Most of the population lived in this outer city in mud or board houses. Estimates of the population run as high as 200,000. It appears unlikely, however, that so many people could have been supported at this site, and a more accurate figure is about half that number. Also in the outer city were several Buddhist temples situated in accord with traditional Chinese practice. The Hua-yen temple was located in the northeastern part of the town, while the

Ch'ien-yüan temple was constructed in the northwestern section.[26]
The ancient, arcane Chinese text entitled the *I Ching* (Book of changes)
had prescribed specific locations for various buildings, and the placement of the two temples conformed to this model[27]—yet another
indication of the Chinese influence on the city. There were probably
other Buddhist temples, as well as several Taoist temples and Muslim
mosques, but their precise location has not been ascertained.

The second section of K'ai-p'ing was the Inner City, which contained the residences of Khubilai and his retinue. Like the Outer City,
it was planned in the shape of a square, though the actual dimensions
of the sides were not equal. From the east to the west totaled 1,836
feet; north to south amounted to 2,016 feet. A brick wall ten to sixteen
feet in height surrounded the whole Inner City, and four turrets were
built in each side of the square. The English traveler S. W. Bushell,
who explored the site in 1872, and the Japanese archeologists who
excavated the area in the 1930s found only a high earthen platform
near the northern wall.[28] No other building could be identified, and
"nothing [was] left in the grass but the rocks which were used for
solidifying the ground preparatory to the erection of the buildings, to
tell the tale of glory of centuries ago."[29] The Imperial Palace, known
to the Chinese as the Ta-an ko (Pavilion of Great Harmony), was
built on this earthen platform, which measured about five hundred
feet from east to west and one hundred and fifty feet from north to
south. The platform, which was reinforced on various sides with
wooden beams or posts, was needed because the land was marshy.
Underneath the platform, "since the water was imprisoned in the
bowels of the earth, it came out in the course of time in other places in
meadows some distance away, where it flowed forth as so many
springs,"[30] making for a picturesque scene. This platform must have
been the site of the magnificent marble palace that so impressed
Marco Polo in the city he referred to as "Ciandu." Inside the palace, he
wrote, "the halls and rooms and passages are all gilded and wonder-
fully painted within with pictures and images of beasts and birds and
trees and flowers and many kinds of things, so well and so cunningly
that it is a delight and a wonder to see."[31] Palaces and government
buildings were scattered around the Inner City, but the Japanese
archeologists who explored the site in the 1930s were unable to
identify their exact locations. The town was apparently not as meticulously planned as other capitals of the middle period in Chinese
history, but its buildings were certainly luxurious. The palace was

made of marble and innumerable tiles and glazed roof tile decorations have been found on the site.[32]

K'ai-p'ing's principal innovation to the typical plan for a Chinese capital was its hunting preserve, the third section of the city, though a few Chinese dynasties had established small hunting parks. Located west and north of the Outer City, it was composed of meadow lands, woods, and streams. An earthen wall also enclosed the park, moats were found outside the walls, and four gates on various sides led into the site. Precious little of this magnificent man-made park has survived. The woods, streams, and buildings are all gone. It is only through Marco Polo that we are afforded a vivid description of this beautiful meadow and the buildings erected there. According to him, fountains and streams dotted the landscape. A variety of tame animals, principally deer, were kept in the park for Khubilai's hunts. Another diverting pursuit in this vast stretch of land was falconry. In the center of the park was a palace with a cane roof. The cane pillars were gilded and varnished, and the ceilings were painted with beasts and birds. Each cane was "fixed with nails for protection from winds, and they make those canes so well set together and joined that they protect the house from rain and send the water off downwards." Roaming in the park were special breeds of white mares and cows whose milk "no one else in the world dares drink . . . except only the great Kaan and his descendants."[33] "Xanadu," as Coleridge referred to Shang-tu, did indeed have a "stately pleasure dome."[34]

K'ai-p'ing was, in many ways, ideally situated. In summer it was much cooler than North China, and once he became the Great Khan, Khubilai spent June, July, and August there, away from the stifling heat of his capital in Peking. Surrounded on all sides by mountains and with abundant trees, animals, and birds, it offered a fine location for a town and could sustain a population of a moderate size. Whether Khubilai perceived of K'ai-p'ing as a capital is difficult to tell; he may have conceived of it simply as a summer residence. Whatever his view of K'ai-p'ing, in building it he was inevitably edging toward the values and lifestyles of his sedentary subjects.

Just as inevitably, his new orientation was bound to arouse opposition. Mongols espousing the traditional values were perturbed by his seemingly favorable attitude toward the Chinese, and from this time on they resisted his policies. This divisiveness weakened the Mongols and undermined their efforts at ruling the vast territories they had subjugated. Khubilai appeared to have succumbed to the attractions of Chinese civilization. Mongol traditionalists viewed his possible "conversion" to Chinese values as a threat to their way of life, and some were determined to destroy him before he could subvert their customary nomadic pastoral economy.

Surely Möngke had his reasons to listen to accusations of his younger brother's pro-Chinese, and possibly treasonous, attitudes and policies. He may have resented Khubilai's resounding success in the Ta-li campaigns. Khubilai, after remaining in the shadows for much of his young adulthood, was now becoming more prominent. Möngke may have been envious of his younger brother's new-found fame. He also could not have been happy with Khubilai's establishment of a luxurious residence at K'ai-p'ing, with palaces that rivaled and even surpassed the lavish residences of the Great Khan in Khara Khorum. The capital in the Mongol heartland, he must have believed, ought to be the real showpiece in the empire. Competition from Khubilai's newly constructed town was not welcome.

But even more important than these petty, perhaps ephemeral concerns was the fear that Khubilai was identifying with his subjects. Möngke's officials repeatedly attempted to arouse his suspicions of his younger brother. They accused Khubilai of using Chinese laws to administer his domain and of eschewing the traditional Mongol precepts.[35] Möngke still perceived of Khara Khorum as his capital and Mongolia as the center of the Mongol domains, but Khubilai's establishment of a principal residence in the sedentary world challenged the traditional Mongol society. Möngke must have been persuaded to eliminate the pernicious threat posed by his younger brother.

At any rate, in 1257, Möngke sent two of his trusted aides, Alandar and Liu T'ai-p'ing, to Khubilai's domain to investigate revenue collection.[36] Several Chinese sources imply that the stated objective of the mission was a pretext for bringing about Khubilai's downfall. The two emissaries would, if necessary, fabricate a case against Khubilai. After a hasty inspection of the tax records, they uncovered what they said were numerous infractions, evasions, and transgressions of the law. They immediately rounded up a number of high-ranking officials and executed them, without benefit of a hearing. Officials with unusually strong links with the great Mongol noble families escaped this fate. The celebrated Chinese military leader Shih T'ien-tse was one of these renowned officials whose own prominence or whose powerful supporters kept them from harm.[37] Others were not as fortunate, though there is no evidence of a terrible bloodbath. Having concluded the preliminary purge, Alandar set up an agency translated into Chinese as the Kou-k'ao chü to audit the records of the tax collection bureau and to scrutinize the activities of Khubilai's officials.[38] They were intent on reducing the number of Chinese in the local administration. The purge would no doubt continue until Khubilai himself was threatened. Already he had been relieved of some of his responsibilities, including the vital responsibility of tax collection, and it appeared that his position in the Mongol hierarchy was highly unstable.

Thus Khubilai's options were limited. He could defy his older brother, seek to oust the emissaries, and await the consequences. Möngke would probably have retaliated with a punitive expedition to crush his recalcitrant younger brother. This fraternal war would surely have weakened the Mongols and probably have led to Khubilai's defeat. Khubilai had little hope of securing much support from the Mongol nobles, since in their eyes he would be the insolent, rebellious younger brother. This option was thus impractical for Khubilai.

The Chinese sources give Khubilai's Confucian and Buddhist advisers credit for persuading him to adopt a second option. By their accounts the Confucian scholar Yao Shu pleaded with Khubilai not to be precipitous in his response, and Na-mo, whom Möngke had appointed the leader of the Buddhists in the Mongol empire, urged Khubilai to be even more reverential toward his older brother.[39] They both implied that if Khubilai were hostile he would simply confirm the scurrilous insinuations against his character made by Möngke's advisers. A more effective response, they proposed, was to correct the erroneous and misleading impressions conveyed by Khubilai's enemies at Möngke's court. Adopting this advice, Khubilai sent a Chinese named T'an Ch'eng and a Mongol named Kökö (Chin.: K'uo-k'uo) to Möngke to present his case.[40] Apparently the mission was unsuccessful, because in December of 1257 Möngke was still implacably hostile to Khubilai. A more impressive demonstration of compromise and conciliation was needed. Now Khubilai's advisers suggested that he go in person to Möngke's court in Khara Khorum to dispute the allegations against him. They recommended that he steer clear of political issues and appeal to Möngke brother to brother without reference to the larger questions on which they differed.[41] Khubilai did exactly as they suggested, the Chinese sources relate, and the meeting of the two brothers was a success. After the brothers fell into each other's arms, they say, all traces of the conflict vanished.

But how adequate is this as an explanation? Both Möngke and Khubilai were hard-headed realists and rarely allowed their emotions to shape their policies. Sentiment, even in the form of a tearful re-union, would not often motivate them on critical policy decisions. Family feeling certainly did not inhibit Möngke at his accession to the khanate, when he conducted a ruthless purge directed at his cousins, aunts, and more distant relatives. Fraternal strife was not unknown among the Mongols, and within a couple of years Khubilai himself would engage in a bloody struggle for the succession with his own younger brother. The touching reconciliation described in the Chinese accounts may have happened, but the explanation for it does not lie in fraternal affection alone.

In January of 1258, Möngke faced two critical, divisive issues that could undermine his rule. First, a religious conflict between the Buddhists and the Taoists had escalated into pitched battles, destruction of temples and monasteries, and confiscation of valuable religious artifacts. Möngke needed to achieve a reconciliation, or at least stability, to promote his political and economic objectives. The second task was to conquer Southern China, by far the wealthiest region of the Middle Kingdom. Subjugation of the South would not only make Möngke appear more awesome to the Chinese but might also increase his stature among Chinese officials and scholars, whose country had not been unified for over three centuries. Both issues confronting Möngke involved China, Khubilai's bailiwick, and without Khubilai's assistance, Möngke would face grave difficulties in dealing with them. Khubilai had won the confidence of many Northern Chinese, and his Chinese advisers could be helpful in resolving the Buddhist-Taoist dispute as well as in gaining the allegiance of Chinese in the South. Thus Möngke could ill afford to cast Khubilai aside and alienate his younger brother's Chinese allies. Möngke's innate pragmatism would certainly not countenance such a drastic, self-defeating gesture. Thus the tearful reconciliation with Khubilai. This assessment strikes me as more realistic than the Chinese version. Though I do not rule out the possibility that the dramatic scene portrayed in the Chinese chronicles occurred, I believe it occurred only after both Möngke and Khubilai had rationally evaluated the folly of a split between them.

KHUBILAI AND THE
BUDDHIST-TAOIST DEBATE

Though Möngke imposed stricter surveillance of Khubilai's lands and was more careful in granting Khubilai additional territory in North China, the Great Khan also offered his younger brother additional responsibilities. Shortly after their meeting and the purported settlement of their disagreement, Möngke authorized Khubilai to preside over a debate between Buddhist and Taoist clerics that would put an end to the mounting hostility between the two groups. Khubilai quickly convened a meeting at K'ai-p'ing, to which he invited Buddhists, Taoists, and presumably impartial Confucian scholars and advisers and court officials. This conference for the first time gave Buddhists and Taoists the opportunity to air their views and to have the secular authorities adjudicate their dispute. Khubilai had been entrusted with a vital task: he was to judge the conflicting claims of the two religions.

Power, not ideology, motivated the struggle between the Buddhists and the Taoists in the 1250s.[42] A variety of different Taoist sects, as many as eighty-one by one account, had proliferated, stretching all the way from the ascetic Ch'üan-chen order to the more worldly Cheng-i sect, which emphasized fortune telling, astrology, and magic.[43] Some of them clearly lusted after worldly gains and access to political power, desires that placed them on a direct collision course with the Buddhist sects. During the Mongol era, the Taoists appear to have been the more rebellious of the two groups, but this impression may derive from the bias of the Buddhist sources upon which we are dependent.[44]

A new element, the Tibetan Buddhists, contributed to the developing controversy and hostility. During Möngke's reign, a growing number of Tibetan Buddhists started to appear in North China. In 1252, Mongol troops, under orders from the Great Khan, had invaded Tibet and had finally pacified that land. In Tibet, lamas had been politically involved, often seeking and securing assistance from the political authorities in disputes with the native Bon shamanists. Once they had overcome the shamanists, the lamas themselves frequently acted as secular governors within their jurisdictions. To rule effectively over their people, they had incorporated some Bon beliefs into their version of Buddhism, introducing a strong element of magic. Though the ideology of their Tantric form of Buddhism was difficult to explain, its mysticism, magic, and astrology were appealing to ordinary people. The lamas' claims of magical abilities in particular attracted the Mongols, who favored religions with tangible benefits or noticeable, awesome powers. The lamas' experience in Tibet, which had instilled in them an appreciation of the role of politics in religious disputes, made them valuable allies for the Chinese Buddhists.[45]

Thus the stage was set for the Buddhist-Taoist struggle under the Mongols. Both groups sought supremacy and both were willing to appeal to the secular authorities for assistance. Each resented any special favors granted to the other by the government. Each desired the patronage of the Mongol court, and actively attempted to ingratiate itself with the Mongol ruling elite. Because their secular ambitions were at odds and irreconcilable, a conflict between them could not be averted.

The Taoists had taken the offensive by affirming the *hua-hu* ("convert the barbarians") theory, which had been most fully developed in the *Hua-hu ching* (Classic of the conversion of the barbarians) by Wang Fu (alias Chi Kung-tz'u), a fourth-century work. According to this interpretation, the Taoist sage Lao Tzu had died not in China but in the Western Regions, which in this case refers to India. Transforming himself into one of the eighty-one incarnations he eventually adopted during his lifetime, he became known as the Buddha and started to propagate the teachings of Buddhism. He reached India where he began to convert the local people. In effect, the Buddhist sutras derived from Taoist writings.[46] The *hua-hu* theory implied that Buddhism was a simple and corrupted form of Taoism, developed by Lao Tzu to appeal to the less sophisticated foreigners in the West, and that Taoism was superior to and more significant than Buddhism.[47] Naturally the Buddhists found it most offensive.

Another part of the Taoist arsenal was a second work, also fabricated, known as the *Pa-shih-i hua-t'u* (Illustrations of the eighty-one conversions). Unlike the *Hua-hu ching*, the *Pa-shih-i hua-t'u* did not consist of a reasoned argument against Buddhism or a scornful characterization of the religion as inferior. Instead, it was comprised of portraits of eighty-one incarnations of Lao Tzu. In one of these paintings, he appeared as the Buddha—still another indication that the sacred figure in the Indian religion was inferior to the Chinese sage.[48] Infuriated by such slights the Buddhists soon found ways to retaliate.

Their response to the Taoists' disparaging, even scurrilous, *hua-hu* theory was to create their own version of the relationship between Lao Tzu and Buddha. They claimed that Buddha was born in 1029 B.C. and had departed this world in 950 B.C. Thus his religious enlightenment had preceded Lao Tzu's birth by at least three centuries, and, by virtue of earlier birth, he was superior to Lao Tzu. But some texts went further, contending that Lao Tzu and even Confucius were merely disciples of the Buddha, even quoting passages from the *Hua-hu ching*. Here, said the Buddhists, Lao Tzu portrayed himself on a lower level than Buddha, depicting himself as Mahākāśyapa, the leader of the disciples after Buddha's death and the compiler of the earliest Buddhist canon.[49]

The Taoists acted first in this struggle.[50] Capitalizing on the patronage of the Mongol khans, they sought to intimidate the Buddhists by circulating numerous copies of the *Hua-hu ching* and the *Pa-shih-i hua-t'u*.[51] The Buddhist accounts, on which we are dependent for information about these events, also complained that the Taoists defaced and destroyed Buddhist paintings and sculptures, turned Buddhist temples and monasteries into Taoist ones, and appropriated land formerly farmed by Buddhist monks. Such active harassment clearly threatened the Buddhists and necessitated a response. The Buddhist sources narrate the history of the Buddhist-Taoist struggles, including the tumultuous debates that were convened in the 1250s and continued sporadically until 1281.[52] They give the Taoist viewpoint short shrift, and what emerges, therefore, is an account highly favorable to the Buddhists.

The principal judge, Khubilai, had by this time been exposed to Buddhism and Taoism as well as to other religions within China. If we judge from his later utterances and actions, he was much more sympathetic to the Buddhists than to the Taoists. For example, in a conversation with Marco Polo, Khubilai described his religious views, by a curious omission.

> There are four prophets who are worshipped and to whom everybody does reverence. The Christians say their God was Jesus Christ; the Saracens Mahomet; the Jews Moses; and the idolaters Sagamoni Burcan [the Shakyamuni Buddha], who was the first god to the idols; and I do honour and reverence to all four, that is to him who is the greatest in heaven and more true, and him I pray to help me.[53]

He overlooked, probably deliberately, the fifth prophet, Lao Tzu, and his religion, Taoism. From the time of his introduction to Buddhism, he had seen its value to him. He had been impressed with Hai-yün, the first important Ch'an Buddhist monk he had encountered. In one of their dialogues, Khubilai had asked, "Among the three religions [Buddhism, Taoism, and Confucianism] which one is the most honorable, which has the best law, and which is the outermost?" Hai-yün responded:

> Among all sages, only Buddhist monks are not tricky. Therefore from ancient times, Buddhism has always been held above the others. Consequently, according to the royal decree of the imperial ancestors, the empress mother [Töregene] proclaimed that Buddhist monks should stand at the head and that no Taoist priest should be allowed to be placed before a monk.[54]

By such statements Hai-yün attempted to prejudice Khubilai against the Taoists. The Ch'an monk also introduced Khubilai to Liu Ping-chung, who became an influential adviser and a promoter of policies that benefited the Buddhists.

But Khubilai increasingly turned to Tibetan Buddhism. Because Ch'an, a meditative quietistic sect, had scant immediate utility, its attractiveness to the pragmatic Mongol prince was limited. The purported magical powers of the Tibetan Buddhists were much more appealing. Moreover, the politically experienced lamas could be useful political allies for Khubilai. Rewarding and patronizing them would eventually benefit him. As early as 1253, Khubilai had invited the Sa-skya Paṇḍita, the most renowned of the Tibetan Buddhist monks, to an interview.[55] The Sa-skya Paṇḍita had died in 1251, however, and his nephew, the 'Phags-pa lama (1235–80), accepted the invitation. The Tibetan sources offer a fanciful, legendary account of the first encounter between Khubilai and the 'Phags-pa lama. As soon as they met, one Tibetan text reports, they became inextricably interrelated, "like the sun and moon in the sky."[56] Khubilai became the patron and the 'Phags-pa lama served as his religious confidant. The Great Khan presumably provided the political and military support for 'Phags-pa's efforts to dominate Tibet while the lama supplied Khubilai with religious instruction.

Khubilai at first had been much more interested in another Tibetan who passed through his domains, however. This Tibetan monk, named Karma Pakshi (1204–83), was a leader of the Black Hat order of the Karma-pa sect. Renowned for his magical and supernatural powers, Karma Pakshi reputedly could enter into a trance and then perform miracles.[57] When Khubilai learned of his remarkable abilities, he invited him to remain in his camp. Karma Pakshi declined the

Mongol prince's invitation, however, and set forth for Möngke's palaces at Khara Khorum.

Karma Pakshi's rejection of Khubilai finally permitted the ʿPhags-pa lama to demonstrate his value. The ʿPhags-pa lama took advantage of this opportunity to ingratiate himself with the khan. Perhaps as important, he struck up a relationship with Khubilai's wife Chabi, an ardent Buddhist. According to the Tibetan and Mongol sources, under the influence of the ʿPhags-pa lama's views she reputedly mediated a dispute over precedence between Khubilai and the Tibetan master. For his part, the ʿPhags-pa lama was willing to serve Khubilai as long as the Mongol Khan accorded him a higher status. As a Buddhist monk, the ʿPhags-pa lama proclaimed himself to be superior to the temporal authorities, but as a Mongol khan, Khubilai perceived himself to be superior to everyone in his domains. Chabi helped to reconcile these conflicting claims and permitted them to work together. Under the new scheme, the ʿPhags-pa lama had precedence in spiritual and religious affairs while Khubilai was granted jurisdiction in temporal matters. When Khubilai received private religious instruction from the lama, he would sit on a lower platform than the Tibetan cleric. But when Khubilai conducted court business in public, he would sit on a higher platform than the ʿPhags-pa lama.[58] Both men readily accepted the compromise.

In short, Khubilai went into the debates already leaning toward the Buddhists, particularly the Tibetan lamas. Since the presiding official already favored the Buddhists, he would surely offer them whatever support he could. Thus, the outcome was predetermined. No matter what the Taoists did, they were bound to lose.

In 1258, the debates were convened by Khubilai in his newly built town of K'ai-p'ing. The Chinese and Tibetan Buddhists, who must have known that Khubilai was prejudiced in their favor, were determined to press their advantage in order once and for all to be rid of their Taoist antagonists. The Chinese abbot Fu-yü and the Tibetan lama ʿPhags-pa were the two most prominent Buddhist dignitaries at these meetings. The Taoists, whose leader Chang Chih-ching was relatively inexperienced and apparently not a skillful debater, were less well represented. And the other Taoist spokesmen were generally colorless and unimaginative.[59]

The debate centered on the two texts that had been circulated by the Taoists. The ʿPhags-pa lama cross-examined his Taoist counterparts about the authenticity of the *Hua-hu ching*. He sought proof of its date and authorship, and compelled the Taoists to acknowledge that neither Lao Tzu nor the early Chinese historians mentioned the text. The first great universal history of China, the *Shih-chi* by Ssu-ma Ch'ien, written in the first century B.C., did not refer to the *Hua-hu ching*, an omission that undermined the Taoists' credibility. The ʿPhags-pa lama suggested that the two Taoist documents were forgeries, an extremely damaging suggestion that the Taoists were unable to refute. There was no textual verification for the early existence of the *Hua-hu ching* and the *Pa-shih-i hua-t'u*.[60] The Taoists' scholarship was on shaky grounds here.

Khubilai actively participated in the debates. He was not simply a passive witness to these discussions, but frequently asked leading questions, commented on the statements of the debaters, and presented his own views. And he clearly revealed his own pro-Buddhist sentiments. By this time, he was convinced that the Buddhists had won the ideological debate. But he offered the Taoists one last opportunity to save face by challenging them to perform the magical and supernatural feats at which they repeatedly claimed to be proficient. The Taoists were unable to demonstrate any otherworldly powers, however, and Khubilai's faith in their abilities was further eroded.

In the end, Khubilai decreed the Taoists to be the losers in the debates and punished their leaders. He ordered his retainers to shave the heads of seventeen prominent Taoists and to compel them to convert to Buddhism. All copies of the two forged texts were to be burned, and even copies of the writings and paintings found in steles, pillars, and walls were to be erased or destroyed. The Buddhist temples occupied by the Taoists, numbering around 237, and the properties the Taoists had confiscated were to be restored to their rightful Buddhist owners.[61]

These penalties were certainly a blow to Taoism, but they were not devastating. Taoism was not proscribed, nor were any Taoists imprisoned or executed. After all the accusations of Taoist excesses and crimes, it appears that Khubilai was surprisingly lenient, perhaps out of unwillingness to alienate the large Taoist community in North China.[62] Taoism was popular among all classes in China, and a vindictive purge would have aroused and enraged the Taoists and thus would have impeded Khubilai's efforts to govern. His mother had advised him to avoid such religious disunity, and Khubilai must have accepted this as wise counsel. Slapping the hands of the leading Taoist dignitaries was sufficient to warn them to avoid further bullying of the Buddhists.

For a time, the Buddhist-Taoist conflict appeared to subside. Naturally Khubilai's efforts were applauded, and his prestige among the Mongol hierarchy was bolstered. Moreover, he had won over some Chinese scholars with his skills at presiding and mediating over the debates. They were impressed by his intelligence and his moderation, and he had demonstrated credibility as an executive. With this victory, he was prepared for his next challenging assignment.

MÖNGKE'S CAMPAIGN AGAINST THE SOUTHERN SUNG

The task with which Möngke now entrusted Khubilai was indeed a challenge—to lead one of Möngke's four armies in the conquest of Southern China. The Mongols needed to gain the submission of the Southern Sung dynasty if they intended to secure their control of North China and prevent Chinese nationalists in the North from rallying around the Southern state. The Southern Sung was a reminder that the Chinese had an alternative, and its existence was a threat to Mongol rule. Möngke may also have been eager to divert his troops, to keep them occupied as well as to have them maintain their military skills. He therefore decided to mount the campaign to crush the Chinese in the South, in which Khubilai was to play a vital role.

Möngke's plan raised some questions. Several leaders in his entourage objected that the South was hot and a breeding ground for diseases, implying that the Mongol armies would suffer much more than in the cool climates to which they were accustomed. The Mongol forces, the critics contended, would get mired because of these unfamiliar conditions. However, Möngke responded forcefully that he wished to complete the task that his ancestors had begun.[63] He overrode all opposition with this response and with his evident desire to conquer the rest of China.

Victory over the Sung would require more advanced techniques in warfare. China south of the Yangtze River had some of the largest cities in the world. The capital at Lin-an (modern Hangchow), for instance, was the world's most populous city, with a population conservatively estimated at approximately 1.5 million.[64] By contrast, Venice, one of the commercial centers of Europe, had 100,000 inhabitants. The techniques of siege warfare that the Mongols had developed in their campaigns in North China would truly be tested now. Heavy artillery would be needed in besieging these towns, for catapults that could hurl big rocks and stones were essential. Cavalry warfare, which had been the Mongols' main strength, was not suited to either the terrain or the society of South China. Here, their success would depend upon infantry and upon sieges of the principal cities.[65] For assistance in planning and executing such campaigns, they turned to both their Chinese advisers and the Muslims in their employ.

Having concluded that his troops were capable of defeating and occupying South China, Möngke decided to deploy his forces along four fronts, to keep the Sung armies from concentrating on defending any one region. They would be dispersed along a wide expanse of territory in order to counter the Mongol assaults. Despite this advantage, Möngke still meticulously planned his campaign. His youngest brother, Arigh Böke, remained in Khara Khorum to protect the capital and to manage the daily operations of the Mongol state. Mongol custom dictated that the youngest be placed in charge of the family hearth or lands, and Möngke adhered to tradition in assigning Arigh Böke that task.

With preparations made and plans in place, in June and July of 1257 Möngke made a pilgrimage to Chinggis's old palaces. There, he conducted the ritual sacrifices that were designed to ensure success in a new venture.[66] In the following month, he made the proper offerings to Heaven, scattering the milk from his own special herd of mares on the sacred ground around his palace.[67] Having performed his duties as a good Mongol ruler, he was prepared to start marching toward the south. By May of 1258, he had crossed the Yellow River and assembled his forces at Liu-p'an shan, just southwest of modern Ku-yüan hsien in the modern province of Ning-hsia. The number of troops under his command is unclear. The figures given by Persian historians appear to be grossly inflated. One source credits Möngke with a force of 600,000 men, while another claims that Khubilai alone led a contingent of nine *tümen* (approximately 90,000 troops).[68] The Chinese figures are generally much lower.[69] When Möngke succeeded in capturing an important town in Szechwan, he left a force of 3,000 men as guards.[70] Had he truly commanded the sizable army claimed for him in the Persian chronicles, he surely would have stationed a larger detachment to protect his hard-won gains.[71]

Specific objectives were assigned to each of the four armies. The troops under Möngke's personal command were to head south from his base in the northwest, occupy the southwestern province of Szechwan, and then march eastward. Khubilai's troops were directed to move south from his newly constructed town of K'ai-p'ing to the central part of China and cross the Yangtze River at O-chou (Wu-ch'ang in modern Hupei), where they were to defeat the Sung forces. There they would rendezvous with the detachments led by Uriyang-khadai, the third army, who were to march northeast from Yünnan. The fourth army, led by a grandson of one of Chinggis Khan's brothers, was to move from Möngke's base in Liu-p'an shan eastward toward Hsiang-yang, just northwest of O-chou. Eventually it too was slated to join Khubilai's and Uriyangkhadai's troops.[72] The plan clearly was to isolate the eastern and western sections of the Southern Sung. By concentrating on pacifying southwest and central China, the Mongols hoped to pressure the core of Sung strength, which was centered in the east. They also hoped that a quick victory in the west would persuade the Sung to capitulate and would minimize Mongol losses.

Möngke's troops faced the greatest difficulties. His route of march was the most strenuous and the least well explored and traveled. The heat in the southwest was oppressive, and the hilly terrain treacherous and easily defensible. The natural environment favored the defenders, and they capitalized on their familiarity with the landscape to delay Möngke's progress. Cavalry, one of the Mongols' main strengths, was not a great asset in this expedition. Instead, sieges of enclaves and towns dominated the military action. Though the Mongols had become much more proficient in siege warfare, this military tactic was not their forte. Moreover, the defenders were perhaps more tenacious than the Mongols had anticipated. Möngke was to be stalled in the southwest for more time than he would have liked.[73]

Yet his campaign started auspiciously. By March of 1258, his troops had overrun the city of Ch'eng-tu, one of the vital strongholds in Szechwan. Their next objective was the region around Ch'ung-ch'ing, where the main obstacle was the town of Ho-chou. Wang Chien, the Sung general, was determined to guard the town and to repel the Mongol invaders. He did not appear to be intimidated by the forces arrayed against him and was unwilling to surrender. As a result, Möngke's forces made slow progress.[74] In March of 1259, a year after his victory in Ch'eng-tu, Möngke held a banquet for his leading generals to discuss future strategy. After much food and drink, they began their deliberations. Once again, one of Möngke's most trusted advisers expressed reservations about campaigns in lands so different from the areas of the Mongols' earlier successes. He reemphasized the threats of disease and intense heat. Yet Möngke pushed aside these objections and resolutely pressed forward with his plans to occupy Ho-chou by whatever means he could. His efforts were, however, doomed to failure.

For five months Möngke campaigned in the Ho-chou region. His troops repeatedly attacked the town from late March to early May, but to no avail. Both sides, according to the sources, suffered severe losses. Möngke was not deterred, however. He persisted, but his troops were hampered by heavy rainstorms in May and early June.[75] His campaign bogged down during this wet season. As soon as the rains ended, his forces assaulted the town, but Wang Chien's troops could not be budged. On one of the last assaults, a certain Wang Te-ch'en led his forces in setting up ladders to storm the city walls. As he was climbing a ladder, he spotted Wang Chien and urged the Sung general to submit. Wang Chien responded by hurling rocks at the attackers, one of which hit and killed Wang Te-ch'en.[76]

On August 11, within a few days of this bloody but inconclusive attack, Möngke died in the nearby hills at Tiao-yü shan. Some of the sources attribute his demise to an arrow wound that he received during the siege of Ho-chou.[77] Others, including the Yüan shih, assert that he succumbed to dysentery.[78] Rashīd al-Dīn states that Möngke was a victim of a cholera epidemic.[79] Whatever the cause, Möngke's death reverberated throughout the Mongol world and profoundly influenced its future course.

THE STRUGGLE FOR SUCCESSION

With Möngke's death, the top echelons of the Mongol world came to a standstill. Möngke's own campaign in the southwest ended abruptly. His troops retained the territory they had occupied but registered no additional gains. Nor did they make any further efforts to link up with the other Mongol armies seeking to pacify the Sung. Möngke's corpse was transported to northeast Mongolia and buried alongside his father, Tolui, and his grandfather, Chinggis. Another two decades would elapse before the Mongols finally vanquished the Sung.

Möngke's own expedition was not the only one to be temporarily sidetracked: Mongols as far away as the Middle East were affected by the Great Khan's death. Möngke's younger brother Hülegü, who had expanded the lands under Mongol control to the Syrian border, halted his advance and headed back toward Mongolia. Leaving a token force under the command of the Nestorian Ked Bukha, he rushed back to take part in the *khuriltai* that would elect the new Great Khan. Once he had temporarily halted his advance in the Middle East, he never regained his momentum. Just as the death of Ögödei had prompted the Mongols to abandon their campaign in Eastern Europe, the death of Möngke terminated their plans for further expansion in the Middle East and Asia Minor. In addition, Hülegü's absence, as we shall note later, offered the Muslims both a respite and an opportunity to attack the small detachments led by the unfortunate Ked Bukha. Thus they were able to avenge themselves by administering the first critical defeat to the thirteenth-century Mongols.

Once more, the lack of an orderly succession to the Great Khanate had brought dislocation and disruption to the Mongol world. Without a specific line of descent, a *khuriltai* had to be convened to select the new ruler. We have seen how the circumstances surrounding the election of Möngke—the disputed election, the purges that followed his enthronement—exacerbated the difficulties and tarnished the image of the *khuriltai*. It appeared that the leader with the greatest military power (Batu, for example, in the case of Möngke's appointment) could sway the election. Raw military power, not any particular principle of succession, provided the strongest challengers for the khanate. If two leading candidates thought themselves to be equally qualified, then the danger of a confrontation was magnified. Such divisiveness scarcely promoted stability within the Mongol domains. Möngke's enthronement in 1251 had clearly alienated the descendants of Ögödei and Chaghadai, two of the four Mongol royal families. They certainly sought an opportunity to reassert their claims to the Great Khanate, and Möngke's death offered just such a possibility.

The actual struggle for the throne, however, was conducted within the house of Tolui. Two of Möngke's younger brothers, Khubilai and Arigh Böke, wished to replace him. Hülegü, the third of his brothers, who had established his own domain in West Asia, did not contest the throne. Though he did not decisively influence the outcome of the struggle, he favored his older brother Khubilai as Great Khan. His support for Khubilai probably stemmed in part from their common identification with the sedentary world. Arigh Böke, however, had remained in the Mongol homeland while his brothers traveled to the centers of the great civilizations in the south and west. His concerns and life were more parochial and confined, and he preferred the world of the steppes to the world of the sown. He emerged as the defender of the traditional Mongol ways and values, a leader of the more conservative elements among the Mongols, who felt dispossessed, isolated, and threatened by the growing fondness for sedentary life. These elements considered Khubilai and Hülegü to be among the worst offenders, as they were attracted by the civilizations they had helped to conquer, sought advice and assistance from the subject populace, and spent most of their time not in Mongolia but in either China or Persia. Appalled by the changes they observed in Khubilai, Hülegü, and some of their other leaders, this discontented group of conservatives turned to Arigh Böke to represent them.

Since Arigh Böke ultimately lost the contest, the sources yield pitifully little information supporting his claims. They portray him as a usurper, duplicitous and power-hungry, who initiated the succession crisis by plotting to take the throne illegally. Encouraged by his advisers, he surreptitiously maneuvered to frustrate the wishes of the Mongol nobility and to succeed to the khanate before anyone else could lay claim to the throne. This version of events is simplistic and unduly harsh toward Arigh Böke, however. Despite his protestations, Khubilai was as eager as Arigh Böke to ascend to the throne. The *Yüan shih* tells us that Khubilai thrice refused the offer of the Khanate, but his refusals were ritualistic.[80] He was simply abiding by the rules of etiquette developed by his immediate predecessors. It would have been unseemly to appear too anxious to accede, and he was living up to the expectations of the Mongol nobility. He was just as willing as his younger brother to employ any tactics to attain his objective of becoming the Great Khan. A brief recounting of the events leading to Khubilai's assumption of the Khanate reveals his desire and drive for power.

Sometime in 1258, Khubilai learned of Möngke's plans for the expedition against the Sung. In the last month of the year, he set out from his palace in K'ai-p'ing toward the south. He dispatched an advance guard under General Batur to gather and prepare supplies for his troops on their march. Seeking to duplicate his successful Ta-li expedition, he warned his officers against indiscriminate killing of Chinese and cautioned that those who disobeyed this injunction could be punished and even executed.[81] Clearly he hoped to gain the allegiance of the Chinese by this evidence of his leniency and flexibility. By August of 1259, he had crossed the Huai River (in the modern province of Honan) and had dispatched his close adviser, Lien Hsi-hsien, a Uighur, to the T'ai-shan area (near Huang-an hsien in modern Hupei) to call on the local people to submit. After Lien's departure, Khubilai continued on his southward march, reaching the northern banks of the Yangtze River early in September. Ten days later, he learned of Möngke's death from a messenger sent by his half-brother Möge, who asked him to return to the north for the election of the new Great Khan. According to the *Yüan shih*, Khubilai refused, saying, "I have received Imperial orders to come south. How can I return without merit?" [82] Rashīd al-Dīn recounts the same incident and quotes Khubilai as saying, "We have come hither with an army like ants or locusts: How can we turn back, our task undone, because of rumors?" [83]

Whether these dialogues actually took place, or were later fabrications meant to illustrate Khubilai's selflessness and heroic stature, is difficult to determine. His motives for pursuing the campaign against the Sung for another two months are unclear. He must surely have realized that the speedy election of a Great Khan was vital. Perhaps he wanted or needed a success over the Sung to prove his abilities. Neither Ögödei nor Möngke had been able to defeat the Sung or to impose a settlement on the Southern Chinese. A triumph here would naturally impress the forthcoming *khuriltai*. Moreover, if a dispute over the succession arose, he could count upon some of the resources of Southern China in any contest for the khanate. For these reasons he ignored the request of his half-brother to return to the north.

Thus Khubilai was intent on crossing the Yangtze and seizing territory across that river. A few weeks after rebuffing Möge, he ordered his troops to launch a strike on the opposite bank. His generals, deterred by the wind and thunderstorms that swept across the river at that time, recommended that Khubilai wait until conditions were more conducive for an attack against the Sung side. He overrode their objections, however, and demanded immediate preparations for a crossing.[84] The flags were lifted, the drums beaten, and the troops crossed over to the other side. As soon as they landed, the sky cleared and a battle ensued. Both sides suffered numerous casualties, but the Mongols had established a base south of the Yangtze.

Their next objective was O-chou. This town along the Yangtze was not as easily stormed. It was heavily fortified, and a long siege appeared to be in the offing. The Chancellor (Ch'eng-hsiang) of the

Southern Sung, Chia Ssu-tao, had also dispatched reinforcements to the besieged town.[85] The Sung general Lü Wen-te arrived from Ch'ung-ch'ing and, incredibly enough, on the night of October 5 eluded the Mongol forces and led his troops into O-chou.[86] This breach of the siege indicates that the Mongols were not in total control of the area. Khubilai, however, was eager to capture O-chou, since a victory would bolster his prestige in the Mongol world, and appeared unwilling to accept a compromise. Chia Ssu-tao, who wished to preserve the territory of the Southern Sung at any cost, sent Sung Ching, one of his generals, to negotiate a settlement. Chia harked back to the conditions accepted in 1005 by the Khitans, a group from Manchuria who had threatened the survival of the Northern Sung dynasty. By the Treaty of Shan-yüan, the Khitans had agreed not to make incursions on Chinese territory in return for an annual tribute of silk and silver from the Sung.[87] Now Chia Ssu-tao attempted to work out a similar arrangement with the Mongols and authorized Sung Ching to offer Khubilai a yearly payment of silver and textiles in return for a pledge to maintain the Yangtze as their common border, but Khubilai rejected the agreement. Chao Pi, a Confucian adviser who acted as Khubilai's representative in a meeting with Sung Ching, was scornful of the Sung proposal, noting that "now, after we have already crossed the Yangtze, what use are these words?"[88] The Mongols had already won, by force, the territorial concessions that the Sung envoy was willing to grant them. Why abandon the campaign, Khubilai must have reasoned, when they were on the verge of victory? There was no need to compromise; time was on his side, and his military efforts were bearing fruit.

The succession crisis saved the Sung at this juncture. The struggle for the khanate had heated up considerably in the few months following Möngke's death, and Arigh Böke had garnered substantial support for his candidacy. One of Möngke's wives, along with Möngke's sons Asutai and Ürüng Tash, threw in their lot with him.[89] Ögödei's grandson Durchi, Chaghadai's grandson Alghu, and Jochi's grandson Khurumshi, among others, also pledged their support. In addition, Arigh Böke had influential allies outside the royal family, among whom was Bolghai, the most important official during Möngke's reign. Thus arrayed, he now made his move. Arigh Böke appointed Alandar as the commander of his armies and ordered him to raise troops north of the Gobi while Durchi recruited forces for him south of that dreaded desert. Late in November, Durchi headed toward Yen, the region around modern Peking, which he hoped to overwhelm.[90] Alandar began a march toward Khubilai's new town of K'ai-p'ing. Khubilai's wife Chabi, who had stayed behind while her husband went on campaign, tried to stall Alandar's advance; she also dispatched an envoy to inform Khubilai of his younger brother's plans. Khubilai was left without options. He would have to abandon the siege of O-chou and depart for the north to counter Arigh Böke. Accepting the inevitable, he withdrew most of his troops from O-chou and went to assert his claims, leaving behind a token force under Batur to preserve some of their gains.[91]

Rashīd al-Dīn's version of this story is even more critical of Arigh Böke's alleged duplicity. The Persian historian tells us that Arigh Böke was recruiting troops (*cherig* and *turqaq*) but sought to conceal this effort. When Khubilai asked Arigh Böke's messengers about the ugly rumors circulating concerning the troops, they responded, "We slaves know nothing. Assuredly it is a lie."[92] Khubilai's suspicions were aroused, however, and he transmitted a message to Arigh Böke conveying his suspicions. Arigh Böke immediately sent an envoy to "speak sweet" to Khubilai and to inform him that "he had cancelled the raising of *turqaq*s and *cherig*s."[93] Actually he had no such intention, and continued to build up his army for an eventual confrontation with Khubilai. The denouement occurred when, in an effort to trap and seize his adversary, Arigh Böke invited Khubilai and "all the [other] princes" to meet to mourn the death of Möngke. However, recognizing that he would be detained as soon as he set foot in Arigh Böke's land, Khubilai rejected the invitation, on the pretext that "we have not yet returned from the campaign."[94] Arigh Böke realized at that point that he could not deceive Khubilai, and he prepared for war. Spreading the rumor that his older brother Hülegü and Berke, the ruler of the Golden Horde in Russia, backed his candidacy, he cultivated the support of as many Mongol nobles as he could muster. Now, neither side could turn back from the confrontation. Is Rashīd al-Dīn's account reliable? Clearly it is weighted against Arigh Böke. I believe that each side must have provoked the other, because both nobles yearned for the top position.

When Khubilai reached K'ai-p'ing in the spring of 1260, numerous princes reportedly urged him to accept the leadership of the Mongol world. The *Yüan shih* says that they "begged" him to take the throne. After three ritual refusals, he finally acceded to their wishes, and on May 5, in K'ai-p'ing, a hastily convened *khuriltai* elected him Great

Khan. His election was extraordinary, for all of the previous Khaghans had been chosen in assemblages that met in Mongolia or Central Asia. Therefore, its legitimacy could be and was challenged repeatedly. However, in choosing to enter the fray against his younger brother, he had taken the first step toward the most important position in the world at that time, and within a few years he would be recognized as the legitimate ruler of the Mongols.

THE GREAT KHAN

Khubilai's election in May of 1260 was contested.[1] Arigh Böke was the first to challenge Khubilai's selection, but his challenge would not be the last. An aura of illegitimacy would continue to haunt Khubilai throughout his reign, and attempts were made by several Chinese and Mongol leaders to depose him as the Great Khan and as the Emperor of China. His principal antagonists were conservative Mongols, who were suspicious of his apparent identification with China, and native Chinese, who detested alien rule. Whatever policies he chose were bound to alienate one of these two groups. Neither side would be totally propitiated, and each, when angered by one of his decisions, could point to the irregularity of his election as a justification for rebellion. Facing such threats to his rule, he repeatedly sought ways to assert his legitimacy. This desire to be accepted by his Chinese and Mongol subjects as their rightful ruler may indeed have motivated some of his later military campaigns. The story of his selection must be told in detail, as in later years it would continue to provide fuel for attempts to depose him.

ARIGH BÖKE'S CHALLENGE

In June of 1260, Arigh Böke was proclaimed the Great Khan.[2] Both Arigh Böke and Khubilai were now Great Khans and attracted support from various segments of the Mongol royal family, though Arigh Böke seems to have had an edge. Three of the ruling houses in the Mongol world supported him. Berke, the Khan of the Golden Horde after Batu's death in 1257, favored Arigh Böke, in part because of his animosity toward Khubilai's ally and other brother Hülegü. Berke had converted to Islam, and the Muslims considered Hülegü to be an enemy.[3] Berke and Hülegü both claimed possession of the region of modern-day Azerbaijan, an issue that generated bitter hostility between them. They would naturally support different candidates for the Great Khanate. Arigh Böke also had the backing of the Chaghadai khanate of Central Asia. Its ruler, Alghu, was, in fact, one of those who strenuously urged Arigh Böke to take the throne. Many members of the family of the late Khaghan Möngke had allied themselves with him. Khubilai's principal ally and the one he truly counted on for assistance was Hülegü, the Il-Khan of Persia, but Hülegü was facing a crisis.

Once Hülegü had heard the news of Möngke's death, he had decided to return to his homeland. He had just gained one of his most impressive victories when, with the help of King Het‘um and his Armenian troops, Hülegü had captured the city of Aleppo on January 25, 1260. The Armenian sources reveal that Het‘um, a beleaguered Christian surrounded by Muslims and Muslim sympathizers in the Middle East, Russia, and Turkey, provided 40,000 soldiers and 12,000 cavalry to the Mongols for the siege of the Syrian city.[4] Het‘um felt safer with the Mongols than he did with the Muslims. That Hülegü's wife was a Christian was no doubt a consideration in Het‘um's decision to offer assistance. With this victory in hand, Hülegü believed that he could return, with confidence, to Mongolia for the *khuriltai* to select the new khan. His second-in-command, Ked Bukha, was assigned to conquer Damascus and then to occupy the rest of Syria.[5] His relentless drive appeared to be unstoppable, and he calculated that his troops, under the leadership of Ked Bukha, could do without him.

But this calculation proved mistaken. The Mamlūk rulers of Egypt (who were originally the Turkish slaves of the Egyptians but had usurped power in the thirteenth century) soon learned that Hülegü had gone toward the east, leaving behind only a small detachment under Ked Bukha.[6] Baibars, one of their commanders, recognized that the Mamlūks had a magnificent opportunity to smash the undermanned Mongol forces and thus undermine the Mongols' image of invincibility and boost the confidence of the Muslim world in its struggle with the Mongols.[7] Baibars therefore led his troops north to confront Ked Bukha's troops. On September 6, 1260, the two armies clashed in a historic battle at ʿAin Jālūt in the Galilee. Ked Bukha's forces, totaling perhaps 10,000 soldiers, were vastly outnumbered and outmaneuvered. The Mamlūks used the tactic of retreat, which had worked so often for the Mongols. After a few hours of fighting, the Mamlūks began to withdraw from the battlefield and the Mongols, believing that they were routing the enemy, kept advancing and were lured into a deadly trap.[8] As the Mongols pursued the retreating Mamlūk detachment, they suddenly noticed other Mamlūk forces starting to appear on all sides. The Mamlūk armies surrounded and pounced upon them. By the end of the day, the Mongol troops had been vanquished, and Ked Bukha had been captured and beheaded.[9] The Mongols had finally been halted.

On learning the news of the defeat at ʿAin Jālūt, Hülegü hastily retraced his route. Before he could avenge himself on the Muslims, however, he became embroiled in a war with the Golden Horde. He faced a formidable threat in Berke, the ruler of the Mongol forces in Russia, who, emboldened by the Mamlūk victory over the troops of the Il-Khan, declared war on Hülegü.[10]

Meanwhile, back in K'ai-p'ing, with Hülegü diverted by his war with the Golden Horde, Khubilai found himself on his own. Left to his own devices, he first sought to justify himself and to portray his younger brother Arigh Böke as an illegitimate usurper. No doubt under the influence of his Chinese advisers, he couched his argument in Chinese terms. Within a month after accepting the throne, he issued a proclamation (actually written by his adviser Wang O), seeking to associate himself with the Chinese emperors of old. He admitted that though the Mongols' military skills were superior, their governing skills were not as highly developed. A sage was needed to unite the peoples of China and to curb the excesses of the army led by Arigh Böke. Khubilai offered himself for this task, noting that he cultivated goodness and love and had repeatedly assisted the masses. He advocated a reduction of taxes and other burdens on the people. Feeding the hungry would, he stressed, be his first priority, but he also emphasized that he would govern in accordance with the traditions of the ancestors, a view that was surely meant to ingratiate him with his Chinese subjects. He concluded with a ringing call for the military and civilians and those within his domains, as well as those outside who challenged his rule, to cooperate in the interests of the empire.[11] His exhortation barely differed from those of traditional Chinese emperors.

He appealed to his Chinese subjects for help in reunifying China under his rule, but he did so within a Chinese context. A few days after issuing his proclamation, he adopted a Chinese reign title, Chung-t'ung (Central Rule), like a typical Chinese emperor.[12] In addition, he created government institutions that either resembled or were the same as the traditional Chinese ones. The Chung-shu sheng (Secretariats) and the Hsüan-wei ssu (Pacification Commissions), ten of each of which were organized throughout his domains, were only slightly different from the governing bodies of China during the Sung and earlier dynasties.[13] Khubilai wished to signal to the Chinese that he intended to adopt the trappings and style of a Chinese ruler.

Though Khubilai won over many Chinese in the North with his actions, he failed to influence the Southern Sung. In fact, the Chinese dynasty took advantage of Khubilai's troubles in the North to recover the territory that the Mongols had earlier seized. The Sung minister Chia Ssu-tao ordered his troops to attack the small detachment guarding Khubilai's newly acquired lands. They crushed the Mongol forces and reoccupied their old lands. Chia deliberately portrayed this minor battle as a great victory, misleading the Sung court and stiffening its resolve against compromising with the "barbarian" intruders from the north.[14] Meanwhile, Khubilai's response was feeble. With his armies needed in the civil war against Arigh Böke, he could not afford to send a punitive force to deal with the Sung. Instead, on May 21, 1260, he dispatched an embassy led by Hao Ching, one of his Confucian advisers, assisted by Ho Yüan and Liu Jen-chieh, to the Sung court to seek a diplomatic settlement of the disputes. Chia Ssu-tao's response was predictable if unwise: he detained Hao Ching and the rest of the embassy.[15] This tangible evidence of Sung hostility, however, would only spur Khubilai and his fellow Mongols to repay them in kind, and eventually they did. But for the time being Khubilai was much more concerned with Arigh Böke.

Khubilai's main strategy was to deny use of the plentiful resources available in the sedentary world to Arigh Böke. Based in Khara Khorum, Arigh Böke needed to import most of the troops' provisions, and Khubilai was determined to cut him off from his supply centers. The Uighur territory, with its capital in Besh Balikh, was one of these centers.[16] The Mongol representative in Besh Balikh, Ögödei's son and

Khubilai's cousin Khadan, supported Khubilai. By 1262 Khadan had overpowered the forces favoring Arigh Böke. Khadan was also helpful in safeguarding the old Tangut territories in northwest China from Arigh Böke's incursions. His troops occupied Kansu, thereby denying Arigh Böke access to the supplies of that region. Khubilai himself had forces stationed in Yen (in the vicinity of the present city of Peking, later the site for Khubilai's capital in North China), the third of the possible supply centers for the Mongols of Khara Khorum. Arigh Böke was left with only one zone, the Yenisei valley northwest of Khara Khorum.[17] Recent Soviet studies indicate that the farmers in the Upper Yenisei grew wheat, millet, and barley, and that the craftsmen produced daily necessities, weapons, and agricultural tools for the Mongols.[18] Arigh Böke relied principally on this area for the supplies that were so essential to his survival.

But this single base in the Upper Yenisei was a precarious source of supplies for an army bent on defeating a force with the resources of Northern China and Central Asia at its disposal. Yet Arigh Böke was limited to the Upper Yenisei after the fall of 1260. Khubilai had led his troops toward Khara Khorum, and Arigh Böke had rapidly retreated to the Yus, a tributary of the Yenisei river.[19] Both armies set up their winter camps and awaited the spring for their confrontation. Rashīd al-Dīn accuses Arigh Böke of seeking to delude Khubilai by falsely agreeing to submit. The Persian historian reports that Arigh Böke confessed to Khubilai that "we ... committed a crime and transgressed out of ignorance. Thou art my *aqa* [elder brother], and thou knowest thy power. I shall go whithersoever thou commandest and shall not deviate from the *aqa*'s command. Having fattened and satisfied my animals I will present myself before thee."[20] But Rashīd al-Dīn reprovingly notes that instead, Arigh Böke was treacherously preparing to attack Khubilai's troops. Even if this accusation was true, it seems unlikely that such a transparent ploy would fool Khubilai.

Arigh Böke's "pledge" did not deter Khubilai himself from preparing for battle. In a short span of time, he secured his base in Yen by stationing an army of 30,000 there; he commanded his civilian officials to buy 10,000 horses and to transport them to K'ai-p'ing to be used by the military; and he had 100,000 *shih* (piculs) of rice sent from the region around modern Peking to K'ai-p'ing.[21] A few weeks later he requisitioned still another 15,000 troops from North China and 10,000 outfits, composed of fur hats and boots and trousers, from his old appanage in Chen-ting and from Peking and I-tu (an important district in the province of Shantung).[22] Simultaneously, he sought to strengthen the border defenses of North China. An army of 7,000 men went to Yen-an, and another, commanded by Khubilai's Confucian adviser Lien Hsi-hsien, headed for Sian. Lien Hsi-hsien defeated Liu T'ai-p'ing, Arigh Böke's principal supporter in the region, near Sian and gained control of the grain storehouses that could have been used to supply Arigh Böke's forces.[23] After this victory, he moved westward and ousted Arigh Böke's supporters from the northwestern towns of Liang-chou and Kan-chou. Simultaneously, he dispatched some of his crack troops south to Szechwan to ensure supremacy in that vital province.[24] Khubilai's forces thus had cleared out nearly all the enemy from Northwest and Southwest China. Khubilai rewarded his successful underlings lavishly, perhaps to guarantee their loyalty and to avert defections. Lien Hsi-hsien was promoted to Prime Minister of the Right in the Secretariat, and Khadan was given 5,000 *liang* (taels) of silver and 300 bolts of silk. Somewhat lesser gifts were offered to lesser functionaries.[25]

Meanwhile, Arigh Böke was not idle. He wanted at all costs to maintain access to Central Asia, and his main offensive thrusts were directed toward this objective. The armies led by Alandar were assigned to keep the roads to Central Asia open. Khubilai's troops, however, were ready for them. Late in 1260, Khadan intercepted Alandar near Hsi-liang, an important town in Northwest China, crushed the latter's forces, and beheaded Arigh Böke's unfortunate supporter.[26] Arigh Böke's next ploy was to effect a direct alliance with the Chaghadai khanate in Central Asia.[27] Since Chaghadai's grandson Alghu was part of Arigh Böke's entourage, Arigh Böke did, in fact, have a direct connection with the Mongol rulers of that region. He persuaded Alghu to rush toward and lay claim to Central Asia, where the khan, Khara Hülegü, another of Chaghadai's grandsons, had just died. Khubilai, having the same notion, also wanted to fill the vacuum in the Central Asian leadership with his own candidate, another of Chaghadai's grandsons, Abishkha, whom he helped to return toward Central Asia. Arigh Böke's forces, however, managed to intercept, detain, and finally kill Abishkha.[28] The more fortunate Alghu reached his destination and was invested as the Chaghadai Khan. Arigh Böke appeared now to have an invaluable ally in Central Asia, an ally who could supply him with the grain and other supplies he so desperately needed. As long as Alghu retained his power and remained on good terms with Arigh Böke, the latter had a chance in his struggle with Khubilai. Control over or at the very least good relations with the Chaghadai Khanate and its resources was vital for Arigh Böke.

Before Arigh Böke could determine whether the Chaghadai Khan was a solid ally, he encountered Khubilai's troops in a crucial battle in 1261. Rashīd al-Dīn persists in accusing Arigh Böke of duplicity and of provoking the battle with Khubilai's forces. He writes that Arigh Böke did not intend to make peace with Khubilai and was instead preparing his men and animals for war. By the fall of 1261, Arigh Böke had, according to the Persian historian, "fattened his horses" and surreptitiously headed for a confrontation. He "did not keep his word but broke his promise and again went to war against the Qa'an [Khan]. When he came to Yesüngge [one of Khubilai's generals], who was stationed on the frontier of the region, he sent a messenger to say that he was coming to surrender. Having thus rendered him careless he fell upon him, routed and scattered him and his army. . . ."[29] Learning of Arigh Böke's treachery, Rashīd al-Dīn goes on, Khubilai gathered his forces for battle, and in November the two armies clashed at Shimultai, not far from the Chinese border. Arigh Böke's troops were defeated and compelled to retreat.[30] Yet within ten days they had regrouped sufficiently to engage Khubilai's forces. The ensuing battle, fought farther north along the western slope of the Khingan Mountains in eastern Mongolia, was a standoff. Khubilai himself did not take part, and Arigh Böke's army probably encountered only a small portion of Khubilai's troops, for, notwithstanding the indecisiveness of this last battle, Khubilai had clear-cut and sole control over Mongolia and had placed enormous pressure on Arigh Böke's base in the Yenisei.

Arigh Böke was now compelled to turn to his "ally" in Central Asia. Alghu had, in his year in Central Asia, succeeded in crushing opposition to his regime and in tapping the resources of the region. Arigh Böke had been so eager to obtain supplies from the Chaghadai region that he had given Alghu sole responsibility for collecting revenue, scarcely considering that Alghu might eventually seek to exceed his authority. Alghu naturally wished to keep the goods, horses, and precious metals for himself. Once he realized that Arigh Böke was vulnerable, he challenged his erstwhile ally, refusing to share the proceeds of the taxes he had imposed and gathered. When Arigh Böke's envoys arrived in his lands and requested a division of the spoils, he forestalled a response. They grew impatient and sought an immediate reallocation of the taxes. Now compelled to act, Alghu executed them, precipitating a conflict with his ruler.[31]

Arigh Böke departed from Mongolia to Central Asia to assert his supremacy. Khubilai filled the vacuum created by Arigh Böke's departure, moving into and making himself master of Mongolia and offering grain and warning his officials not to exploit the people in this newly pacified region. Khubilai did not chase after Arigh Böke because, as Rashīd al-Dīn writes, "messengers arrived and reported that because of his absence, madness and confusion had appeared in the land of Khitai. He therefore returned to his capital there."[32] He had to contend with a rebellion in China itself and returned to K'ai-p'ing to devote his full attention to what he perceived to be the more dangerous threat to his throne. Not having Khubilai's army harassing him, Arigh Böke could wage war against Alghu without fear of an attack from the rear. He marched his troops toward the Ili River in northern Sinkiang, and his advance guard, under Khara Bukha, encountered Alghu's forces, who soundly trounced them. Khara Bukha was killed, and Alghu was buoyed up by this initial victory. Alghu did not have a chance to celebrate, though, because his troops were routed shortly thereafter. Arigh Böke occupied Alghu's base at Almalikh and forced Alghu to flee to the western oases of Central Asia, Khotan and Kashgar.[33]

Arigh Böke's apparent success proved to be a pyrrhic victory. His new headquarters at Almalikh lay in the steppes, and he still lacked the essential supplies for his war of attrition with Khubilai. He had no dependable source of grain and weapons, and Alghu's forces blocked access to the resources of the southerly, more fertile regions of Sinkiang. Arigh Böke was probably worse off now than he had been. His own actions, according to the hostile record of Rashīd al-Dīn, exacerbated his difficulties. He treated the prisoners he had captured in his struggles with Alghu with undue harshness, torturing and killing many of them, even those who had not fought against him. Such deliberate violence alienated his supporters and prompted defections from his ranks. The defections increased during the particularly severe winter of 1263. Famine threatened the survival of Arigh Böke's soldiers and country, and many men and horses perished. By spring, even some of his most ardent supporters had deserted him. One of Hülegü's sons, Jumukhur, claiming illness, departed for the western Central Asian town of Samarkand. Möngke's son Ürüng Tash requested his father's jade seal (*tamgha*) from Arigh Böke. When Arigh Böke's messengers arrived with the seal, Urüng Tash took it, left, and submitted to Khubilai. Alghu, noticing Arigh Böke's difficulties, regrouped his forces and prepared to expel his former ally and current enemy from the Ili River region.

By 1264, Arigh Böke's options were limited. Without his full complement of forces and supporters, he was no match for Alghu. Retreat from Alghu meant incursions on Khubilai's territory, which would prompt Khubilai's swift retaliation. Arigh Böke decided instead to surrender to Khubilai. He reached K'ai-p'ing (which had been renamed Shang-tu in 1263), and was ushered into Khubilai's presence. After an awkward moment, the two brothers embraced and appeared to have a reconciliation. Here again Rashīd al-Dīn cannot resist a swipe at Arigh Böke. He tells us that Khubilai wiped his brother's tears and gently asked, "Dear brother, in this strife and contention were we in the right or you?" Arigh Böke responded maliciously, "We were then and you are today." [34] Rashīd al-Dīn meant to show, through this brief dialogue, Arigh Böke's ingratitude and lack of appreciation for the brotherly compassion that had just been showered on him. But, given the Persian historian's prejudice against Arigh Böke, it seems unlikely that this dialogue actually took place. In any case, Khubilai initially did not punish his younger brother. His inaction, however, alienated many of his supporters, who did not believe that Arigh Böke and his retainers should go unpunished. Some of them protested, and Hülegü's objections particularly impressed Khubilai, who sought to pacify his fellow Mongols by, according to Rashīd al-Dīn, not admitting Arigh Böke "to his presence for a whole year." This mild punishment apparently did not satisfy the Mongols; a purge of the disloyal elements who had supported Arigh Böke was required. After interrogating Arigh Böke to find out who had incited him to challenge his older brother's claim to the throne, Khubilai declared Bolghai, the most influential official during Möngke's reign, to be one of the principal conspirators and had him executed. Nine other prominent retainers in Arigh Böke's camp suffered a similar fate.

Now the time had come to judge Arigh Böke. Khubilai felt insecure about being the sole judge of his younger brother, however, and decided to convene a *khuriltai* to determine Arigh Böke's fate and, just as important, to confirm his own accession to the Great Khanate. His messengers fanned out to the principal khanates in Persia, Russia, and Central Asia to summon the rulers to the convocation. The response was unenthusiastic: all three khans offered excuses for a delay in attendance at court. Berke, the ruler of the Mongols in Russia, and Hülegü, the khan of Persia, were at war, and neither could afford to leave his domain while conflict raged. The Chaghadai khan, Alghu, pleaded that he himself had not been confirmed and thus could not act as a judge in Arigh Böke's case. These three khans did not, in any case, last long. Hülegü died in 1265, shortly after Khubilai's messengers reached him, and Berke and Alghu survived him by only a year. Khubilai now had the leeway to deal with Arigh Böke as he chose.

Arigh Böke saved Khubilai from great anguish by contracting an illness and dying early in 1266. His demise was convenient for Khubilai, and this very convenience has cast doubts on the circumstances of his death. The unexpectedness of his illness and the suddenness of his passing gave rise to suspicions of foul play. Arigh Böke was a vigorous man in his late forties, and there are no intimations of a serious malady before this time. Some scholars have suggested that his death was unnatural, and a few believe him to have been poisoned. Certainly, his presence was a constant reminder that Khubilai's accession was irregular, and eliminating him might have contributed to greater stability in Khubilai's domains. But this interpretation of Arigh Böke's death is conjectural. The present sources do not solve the riddle of his death.[35]

Even discounting Arigh Böke's challenge, Khubilai still faced other threats to his authority. His right to the position of Great Khan was not incontrovertible. He had not received the blessings of a *khuriltai* composed of the leading Mongol nobles and khans. His election had taken place in K'ai-p'ing, not in the traditional center of the Mongol homelands. When he attempted to convoke a second *khuriltai*, the three main khans demurred, citing difficulties within their own domains. Nevertheless, they continued to pay homage to Khubilai as the Great Khan, and each of the regional khanates sought his confirmation when a new khan was to be appointed. Yet an aura of illegitimacy continued to surround Khubilai. Indeed, some of his later domestic and foreign policies may have stemmed from his desire to gain the wholehearted support that so long eluded him.

THE REBELLION OF LI T'AN

His acceptance as the Emperor of the Chinese was also tenuous and rivaled. As long as Sung emperors ruled from Hangchow, many Chinese would owe their allegiance to their native ruler. To gain the unqualified support of his Chinese subjects, Khubilai still needed to topple the Sung. Even closer to him, challenges to his supremacy were mounted. For the first two years of his reign, he faced discontent in North China, which finally erupted into a local rebellion in 1262.

The rebellion erupted in the province of Shantung, where the rebel leader Li T'an ruled the I-tu district.[36] The Chinese sources yield little information about him until the time of Möngke's campaign against the Sung. In 1258, Möngke asked Li to join him in Central China to head south against the Chinese dynasty. Li argued that I-tu was an important thoroughfare that needed protection, and he received Möngke's permission to remain behind.[37] He led his troops on raids and attacks against Sung coastal towns, occupying Hai-chou and Lien-chou. The Chinese sources, which are hostile to Li—the *Yüan shih* classifies him as a "rebellious minister"—imply that his campaigns were attempts at self-aggrandizement. The Sung forces were diverted by the attacks of Möngke, Khubilai, and Uriyangkhadai, leaving Li with scant opposition in the coastal towns. Li, according to the *Yüan shih*, was scarcely interested in the progress of Möngke's campaign. His prime concern was to seize additional territory for himself, but the Mongols were unaware of his real intentions.

When Khubilai acceded to the throne in 1260, he did not harbor any suspicions of Li's activities in the east. It is true that he appointed Sung Tzu-chen as the Pacification Commissioner (Chin.: Hsüan-fu shih) of I-tu, Chi-nan, and the adjacent lands in Shantung, but he also promoted Li to Military Commissioner (Chin.: Ta tu-tu) of the Chiang-Huai region.[38] After his promotion, Li informed Khubilai that Sung prisoners he had captured revealed to him that the Sung leaders Chia Ssu-tao and Lü Wen-te had 2,000 boats with an army of 75,000 soldiers poised for an attack on Lien-chou. He explained that the city wall needed to be repaired and the city prepared for the Sung assault. Khubilai gave him 300 ingots (Chin.: *ting*) of silver to cover the costs of these defense measures. Li made a further request, for permission to cross the Huai River to badger the Sung in their own land. But, though Khubilai clearly prized Li's support, he did not grant his Chinese underling the authority to press forward against the Sung, perhaps fearing that Li would become overly powerful.[39] Khubilai recognized that Li already had a strong position because of his army and the resources at his disposal. Shantung's reserves of salt and copper gave Li the wealth he needed for his military expeditions. Khubilai's decision may have alienated Li, but it appears likely that Li intended to challenge the Mongols in any case. Li did not at this time disobey

Khubilai's orders, but went out to meet the advancing Sung forces. Early in 1261, he reported to Khubilai, who had provided him with grain and other supplies, that he had defeated the Sung armies at Lien-chou. Khubilai rewarded Li and offered gold and silver tallies to his leading military commanders.[40] In the next few months, Li reported other victories against the Sung.

Then, late in 1261, Li began to detach himself from Khubilai. He may have received assurances of support from the Sung leaders in the event that he broke with the Mongols, and he must have calculated that trade and other economic relations with the Sung offered more benefits than with the Mongols. As an ethnic Chinese, he may, in addition, have felt loyalty to the Sung. Whatever the motivation, Li prepared to break away from Khubilai. He did not fulfill his obligation of sending horses to Khubilai's armies fighting against Arigh Böke, and he arranged for his son Li Yen-chien, who had been kept as a hostage at the Mongol court, to slip away from his Mongol captors and to rejoin him in I-tu.[41]

With his son safely away from the Mongols and possibly with assurances of help from the Sung, Li could sever relations with Khubilai and the Mongols. On February 22, 1262, he rebelled against those whom he had earlier accepted as his overlords. He "plundered," to use the pejorative language of the *Yüan shih*, the storehouses in I-tu, "massacred" the Mongol soldiers in the area, and turned over Lien-chou and Hai-chou to the Sung. His troops "pillaged" the towns near I-tu, and within the month "ransacked" the town of Chi-nan.

Though Khubilai was absorbed in his struggle with Arigh Böke, he quickly perceived the threat posed by Li and acted to dispose of it. He sent a number of his most trusted military men to cope with Li in Shantung. Along with the military went Chao Pi, one of his most influential advisers.[42] Khubilai was determined to crush the Chinese rebel before other Chinese in the North were infected by overt anti-Mongol sentiments. His troops repaired the defenses of the towns that could be endangered by Li's forces and garrisoned them. Once his territory was secured, Khubilai ordered Shih T'ien-tse and Shih Ch'u to take the offensive against Li. In late March or early April, the two armies clashed not far from Chi-nan. Li was routed and 4,000 of his troops were killed.[43] Li retreated to Chi-nan with his remaining forces. His army was reeling and on the defensive, and the pursuing Mongol-Chinese joint force continued to put pressure on him.

By mid-April, some of his leading generals began to desert him.

They submitted to the Mongols and claimed that Li had coerced them into joining him. Wishing to encourage others to desert, Khubilai pardoned these former enemies. He also warned his soldiers not to harm the people in the newly repacified area and not to do any unnecessary damage to property, hoping in this way to attract more defectors. His strategy worked, as more and more of Li's troops deserted. Simultaneously, Shih T'ien-tse besieged Li's center in Chi-nan. Cut off from supplies and weapons, Li's forces started to escape from the besieged town and voluntarily submitted. By early August, Li T'an knew that he had lost. He went to the nearby lake of Ta-ming and tried to drown himself, but the Mongols rescued him in order to execute him properly. They placed him in a sack and had him trampled by their horses.[44] By Mongol custom, the blood of the enemy leader must not be spilled. Trampling to death was the preferred method of executing foreign rulers.

Execution was also the fate of Wang Wen-t'ung. Before Khubilai assumed power as the Great Khan, he had recruited this talented Chinese for his staff of Confucian advisers.[45] Early in Khubilai's reign, Wang had been appointed the Chief Administrator (Chin.: P'ing-chang cheng-shih) in the Secretariat (Chung-shu sheng), subordinate only to the two prime ministers, and he became one of the most influential ministers in the government. He had played a role in setting up the circuits (lu) that were to rule China, in proposing the use of paper money, and in promoting commerce. He also contributed to the tax system devised by Khubilai and his advisers to raise the revenues needed both for the campaign against Arigh Böke and for the establishment of a government. Khubilai began to rely on Wang for important official matters. Unfortunately for Wang, however, his daughter had married Li T'an, and Wang appeared to be implicated in his son-in-law's rebellion.[46] He had, on several occasions, sent his son to Li T'an with reports on Khubilai's movements and activities. The court also discovered incriminating letters from Li T'an to Wang. Wang was relieved of his duties, and Khubilai convened a meeting of some of his principal Confucian advisers, including Yao Shu and Tou Mo, to solicit their views on Wang's punishment. They suggested that Wang be executed, and one particularly enraged adviser rec-ommended that he be hacked to pieces.[47] With their unanimous support, Khubilai ordered the execution of Wang Wen-t'ung and Wang's son, who had served as an intermediary between his father and Li T'an. Wang's "treachery" was widely publicized, and his specific infractions were disclosed in great detail to the Chinese public. He was reviled not only for the duplicity of his attitudes and behavior toward his Mongol overlords but also for harming the interests of his own people. It was surely no accident that Khubilai sought the counsel of his Chinese advisers in deciding on the proper punishment for Wang. Khubilai wished to demonstrate that Wang had betrayed not only the khan but the Chinese as well. What better way than to have Wang condemned by his fellow countrymen.

Despite the closing of the ranks by his Confucian advisers, this incident left its mark on Khubilai, who became increasingly suspicious of the Chinese. A rebellion in a key economic area had been led by an important Chinese leader with the covert support of one of his most trusted and invaluable ministers. From this time on, he hesitated to rely on his Chinese aides to rule China. Afraid that dependence on the Chinese might imperil his reign, he sought assistance from non-Chinese advisers. Even before he became the Great Khan, he had been wary of relying solely on his Chinese counselors. But Li T'an's rebellion prompted a sharper reaction to such dependence. Khubilai now realized that he needed to recruit non-Chinese advisers to counter the influence of the Chinese in his employ and reduce the threat of a devastating rebellion. Moreover, among Khubilai's principal enemies were the Chinese of the Southern Sung. Could he count on his Chinese advisers to remain loyal in the battle against their own countrymen? Khubilai was uncertain. Yet depending on foreigners also had its perils, for to do so might provoke further Chinese discontent. Khubilai's position had always been ambivalent, but Li T'an's revolt was nonetheless a turning point.

Physically, he was prepared for the policy decisions that were required. A Chinese portrait of him painted around this time shows a robust, determined man. He wears a simple white cloth garment; no silks or furs adorn his body. His black and white hat is hardly lavish, and his mustache and beard are trim and obviously cared for. Most important, the picture shows that Khubilai had not yet abandoned himself to sensual pleasures. Though certainly not gaunt, neither was he obese, as he became toward the end of his reign.[48] Probably food, Chinese or any other kind, had not yet become a consuming passion; nor does he show any sign of being a heavy drinker, as later he would become. His alertness and robustness contrast sharply with his appearance in a painting executed in 1280. Two decades after assuming power in China, he had become grotesquely fat. He had also begun to lose touch with political affairs, whereas early in his reign he had taken an active part in decision-making and was in good physical condition, able to undertake the vital task of establishing a government for China, by now the crown jewel of his domains.

THE ROLE OF CHABI

Chabi was the ideal helpmate in Khubilai's effort to rule China. It was she, for instance, who urged him to return to the North from his campaign against the Sung and counter the threat of Arigh Böke. Without her timely warning, Khubilai would have been in a weaker position to cope with his brother. She aspired to be the empress of a powerful state, not simply the wife of a tribal chieftain. She had wide-ranging interests and was not limited by Mongol pastoral traditions. In the early years of Khubilai's reign, for example, four members of the Imperial Guard, according to the *Yüan shih*, proposed that the areas around his capital be turned into pastureland for the Mongol horses. This proposal fit in with the traditional Mongol economy, but it made little sense in the agrarian economy of North China. Chabi sensed the folly of the proposal and objected violently. She reprimanded Liu Ping-chung, one of the most influential of Khubilai's Chinese advisers, for not speaking up against the proposal, noting, "You Chinese are intelligent. When you speak, the emperor listens. Why have you not remonstrated with him?"[49] Khubilai quickly rejected the proposal. The Mongol nobles were thus not permitted to encroach on the agricultural land of the Chinese peasants who lived around the capital.

Chabi's personality, interests, and activities eventually initiated trends at court. She was regarded as extremely frugal and rarely threw anything out, and numerous perhaps stereotyped anecdotes about her parsimoniousness appear in her biography in the *Yüan shih*. With her encouragement, the court ladies collected the strings from old bows and made them into thread, which could then be woven for cloth. She salvaged old animal pelts and used them as rugs. Her practicality is also evident in the new fashions she introduced. Khubilai was concerned that Mongol hats were "without a front" and that those who wore them received little protection from the blazing desert sun. So Chabi designed hats with a rim, and Khubilai ordered all new hats to

4.   Portrait of Khubilai Khan. National Palace Museum, Taipei.

be modeled on Chabi's creation. Later she designed a sleeveless garment that could be worn comfortably in combat.[50]

She was also in fashion when she expressed an interest in earlier
rulers of China. Like Khubilai, she was entranced by the great Emperor T'ai-tsung (r. 624–49) of the T'ang dynasty, and she prodded a
Chinese scholar to explain the exploits and the character of the T'ang
ruler to the court. Since T'ang T'ai-tsung was the most renowned
emperor of the last truly powerful Chinese dynasty, it is only natural

5.   Portrait of Chabi. National Palace Museum, Taipei.

that Khubilai would wish to emulate him and that Chabi would invite comparisons between her husband and the illustrious T'ang ruler.[51] Chabi and Khubilai must have realized that it would be easier for Khubilai to govern the Chinese if he succeeded in identifying himself with a major figure in the Chinese tradition. In sum, Chabi was just as anxious as her husband to set up a government in China.

EARLY ORGANIZATION UNDER KHUBILAI

At the onset of his reign, Khubilai's Chinese advisers had also bombarded him with proposals for the organization of his administration. Many of them were similar, looking toward the creation of a Chinese-style administration. The sixteen points advocated by Hao Ching, Khubilai's envoy who had been detained by the Southern Sung, are typical of this genre and embody some suggestions that Khubilai accepted. Hao first proposed that Khubilai convene a representative group of scholars and officials to discuss a new political system. The most important priority of this group ought to be defense, and the death penalty should be mandated for defectors and traitors, though a partial amnesty would be offered at the beginning of the dynasty to those who forswore opposition. The ruler should be open in his dealings with others, should clearly delineate proper rewards and punishments, and should be decisive. However, he would need a central administration and ministers with some power because he could not make all the decisions. The central government ought to be based in North China because that area was the true heartland, but a subsidiary administration should be retained in Khara Khorum and military districts should be established on the border. The ruler should take special pains to maintain good relations with princes of the blood; even so, inspectorates should be organized to control the appanages and to limit their possible abuses of power. He should also strive to reduce the number of officials and to amalgamate offices so as to bring expenses under control and to limit the cliques among the official class. Taxes on the people should be kept at a minimum, and extraordinary levies imposed by the Sung and other dynasties to cover their expenses ought to be abolished. Paper money should be widely circulated as a unit of currency, and government monopolies on salt and iron should be retained, though the number of officials supervising these monopolies ought to be decreased. After all these steps had been taken, the ruler ought to name a crown prince to ensure the continuity of his dynasty.[52]

Khubilai eventually adopted many of Hao's ideas, which echoed those of numerous other Confucian scholars. But the return to the traditional system of Chinese government that they envisioned was not exactly what Khubilai had in mind. Khubilai wanted his administration to attract the support of the Chinese but also reflect and protect Mongol concerns. He was unwilling to turn over too much authority to his Chinese advisers. Nor was he eager to lift his whole administrative apparatus from those of traditional Chinese dynasties. He desired a structure that suited his own needs. Thus he was unwilling, for example, to reinstitute the civil service examinations. These difficult exams, based on knowledge of the Confucian classics, had been the principal means of recruiting officials from the Han dynasty on. Khubilai, however, wanted a free hand in selecting his own officials and was unwilling to be bound by Chinese practices. Preparations for the exams required repeated exposure to and empathy for Confucian doctrines, and Khubilai was not anxious to commit himself to a coterie of advisers shaped by the one prevailing ideology.[53] Already one of his Confucian Chinese advisers, Wang Wen-t'ung, had proven disloyal. How many more would prove untrustworthy in helping the Mongols to rule the Chinese? Khubilai did not want only Confucians staffing his government, nor did he want the civil service exams to be the only vehicle for recruiting officials. What he wanted, rather, was the power to appoint his own underlings. Since the exams were among the most characteristic features of Chinese civilization, their absence during Khubilai's reign signified an important deviation from traditional Chinese practices.

In other ways, too, Khubilai deviated from Chinese practices. He divided the population into three, and later four, groups, with the Mongols occupying the most prominent positions. Next were the so-called *Se-mu jen* (miscellaneous aliens), consisting mostly of Western and Central Asians, who because they performed valuable services for the Mongols were accorded higher status than the indigenous peoples. Third were the Northern Chinese, as well as the Jurchens of the earlier Chin dynasty, who were classified as the *Han-jen* and were the lowest-ranked group until the Mongol conquest of the Southern Sung in 1279. Finally came the Southern Chinese, the *Nan-jen*, the least desirable and least trustworthy group.[54] The two Chinese groups were excluded from some of the most important civilian positions, which were reserved for the Mongols or their Central Asian underlings. Although Chinese who were recruited as advisers were often actually more influential than high officials, their status was not as well defined.

Khubilai adopted these policies partly for a simple, pragmatic reason: the Chinese vastly outnumbered the Mongols in China. One source estimates that the Mongols had a few hundred thousand people residing in China, whereas the Chinese population of the North amounted to about ten million and the Chinese of the Southern Sung accounted for another fifty million.[55] Given the disparity in numbers, the Mongols needed to retain control of the leading positions in government if they were to survive and avoid being engulfed by the more numerous Chinese. They had to be at the forefront in order to retain power and to preserve their unique cultural heritage. With the numerical odds against him, Khubilai surmised that he had to emphasize Mongol leadership.

First, however, he had to gain control over the Mongol leadership. Many Mongol nobles had been granted appanages (in Chinese, *fen-ti*) since the time of Ögödei. They considered themselves supreme within these areas and brooked scant interference. Khubilai, needing to assert the central government's power over these largely autonomous territories, could not tolerate challenges to his authority from the appanages. They had to be placed under the supervision of a central government, and Khubilai intended to restrain them through institutions he would establish.[56]

Khubilai thus faced the task of imposing limits on not only the Chinese but also the Mongols, a more difficult task than that of the typical Chinese emperor. He also aspired to a loftier position—to be a universal sovereign, rather than merely a Chinese emperor. These aspirations, however, remained unfulfilled. The other main territories within the Mongol domains—Central Asia, Persia, and Russia— began to assert their independence at the start of his reign. Though they respected his title of Great Khan, they were moving toward self-government. The so-called Mongol empire was separating into a series of distinct political units—the Golden Horde of Russia, the Il-Khanate of Persia, the Chaghadai Khanate of Central Asia, and the Great Khanate of North China and Mongolia. Khubilai could not count on unanimity among the Mongol elite, which was symbolized by the convening of *khuriltai* for the discussion of major military policies and the acclamation of a new ruler.[57] Nonetheless, he persisted in perceiving himself as more than a Chinese emperor and he adopted the trappings of a ruler of the Mongol empire, even though his power was confined mostly to China and Mongolia. Eventually, however, he was realistic enough to adjust to these circumstances and to create a government suited to the Mongol domains in East Asia.

The institutions he set up would thus be familiar to his Chinese subjects, resembling the Chinese ones without being mere replicas. Within a month of his accession in May of 1260, for example, he organized a Secretariat, with Wang Wen-t'ung as its principal administrator and Chang Wen-ch'ien as his chief assistant.[58] The Secretariat took charge of most civilian matters. In 1263, he established the Privy Council (Chin.: Shu-mi yüan) to supervise military affairs. Five years later, the Censorate (Yü-shih-t'ai), the last of the major agencies, was formed to inspect and report on the officials throughout Khubilai's Chinese domains. Each of these agencies had branches (hsing) in the various provinces to implement the policies determined at the capital. Along with these agencies, which had responsibilities throughout the country, there were a myriad of special offices that catered to the khan and his court, for example, the Bureau for Imperial Household Provisions and the Directorate for the Imperial Accessories.[59]

Khubilai simplified and streamlined the civilian administration. He abandoned the Chancellery and Department of State, agencies that had lasted since the T'ang dynasty, but maintained the Secretariat, which was granted sole jurisdiction over civilian affairs. With only one agency in charge, the civilian government would presumably run more smoothly. All reports to the throne were filtered through the Secretariat, which drafted the laws and resolved "legal cases involving capital crimes and had a staff of judges [tuan-shih kuan] to help in this work."[60] The Head of the Secretariat (Chung-shu ling) would, with Khubilai's approval, make major policy decisions, which would then be carried out by one of the ministries. The Prime Ministers of the Left (Tso ch'eng-hsiang) and the Right (Yu ch'eng-hsiang) would advise the Emperor and were to be responsible for the six functional ministries, which implemented government policy and substituted for the Head of the Secretariat when he was ill, traveling, or otherwise unavailable.

The Head was also the direct supervisor of the six functional ministries, agencies that had been a characteristic feature of Chinese government since the T'ang. The Ministry of Personnel oversaw the civilian officials. The Ministry of Revenue conducted censuses, collected taxes and tribute, and regulated the circulation of money. The Ministry of Rites managed court ceremonies, festivities, music, sacrifices, and entertainments and greeted foreign envoys. The Ministry of War operated military commands and colonies and postal stations, requisitioned military supplies, and trained the army (though the Privy Council assumed most military functions). The Ministry of Justice enforced the laws and administered the prisons. Finally, the Ministry of Public Works repaired fortifications, managed dams and public lands, and devised rules for artisans.[61]

Under the local administrative structure devised by Khubilai and

his advisers, China was divided into provinces, each under the jurisdiction of a branch office of the Secretariat. After the conquest of the
Southern Sung in 1279, China consisted of ten such provinces, with
the Metropolitan Province, the khan's own domain, which consisted
of modern Hopei, Shantung, Shansi, and part of Inner Mongolia, as
the vital part.[62] A Prime Minister (Chin.: Ch'eng-hsiang) was the chief
administrator in each province and was assisted by officials with titles
similar to the ones in the central government Secretariat. The provinces were further subdivided into about sixty Pacification Commissions (Hsüan-wei ssu), which were composed of about one hundred
and eighty circuits (lu). The General Administrator (Tsung-kuan) was
frequently a Chinese. Parallel to the General Administrator were the
local commissioners (Mong.: darughachi) often sent to these circuits.
These commissioners were often to be Mongols or Central Asians, and
their functions overlapped with those of the General Administrators.
In effect, each served as a check on the other.

One of the major differences between Mongol rule and that of the
Chinese dynasties was the emphasis on control. Arigh Böke's challenge, Li T'an's rebellion, and Khubilai's contested succession to the
throne made him cautious about trusting his officials, whether Mongol or Chinese. Khubilai was concerned that the officials, many of
whom were not Mongols, remain loyal, honest, and incorruptible.
Moreover, even in the Mongol domains, he was eager to reduce the
authority of the appanages. Thus he delegated more power to the
Censorate than had any earlier dynasty in Chinese history. Like the
Secretariat, the Censorate was divided up into branches that oversaw
the local officials. Censors periodically toured the country to ferret
out financial and political abuses by the court, the military, or the
local governments. As one student of the Censorate notes, "The
[Mongol] censorial system was . . . far more pervasive than any preceding one, and its degree of tightly knit centralization was never
exceeded in China's censorial history. The Mongols' surveillance
apparatus can be reckoned as one of the institutional marvels of
Chinese history."[63] Having coped with the rebellion of Li T'an,
Khubilai wanted to defuse or destroy any opposition before such
dissent erupted into armed insurrection. Surveillance and control
were vital.

His attitudes and policies were other telling indications of his
deviation from traditional Chinese practices. Khubilai's principal objective was to *control* the officials and to restrict their abuses of power.

His regulations and edicts were designed to prevent officials from capitalizing on their positions to intimidate the populace and to undercut, through their abuses, the prestige and authority of his government. Officials who were laggardly or lacked zeal in carrying out their duties might be beaten or even executed. Those who accepted gifts or bribes from the people they supervised or lied to their superiors were flogged. A severe infraction would lead the court to relieve the official of his position. Precise punishments were specified for various forms of venality and corruption and for dereliction of duty. Officials who employed public facilities or the service personnel for their own private gain were to be severely punished. Similarly, officials who imposed excessive taxes or corvée or in any way exploited their subjects were treated harshly.[64]

Some recent studies have suggested that, in actual practice, Khubilai's efforts at control were fruitless. The Central Secretariat apparently functioned effectively only in the Metropolitan Province, Khubilai's own domain. It seems to have had little influence on the other provinces. One modern scholar writes that "with the important exception of the appointment of officials, [the central government's] engagement in empire-wide administration was at best transitory or limited to very restricted activities."[65] The powerful branch secretariats often ignored the directives of the Central Secretariat. Many agencies had overlapping functions, prompting numerous delays in decision-making. Khubilai's dominance over local affairs was not as pervasive as he wished. Similarly, his controls over his officials were limited. Throughout his reign, he issued admonitions and edicts aimed at corrupt officials, but, as we shall see in chapter 7, bribery and graft remained serious problems that the Censorate was unable to prevent. Yet by the early 1260s Khubilai had devised an administration for China that, at least on paper, appeared to be workable.

Having established a government for China, Khubilai was prepared to implement his economic and social objectives in the country. He had devised a system that in theory ensured Mongol control of China. The actual government offices were not unfamiliar to the Chinese, for many of them were merely modifications of traditional institutions. Khubilai planned to recruit Chinese for his government, but the Mongols and their Central Asian underlings would supervise them. The Censorate and the tight regulations were designed to prevent most of these Chinese officials from acts of sabotage or disloyalty. Khubilai was thus free to initiate the policies that he wished to pursue.

The Conqueror

Like his Mongol predecessors, Khubilai knew that he had to persist in territorial expansion. His military forces were poised for further engagements. In Mongol eyes, his success as a ruler would be measured at least in part by his ability to add wealth, men, and territory to his domain. Similarly, Chinese ideology held that a good ruler's virtue and the glory of his state would induce foreigners to submit to Chinese civilization.[1] To enhance his credibility as a ruler of the Mongol and Chinese worlds, Khubilai needed to pursue an assertive, even aggressive, foreign policy. The questions about Khubilai's seizure of power also prompted him to prove himself and quell any lingering doubts about his right to rule. Inasmuch as he had been challenged by his own brother, there was a real question of his authority as the ruler of the Mongol world. What better way to undercut such doubts than for him to bring additional lands under Mongol political control?

Khubilai's principal objective was to overwhelm the Southern Sung. Though he controlled the traditional center of China, he was not the master of the region south of the Yangtze River. Since the early T'ang dynasty, the South had become increasingly prominent. It was much more fertile than the North, and seaborne trade had enriched its coastal towns. Khubilai needed to subjugate the Southern Sung, both to gain the respect of the Chinese and to eliminate the perennial threat posed by the hostile dynasty that lay claim to land already under his jurisdiction.

Still another concern was the security of his borders. The southern border with the Sung clearly required stability, if not pacification. The northeastern frontier, which constituted the border with Korea, did not pose a threat, but at the time of Khubilai's enthronement Korea was only beginning to accept Mongol jurisdiction. Along the Central Asian border, there *was* a real threat to Khubilai's aspirations, with Ögödei's grandson Khaidu challenging Khubilai's supremacy in Central Asia and making sporadic forays along China's northwestern borders. This leader of the Central Asian nomads would also prove troublesome to the northernmost of Khubilai's domains, Mongolia. All of these defense concerns prompted Khubilai to maintain and increase the number of his troops and to initiate military expeditions toward the northwest and north.

THE CONQUEST OF SOUTHERN CHINA

His most vital objective was Southern China. He wished to gain access to the resources of the Sung. Moreover, though the Sung military was relatively weak and did not pose an immediate threat, the area remained a potential trouble spot. The Chinese desired reunification of their lands. Should the Sung Chinese marshal a more effective fighting force, one of their first goals would surely be the reconquest of the North. Under Möngke, there had been a fruitless effort to pacify the Sung. Since in the 1260s Khubilai held the upper hand, he sought to subjugate the South before it could recoup its military strength. Conquest of the South thus offered valuable political and military benefits. And the economic value of such an expedition, if successful, could also not be discounted. Merchants from South China had developed a lucrative trade with Southeast Asia, India, and as far away as the Middle East. The products, profits, and revenues to be gained from this commerce were no doubt additional inducements for Khubilai. The land in South China was also more fertile, a vital consideration for the North, whose population often outstripped its food supplies. If Khubilai expanded southward, he could ensure an adequate grain reserve for his subjects in North China.

But the conquest of South China was not going to be easy. The Mongol armies and cavalry were not accustomed to the temperatures and lands of the South. The Mongols' horses faced innumerable obstacles. The warm temperatures and the forests were far more difficult environments than the steppelands, and the steeds could not really adjust to the heat. There was hardly any fodder for them to graze on, since in the South crops were planted on every available plot of arable land.[2] The Mongols themselves were not ready for the diseases of the tropics and semi-tropics, where parasites and mosquitoes transmitted diseases to which they had not developed resistance.[3]

Then, too, the Mongol troops needed to employ military techniques they had scarcely, if ever, used before. As befitted a state so involved in overseas trade, the Sung had a powerful navy, and perhaps as important, some of its leading cities would have to be attacked by maritime forces. The Mongols would be required to construct boats, recruit sailors, and become more proficient in sea warfare. They did, in fact, with the help of their Chinese, Korean, and Jurchen subjects, develop a navy capable of subduing the Southern Sung. They at least shared a land border with the Sung, and some of the battles took place on land, to which they were accustomed and on which they were at this time almost invincible. However, the subjugation of the Sung would entail vast fiscal and military resources.

Despite its military weakness in the late thirteenth century, the Sung was still a formidable foe. The city of Hangchow as well as some of the other great urban centers had vibrant, sophisticated cultures. Luxurious restaurants, tea houses, and theaters were located throughout these cities. "The passion for luxury and pleasure was particularly strong in Hangchow. No other town had such a concentration of wealth. The riches and elegance of the upper classes and of the prosperous merchants account for the importance of the luxury trade."[4] Exotic and exquisite foods, including "sweet soya soup at the Mixed Wares Market, pig cooked in ashes in front of the Longevity-and-Compassion Palace, ... scented shell-fish cooked in rice-wine, goose with apricots, lotus-seed soup, pimento soup with mussels and [fish] cooked with plums,"[5] were served in the numerous restaurants that dotted the city. The Southern Sung possessed considerable wealth, deriving primarily from the fertile land but also from overseas commerce.[6]

The Sung government, recognizing the potential revenue to be garnered from trade, helped to promote commerce by engaging merchants to supervise the state monopolies and by allotting them relatively high status in society.[7] The court appointed Maritime Trade Superintendents (T'i-chü shih-po shih) in various ports to manage the trade and to ensure that it received the imports it required and the taxes it mandated. The Maritime Trade Superintendents opened nine ports to foreign trade, and Ch'üan-chou, in modern Fukien province, became the largest of these harbors.[8] Simultaneously, the court actively encouraged commerce on the many lakes and rivers in its domain. The cities in the southeast coastal areas were, in this way, linked to the hinterland, providing a market for the cash crops produced in the interior. Boat traffic in the canals, lakes, and rivers increased dramatically. Despite the court's numerous restrictions on both foreign and domestic trade, merchants still profited and generally cooperated.

As seaborne commerce continued to flourish, the Sung's interest in and concern for shipping, and as a result for naval power, grew. Its naval technology made dramatic advances. A wide variety of sizable ships was developed. Such weapons as "flaming arrows, rockets, flame-throwers, and . . . bombs cast by catapults" and fragmentation bombs were only a few of the innovations introduced by Sung inventors.[9] Though defense against piracy was the original spark for the development of the navy, another consideration was the threat of the "barbarians," first the Chin dynasty and then the Mongols, in the North. Government officials knew that strength on the seas would balance the effective, and seemingly invincible, land forces of their "barbarian" enemies. The Sung's control of the seas would defuse the Mongols' advantage in cavalry and land warfare.

The Sung court had founded shipyards in such towns as Hang-chow, Kuang-chou (now known as Canton), Ming-chou, and Wen-chou, to build boats to be used both in the coastal areas and on the Yangtze River. After its expulsion from North China by the Chin dynasty in 1126, it created government offices for the defense of the river (Yen-chiang chih-chih shih, or "Military Commissioner of River Defenses") and the coastal areas (Yen-hai chih-chih shih, or "Military Commissioner of Coastal Defenses").[10] The navy remained a potent and effective force for approximately a century, but it began to deteriorate as the Sung itself declined. Corruption and laxity contributed to low morale among naval officers, poor training and lack of fitness among the crews, and a paucity of well-equipped fighting ships. As one official commented in 1239, "they [the sailors] cannot ride the waves and thrust with their spears. This is the result of thirty years of neglect."[11] (His critique was somewhat overstated in order to rouse the government into action.) Despite the decline in the Sung navy, it still appeared superior to the Mongol sea forces.

Serious evidences of decay resulted from the economic and political dislocations in the Sung system. The government confronted some of the same difficulties that had engulfed earlier Chinese dynasties. Like the Han and the T'ang dynasties in various periods in their history, the Sung government was faced with severe financial problems. Large landowners had accumulated vast estates, whether through chicanery, oppression of the peasantry, or good management. Many of these landlords either were officials themselves or else had close relatives in the bureaucracy. In any case, they achieved a tax-exempt status through their official connections. As more and more land was removed from the tax rolls, the government's fiscal crisis worsened. The court could not meet its rapidly rising military expenditures. By 1260, when Khubilai ascended the throne in the North, the abuses of the landlords and officials in the South imperiled the dynasty. The evasion of taxes had to be restricted if the Southern Sung was to survive. Again in the same pattern as earlier Chinese dynasties, the Southern Sung suffered from excesses and hunger for power among the court retinue. Though eunuchs were not as politically dominant as they had been in the Later Han and T'ang dynasties, they were present at court and were potential challengers for political power.[12] Similarly, the relatives of each succeeding empress and the members of the imperial clan sought high offices on the basis of their connection to the throne.[13] All of these assorted groups needed to be restrained if the Sung was to weather challenges from the Mongols.

In the 1260s and 1270s, the Chancellor, Chia Ssu-tao, attempted to initiate reform to prevent such abuses. Like many reformers throughout Chinese history, he has been harshly criticized in the traditional histories.[14] These accounts, which were written by members of the landlord and official classes, would be unsympathetic to an official who sought to revoke the privileges and to root out the excesses of these classes. They picture Chia as a villainous minister, and it is only through inference and a careful sifting of the biased evidence that a more balanced portrait may be drawn.[15] Chia, in this modern view, tried to persuade the emperor to issue edicts to curb official profiteering. He also used public letter boxes, "where people could place complaints or denunciations,"[16] as another way of bringing official misdeeds to light. His proposals aroused considerable opposition from the officials and their landlord allies. Chia dealt with his opponents by purging several dissident officials, and even executing a few. To replace these disgraced bureaucrats, he promoted his own cronies and low-ranking officials, bypassing some more experienced men. These policies, in turn, swelled the size of the opposition groups. Such political turbulence and divisiveness made the Sung vulnerable to challenges by a unified, powerful force such as the Mongols.

Khubilai, for his own purposes, was intent on becoming the master of Southern China. Yet he was initially not belligerent. As we discussed in chapter 3, he had sent his envoy Hao Ching to the south in 1260 to propose a peaceful solution. If the Sung would acquiesce in his reign as the Son of Heaven for all of China, in return he would give them limited self-rule and a chance to enjoy the prosperity offered by the Mongols' toleration and support of commerce. Hao Ching supplemented Khubilai's proposal with his own letter, a paean to Khubilai in which he identified the Mongol ruler as a typical Chinese-style emperor surrounded by Confucian advisers and governing with the proper moral standards.[17] On the other hand, he warned of the possible consequences of lack of cooperation with Khubilai. The Mongols, he pointedly reminded the Sung court, had awesome military power. Military resistance was pointless. He cited parallels from Chinese history in which a Chinese dynasty, including the Sung itself, had made an accommodation, generally by the payment of tribute, with the so-called barbarians. As noted earlier, the Sung responded by detaining Hao. Chia Ssu-tao and the officials who supported him had decided to resist. When Khubilai dispatched two envoys, Ts'ui Ming-tao and Li Ch'üan-i, in the spring of 1261 to seek Hao's release, the Sung simply rejected their appeals.[18]

Khubilai was undeterred and made additional conciliatory gestures. In 1261, he himself released seventy-five Sung merchants whom his troops had captured along the border; in the following year, another forty traders were allowed to return; and two years later, he pardoned fifty-seven merchants.[19] As late as 1269, he released still another forty-five merchants.[20] In 1264, Khubilai rebuked his military leaders for executing two captured Sung generals without an investigation or trial. Khubilai, trying to encourage defections in the Sung army, was displeased with such reckless and thoughtless actions. More characteristic of his policy was his granting of land, clothing, and oxen to Sung defectors.[21] This policy achieved results, for defectors trickled in throughout the early 1260s. Liu Cheng, who later campaigned actively against the Sung, was the most prominent of these collaborators.[22]

Yet these gestures did not lead to a cessation of hostilities. Skirmishes between the two armies are repeatedly recorded in the Chinese histories. Sung troops raided across the border in August of 1260, November of 1261, and March, May, and June of 1262.[23] Khubilai's forces retaliated in February of 1261 and again in July of 1262.[24] Early in 1265, the first major battle erupted. The two armies clashed near Tiao-yü shan (in Szechwan province), and Khubilai's troops not only won the battle but also captured 146 ships.[25]

The confiscation of the ships demonstrated Khubilai's growing awareness of the need for a navy. Khubilai had, by this time, recognized that victory over the Sung required a strong waterborne force and set about either to capture or to construct ships. His efforts were impressive, for, as one historian of the navy in China writes, "the alacrity with which the Mongols, a nation of horsemen unacquainted with the sea, took to naval warfare was amazing."[26] The Sung defector Liu Cheng was one of the most ardent proponents of a shipbuilding program. Without ships, he argued, the Mongols could not subjugate the Sung. His advocacy and Khubilai's support, which led to the establishment of four sections or "wings" (Chin.: *i*) in their navy, bore fruit in one of the decisive early battles between the two sides.

The encounter at Hsiang-yang, starting in 1268, marked the turning point in the struggle.[27] It was the longest campaign in the war and the one that the *Yüan shih*, Rashīd al-Dīn, and Marco Polo all described in some detail. Marco even claimed to have participated in the siege of the town, an impossible sequence, since the siege ended in a Mongol victory two years before he reputedly reached China. Hsiang-yang and the adjacent town of Fan-ch'eng were located along the northern border of the modern province of Hupei. They were on opposite banks of the Han River, which flowed into the Yangtze River farther south at the modern town of Wu-ch'ang. Their significance lay in their strategic location: they were the last strongholds en route to the Yangtze River basin. They protected the paths to the Middle Yangtze basin and the southeast as well as to the western regions of the Southern Sung. Seizure of the two towns would offer the Mongols a base for assaults on the rest of the South. The Chinese had constructed excellent fortifications at Hsiang-yang, Rashīd al-Dīn's informants later told him, and Hsiang-yang had a "strong castle, a stout wall, and a deep moat."[28] The Sung authorities appointed Lü Wen-huan as the commander of this well-defended, seemingly impregnable town.[29]

To overcome the resistance of the Sung forces at Hsiang-yang, the

Mongol troops were required to display their newly developed skills in siege and naval warfare. They counted at first on starving out the Sung defenders, but they soon discovered that they would have to block supplies sent by boat to Hsiang-yang. What they needed was naval supremacy over the Han River stretching as far as possible south to the Yangtze. The Sung would try to dispatch supplies and reinforcements by water transport. It was essential for Khubilai's forces to prevent them from doing so. To overcome the resistance of the defenders, Khubilai's troops would eventually have to storm the castle and fort. But the Sung troops were so well entrenched that the Mongols realized they would suffer heavy casualties. They needed artillery support to avert such losses.

The leaders Khubilai chose for this campaign reveal once again his policy of personnel recruitment. He did not appoint Mongol commanders exclusively; nor did he choose the entire leadership from any single ethnic group. Liu Cheng, the recent defector who informed Khubilai of the Sung's political and military weaknesses, and Shih T'ien-tse, who had joined the Mongols even before Khubilai's accession, were the most prominent Chinese generals. Arigh Khaya, who proved to be one of the most successful commanders, was a Uighur;[30] A-chu (Aju, in Mongol) was the principal Mongol delegated to participate in the siege;[31] and Ismaʿil and ʿAla al-Din, who designed the artillery for the final assault on Hsiang-yang, were Middle Eastern Muslims.[32] Koreans and Jurchens built the ships used during the siege. The leaders and troops who converged on Hsiang-yang constituted what we would today describe as an international force. Here was still another example of Khubilai's genius in attracting non-Mongols to his cause and employing them for his purposes. He was willing to recruit non-Mongols and grant them authority, even over military matters. The troops they commanded also were composed of different ethnic groups.

The commanders entrusted by Khubilai with this vital military objective took almost five years to occupy Hsiang-yang. They moved gradually to tighten their blockade of the town, but even so they did not foresee the lengthy siege that ensued. The inhabitants of Hsiang-yang had stored vast quantities of provisions, and a few ships on occasion slipped through the Mongol blockade to supply essentials to the beleaguered Chinese population. These sporadic successes prolonged the siege. The Chinese chronicles provide few details on the fighting. However, they do reveal that the siege was not continuous.

There were brief periods during which the siege was lifted, suspended, or less than totally effective. Unfortunately, the reasons for these lapses are not discussed in the sources.

The first step leading to the blockade was the order early in 1268 to officials in Shensi and Szechwan to construct five hundred boats. Liu Cheng planned to use these vessels to control access to the Han River. Within a few months, he began to build fortifications at Po-ho-k'ou and Lu-men shan, south of Hsiang-yang, to prevent boats with supplies from reaching the town.[33] By October, Khubilai had assigned the Mongol commander A-chu to lay siege to Fan-ch'eng as well.[34] The Sung troops at Hsiang-yang panicked at this point. On December 6, they tried to break through the Mongol-led forces. The attempt was abortive, and the Chinese histories record that Khubilai's troops captured and beheaded innumerable enemy soldiers.[35] The besieged Chinese soldiers did not make the same mistake for some time. Instead they awaited supplies and men from their compatriots in the South. They did not need to wait long. In August of 1269, the Sung general Hsia Kuei, with three thousand boats, attacked Lu-men shan. However, the Mongol forces not only defeated him but also captured fifty of his boats.[36]

Khubilai was by this time apparently dissatisfied with the course of the siege. In February of 1269, he had already sent Shih T'ien-tse, one of his most trusted military aides, to inspect the placement of his forces around Hsiang-yang and to proffer suggestions for improvement. The very next month he authorized reinforcements of twenty thousand troops for A-chu and Liu Cheng,[37] and in April, adopting Shih T'ien-tse's suggestion, those two military commanders connected the ramparts from Po-ho-k'ou to Lu-men shan, making entrance and exit from Hsiang-yang even more difficult. These steps were insufficient, for A-chu and Liu Cheng requested seventy thousand men and five thousand ships in April of 1270.[38] Even so, they could not compel the Sung defenders to submit. A stalemate prevailed.

The Sung court remained adamant in its unwillingness to yield. The Chinese sources revile Chia Ssu-tao for obsessively pursuing a mistaken policy and for deliberately misleading the emperor about the gravity of the Mongol threat. Chia had, according to these accounts, lulled the court into minimizing Mongol power by falsely claiming to have defeated Khubilai's armies in 1260. He had persisted in deceiving the Sung authorities, but a loss at Hsiang-yang would undermine his credibility. Therefore, he could not allow his troops in that town to surrender. Some sources suggest that he kept the emperor ignorant of the Mongol siege at Hsiang-yang. These accounts are simply absurd. Leading court officials knew full well of the condition of the besieged town, and one sinologist has recently observed that "repeated rewards and gifts for the troops garrisoned in Hsiang-yang and elsewhere are recorded in the Basic Annals of the *Sung shih*, and an imperial decree rewarded with promotion and gifts of money several brave officers who had smuggled official letters into the besieged town of Hsiang-yang." [39] No single Sung official can be castigated for the unyielding position of the court, which appeared to be united in its refusal to make concessions to the Mongols. Leading Sung officials as a whole underestimated Mongol capabilities, and they would not readily surrender at Hsiang-yang. They were determined to provide supplies to the garrison based near the Han River.

The Sung troops at Hsiang-yang were just as determined not to surrender without a fight. They had sufficient provisions of food and water and had shortages only of clothing, salt, and other not absolutely essential goods. Thus they could withstand a siege for a prolonged period. They did occasionally, however, send detachments to batter their way through the blockade. An attempt on March 18, 1270, was typical.[40] Forces numbering ten thousand soldiers and cavalry with over one hundred boats tried to battle their way through the Mongol fortifications. The Mongol troops were prepared. Liu Cheng had several hundred boats at his disposal; the forts at Lu-men shan had recently been strengthened; and an infusion of freshly arrived soldiers was ready for the onrushing enemy. After a ferocious battle, the Sung forces, having suffered heavy casualties, were forced to return to their base in Hsiang-yang.

The Sung court, aware of its responsibilities, continued to dispatch supply boats to the beleaguered troops. Most of these boats did not reach their destination, as the Mongol siege appeared almost impenetrable. Yet the court persisted in its efforts to penetrate the blockade. In August of 1269, the Sung general Hsia Kuei headed toward Lu-men shan with three thousand boats, but he was defeated and lost more than two thousand men and fifty boats.[41] In October of the following year, Fan Wen-hu tried to accomplish what Hsia had failed to do. His losses amounted to a thousand men and thirty boats.[42] Another recorded relief effort took place in August of 1271. The attempt failed dismally, and two thousand Sung soldiers died. In September of 1272, one party of Sung troops, originally consisting of three thousand men, did fight its way into the town. But their campaign was a pyrrhic victory. Chang Shun, one of the two commanders, was killed, as were substantial numbers of his men. Many of the supplies they had transported were lost or destroyed. When the remnants of the relief forces tried desperately to depart from the fort they had only recently and arduously reached, they found themselves trapped. Their leader was captured, as were many of the troops he led.[43]

The Mongol blockade was, to be sure, eminently effective, but the Mongol forces were unable to wear down the Sung defenders. They had cut off Hsiang-yang and Fan-ch'eng from the rest of the Sung state, but they could not subdue the stubborn garrisons. There was no way to rush the forts without incurring heavy casualties and with any guarantee of success. Yet if the Mongol-led forces simply maintained the siege without any offensive action, they could be tied down indefinitely. They needed help to break the stalemate.

Two Muslim engineers provided the assistance that the Mongols sought. Khubilai had turned to his nephew, the Il-Khan Abakha of Persia, for the expertise essential for crushing the resistance at Fan-ch'eng and Hsiang-yang. In 1271 Abakha responded to Khubilai's appeal by sending Ismāʿīl and ʿAlā al-Dīn.[44] After a brief stay at the Mongol court, the two Muslims in late 1272 went to the battle zone, surveyed the scene, and set to work to build war machines. They built a mangonel and a catapult capable of hurling huge rocks over a considerable distance.[45] In December, the Mongol troops began to use these devices in an attack on Fan-ch'eng. With such strong artillery support, Arigh Khaya could finally storm the fort. Battered by a barrage of rocks and projectiles, the remaining Sung forces could not withstand the onrushing Mongol troops, and Fan-ch'eng fell within a few days. When reports of the collapse of the Fan-ch'eng garrison reached Lü Wen-huan, he quickly recognized that his own men at Hsiang-yang could not resist such a massive artillery assault. But he did not submit immediately. The Muslim engineers therefore "inspected the strength of the position and set up an engine at the southeast corner of the city. The missile weighed 150 catties. When the machinery went off the noise shook heaven and earth; everything that [the missile] hit was broken and destroyed."[46] Late in March, acknowledging the superior firepower of the opposition, Lü finally surrendered.[47] A siege of almost five years' duration had ended, and a vital symbol of Sung resistance to the "barbarians" had suddenly been wiped out.

The morale of the Sung court must surely have sunk. One of their important defensive positions had been overwhelmed. Chia Ssu-tao, the principal strategist and policymaker, found himself discredited. He tried to regain some of his lost prestige by going in person to lead the Sung army. He also sought to raise additional revenues for the growing military expenditures by imposing taxes for the first time on the Buddhist and Taoist monasteries. But both of these efforts backfired on him. Buddhist and Taoist leaders, who earlier either supported or were indifferent to him, now became hostile. His military exploits wound up as fiascoes. After the fall of Hsiang-yang the Mongols were certain to move southeastward toward the Sung capital at Hangchow, and Chia decided to meet the advancing enemy northwest of the city.

By this time, Chia faced a more unified Mongol army and an extremely capable Mongol general. In a memorial to Khubilai written some months after the collapse of Hsiang-yang, Shih T'ien-tse recommended that one man be appointed as overall leader of the invading Mongol troops. Shih argued that the lack of such a leader caused confusion, delays, and strife. Shih, who was at this time deathly ill, was not promoting his own career here; he knew that a proper chain of command was vital for success in military operations.[48] Khubilai agreed with his loyal and old friend and companion, and in the summer of 1273 chose Bayan, probably the most gifted and successful military man of his generation, to assume command over the expeditionary forces. A Turk descended from a long line of military officers who had served under the Great Khans, Bayan had, as a youth, accompanied Khubilai's younger brother Hülegü on his campaigns in Persia and the Middle East. He returned eastward in the mid-1260s and quickly established a reputation as an outstanding official. Khubilai noticed that "whenever he [Bayan] participated in planning affairs of state, he frequently excelled [other] courtiers."[49] Khubilai offered him progressively greater responsibilities until his crowning assignment as commander-in-chief of the troops in China.

Throughout late 1274 and early 1275, Bayan moved inexorably forward against the Sung. He adopted the same tactics that had proved effective for the Mongols for decades. He would demand submission whenever he arrived in the neighborhood of an unpacified town or fortification. If the inhabitants or the military refused his order, they would be subject to attack by the catapults and flame-throwers designed for the Mongols by the two Muslim engineers. Some Chinese defected or submitted without much prodding. Generals such as Lü Wen-huan and Fan Wen-hu recognized the military superiority of the Mongol-led troops and simply joined them to avoid a foolish, suicidal last stand. Other Sung officials, embittered by Chia Ssu-tao's reforms, thought they would fare better under Mongol rule. Still others perceived of the Mongols as the only group that could unify North and South China. Whatever the motives, the number of defectors or at least those willing to surrender increased as Bayan marched south.

Bayan's troops seemed and were unstoppable. In January of 1275, they decided to traverse the Yangtze at Han-k'ou. A fierce naval and land battle ensued, and "those who were beheaded and those who died by drowning were innumerable."[50] The Sung forces were compelled to retreat from the banks of the Yangtze. In mid-March, Bayan finally met his chief adversary Chia Ssu-tao in Ting-chia chou, a site within striking distance of Yang-chou. Chia is said to have led a force of 130,000 men. The number of troops under Bayan's command is difficult to estimate, but the critical difference between the two armies was not size but equipment. The catapults employed by Bayan's forces not only intimidated and terrorized the enemy but also inflicted heavy casualties. Chia's troops began to desert him, and he finally had to gather the remaining forces and retreat.[51]

His enemies at court now had the opportunity they sought. They did not fault the Chinese soldiers for the repeated losses. Instead, they criticized Chia for seeking to appease the Mongols as early as 1259 and for recruiting incompetent military men when he did decide to stand up to the "barbarians." An official named Ch'en Wen-lung, for example, demanded not only that Chia be dismissed but also that some of his military appointees be relieved of their responsibilities. Even Chia's protégés now turned against him. Ch'en I-chung, an administrator of the Bureau of Military Affairs whose career had been immeasurably bolstered by Chia, called on the court to impose stiff penalties on his former patron. Fang Hui, a poet and official who had been excessively sycophantic in his dealings with Chia, now demanded the execution of the object of his flattery.[52] Blaming Chia for the Sung army's losses to Bayan, these officials had him relieved from his government offices and stripped of his rank. Even such degradation did not satisfy his enemies, and they had him banished to the southern province of Fukien. En route, the commander of the detachment sent to accompany the former Sung Chancellor killed him. The controversial Chia Ssu-tao was dead, but many among both his supporters and opponents had become so disenchanted that they hastened to submit to Bayan. To encourage more defections, Khubilai sent a message, via his Confucian minister Lien Hsi-hsien, to Bayan to prevent his soldiers from plundering in the regions they had recently captured. This was apparently one of Khubilai's few admonitions to his commander, for, as he said, "that a general during the campaign need not follow Court orders is sound military law."[53] After several mopping-up operations, Bayan approached Yang-chou, assigned some of his commanders to besiege the city, and moved toward his ultimate goal, the city of Hangchow.[54]

The Sung court at Hangchow was in a state of confusion and chaos. The young emperor, Tu-tsung, who had reigned since 1264, had died suddenly on August 12, 1274. He had three sons, all of whom were minors. The second son, the four-year-old Hsien (1270–1323), succeeded him because his mother, the Empress Ch'üan, was Tu-tsung's legal wife; his older half-brother was the son of a concubine. Real political power remained, nonetheless, in the hands of Hsien's grandmother and regent, the Empress Dowager Hsieh (Hsieh Huang-hou, 1208–82).[55] She was old and ill, however, and the political crises of 1274–75, culminating in the downfall of Chia Ssu-tao, left her with few reliable advisers. Defections had also robbed her of potential counselors. As the Mongols advanced toward Hangchow, she became increasingly anxious about the very survival of the dynasty. Wen T'ien-hsiang (1236–83), by this time one of the most prominent of the civil officials, proposed now that the imperial family leave the city and head for a more secure sanctuary in the South.[56] Chang Shih-chieh (1236–79), the most eminent military commander, seconded Wen's suggestion, but the Empress Dowager was apparently unwilling to abandon the capital. As Bayan's forces approached the city, however, she finally compromised. She had the Emperor's brothers escorted out of Hangchow to a location in the south, but she and the Emperor remained behind to rally the local people.

Meanwhile, Bayan's troops occupied one town after another. In most cases, the Sung military and the inhabitants simply surrendered. The Sung positions were crumbling. Even so, the Empress Dowager wished to effect an accommodation between equals rather than to submit as a conquered subject. On December 23, 1275, she dispatched an envoy to persuade Bayan to abandon his expedition in return for regular tribute payments from the Sung court. The Mongol commander was too close to victory to accept such meager spoils. Citing the Sung's treachery in detaining Hao Ching and in killing one of Khubilai's envoys, he curtly dismissed the Empress Dowager's emissary.[57] Chastened by Bayan's rejection of this offer, the Sung court decided to make a more attractive proposal. On January 11, 1276, it made a more specific offer: the Sung would present yearly tribute of 250,000 taels of silver and 250,000 bolts of silk.[58] Bayan was not enticed by this substantial offer. He wanted and would settle for nothing less than unconditional surrender. Only in late January, after the Sung emperor had described himself as a subject of Khubilai's, did Bayan consent to negotiate with the Sung envoys. After several abortive meetings between their representatives, the Empress Dowager submitted the Sung dynasty's seal to Bayan, an unambiguous symbol of capitulation.[59]

However, within the week Bayan learned that Chang Shih-chieh was escorting the Emperor's two half-brothers south. Bayan's underlings gave chase, but the Sung party eluded them.[60] The Mongol commander chose temporarily to ignore the apparent duplicity of the court in enabling part of the imperial family to flee. Therefore, when the Sung emperor came in person to submit to the new masters of the city, Bayan graciously accepted the surrender. Later he noted that as a result of the submission, "the South and the North have become one family."[61] He directed his officers to conduct a census of Hangchow's population and to register its granaries and treasuries. Simultaneously, he ordered that the Sung royal family be treated with respect. He prohibited his men from pillaging the tombs of the Sung emperors and from plundering their treasuries.[62] Having admonished his forces, Bayan, accompanied by the Emperor and the Empress Dowager, returned north to Khubilai's court in Shang-tu.

Khubilai treated the Sung rulers fairly well. Though he confiscated some of the imperial family's robes, crowns, jade tablets of authority, jewelry, and other treasures, he was not as vindictive as he could have been.[63] He granted the deposed Emperor Hsien the title "Duke of Ying" and provided the young man with the luxuries to which he had grown accustomed. Eventually Hsien was exiled to Tibet, and, in 1296, he took monastic vows.[64] Khubilai also promised similarly benevolent and generous treatment to ordinary Sung officials and people. All who had submitted would be pardoned, and Khubilai ordered that Confucians, Taoists, and Buddhists all be treated respectfully. He pledged government support or subsidies for widows, orphans, and the childless elderly.[65] He transmitted, in this way, an important message: he would not tolerate plunder of the newly conquered regions. Instead, he would adopt the same policy in the South that he had implemented in the North, to promote the recovery of war-ravaged lands and seek economic growth and development.

An account in the Yüan dynastic history, which may or may not be apocryphal, portrays the image that Khubilai and his wife Chabi wished to convey about their attitude toward the deposed Sung rulers. After their audience with Khubilai, the Sung Empress Dowager Hsieh and the Empress Ch'üan were provided with residences in Ta-tu (modern Peking). Two of their attendants, one surnamed Chu and the other surnamed Ch'en, were so distressed by their mistresses' humiliation that they hung themselves. Khubilai, infuriated and perhaps embarrassed by these suicides, exposed their corpses and hung their heads in Empress Ch'üan's quarters.[66] Chabi was outraged by Khubilai's barbaric action, and she demanded that Empress Ch'üan, together with the Empress Dowager Hsieh, be allowed to return to South China. Khubilai was chastened by his wife's tongue-lashing, but he still responded that it was not feasible to permit the empresses to return to the South. Chinese loyalists in the South would create disturbances, and the empresses' safety could not be guaranteed. Instead, Khubilai recommended that they remain in Ta-tu, and he pledged that they would be well cared for. Chabi was accorded the responsibility of seeing to their needs, and she apparently treated them generously. The Empress Dowager Hsieh stayed in Ta-tu until her death in 1282 or 1283, and the Empress Ch'üan joined a Buddhist nunnery, where she died sometime after 1296. Such consideration for the Sung imperial family stored up enormous goodwill for the Mongol rulers.[67]

Despite the capture of Hangchow, the conquest of the Sung was still not completed. Learning of the fall of the capital, the Sung loyalists who had fled to the South gathered together in Fu-chou on June 14, 1276, to witness the coronation ceremonies for the seven-year-old Emperor Shih (1268–78), the captured Emperor's older half-brother. At precisely the time when a forceful, dynamic ruler was required, another child emperor had been enthroned. Ch'en I-chung became the overall leader, and Chang Shih-chieh, Wen T'ien-hsiang, and Lu Hsiu-fu (1238–79) had responsible positions. All four sought to dominate, and there was no higher authority to reconcile their differing views. The conflicts led at one time to the banishment of Lu Hsiu-fu for daring to question Ch'en's policies.[68] As these leaders continued to wrangle, other officials wearied of this internecine strife and began to defect in droves to the Mongols. The Sung general Hsia Kuei, for example, defected bringing with him three big and six small prefectures and thirty-six districts in western Huai-nan, bordering on the Mongol lands.[69] Lack of unity weakened the Sung's ability to retain the loyalty of its own people.

Such disunity emboldened the Mongol-led forces to advance southward as rapidly as possible. The Uighur Arigh Khaya was assigned to pacify the southwestern domains of the Sung. With 30,000 troops under his command, he began to move toward the modern province of Kwangsi in July of 1276.[70] En route, he brought Ch'angsha under Mongol control, and by April of the following year he had fought his way into Northern Kwangsi. He apparently took Khubilai's injunctions to heart, for within a few days after his troops occupied Kwangsi, he instituted a civilian administration and began to further the economic recovery of the region.[71] Meanwhile in the East, the Mongol troops under the command of a certain Sodu pursued the rest of the Sung royal family all down the southern coast of China.[72] From the port of Ch'u-chou, which he had seized late in 1275, Sodu quickly moved toward the south.[73] By the end of 1276, his troops had begun to converge on Fu-chou, the city in which the child Emperor Shih had only recently sought sanctuary. With the Mongol forces only a few days' march away, the highest Sung officials decided once again to retreat. They spurned any suggestion of surrender. Going out to sea, they sailed south and docked at the busy port of Ch'üan-chou.

On their arrival, they started to negotiate with P'u Shou-keng, the remarkable Superintendent of Maritime Trade at Ch'üan-chou.[74] Descended from a line of prosperous Arab merchants who had originally settled in Kuang-chou, P'u was appointed the Superintendent of Maritime Trade in Ch'üan-chou because of his help in crushing the piracy that plagued the city. His position afforded numerous opportunities for enrichment. Gifts from grateful merchants and officials, as well as bribes and graft, contributed to P'u's wealth.[75] His power and prosperity made him an alluring figure for both Khubilai and the fleeing Sung royal family. Both sides attempted to gain his allegiance, recognizing that P'u had access to ships vital in the naval warfare that appeared to be crucial in their future struggle. When the Sung loyalists reached Ch'üan-chou, they immediately sought boats and supplies, but P'u found them to be high-handed and arrogant. They appeared to be requisitioning, not requesting, what they wanted. Restraining his anger, he invited them to stay longer in Ch'üan-chou. Simultaneously, he moved closer to an alliance with the Mongols. Chang Shih-chieh and the other Sung supporters were, however, suspicious of P'u's intentions and loyalties. As one scholar observes, "it is quite probable that when P'u Shou-keng asked the emperor to come within the city, he intended to take him prisoner." [76] The Sung loyalists thus fled from Ch'üan-chou early in 1277. By April, if not earlier, P'u had formally elected to cooperate with the Mongols and sent notice of his intentions to Khubilai's court. [77] Khubilai was elated, for P'u's transfer of loyalty bolstered the Mongol navy. He ingratiated himself with the Arab official by appointing him the military commander of the provinces of Min (modern Fukien) and Kuang (modern Kwangtung). [78] By this means, Khubilai assured that he would have access to P'u's superior ships. P'u had a scare later in the year. Chang Shih-chieh rounded up a fleet of fine ships and blockaded the port of Ch'üan-chou, and P'u appeared to be in some difficulty. Within two months, however, Khubilai dispatched Mongol reinforcements to rescue P'u, and Chang was compelled to withdraw to the South.

The Sung loyalists continued on their peripatetic ways. After departing from Ch'üan-chou, they moved around from one port to another, stopping first at Ch'ao-chou, then moving on to Hui-chou. They wound up in Kuang-chou for most of 1277. But they would not remain unmolested. Sodu would not be deflected from his ultimate objective of crushing the Sung opposition. [79] Whenever he faced resistance, he smashed it with the catapults and other war machines introduced by the Muslims. [80] He tried to initiate negotiations in November of 1277, but Chang Shih-chieh flatly refused his offer. Following this rebuff, Sodu attacked and occupied Kuang-chou, and by February of 1278 his troops also marched into Ch'ao-chou. [81] While fleeing once again, the Sung refugees encountered a bad storm on January 6, 1278. The Emperor's ship sank, and he and Chang Shih-chieh barely escaped with their lives. The pressures, the rugged life, and the different climates and environments all took their toll on the young, somewhat sickly Emperor, and on May 8 he died, just before his tenth birthday. [82]

His death was a heavy blow for the Sung loyalists, but Chang Shih-chieh managed to rally them for one last time. He enthroned the dead Emperor Shih's half-brother Ping and, together with Lu Hsiu-fu, ruled in the child emperor's name. By this time, the remaining Sung refugees were based in the southeastern extremity of China. In fact, they had now settled in an island called Nao-chou off the Lei-chou peninsula. They knew that their residence would offer only a temporary respite from Mongol attacks. What was to be done? Ch'en I-chung proposed that the emperor seek asylum in Champa (in modern times, the southern regions of Vietnam). Since many of the people of Champa were originally of Chinese descent and since they too feared a Mongol invasion, they might welcome the young monarch. They might also be delighted with the prestige of safeguarding the ruler of a great empire. Ch'en voyaged to Champa to discover if its rulers would harbor the Sung emperor.[83] Awaiting Ch'en's return, the Sung refugees found themselves unable to remain and rest in Nao-chou. The Mongol armies occupied Lei-chou, preventing an escape toward Champa. The Sung loyalists set out to sea again and found temporary refuge on the island of Yai-shan, not far from Kuang-chou, which was already in Mongol hands.

The Mongols prepared for an assault on the beleaguered Sung troops. Early in 1279, their forces converged in the south on Yai-shan. Knowing that he could not counter the Mongols' firepower, Chang Shih-chieh tried to elude the blockade around Yai-shan. But on March 19, only sixteen of his vessels broke through the encirclement of the Mongol fleet.[84] The Sung emperor's ship was one of the casualties. Lu Hsiu-fu, who realized that the ship was sinking, is reputed to have taken the child emperor in his hands and jumped overboard to his death. The last Sung emperor had perished at sea, and the Sung dynasty had at last fallen to the Mongols.

Most of the remaining Sung loyalists either surrendered or committed suicide, but a few vowed to continue the struggle. Chang Shih-chieh, the most notable of these leaders, conceived of finding a descendant of the Sung royal family in Champa or Annam who could be enthroned as the Emperor. With this optimistic view in mind, he departed for those Southeast Asian lands. Good fortune was not with him, though, as his ship encountered a hurricane in June of 1279 and he lost his life. Ch'en I-chung had reached Champa but could not return once he learned that the last Sung emperor had died. He remained in Champa, paving the way for the arrival of other Sung refugees. In 1283, when the Mongols invaded Champa, he appears to have fled to Siam, where he resided until his death.[85] Wen T'ien-hsiang, who had been captured by the Mongols, refused to serve or cooperate with the new masters of the South and, as we shall see, was eventually executed for his hostile attitude toward the Mongols.

By 1279, Khubilai had crushed the remnants of the Sung dynasty. He now faced perhaps a more difficult task, however, for he needed to gain the allegiance of the people of the Sung whom he had just subdued. To win their confidence, he could not appear to be merely a "barbarian" conqueror interested solely in exploiting the resources of South China. Khubilai needed to establish a government that served the Mongols yet did not overly oppress the local people. Continuity in some policies and personnel would also smooth the transition to Mongol rule. Khubilai tried almost as soon as the Sung fell to prevent his forces from alienating its people. In September of 1278, he ordered Sodu and P'u Shou-keng to treat his new subjects with proper respect, and he advised his military officials to permit the commoners in the new territories to devote themselves to agriculture and their trades.[86] Their property, he cautioned, was not to be expropriated. He made similar pronouncements throughout the early years of his rule concerning the territories previously controlled by the Sung. These policies were certainly effective. Few, if any, rebellions and no major insurrections are recorded, and many talented Southerners served the Mongols. Some officials and scholars refused to be recruited and devoted themselves to nonpolitical pursuits, and quite a few remained Sung loyalists at heart. Yet it is remarkable that Khubilai was able to institute Mongol rule with as few difficulties as he did over the land with the largest population in the world. No other territory conquered by the Mongols was as populous or as prosperous. Khubilai's policies, as we shall see, made it possible for the Mongols to govern this vast domain—a success story that ought not to be discounted. From hindsight, we know that Mongol rule over China lasted for less than a century. Yet we should not denigrate Khubilai's achievement. From the standpoint of his contemporaries, Mongol and non-Mongol alike, his success in governing South China is astonishing.

THE SUBMISSION OF KOREA

Khubilai's predecessors had been frustrated in their efforts to pacify Korea. Chinggis in 1218 and Ögödei in 1231–33 had dispatched expeditions to subjugate the country. Though they succeeded in imposing Mongol sovereignty over much of Korea, in 1233 the king himself eluded the enemy forces and crossed over to Kanghwa island, off the eastern coast of the mainland. The Ch'oe family, whose patriarch manipulated and truly controlled the king, remained implacably hostile to the Mongols and refused to submit. The Mongols, diverted by succession problems and by other military campaigns, did not send a punitive expedition until the reign of Möngke. In 1253, Möngke ordered a certain Cha-la-erh-tai to attack the unyielding Korean court; at the end of the year and again in 1258, other Mongol armies crossed into Korea.[87] They overwhelmed the local forces on the Korean mainland, and the Koreans, who were already afflicted with a terrible drought, suffered grievously. Those Koreans who submitted or defected fared well, and the artisans among them, like the craftsmen in other Mongol domains, received special treatment and were often recruited by the conquerors.[88] The Mongol forces, recognizing their lack of expertise in naval warfare, made no effort to go by sea to Kanghwa island—a wise decision that was not emulated by Mongol troops later in Japan and Java. Fortunately for the Mongols, resentment against the oppressive rule of the Ch'oe family surfaced at this time. In 1258, a military coup toppled Ch'oe Ŭi, the head of the clan, and the new leadership sought an accommodation with the Mongols. Crown Prince Chŏn traveled to China to signal the submission of the Koreans and to offer himself as a hostage.[89] Khubilai was the first Mongol prince Chŏn encountered in China. Since Möngke had headed toward Szechwan in the southwest to initiate his attack against the Sung dynasty, Khubilai was the most important figure in Eastern China. Khubilai quickly and graciously accepted the Korean heir into his entourage.

Within a few months, both Möngke and the Korean king died. Khubilai, with the support of his Chinese advisers, decided to gamble on the Crown Prince. He released the young heir, with instructions to return to his native land to claim the throne.[90] The new king would have some authority, but a Mongol resident commissioner would also be stationed in Korea. Khubilai was counting on the loyalty and "virtue," a term used by one of his Confucian advisers, of the new king. Late in 1259, the crown prince, accompanied by an escort of Mongol troops, arrived in Korea and assumed the throne as King Wŏnjong. He quickly demonstrated his loyalty and "virtue" by dispatching the next crown prince as a hostage to Khubilai's court. Khubilai, in turn, bestowed a jade belt and other presents on the Korean prince.[91] For the next decade, relations between the Korean king and the Mongol monarch improved steadily. The Korean king sent periodic tribute embassies to Khubilai's court, and Khubilai reciprocated with lavish gifts and opportunities for trade for Korean merchants.[92] In times of economic distress, Khubilai came to the

Koreans' rescue with supplies of grain and meat. He also repeatedly instructed his troops along the border not to harass, rob, or plunder the Koreans.[93] Similarly, he admonished his Jurchen subjects in Manchuria to refrain from any attacks across the border into Korea.[94] The resulting relations between Wŏnjong and Khubilai were amicable and, in fact, so close that the Mongol emperor sent medicines to the ailing Korean king in 1266.[95]

When Khubilai learned of a revolt directed against the Korean king, therefore, he acted immediately to help his beleaguered Korean ally or what he perceived to be his "vassal." In 1269, a military commander named Im Yon tried to follow the pattern laid down by the Ch'oe clan—that is, control of the monarchy by a military clique. He engineered a coup d'état against Wŏnjong and imposed his own candidate on the throne. Ironically, this usurper was Wŏnjong's younger brother, who consented to be Im Yon's means to power.[96] Within a month of learning of the successful *putsch*, Khubilai had dispatched a detachment of three thousand troops, under the leadership of Wŏnjong's son who had been a hostage at the Mongol court.[97] Early in the following year, the Mongol armies routed Im Yon's forces and reinstated Wŏnjong on his throne. But the military threat persisted. Only in 1273 were the insurgents finally crushed on Cheju Island, off the southern coast of the mainland. Meanwhile Khubilai had cemented his relations with King Wŏnjong. To strengthen the bonds with the Korean monarch, he adopted a tactic that had long been used in East Asia, marital alliance. His daughter known in Chinese as Hu-tu-lu Chieh-li-mi-shih was betrothed to the Korean crown prince; the eventual successor to the throne would thus be Khubilai's grandchild.[98] Throughout the Mongol dynasty Khubilai's heirs pursued the same policy, ensuring strong links with the Korean royal family.

By 1273, Khubilai had brought Korea within the orbit of his newly established dynasty. He imposed obligations on the Koreans but simultaneously provided them with tangible economic assistance. The Koreans were obliged to offer tribute of marmot and otter skins, silver, textiles, and paper. They established, in addition, a special Falconry Office to provide falcons for the hunts that the Mongols, and Khubilai in particular, enjoyed.[99] Korean ceramics, which were more advanced technically than Chinese, were also prized in China. As one historian has observed, "the Korean use of copper oxide [to create a bright red color on the ceramic] predates its use in China by about a century."[100] The Chinese thus valued Korean expertise in pottery. A curious anecdote in the Korean sources reveals that at least one person in the Mongol hierarchy, Khubilai himself, was horrified by the elaborateness and excessive cost of the ceramics. A Korean envoy named Cho offered Khubilai a beautiful vase, and the Great Khan's response was:

> "Painting gold on porcelain—is that to make the porcelain strong?"
> Cho's answer was: "No, it is only to decorate the vase."
> The Khan then asked: "Can the gold be used again?"
> Cho replied: "Porcelain breaks so easily, so also naturally gold. How can it be used again?"
> Khubilai Khan then said: "From now on do not use gold and do not present it to me." [101]

This unusual, almost puritanical response does not seem to jibe with the luxurious lifestyle that foreign observers, including Marco Polo, ascribed to Khubilai and his court. Yet it must be remembered that most of these reports were based on the last years of Khubilai's reign. In his early years as emperor, he devoted himself seriously to the goals of the state and to the assertion of his own legitimacy, undiverted by the luxuries available at the Chinese court. The dialogue with the Korean envoy thus represents his sober early years as emperor, before his standards and values had changed.

In any event, from 1264 to 1294 the Korean monarchs sent thirty-six tribute missions to Khubilai's court.[102] On occasion, Khubilai made special requests. In 1267, for instance, he asked Wŏnjong to send him the skin of a particular kind of fish for his artisans to use in fashioning shoes for him. The swelling in his feet, one of the first symptoms of the gout that would afflict him from that time on, was extremely painful and made proper shoes vitally important. He needed fish-skin shoes and depended on the Koreans for the materials he required. The Koreans also repeatedly offered him medicines as he grew older and sicker.[103]

Khubilai, in addition, made the typical demands of a Mongol khan. He ordered the Koreans to send their population registers (a first step in devising taxes), to set up postal stations, and to offer provisions for Mongol soldiers stationed in Korea.[104] In addition he required certain specific duties of the Koreans. They were obliged to furnish women to serve in his harem or as slaves or servant girls. Members of the royal family also served as hostages at the Mongol court until 1283.[105] The Korean kings of the Koryŏ dynasty, which had ruled since 936, were compelled to accept Mongol resident commissioners in the country.

These commissioners sometimes shared power with the monarchs; often, however, they had more power than the monarchs.[106] The Office of Interpreters that had existed even earlier in the history of the Koryŏ dynasty became more active, with a growing emphasis on mastery of Mongol.[107] Part of Cheju Island was converted into a grazing area for horses and a pastureland for sheep. Many of the horses bred in this southern island were to be presented to the Mongols either as tribute or in trade.[108] By 1273, therefore, Korea had been pacified, and Khubilai did not need to be concerned about rebels along the northeastern border. He had also enforced Mongol economic and military demands on the Koreans.

THE FIRST INVASION OF JAPAN

Perhaps Khubilai's most onerous demand on the Koreans was for assistance in his relations with Japan. That overseas kingdom had, for the most part, isolated itself from the Chinese mainland for four centuries. The Chinese persecution of Buddhism in the middle of the ninth century had alienated the Japanese and convinced them to sever almost totally their mercantile and cultural ties with China.[109] What better way for Khubilai to gain in stature among the Chinese, then, than to reestablish a tributary relationship with the Japanese? The thought of the acclaim he would garner surely prompted his decision to initiate relations with the Land of the Rising Sun. Until this time, Mongol leaders had never engaged in sea combat. Now Khubilai made the fateful decision to obtain the submission of a state across the seas. Though he did not intend to wage a naval war, his Japanese initiative led him to just such a disastrous engagement.

Though the Koreans had grievances against the Japanese, they were not eager to serve as intermediaries in the planned Mongol domination of the Japanese. Since 1223, the Koreans had been subjected to attacks by what the Japanese called *wakō* (*waegu* in Korean or *wo-k'ou* in Chinese), Japanese pirates who plundered the coastal regions. Japanese freebooters capitalized on the distraction of the Mongol invasions of Korea to raid the Korean coast.[110] Such raids persisted until 1263. Yet the Korean court, recognizing that neither the Japanese court nor the Japanese military government sanctioned this piracy, did not declare war against Japan. It merely dispatched emissaries to protest the raids. Once the Japanese freebooters learned that the Mongols had subdued the Koreans and that the Korean peninsula was no longer plagued by hostilities, they ceased their raids. The Koreans had no particular interest, therefore, in participating in Mongol plans to initiate relations with Japan.

Khubilai, however, had other ideas. In the fall of 1266, he sent envoys to inform the Japanese of the new dynasty in China and to invite them to offer tribute to the emperor.[111] The Koreans were expected to help transport the embassy across the seas. Instead, those Koreans who received Khubilai's ambassadors sought to dissuade them from their mission, frightening them with descriptions of the rough seas and turbulent weather around the Japanese islands.[112] The Koreans simply wished to avoid entanglement in Mongol-Japanese relations. Dispirited by the Korean reports of the precarious journey to Japan, Khubilai's envoys hastened back to China. Their account enraged Khubilai, who also found the Koreans to be less than trustworthy. In the summer of 1267, he wrote a stinging letter to the Korean court, reprimanding his "subjects" for not only failing to assist but actually discouraging his envoys from reaching Japan.[113] He was determined to try again, and would brook no interference from the Koreans. In 1268, he sent another embassy, and this time the Koreans cooperated with it. The leaders of the mission, an official from the Ministry of Rites and another from the Ministry of War, were instructed by Khubilai to notify the Japanese of his accession and to indicate that they were expected to send tribute embassies.[114]

The Japanese did not welcome the embassy, and by their actions thus made themselves vulnerable to the more vigorous enforcement of Khubilai's policies. The Japanese court, based in Kyōto, was virtually powerless; real power was in the hands of the Bakufu, or military government, centered in Kamakura. Within the Bakufu, the Shōgun's Regent, Hōjō Tokimune, was the ultimate decision-maker, and he had no intention of acquiescing to the Mongols. Counting on the strength of the samurai (warrior) class, and on the insularity and what he perceived to be the inaccessibility of the Japanese islands, he and his predecessor as regent, Hōjō Masamura, had rebuffed the overtures of the Mongol embassy.[115] After some preliminary discussions of the appropriate response to Khubilai's letter, a missive in which Khubilai referred to the Japanese emperor as the "king of a little country," [116] the Bakufu simply sent the Mongol away without any message from the Japanese government. Though court officials drafted a conciliatory letter and sent a copy for approval to the Bakufu, the Shōgun's Regent vetoed the dispatch of this missive.[117] Undiscouraged by this response, Khubilai, early in 1271, sent still another embassy with the same message as his other ambassadors.[118] The envoys' Korean escorts secretly alerted the Japanese to the threat posed by the Mongol military, yet once again the Japanese refused to permit the Mongol envoys access to the court. On their return, the envoys captured two Japanese fishermen and brought them back to China. Khubilai entertained the fishermen and demanded that they request their ruler to show the proper respect for the emperor of China and the khan of the Mongol domains by sending a tribute embassy. Then he had them escorted to Korea on their return journey to Japan. Khubilai's release and return of the detained fishermen elicited no response from the Japanese.

By now, Khubilai was perplexed and annoyed at the "insolence" of the Japanese. He could not allow them to defy him indefinitely. In neither of his two roles, as Khan of Khans of the Mongols or as Emperor of China, could he afford to be humiliated by a foreign state. Mongol custom demanded the proper reception of envoys, and Chinese custom required acceptance of the Emperor as the supreme ruler of all lands. Such clear-cut mandates meant that Khubilai could not continue to tolerate the slights endured by his envoys in Japan. Before adopting a more forceful policy, however, he sent still another envoy to the Japanese. Chao Liang-pi (1217–86), the emissary whom he chose, set forth in the spring of 1272 and landed at Imazu on the eastern coast of the island of Kyūshū in October of the same year.[119] When his demand for a meeting with the Emperor was curtly rebuffed, he issued an ultimatum: the Japanese Emperor had two months in which to respond to Khubilai's letter. The court was willing to provide a bland and nebulous response to the Mongols, but the military government rejected any compromise. The warriors in Kamakura prevailed, and they had the Chinese envoys expelled. The Bakufu's brusqueness has been described as "equivalent to a declaration of war by Japan."[120] Chao Liang-pi returned to China in the sixth month of 1273 and reported to Khubilai on Japan's land and customs, and probably on its defenses.[121] What aroused Khubilai was Chao's description of the insulting reception he had been given. Khubilai could no longer procrastinate, for delays were only allowing the Japanese to be more brazen. A few months prior to Chao's return the Mongols had won their major victory at Hsiang-yang against the Southern Sung, so now Khubilai could divert a small part of his army to the pacification of the Japanese. At the same time his campaign against Japan could be justified as part of his subjugation of the Sung. The Japanese had been engaged in a lively commerce with Khubilai's Chinese adversaries in the South. By defeating the Japanese, he could sever the trade links between his two enemies, thus weakening the Sung.[122]

Khubilai had, for some time, been preparing for the invasion of Japan. He had ordered the Koreans to build ships that would transport his troops across the Sea of Japan to attack the southernmost of the Japanese islands. In November of 1274 a mission, composed of 15,000 Mongol, Chinese, and Jurchen soldiers and 6,000 to 8,000 mostly disgruntled Korean troops (who were not eager to take part in the campaign) and guided by about 7,000 Korean sailors, departed from Happ'o (near modern Pusan) for Japan.[123] Loaded into 300 large ships and 400 to 500 small vessels, the troops first landed in the offshore islands of Tsushima and Iki and easily vanquished the Japanese forces stationed there. Yet the force that Khubilai had sent to overwhelm the Japanese was neither sizable nor imposing. He surely underestimated the resistance that the Japanese were capable of offering.[124]

The crucial battle would naturally be fought in Kyūshū. Although the Japanese knew that the Mongol mission was on its way, their preparations were rudimentary. Their economy could not sustain the maintenance of a sizable army in Kyūshū, nor did they have the politically unified and centralized state needed to field a strong fighting force. They could not match the Mongols' long-range weapons, which included crossbows and various projectiles. Their commanders were not as experienced or as battle-hardened as the Mongol military leaders. The Japanese troops were proficient in hand-to-hand combat, but the Mongols positioned themselves in tightly knit group formations, a tactic unfamiliar to the Japanese.[125] Therefore, when the Mongol forces landed on the east coast of Kyūshū at Hakata on November 19, the Japanese were at a decided disadvantage. The Mongols' battle stance and their plan of attack baffled the Japanese, as did the drums and bells that preceded a Mongol advance. By the end of the first night, the Japanese forces had suffered serious losses of manpower and equipment. Their remaining troops were in a weak position. A rout appeared to be in the making, and that night only the cover of darkness saved them.

Nature, however, provided even greater protection for the Japanese. That same night, a gale-like storm erupted. The Korean sailors quickly persuaded the Mongol commanders that they needed to return to their ships and head for the open seas until the storm subsided. Otherwise their vessels would founder on the rocks along the coast, and their sole means of retreat would be lost. The Mongols reluctantly agreed and began to withdraw from Hakata.[126] A few Japanese pursued and killed some of the retreating Mongol soldiers. The bulk of the Mongol casualties suffered that night, however, were at sea. The winds, the waves, and the rocks shattered several hundred ships, and, according to some accounts, 13,000 lives were lost.[127] The Japanese had been saved by this storm. The expedition ended disastrously for the Mongols, and the remaining Mongol forces sailed for home to report the fiasco to Khubilai.

Since the Great Khan was fully engaged in the attempt to suppress once and for all the Southern Sung, he could not immediately avenge himself on the Japanese. Instead, in 1275, he dispatched another embassy, led by Tu Shih-chung and Ho Wen-chu, to Japan to seek what he wanted without resort to another invasion.[128] The Japanese authorities, cocky with their recent success and trusting the gods who had saved them, widened the breach between themselves and the dynasty in China by executing the unfortunate envoys.[129] This was one of the most heinous offenses that could be committed against the Mongols. Khubilai could not allow such an outrageous act to go unpunished; however, some years would elapse before he was able to send a punitive force to the Japanese islands.

He had, by the mid-1270s, pacified the Koreans and even made them accomplices, reluctant though they may have been in his attack on Japan. But he had failed with the Japanese. He had more pressing concerns elsewhere, however—threats to the territorial integrity of his state, for example. Central Asia offered much more serious challenges to his political authority. He had to deal with that region first before devoting his attention once again to the Japanese.

CAMPAIGNS AGAINST KHUBILAI

In Central Asia Khubilai confronted a foe who wished to wrest control of his khanate. Here, in contrast to Korea and Japan, which posed no true threats to his own position, he faced a hostile challenger who could claim his own throne. In Korea and Japan, Khubilai sought to consolidate and expand Mongol territorial and economic gains, but in Central Asia his enemy wished to detach lands that had been conquered by Khubilai's Mongol predecessors. The threat was even graver because his principal antagonist was not only a Mongol, but also a member of the royal family, a descendant of the Great Khan Ögödei. With his East Asian neighbors, all that Khubilai required was *pro forma* acquiescence to his authority as a ruler. Once he had this pledge, he would scarcely meddle in their internal affairs. Central Asia, on the other hand, shared a common border with Khubilai's domains and was ruled by a fellow Mongol. Without control over, or at least peaceful relations in, this vast territory, Khubilai's frontier lands in Northwest China would be subject to hit-and-run attacks, the kind that Inner Asian nomads had perennially inflicted on Chinese farmers. After these raids, the nomads could simply flee into the vast open spaces of the Central Asian steppes or deserts to evade their pursuers.[130] Even more threatening was the proximity of Central Asia to Mongolia. The traditional Mongol homeland was vulnerable to attack from Central Asia. For Khubilai to abandon his native territories was unthinkable.

In addition, Central Asia was vital to Khubilai's grandiose plans for long-distance trade. It was the crossroads in commerce between China and India, the Middle East, and Europe. Caravans transporting goods across Eurasia counted on stops in the towns and oases of Central Asia both to trade with the local inhabitants and to replenish their supplies. These halting places were essential for the survival of the caravan trade. Similarly, the towns and oases needed the farming enclaves nearby for their food and supplies.

Khubilai's cousin Khaidu was responsible for the hostile stance of Central Asia. Khaidu, as a representative of the Mongol nomadic values, prized certain traditional virtues.[131] Stories that circulated about his daughter Khutulun demonstrate some of those values. Even if these stories are apocryphal, as some historians have suggested, they still reflect some of the values most admired by Khaidu.[132]

Following in her father's footsteps, Khutulun relished the military life and took part in combat. Marco Polo described her as "very beautiful, but also so strong and brave that in all her father's realm there was no man who could outdo her in feats of strength."[133] Though her parents wished her to marry, she would not consent until a prospective suitor bested her in contests of physical strength and endurance and military skill. She accepted any challenge as long as the young man gambled one hundred horses for the chance to defeat and thus to betroth her. In time, it was said, she accumulated ten thousand horses as a result of her victories in these contests.

Finally, in 1280, a handsome, self-confident, and skillful young prince arrived in Khaidu's court to challenge Khutulun. He was so confident of victory that he wagered one thousand horses on his ability to defeat her in a wrestling match. Khutulun's parents were delighted with the imposing and wealthy prince and "did privily beseech their daughter to let herself be vanquished." Khutulun responded haughtily that "never would she let herself be vanquished if she could help it; if, indeed, he should get the better of her then she would gladly be his wife." [134] She nonchalantly went her own way. Among the Chinese of that day, the young and the female were dominated by the old and the male, but Mongol noblewomen had minds of their own and did not hesitate to assert their views. Khutulun had no intention of "throwing" the wrestling match; the prince would have to defeat her in honest competition. The great day arrived, and, surrounded by a large, expectant crowd, the two combatants began to grapple with each other. Khutulun and the prince were evenly matched. For a long time, neither could gain the upper hand. But, with a sudden movement, Khutulun flipped her opponent to the ground, winning the contest. Embarrassed by his loss to a "mere woman," the prince hastily departed, leaving his thousand horses behind.

Father and daughter, from this time on, went together on military expeditions. Khaidu was amazed and delighted by her military prowess: "not a knight in all his train played such feats of arms as she did. Sometimes she would quit her father's side and made a dash at the host of the enemy, and seize some man thereout, as deftly as a hawk pounces on a bird, and carry him to her father." [135] Khutulun represented the virtues Khaidu found most praiseworthy. She was proud and brave and she valued physical strength and endurance. She enjoyed the life of the warrior, not the life of the governor. Her habitat was the open spaces, not a grand palace in a populous though splendid capital city. She sought a mate who was proficient in combat, rather than in scholarship or in ruling. In short, she favored the pastoral, nomadic society over a sedentary, agricultural society ruled by a central government and staffed by a bureaucracy. Her father would naturally come into conflict with Khubilai.

Our view of this struggle is biased by the available sources, which favor Khubilai. Khaidu is treated as a rebel rather than as an upholder of traditional Mongol values. He is depicted as duplicitous and cruel, and the conflicts with Khubilai were, according to the sources, due to his treachery. One example shows the way he is generally portrayed:

> Qubilai Qa'an sent messengers to them, seeking to win them over, and said: "The other princes have all presented themselves here: why have you not come? It is my heart's desire that we should brighten our eyes with the sight of one another. Then, having consulted together on every matter, you will receive all manner of favors and return home." Qaidu had no mind to submit and gave the following excuse: "Our animals are lean. When they are fat we will obey the command." He delayed on this pretext for 3 years.[136]

But such depictions of Khaidu are surely unfair. He was not simply treacherous; nor was he a renegade, as he is often portrayed in the Chinese sources.[137] Plunder was not his sole or even his primary objective. To him the vital task was to preserve the nomadic society, without the inroads imposed on it by Khubilai. He did not intend to destroy the flourishing towns in the region or to dismantle their commercial bases. In fact, he constructed new towns and rebuilt cities that had been damaged earlier in the various stages of the Mongol conquests. He found a new location for Andijan, somewhat northwest of the eventually dominant trading emporium of Kashgar, and had the town reconstructed there.[138] It soon became a vibrant economic center for the western regions of Central Asia. Tirmidh, which had suffered terrible devastation during Chinggis Khan's invasion of Central Asia, was another town that benefited from Khaidu's promotion of economic revival. Farther south and west of Andijan, he restored Tirmidh both in its earlier capacity as a center of Islamic theology and as a vital halting place for the caravans crossing Central Asia.[139] These few examples offer sufficient proof that Khaidu did not recklessly seek to devastate the oases and towns of Central Asia or to expand the territories available for herding at the expense of the region's traditional economy.

His attitude and policies toward the governance of the region also yield clues of some accommodation with the sedentary cultures of Central Asia. He did not, of course, create a centralized, stationary government with a carefully selected, able group of bureaucrats. Nor did he enact well-defined regulations and laws by which the government implemented its policies. Those kinds of compromises were out of the question. Yet he sought to provide security for the non-nomadic peoples in his newly carved-out domains. He actively discouraged the pillaging of the towns and must have instructed his underlings not to harass their inhabitants. Instead of pillaging, he levied taxes on the towns, and the revenues he derived were used to support his forces.[140]

Such limited compromises bolstered Khaidu's position in Central Asia. The divisive conflicts between the townspeople and the nomads were muted. Despite these conciliatory gestures, however, Khaidu still identified with the nomads and believed that Khubilai had capitulated to the sedentary world. To Khaidu, the principal defender of the traditional Mongol way of life, Khubilai had betrayed his Mongol heritage and could not be trusted.

The precise date for the onset of hostilities between Khubilai and Khaidu is difficult to establish. Khubilai had repeatedly requested that Khaidu come to his court, but the Central Asian ruler had just as often deflected these invitations. Both knew that a confrontation was imminent. Khubilai became increasingly concerned about Khaidu's intentions. Already, on July 9, 1266, Khubilai had appointed his son Nomukhan as Pei-p'ing wang (Prince of the Pacification of the North), intending no doubt that the young man eventually take charge of the military affairs of North China.[141] Like his older brother Chen-chin, Nomukhan was the son of the union of Khubilai and Chabi. Also like Chen-chin, he had been tutored by a Chinese scholar, but the tutoring began only in 1264. He does not appear to have had the time to absorb much learning from his Chinese tutors; Chen-chin had a more sustained exposure to traditional Chinese education. Unlike Chen-chin, Nomukhan was apparently slated for a military career rather than for a position in the government. He seemed the appropriate person to deal with the unsettled conditions in the west, and in 1271, when he was in his twenties, Khubilai dispatched him to Almalikh, one of the westernmost outposts of the Great Khan's power.[142] Khubilai sent several princes, cousins of Nomukhan's, to accompany him. It turned out to be a disastrous decision, for the cousins engaged in bitter disputes that impeded the expedition and finally led to its failure.

As so often happened outside the predominantly settled world, the two armies hardly had a direct confrontation. Minor engagements characterized most of the actual fighting. Nomukhan rarely, if ever, encountered Khaidu's forces during these battles. With Nomukhan's arrival in Almalikh, Khaidu had moved his troops westward, leaving behind the Chaghadai Khan to contend with Khubilai's son. In the words of Paul Pelliot, "Qaidu's attitude was, for some years to come,

more one of sullen opposition than of open rebellion."[143] Nomukhan
and the Chaghadai Khan clashed on several occasions, and Khubilai's
son appears to have had the upper hand, but the victories do not seem
to have been clear-cut. The conflicts were sporadic and more like guerrilla engagements than traditional battles between two armies.[144]
Khubilai repeatedly sent food and other supplies to Nomukhan, but
they both counted on setting up a supply line in Central Asia.[145] As
soon as Nomukhan received his assignment, he tried to achieve self-
sufficiency. In 1271, he occupied the town of Khotan and speedily
conducted a census there, which was essential for the levying of taxes
and the acquisition of supplies. In the next few years, he started to
expand into the area south of the T'ien Shan (Heavenly Mountains), a
region much more fertile than his base in Almalikh in the northern
steppes, and to develop a supply line from there. Yet the pressure
from the Chaghadai princes persisted.

Despite the supply line, Nomukhan was making little progress in
crushing the dissidents in Central Asia. In 1275, Khubilai sent his
wife's nephew An-t'ung (1245–93), a capable leader who was at that
time the Right Prime Minister (Yu ch'eng-hsiang), to assist Nomukhan.[146] Khubilai had already demanded the return of thirty-four gold
and silver tablets he had earlier bestowed upon Khaidu and the
Chaghadai Khan Barakh, but he received no response to his demand.[147] On arriving at Nomukhan's encampment, An-t'ung quickly
perceived the reasons for the young man's difficulty in overcoming
Khaidu and his other opponents. Factionalism and quarrels divided
the various princes in Nomukhan's army. An-t'ung inadvertently
became embroiled in these disputes, too, when he antagonized Togh
Temür, a grandson of Tolui's and thus Khubilai's nephew.[148] Togh
Temür may have resented that his branch of the house of Tolui had
been shunted aside by Sorghaghtani Beki's sons, particularly Khubilai. However, the sources are silent about his motivations.

In late 1276 the situation worsened, as the princes who accompanied Nomukhan plotted to sabotage his expedition. The conspirators included Togh Temür, Arigh Boke's sons Yobukhur and Melik
Temür, and Möngke's son Shiregi. Each of them may have harbored
feelings that he, not Khubilai or his sons, had a greater claim on the
Great Khanate.[149] Tögh Temür and Shiregi were apparently the principal conspirators. Rashīd al-Dīn writes that they met secretly and
said to each other: "Let us between us seize Nomoghan and Hantum
Noyan [An-t'ung] and hand them over to the enemy."[150] They

sneaked up one night on Nomukhan's encampment and captured Nomukhan, his younger brother Kököchü, and An-t'ung. Nomukhan and Kököchü were delivered to the Khan of the Golden Horde, Möngke Temür, and An-t'ung was sent to Khaidu. The response from Khaidu was disappointing. He equivocated about a possible alliance with the conspirators, responding, "We are grateful to you, and it is what we expected of you. Since there is good water and grass in that region, stay where you are." [151] In other words, he did not want them in his domains. Whether he distrusted them or felt no need for an alliance at that time, he abandoned these potential allies. The conspirators, without the support of Khaidu, feared a possible attack from the Chaghadai forces to the west and from Khubilai's troops to the east. Shortly after receiving Khaidu's discouraging message, they migrated to what they perceived to be a safer location, the Mongolian steppes and the Upper Yenisei. [152]

The fate of the three captured leaders is at first glance baffling, for none of them was harmed. Their captors simply detained them—for almost a decade. Khaidu finally released An-t'ung in 1284, and on January 4 of the following year An-t'ung was once again granted his old position of Right Prime Minister. [153] Nomukhan and Kököchü, who had been escorted as prisoners to the Golden Horde, were fortunate in that one of Tolui's granddaughters (and thus their cousin), Kelmish Akha, was influential at that court. She apparently comforted them during their detention and was, in part, responsible for their release. According to Rashīd al-Dīn, "when Nomoghan ... was captured by his cousins ... and dispatched by them to Möngke-Temür ... Kelmish-Aqa exerted her efforts to secure his restoration to his father with every mark of respect." [154] Her persuasiveness, and perhaps the khan's desire for better relations with Khubilai and the house of Tolui, finally led to the release of Nomukhan and Kököchü. They reached Ta-tu on March 26, 1284. Two months later Khubilai promoted Nomukhan to be the prince of Pei-an (Northern Peace), in recognition of his son's travails in Central Asia and Russia. [155]

Khubilai was not inactive during the decade that elapsed between the seizure and the release of Nomukhan. On learning of the capture of Nomukhan, Khubilai dispatched Bayan, his ablest and most successful general, to retrieve his son. However, Bayan, despite his smashing victories in the campaigns against the Southern Sung dynasty, was frustrated in his efforts. [156] He attempted to engage the enemy, in particular the conspirators who had betrayed Nomukhan, but they continually eluded his troops. In August of 1277, he did rout Shiregi's forces in a battle along the banks of the Orkhon.[157] Shiregi, however, managed to escape. Nomukhan's leaderless troops made some valiant attempts to free their leader, defeating Nomukhan's disloyal aides on several occasions in 1280 and 1281. Yet they could not secure the release of Nomukhan.[158]

Khubilai eventually acknowledged that he could not control Central Asia. He was compelled to accept Khaidu as the *de facto* ruler of the area. Even his most prominent and accomplished general was unable to overwhelm Khaidu and to extend Khubilai's suzerainty into Central Asia. He reluctantly relinquished his position in the steppe-lands north of the T'ien Shan. Nomukhan's base in Almalikh was also abandoned. Yet he wished to retain control of the oases south of the T'ien Shan, which were vital for commerce with the West. His efforts prompted the allocation of substantial resources, but he eventually retreated to the more readily defensible confines of Chinese settlement.

Meanwhile, the success of Khubilai's endeavors rested on his ability to make the towns and oases more self-sufficient. An increase in agricultural production was essential, for the native inhabitants as well as for the Chinese garrisons needed to fend off Khaidu's raids. Khubilai had to move on two fronts, providing troops on the one hand and promoting the interests of local farmers on the other. Encouragement of agriculture in the northwestern sections of the modern province of Kansu and in the oases south of the T'ien Shan entailed the establishment of military colonies, tax remissions, and disaster relief.[159] Neither the Kansu region nor the Tarim River oases were particularly fertile. Khubilai needed to invest substantial resources to implement his scheme. In 1276 he had started to found military colonies in Sha-chou and Kua-chou and provided them with seeds and tools. At around the same time, he instructed Liu En, one of his military underlings, to conduct a census and a land survey of Su-chou and to establish military colonies there.[160] Liu followed his instructions, but the colonies were not secure and were still subject to attack from Khaidu's forces.

Similarly, Khubilai's efforts in the Uighur lands foundered. He wished to use Uighur territory in the modern area of southern Sinkiang as a base in his struggle against Khaidu. Simultaneously, he sought to capitalize on the resources of the area and to deny them to his Central Asian adversary. In 1280, a Chinese commander named

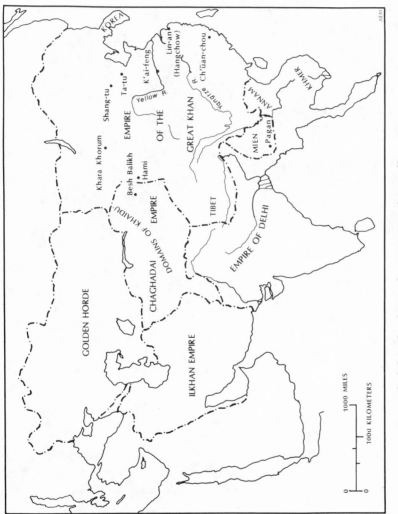

2. Asia at Khubilai Khan's Death—1294. Based on Albert Herrmann, *An Historical Atlas of China*, 42–43.

Ch'i Kung-chih was assigned the task of reimposing Yüan control over the area and regaining the Uighur lands earlier lost to Khaidu.[161] A year later, Ch'i, with about 1,000 soldiers, had reoccupied Besh Balikh, the Uighurs' capital, and had organized military colonies there.[162] But agricultural self-sufficiency remained a distant, seemingly unreachable objective. Khubilai repeatedly approved requests for the shipment of supplies to Ch'i in the next few years. Though the Mongols imposed tax and tribute obligations on the local inhabitants, the actual revenue they garnered was limited. During his raids, Khaidu extorted funds and supplies from the Uighurs.[163] Khubilai was unable to prevent his adversary's hit-and-run attacks, as Khaidu's forces avoided a major battle. The agrarian settlements of the Uighurs were adversely affected:

> The social and economic dislocation occasioned by Khaidu's invasions of Uighuristan was considerable. An agricultural economy based on the extensive use of irrigation is extremely sensitive to the disturbances of war. Vital facilities such as canals and dams are destroyed not only directly by military action, but indirectly by the dispersal of the agricultural population, which results in the disruption of the regular service and repair work necessary to prevent silting.[164]

Lacking protection from the nomads, some Uighurs migrated into China proper, and sometime before 1283, their leader, the *iduq qut*, moved to Yung-ch'ang in Kansu.[165] The final humiliation was the loss of Besh Balikh in 1285 and the capture of Ch'i Kung-chih, the commander whose mission had been to restore Yüan control over the Uighur territories.[166]

From this time on, Khubilai was compelled to abandon any plans for the domination of Central Asia. Like so many Chinese rulers from the Han period (206 B.C.–A.D. 220) on, Khubilai encountered enormous difficulties in seeking to impose his own rule over either the steppelands or the oases in the modern province of Sinkiang.[167] The supply lines needed to maintain both the Yüan armies and the friendly local inhabitants were long and fragile; the constant harassment and the elusiveness of the nomads irritated and intimidated Khubilai's soldiers and allies; and the self-sufficiency he craved for the oases was never realized. The dispatch of troops and the provisions for the natives proved to be costly, an excessive drain on the dynasty's finances. Khubilai's foray was quite simply ineffective. But he did achieve a standstill with Khaidu, with the Central Asian not making incursions into China proper.

Khubilai was more successful in overcoming challenges in Mongolia.[168] After the fall of Arigh Böke, Mongolia enjoyed more than a decade of tranquillity and restoration. Arigh Böke had severely strained the economy of Mongolia during the civil war with his brother, and Khubilai needed to relieve these burdens in order to gain the support of his own people in Mongolia. He initiated such efforts by transporting grain to the poverty-stricken, remitting taxes, and forming military colonies, all in hopes of lightening the load on the local people and enabling them to achieve a measure of self-sufficiency. He founded postal stations to provide a link to his capital in North China and sent artisans to help the natives develop their own expertise in crafts.[169]

One of his principal objectives was to foster the development of agriculture in the steppelands. He issued a directive that those areas in the steppes suitable for agriculture be made ready for farming. To encourage this agrarian development, Khubilai provided oxen and tools to the farmers. In times of crisis caused by natural disasters, he sent emergency rations of grain to the afflicted areas. He appears to have taken special pains to stimulate agriculture in Khara Khorum. The Great Khan Ögödei had promoted farming in areas adjacent to the town, and Khubilai renewed the commitment to a self-sufficient Khara Khorum. Agricultural production in the region of the old Mongol capital increased, but periodically Khubilai and his successors were required to ship grain from China into Khara Khorum. To satisfy the grain needs of Mongolia in general and Khara Khorum in particular, Khubilai therefore stimulated agricultural settlements in the northerly regions of China, specifically in the area of Ning-hsia, from which supplies could be transported to Mongolia. All of these efforts bore some fruit, as the towns did provide grain and manufactured articles to Khara Khorum and Mongolia. Though Khubilai was, on occasion, required to send shipments of grain to relieve shortages, the creation of agricultural settlements linked both Ning-hsia to Mongolia and the two regions to China proper.

He was even able to suppress a rebellion among the Mongol princes in this region. The conspirators who had betrayed his son Nomukhan had migrated to Mongolia and the Upper Yenisei after Khaidu hesitated to welcome them when they turned against Khubilai. The principal conspirators, Shiregi and Togh Temür, then attempted to use this region as a base for an attack on Khara Khorum.[170] Unlike his efforts at pacification in Central Asia, Khubilai's campaigns in Mongolia,

counting in part on his earlier economic program, were extremely successful. The tensions and rivalries within the enemy camp certainly
facilitated his attempts at pacification. Though Togh Temür and
Shiregi and the other leaders were, on the surface, allies, they were
each ambitious and had not settled upon one ruler. Each harbored a
desire to be the principal decision-maker; and these ambitions subverted the unity they needed to resist Khubilai's forces. Rashīd al-Dīn
cites numerous instances of betrayal and duplicity among these erstwhile allies.[171] In 1279, capitalizing on such disarray, Khubilai's
troops overwhelmed Togh Temür in a battle near Khara Khorum. Togh
Temür was subsequently captured and put to death by his own ally
Shiregi.[172] The anti-Khubilai coalition became even shakier after this
blatant evidence of dissidence. Within a year, the princes abandoned
their rebellion and either joined or submitted to the leading Mongols
in China or Central Asia. Shiregi surrendered to Khubilai, who, according to Rashīd al-Dīn, refused to allow his nephew into his presence.
Khubilai instead exiled Shiregi to an "island with a very unhealthy
climate,"[173] where he died shortly thereafter. By 1279, Khubilai had
preserved Mongolia as part of his domain. Central Asia remained
under the control of his principal challenger, however, occasionally
disrupting Khubilai's trade and relations with the West.

Khubilai had proven his military skills; now the question was
whether he could rule the lands he had subjugated.

The Emperor of China

Khubilai wished to be perceived both as the legitimate Khan of Khans of the Mongols and as the Emperor of China. Though he had, by the early 1260s, become closely identified with China, he still, for a time, claimed universal rule. He sought recognition of his status as the undisputed ruler of all the Mongol domains. The Golden Horde in Russia, however, had supported Arigh Böke's candidacy as the Great Khan, and the Central Asian khans had often remained on the side-lines in the struggle between the two brothers. Khubilai was on good terms with the Il-Khans of Persia, but the Mongol rulers there, starting with his brother Hülegü, were essentially self-governing. Though the Il-Khans continued throughout Khubilai's reign to seek formal inves-titure from him, they were virtually autonomous. Thus, despite his successes in China and Korea, Khubilai was unable to have himself accepted as the Great Khan.

China was to be his main base, a realization that dawned on him within a decade of his enthronement as Great Khan. He needed to concentrate on governing China. Though he may have perceived of the Chinese as his "colonial subjects," he recognized that he had to rule China and that to do so he had to employ Chinese advisers and officials. Yet he could not rely totally on Chinese advisers because he had to maintain a delicate balancing act between ruling the sedentary civilization of China and preserving the cultural identity and values of the Mongols. In governing China, he was concerned with the interests of his Chinese subjects, but also with exploiting the resources of the

115

empire for his own aggrandizement. His motivations and objectives alternated from one to the other throughout his reign.

SOCIAL AND ECONOMIC PROBLEMS

The China that Khubilai sought to rule in 1260 faced serious problems. It had not really recovered from the destruction caused by the Mongol conflicts with the Chin dynasty from 1211 to 1234. The battles with the Southern Sung and the wars of succession within the Mongol elite had also contributed to the devastation suffered in North China. Despite Yeh-lü Ch'u-ts'ai's efforts in the 1230s and Möngke's laws in the 1250s, the tax system lacked coherence and regularity. The Chinese peasants were uncertain about the intentions of their Mongol rulers. Would these new overlords simply expropriate their land and convert it into pasture for their animals? Would they devise arbitrary and exorbitant taxes on the peasants? The wars with Arigh Böke in Mongolia and Central Asia and the hostility of the Southern Sung hampered international commerce, and domestic trade had been disrupted by the unrest within China. The Mongols had not developed a code of laws for North China. A combination of the code of the Chin dynasty and the Mongol traditional laws appeared to be dominant, but confusion prevailed; a clear-cut guide to legal and illegal behavior was needed.

The system of education, too, was in disarray. The object of education in the past had been preparation for the civil service examinations. With the suspension of these exams, the Chinese and their Mongol overlords as well began to wonder about the purposes of education. The religious organizations were also confused. The Buddhist hierarchy recognized that Khubilai was sympathetic, but the Taoists did not know to what degree the government would discriminate against them. The Confucians were concerned lest the Mongol emperors ignore or abandon their rituals and their code of conduct. The less popular religions (e.g., Islam) were unsettled about the Mongols' attitudes toward them. In addition, the fates of the Mongol and Chinese militaries were uncertain. What kinds of relationships would these two vastly different forces develop? Would the army play as important a role as it had in traditional Mongol society? The responsibilities of the foreigners, principally Central Asians, brought to China by Khubilai and his predecessors were vague. How would they fit in with the government that Khubilai had just established? The four-class system that he had devised—Mongols, Muslims and Jurchens, Northern Chinese, and Southern Chinese—needed clearer definition. What privileges and responsibilities would each of these groups be granted? What other social divisions would be mandated?[1]

One of the most pressing problems was the apparent depopulation of North China. In 1195, the population of North China under the Chin dynasty amounted to more than forty-five million, six million of whom were Jurchens, and the combined Southern Sung and Chin populations exceeded one hundred million.[2] By 1393, in the early years of the native Chinese dynasty that succeeded the Mongols, the total population of China had declined to sixty million.[3] This remarkable reduction remains unexplained. The wars at the end of the Mongol dynasty must have sharply reduced the population of the North and are a partial explanation for the drop. Even more significant was the inaccuracy of the census caused by evasion and corrupt census takers.[4] Yet some loss in the population of the North is undeniable. The reduction points to misery in North China.[5]

Khubilai needed to respond to these questions and to cope with these problems if he wished to create order in Chinese society. The government agencies he had formed were valuable mechanisms, but they required direction. Khubilai had to articulate the political, social, and economic policies that he meant them to implement. The clearer and the more specific his policies, the more effective his government agencies could be. He had to disclose his plans for ruling, rather than simply exploiting, China, and his officials might then emulate and assist him in seeking to govern the sedentary civilization. He had already promoted the interests of the Chinese peasants in his own appanage in the 1230s and 1240s, but now he had to reveal his intentions to the rest of the Chinese.

However, before embarking on a planned, orderly program to define and clarify his social, political, and economic ideals, Khubilai was required to relieve the misery. The records of the first few years of his reign are replete with accounts of his efforts at relief. He was called upon to decide on appeals for assistance and tax exemption from many regions in his domain in North China, and he often responded by granting such relief. In 1261, he waived taxes on Huai-meng in Honan and other regions because of reports that they were experiencing economic difficulties.[6] In April of 1262, he did the same for the area around modern Peking, Kuang-ning, and other localities that had suffered as a result of the warfare in the north.[7] He also reduced the tax levies on peasants whose mulberry trees and silk-worms had been damaged during these battles.[8] In the same year, he granted paper money to peasants in Ho-hsi whose lands had been devastated by natural disasters.[9] He repeatedly provided grain to widows and orphans without other means of support. In 1262, he ordered his Mongol commissioners to avoid excessive demands of corvée labor on peasants, particularly those who were reclaiming land.[10] And from that time on, he prohibited his officials and his army from making exorbitant demands on the Chinese people.[11] He even rewarded Chinese who submitted but had earlier been hostile, pro-viding them with clothing and other gifts from the court.[12] On the other hand, those Chinese who deliberately sought to avoid the paying of taxes were to be severely punished. Yet a plethora of remis-sions and exemptions and criticisms of exploitative or oppressive officials is recorded in the early years of Khubilai's reign. Khubilai was concerned with the welfare of his Chinese subjects and with the economic rehabilitation of the territory that he hoped to rule.

Some scholars have wondered about Khubilai's own involvement in the social, political, and economic decisions that charted the course for the early years of his reign. Did he take an active role in devising the policies and programs pursued during this time? Or did his Chinese advisers merely present him with proposals that he, with little reflection, then adopted? To be sure, Khubilai did not originate many of the policies that were subsequently implemented. Despite his exposure to and sympathy for the sedentary world, his relative lack of experience in governing an empire like China made him somewhat dependent on advisers. But he did not simply sit back and await proposals; he actively solicited suggestions. One of his officials quotes him as saying: "Those who present memorials to make proposals may present them with the envelopes sealed. If the proposals cannot be adopted, there will be no punishment. But if the proposals are useful, the Court will liberally promote and reward the persons who make the proposals in order to encourage the loyal and sincere ones."[13] Wang Yün, a contemporary observer, tells us that Khubilai participated in the deliberations at court, and that his advisers and officials had ready access to him. In the space of a week in May of 1261, Wang had three audiences with Khubilai to discuss governmental affairs.[14] Other, more influential officials surely met with the khan even more fre-quently. In these early days, Khubilai appears to have been intimately involved with and surprisingly well informed about developments at court and in the country. He was not the creative force behind the numerous policies initiated at that time, but he did influence these policies and on occasion modified them to accommodate Mongol practices.

The programs were also not devised simply by his Chinese advisers. Khubilai had an international staff working for him in the early 1260s. His trusted Tibetan adviser, the 'Phags-pa lama, had received the title of Kuo-shih (State Preceptor) in 1260 and was eventually granted jurisdiction over Tibet.[15] Muslims from Central Asia were encouraged to come to China to supervise trade, and several became financial administrators in the empire. Turks, who had served the Mongols since the time of Chinggis Khan, were even more prominent during Khubilai's reign. They were not simply involved in military campaigns; only seven of the seventy-three Uighur Turks in Khubilai's service were military men. Twenty-one of them were resident commissioners (Mong.: *darughachi*) or local officials, several served as tutors to the imperial princes, and a few translated documents for the court. Khubilai also employed men from other Turkish groups (Khanglis, Kipchaks, etc.) in similar government positions.[16] He was, in effect, recruiting an international corps of advisers, and his economic program necessarily reflected a more cosmopolitan outlook than the programs of earlier Chinese dynasties.

KHUBILAI'S ECONOMIC PROGRAM

One of the pivots of the program was the encouragement of agriculture. In 1261, Khubilai founded an Office for the Stimulation of Agriculture (in Chinese, Ch'üan-nung ssu) and appointed eight officials to initiate programs to support the peasant economy.[17] Khubilai chose Yao Shu to lead the agency, an indication of the value he placed on agriculture.[18] The agency's officials, in turn, selected men knowledgeable in agronomy to help the peasants with their land. Eventually, a sizable hierarchy and bureaucracy were organized to promote the more efficient and productive use of the land.[19] The lands in North China had been damaged by the warfare that had afflicted the territory for half a century, and Khubilai had to initiate policies leading to its recovery. Relief measures, including tax remissions, would be insufficient. Granaries for the storage of surplus grain had to be built as insurance against shortages of food in these devastated lands.

Khubilai's capital would eventually have fifty-eight such granaries, which stored 145,000 *shih* (each *shih* being equivalent to about 133 pounds) of grain.[20] But such measures were palliatives. Khubilai needed to call for more positive efforts to assist the Chinese peasants.

Khubilai's edicts and program reveal attempts to safeguard the interests of the peasants. One of his first instructions to his Mongol underlings was meant to protect the peasants' most valuable possession—their land. Early in 1262, he prohibited the nomads' animals from roaming in the farmlands.[21] He did not wish his own people to encroach upon and perhaps cause additional damage to the valuable territory of the peasants. This edict and other regulations disclose his growing concern for his sedentary subjects. But these measures do not necessarily indicate that Khubilai identified solely with the peasants. It seemed to Khubilai, however, that his Chinese domains could not be properly governed without a flourishing or at least an adequately sustained peasant class.

Khubilai thus sought to help the peasants organize themselves for economic recovery. By 1270, he had found a convenient vehicle for such an organization, the *she*. This new state-sponsored rural organization, composed of about fifty households under the direction of a village leader known as the *she-chang*, had as its principal purpose the stimulation of agricultural production and promotion of reclamation.[22] Khubilai gave the *she* a mandate to help in farming, planting trees, opening up barren areas, improving flood control and irrigation, increasing silk production, and stocking the lakes and rivers with fish.[23] The *she* leader was to compel the indolent to work and to reward the industrious. Khubilai and his advisers conceived of the *she* as a self-help organization for the peasants. The fact that the Chinese themselves were granted responsibility over the *she* was, in this sense, a means of giving them control over their lives.

Khubilai and his advisers intended, however, to graft other functions onto the *she*. Stability was a principal goal. It appears that "many peasants were willing to bind themselves together, not in revolutionary groups designed to change the existing social structure, but in organizations designed to re-establish the old social structure and restore stability to peasant villages."[24] Khubilai also planned to use the *she* as an aid in surveillance and in conducting periodic censuses. Perhaps the most innovative objective was to employ this new organization to promote education. Each *she* had the task of setting up schools for the village boys. The schools were planned to introduce the peasant children to better and more efficient means of farming as well as to provide them with the rudiments of literacy.[25] Although this vision of an educational system, lying outside the confines of the traditional civil service examinations, was not fulfilled,[26] it reveals that the concept of a literate peasantry whose interests the government would protect was embraced by Khubilai and his advisers. No longer would the government concern itself exclusively with the nomads. Peasants would receive a share of the attention of the Mongols.[27] For example, Khubilai required the *she* to establish "charity granaries" (Chin.: *i-ts'ang*) to assist unfortunates during bad harvests or droughts and to provide grain for orphans, widows, and the elderly.[28]

Another way of protecting the peasants was to devise a fixed, regular system of taxation. Khubilai wished to abolish tax farming, a structure that could not easily be controlled and often lent itself to abuses. Perhaps as critical, he sought to reduce the power of the appanages. Under the new system that Khubilai enacted, the payments that peasants had previously made to the appanage would now be remitted to the government and then divided equally between appanage and central government. The peasants would pay annual taxes and need not concern themselves about capricious levies by the appanage holders.[29]

The other principal burden on the peasants, corvée obligations, was as onerous as the taxes. Khubilai embarked upon a series of public works projects, such as the extension of the Grand Canal, that necessitated vast investments of labor and capital. The postal relay system, which linked the Mongol capital to the rest of China, also entailed corvée in the form of supplying labor and horses, and provisions for both men and animals. Such corvées were clearly burdensome obligations; however, Khubilai sought, throughout his reign, to limit excessive demands on the population. On occasion, he waived the taxes on those particularly called upon for corvée. He repeatedly issued regulations demanding that his official envoys and troops not make extralegal impositions on the peasants. To be sure, the fact that these injunctions to his own personnel had to be repeated indicates that abuses persisted.[30] Yet it is clear that Khubilai, unlike some of the more conservative Mongols, did not wish merely to exploit the Chinese peasants or to compel them to abandon their farms so that the land could be used for grazing.

Another group he sought to protect was the artisans. Khubilai set up a number of offices in his government both to organize and to safeguard the welfare of craftsmen. These household agencies were charged with providing jewelry, clothing, and textiles for the private use of the court.[31] Moreover, public works projects required the services of highly skilled craftsmen. To garner their allegiance and to help them prosper, Khubilai enacted regulations favoring artisans. The government offered them rations of food, clothing, and salt and exempted them from corvée labor. It also permitted them to sell some goods on the open market.[32] Thus, artisans were in an enviable position during Khubilai's reign.[33] Though the usual complaints of official corruption were magnified by the onerous demands and graft of the supervisors of the artisans,[34] the court certainly attempted to prevent such abuses and exploitation, and craftsmen, in general, benefited from Mongol rule.

Merchants also prospered during Khubilai's reign. The Chinese dynasties of the past had occasionally imposed restrictions on merchants, and powerful segments of the Confucian official class disapproved of trade. Merchants were traditionally perceived as parasitical, crafty, and avaricious, and the various Chinese courts attempted to regulate their activities as well as their profits.[35] Khubilai did not share this bias against merchants; in fact, he accorded them high status.[36] Trade within China prospered, and foreign commerce also flourished. Muslim merchants served as intermediaries in the overland trade from China to Central Asia, the Middle East, and Persia. They imported camels, horses, carpets, medicines, and spices and exported Chinese textiles, ceramics, lacquerware, ginger, and cassia.[37] From the southeastern port cities of Ch'üan-chou and Fu-chou, they transported Chinese ceramics, silks, and copper cash westward, returning with precious stones, rhinoceros horns, medicines, incense, carpets, pepper, nutmeg, and other spices.[38] Some Chinese ceramics, in fact, were designed for export. The Chinese exhibited a "genuine willingness . . . to supply wares in forms agreeable to Muslim taste."[39]

Individual merchants, as well as merchant associations known in Mongolian as *ortogh*, eventually contributed to the Mongol economy in China. The new dynasty's regulations required foreign merchants to convert their precious metals into paper currency as soon as they set foot in China.[40] This policy was extremely profitable for the court, and the merchants abided by the regulation because it granted them entry into the lucrative trade with China. The *ortogh* also performed

invaluable services for the court and were cultivated by it. In the
years of the Mongol conquests, for instance, they provided badly
needed loans to the Mongol nobility.[41] In 1268, Khubilai, as a reward,
created the General Administration for the Supervision of the
Ortogh. This office loaned funds (known as *wo-t'o-ch'ien*, or "*ortogh*
money"), which it obtained from the Mongol elite and from the
government, to the *ortogh* at 0.8 percent monthly interest, which was
lower than the 3 percent monthly interest charged to most borrowers.[42] The *ortogh* used this money either to finance trade caravans
or to loan funds at a higher rate of interest to Chinese merchants.
Khubilai's policies were thus extremely beneficial to traders. The tax
imposed upon commercial transactions amounted to only three and
one-third percent.[43] Even the excesses of the merchant associations
were tolerated. Some of the merchants, for instance, would comman-
deer soldiers to protect them on their travels, while others used
improper methods to force borrowers to repay their loans promptly.[44]
The dynastic sources record numerous complaints about abuses by
merchants, but stern warnings, rather than stiff punishments, were
the main tactic used to control the *ortogh*.

To facilitate trade and to promote the welfare of the merchants,
Khubilai initiated the use of paper currency throughout his domains.
Khubilai was the first Mongol ruler to seek a countrywide system of
paper currency. The Chinese sources credit Liu Ping-chung with
persuading Khubilai to adopt paper money for North China. But
Khubilai did not need Liu's prompting to notice the benefits and
utility of paper currency. Here again the chronicles tell the story of a
sage Chinese adviser inveigling an ignorant, unsophisticated Mongol
ruler to sanction an innovative, brilliant policy. Whether or not that
story is true, Khubilai invalidated the local paper currencies that had
circulated under the earlier Mongol khans and called upon the people
of North China to surrender gold, silver, and copper coins to the
government.[45] He was determined to impose government controls on
the currency and to replace coins with paper money.

In his first year in power, Khubilai devised three types of paper
currency, one of which remained in use throughout his reign. The
first, known in Chinese as the *ssu-ch'ao*, was based upon silk, but the
two others, the *Chung-t'ung yüan-pao-ch'ao* and the *Chung-t'ung yin-
huo*, were backed by a silver reserve. The *Chung-t'ung yüan-pao-ch'ao*
eventually prevailed and won the confidence of the population.[46]
These notes must have been readily available and widely used, for

Marco Polo described them at length in his account of his stay in thirteenth-century China.[47] The system operated well at least until 1276, partly because Khubilai kept tight controls on the amount of paper money printed. Until the conquest of the Southern Sung, the government did not appreciably increase the amount of paper money it produced annually. In 1276, the court, faced with staggering expenses for military campaigns in Southern China and Japan, dramatically expanded the amount it printed.[48] Yet inflation did not get out of hand during Khubilai's reign.[49]

Another form of governmental assistance for the merchants was improvement of the system of transport. Khubilai promoted the building of roads, on either side of which "willows and other trees [had] been planted so that the shadow of the trees [fell] upon the road."[50] In addition, he established postal stations, which, though originally designed to transmit and deliver official mail, also served to facilitate trade.[51] In addition to hosting traveling officials and foreign guests, the postal stations also served as hostelries for merchants. By the end of Khubilai's reign, China had more than 1,400 postal stations, which had at their disposal about 50,000 horses, 8,400 oxen, 6,700 mules, 4,000 carts, almost 6,000 boats, over 200 dogs, and 1,150 sheep.[52] The individual stations varied considerably, but they all had hostels for visitors, kitchens, a main hall, enclosures for animals, and storehouses for grain.[53] Under ideal conditions, the rider-messengers at the postal stations could cover 250 miles a day to deliver significant news, a remarkably efficient mail service for the thirteenth, or any other, century.[54]

Thus, in a variety of ways Khubilai's policies fostered trade and demonstrated his concern for the merchants. In contrast to many Chinese, Khubilai was not biased against traders. And the evidence from contemporary observers indicates that he succeeded: merchants did prosper. Marco Polo, for example, wrote that there were many factories

> in which stay and lodge the merchants and the travelling foreigners, of whom there are many from all parts to bring things as presents to the lord and to sell to the court, and all other men who come there for their business, who come there in very great quantity, between [those who come] for the court of the lord . . . and for this that the town is in so good a market that the merchants and the other men come there for their business. . . . I believe there is not a place in the world to which so many merchants come & that dearer things and of greater value and more strange come into this town . . . than into any city of the world.[55]

Other classes of people and occupational groups also appeared to fare better under Khubilai than under the Chinese emperors. Medicine, for one example, was an occupation favored by the court. The pragmatic Mongol rulers valued medicine and emphasized it as a suitable and attractive profession.[56] Khubilai, himself afflicted with gout and other ailments, was particularly hospitable to physicians. As a pragmatist, Khubilai was impressed by the efficacy of the treatments and medicines offered by the doctors around his court. In 1285, 1288, and 1290 he dispatched envoys to South India to seek not only precious goods but also skilled craftsmen and doctors.[57] Two branches of the Kuang-hui ssu (imperial hospitals), composed primarily of Muslim doctors, were established in K'ai-p'ing and in North China to treat the emperor and the court.[58] Other Mongol officials as well consulted Muslim physicians, and thirty-six volumes of Muslim medicinal recipes were placed in the court library. Starting in 1268, for example, a drug known in Persian as *sharbat* (Chin.: *she-li-pieh*), which was used as a laxative and to counter colic, was imported from Samarkand.[59] Khubilai established an Imperial Academy of Medicine (Chin.: T'ai-i yüan), which specified the criteria for the selection of instructors of medicine and supervised the training of physicians and the preparation of medical texts.[60] The regulations maintained high standards for prospective physicians and therefore members of the Chinese elite in greater numbers than in earlier dynasties were attracted to the field. The physician's calling was lucrative, offered access to influence through the doctor's patients, and conformed to the Confucian emphasis on righteousness and altruism.[61] Moreover, physicians often received exemption from corvée labor and other services and fiscal obligations.[62] With government support, the social status of doctors improved dramatically.[63]

Similarly, Khubilai regarded astronomers and other scientists highly and invited numerous foreign scientists to China. In 1258, the Persians had built an observatory at Marāgheh in Azerbaijan where new astronomical instruments were fashioned and important discoveries were made.[64] In 1267, Khubilai invited the Persian astronomer Jāmal al-Dīn to come to China to transmit these discoveries. He brought along diagrams of an armillary sphere, sundials, an astrolabe, a terrestrial globe, and a celestial globe as gifts for the court. He also offered a new, more accurate calendar, known in Chinese as the Wan-nien li (Calendar for Ten Thousand Years), to Khubilai.[65] Four years later, in 1271, Khubilai finally established the Institute of Muslim

6.   Khubilai's Astronomical Observatory in Peking. Morris Rossabi, photograph.

Astronomy (Hui-hui ssu-t'ien chien). There, the Chinese astronomer Kuo Shou-ching (1231–1316) used the Persian diagrams and calculations to build his own instruments and to devise his own calendar, the Shou-shih li (Calendar Delivering the Seasons), which with minor revisions was employed through the Ming dynasty.[66]

The Muslims contributed also to geographic knowledge and map-making during this period. With Arab and Persian travelers and traders transmitting information about Central Asia and the Middle East, "geography in China [flourished], incorporating data on the non-Chinese world taken from Arab sources."[67] A world map drawn during the Mongol dynasty, probably based on information derived from Muslim sources, gives a fairly accurate rendering of Asia and Europe.[68] And, along with providing inducements for scientists,

Khubilai also favored clergymen and artists, whom the Chinese dynasties had cultivated as well. His attitude toward these two groups
will be discussed more fully later in this chapter.

In sum, Khubilai eliminated some discriminatory practices and
sought to alter the biases against occupational groups that had not
fared well under the Chinese dynasties. Though he sought to treat
farmers with fairness and encourage farm productivity, those not
involved in farming—merchants, physicians, and scientists—were
accorded greater benefits and attracted more court concern. Khubilai
clearly hoped to gain their support in his effort to rule China. The
group whose interests were most damaged by the Mongols was the
landed elite, from whom derived the bulk of the scholar-official class
that had governed China. Khubilai and the Mongols had displaced
them as the rulers of the country. Without the civil service examinations, the Chinese elite had few options. Some acquiesced and served
the Mongols; others abandoned public life to become recluses or
dabble in the arts; and still others, disgruntled with Mongol rule,
formed a potentially disruptive force, particularly in South China.
Khubilai nonetheless attempted to gain their favor by retaining government offices that offered opportunities for scholar-officials. These
included the Han-lin Academy (the Academy of Worthies), which
supervised the Chinese National College (Kuo-tzu hsüeh), the Directorate for the Diffusion of Confucian Texts, the Archives, and the
Imperial Diarists' Office.[69]

KHUBILAI AND THE MILITARY

While concerning himself with social and economic matters, Khubilai
continued to pay attention to the military. He placed real power over
the military in the hands of the Privy Council (Chin.: Shu-mi yüan), an
agency created by the Sung dynasty that he revived in 1263. Khubilai
sought to centralize all of the military under the Council but faced
considerable opposition from the Mongol commanders, who had
traditionally had great independence. Khubilai conceded to them by
creating a separate military for them. The Mongol troops totally under
Khubilai's jurisdiction were organized as the Meng-ku chün (Mongol
Army), while those over which he did not have full control were
called in Mongol the *Tammachi*.[70] These two forces were composed
primarily of cavalry, and a third division, consisting of ethnic
Chinese, was used as the infantry.

All Mongol adult males under the age of seventy were liable for conscription. In addition, certain Chinese families were designated as hereditary military households and were to provide soldiers and supplies for the Yüan armies. But now, having established a bureaucracy and having encouraged sedentary agriculture, Khubilai could not readily mobilize the entire male population for war. He had granted land to the Mongol soldiers as payment for their services, and they simply could not leave their farms to go on military campaigns. Still, they apparently retained their fighting skills and could be relied upon in emergencies. Both the Chinese and the Mongol militaries were exempted from half the taxes imposed on ordinary citizens, but they were forced to provide their own supplies, saving valuable resources for the court. According to a recent study of the army, "the military households ... formed a hereditary military caste with heavy physical and financial burdens."[71]

During Khubilai's reign, the burdens were tolerable. The army remained an effective fighting force, as evidenced by its later successes in Manchuria and in Southeast Asia. But opportunities for graft, corruption, and other abuses were numerous. Officers extorted funds from their men. Moreover, the military administration was not pervasive. Though the Privy Council controlled the region around the capital, local branches, which were often virtually autonomous, controlled the military needs of most other regions.[72]

Some in the traditional Mongol military remained influential even after Khubilai became Emperor of China. Khubilai retained the *kesig*, the old bodyguards of Chinggis, and offered them special privileges and rewards. The men in the *kesig* were generally part of the elite and preserved their positions in the hierarchy. Khubilai needed them to counterbalance the Chinese forces he recruited. Thus, he relied on the *kesig*, not the Chinese, as bodyguards for himself and for those around the court.[73] Similarly, in establishing garrisons throughout his domains Khubilai sensed the need to maintain Mongol dominance. These garrisons, which were stationed in the capital, along the border, in Inner Asia, and in potentially troublesome regions within China, remained under the supervision of Mongol commanders.

Khubilai also perceived Mongol control of military supplies to be essential. He initiated a government monopoly on bamboo, not to acquire income but to prevent the unauthorized use of bamboo for weapons. Since bamboo could be used to make bows and arrows, its use was restricted to the Mongol government, and the Chinese were strictly prohibited from buying and selling it.[74]

Khubilai also recognized the military value of horses and knew that a sensible system of obtaining horses was needed. Now that some Mongols were settling in the sedentary world, they began to face the same problems as the Chinese in acquiring horses. For the expansion of his domain and for defense against his enemies, Khubilai had to have a dependable supply of horses suitable for warfare. Therefore, Khubilai fashioned a "horse administration" and devised regulations guaranteed to protect his steeds. He established the Court of the Imperial Stud to tend his own herds as well as to manage horses assigned to the postal stations and to the imperial guards and armies.[75] Under the regulations issued by his court, one out of every one hundred horses owned by the people was to be turned over to the government. Khubilai also reserved the right to purchase horses, and owners were compelled to sell their animals at official prices. On occasion, he even requisitioned horses without compensating their owners,[76] and offered the following justification: "Horses have already been requisitioned from those Buddhist monks, Christians, Taoists, Mohammedan teachers of North China who had them. . . . Now what need have the monks and Taoists, sitting in their temples, of horses?"[77] There were severe punishments for Chinese families who concealed their horses, as there were for Chinese or Muslim merchants who smuggled them across the border to be sold to Khubilai's enemies. Mongol control over such smuggling was, to Khubilai, essential.

KHUBILAI AND THE LEGAL SYSTEM

Early on, Khubilai recognized that a new legal system was needed. He had inherited a code devised by the Jurchen Chin dynasty, which he employed temporarily but then abandoned in 1271. Even earlier, in 1262, he had instructed his trusted advisers Yao Shu and Shih T'ien-tse to devise a new code that would be suitable in particular for his Chinese subjects.[78] By 1264, the new code had been prepared, but the Chin laws remained in force until 1271. Even after that date, the new code was not implemented. Yet the Mongol laws were not imposed on the Chinese. Precedents derived from the decisions made from 1260 to 1271 were used in determining cases brought to the government or to the courts. Mongol customs, laws, and practices doubtless influenced these decisions, however. The Mongols, with Khubilai's blessing, apparently introduced greater leniency to the Chinese legal system. One hundred thirty-five capital crimes were specified, less than half the number mandated in the Sung law codes. In addition, the annual lists of executions for the early years of Khubilai's reign reveal that the Mongols seldom resorted to such retribution. In 1263, for instance, seven people were executed; in 1265, forty-two; and in 1269, again forty-two, rather minuscule for the size of the population, the nature of the opposition, and the level of violence at that time.[79] As so often in Chinese history, the emperor reviewed sentences of execution, and Khubilai took this responsibility seriously. Once when quite a few prisoners were facing the death penalty, he admonished his officials, saying: "Prisoners are not a mere flock of sheep. How can they be suddenly executed? It is proper that they be instead enslaved and assigned to pan gold with a sieve."[80]

Khubilai often granted amnesties, even to his own political enemies. Following Mongol practice, he permitted criminals to avoid punishment through payment of a fine to the government. This kind of monetary compensation was characteristic of Mongol law. Under Khubilai, the principle of monetary compensation was extended somewhat to more serious crimes. From this time on, compensatory fines, so typical of the Mongols, became part of the Chinese system of justice. The investigation of cases was also modified, incorporating certain Mongol practices. Most cases were handled on the local level, but the more serious ones were subject to review by officials at the provincial government level or even at the level of the central government. These reviews served as a check on abuses of the rights of the accused.

We still do not know enough about Khubilai's legal system to tell whether the statutory reforms and changes in customs actually translated into a more lenient and flexible system. More research is needed to ascertain how effective in practice the legal innovations were. The one indisputable fact is that Khubilai prompted the creation of a legal system that incorporated both Mongol and Chinese elements. And the legal ideals that he had in mind appeared to be more flexible and lenient than earlier Chinese ones. Although the system tended to favor the Mongols, it neither imposed numerous restrictions nor discriminated severely against the Chinese.

Thus, by the mid-1260s, Khubilai had laid the foundations for a stable society in North China. While contending with his brother Arigh Böke and with the Chinese rebel Li T'an, he answered some of the major questions and began to resolve the uncertainties about his plans for China. He had devised methods and institutions for promoting the interests of peasants, artisans, and merchants; he had instituted a fixed scale of taxes and obligations on the Chinese; and he had promoted the use of paper money to facilitate trade and built postal stations to improve communications and transport in his domains. His court rewarded doctors, scientists, and others in formerly servile occupations whom the Chinese had offered little prestige, status, and compensation for their contributions. He also succeeded in developing innovative military and legal systems that included Mongol and Chinese elements. In sum, he appeared to have reconciled some of the disparate Mongol and Chinese elements that confronted him.

KHUBILAI AND THE CONFUCIANS

Khubilai recognized that he had to win over the Confucian Chinese in order to govern the country. One step he took to gain such support was his shift of the capital to North China. The Chinese accounts attribute the construction of the new capital to his adviser Liu Ping-chung.[81] According to these sources, the city was modeled on the plan for an ideal capital outlined in an ancient text known as the *Chou-li*. They portray Liu as the creative force behind the plan, and Khubilai as simply the ruler who ratified Liu's idea. However, it hardly seems credible that Khubilai would not, by himself, recognize the value of setting up his center in the most populous, and unquestionably the most flourishing, part of his domain. He was surely aware of the symbolism involved, and it hardly seems likely that he needed prompting from his Chinese adviser.

In 1266, Khubilai ordered the construction of a capital near the modern city of Peking.[82] The city was originally called Chung-tu (Central Capital) by the Chinese during the Chin dynasty, and in 1272 it came to be known as Ta-tu (Great Capital) in Chinese, Khanbalikh (City of the Khan) to the Turks, and Daidu to the Mongols.[83] Ordinarily the site of a Chinese city was selected through geomancy (*feng-shui*).[84] But the city of Chung-tu was already established; the new city would be built slightly northeast of the Chin dynasty capital. Also, in contrast to the construction of most Chinese cities, to build this new city numerous foreign craftsmen were recruited.[85] The supervisor of the whole project was, in fact, a Muslim.[86] Nonetheless, the city was Chinese in conception and style, with the planners following Chinese models and selecting Chinese architectural forms for most of its buildings. Khubilai wanted Ta-tu to symbolize his efforts to reach out and appeal to the traditional Chinese scholars and Confucians.

Khubilai selected an area for his capital that had not been used by native Chinese dynasties. Sian (in the modern province of Shensi), Lo-yang, and K'ai-feng (both in the modern province of Honan), the three traditional capitals of China, were all located near the Yellow River or one of its tributaries, considerably to the south of modern Peking.[87] The Chin dynasty had established its capital in Chung-tu, but its rulers were Jurchens, not Chinese. Khubilai, too, deviated from Chinese practice and placed his capital outside the area that was the cradle of their civilization. He did so, in part, because he perceived his domain as more than just China. Wishing to retain control over his traditional homeland in Mongolia, he situated his capital farther north than the typical Chinese ones.[88] An administrative center in the North would offer him a listening post and a base from which to assert his authority over his native land. Like the Chinese emperors, Khubilai also had other concerns in determining a site for his capital. The city needed to have good natural defenses, to serve as a communications, transport, and commercial link to the various regions of his domains, and to have access to adequate supplies of food and water.[89] Chung-tu's main deficiency was its insufficient reserves of grain, which Khubilai sought to cope with by importing food from the South. To transport these supplies, he eventually lengthened the Grand Canal to reach all the way to the capital.

In 1267, the Muslim architect known in Chinese records as Yeh-hei-tieh-erh and his underlings and associates began to construct Khubilai's new capital. The city was to be rectangular, to have a circumference of 28,600 meters, and to be enclosed by a wall of rammed earth.[90] Within this outer wall there would be two inner walls that led to the Imperial City and Khubilai's residences and palaces. When it was completed, the Imperial City wall separated Khubilai and his entourage from the officials residing within one of the inner walls and from the ordinary Chinese and Central Asians, whose living quarters were outside the outer wall. The Kao-liang, the Chin-shui, and the T'ung-hui rivers meandered through the city and provided more water for the Imperial City "than ever before in a Chinese capital city."[91] The city was laid out in symmetrical north-south and east-west axes, with wide avenues stretching in geometric patterns from the eleven gates that permitted entry into the city.[92] The avenues were so broad that "horsemen [could] gallop nine abreast."[93]

On all the gates, three on the south, east, and west, and two on the north, were three-story towers that served to warn of impending threats or dangers to the city. Near the eastern wall was the astronomical observatory constructed for Khubilai's Persian astronomers.[94] Within the Imperial City, the hall for receiving foreign envoys, the khan's own quarters and the quarters of his consorts and concubines, the storehouses, and the Scholar's Hall (Chin.: Hsüeh-shih yüan) where the young princes were educated, as well as the other public buildings, were remarkably similar to their counterparts in a typical Chinese capital of the T'ang dynasty or earlier. Lakes, gardens, and bridges, in particular Pei-hai Park, crisscrossed the Imperial City, still another feature of traditional Chinese capitals.

Yet Mongol touches were evident in the décor of some of the buildings. In Khubilai's sleeping chambers, for example, hung curtains and screens of ermine skins, a tangible reminder of the Mongols' hunting and pastoral lifestyle. The main reception hall contained a dais on which were models of reclining tigers, which were "by some mechanical device capable of motion as if they [were] alive."[95] Mongol-style tents were erected in the Imperial Parks, and Khubilai's sons and their cousins lived in them rather than in the palaces. When one of Khubilai's wives was in the last stages of pregnancy, she moved to these same tents to give birth.[96] Finally, Khubilai assigned underlings to gather grass and dirt from the Mongol steppes for his royal altar, another reminder of their pastoral heritage.[97] But amidst these touches of Mongol culture the paramount influence remained Chinese. The decorative motifs included phoenixes and dragons, and the adornments were fashioned of silk and jade, all typically Chinese. Hills, palaces, pavilions, bridges, and parks were all laid out as in a Chinese city.

Possibly the clearest manifestations of the Chinese influence on the city were the temples Khubilai ordered built near his palaces. In particular, the Great Temple (Chin.: T'ai-miao, also known as the Tsung-miao or "Ancestral Temple") illustrated his desire to gain favor with the Confucian elite. Reverence for the ancestors was vital in the Chinese view of life, and the building of the Great Temple indicated that Khubilai intended to maintain the rituals associated with ancestor worship. Though he himself shied away from personal involvement, he planned to promote the ancestral cult of the Chinese, a step that would surely alienate the more conservative Mongols. If there were any misgivings about opposition, Khubilai apparently overrode them.

Khubilai had begun erecting the Great Temple even before he proposed to build a capital.[98] In May of 1263, work on it commenced, and in the following year Khubilai had tablets fashioned for his ancestors. By 1266, eight chambers for his ancestors had been built, each one lodging a tablet for his forebears. One chamber was for his great-grandparents Hö'elün and Yesügei, a second for Chinggis (who was granted the posthumous title of T'ai-tsu), and four others for Jochi, Chaghadai, Ögödei, and Tolui (given the imperial title of Jui-tsung); the final two were for Khubilai's predecessors as Great Khan, Güyüg (Ting-tsung) and Möngke (Hsien-tsung).[99] Once the tablets had been installed in the chambers, the ceremonies and sacrifices of ancestor worship were performed. Khubilai abided by the Chinese belief that the ancestors could intercede in human affairs and needed to be consulted on questions of great importance, but he rarely took part in the ceremonies, instead dispatching Chinese advisers and princes to represent him.

The same motives doubtless prompted Khubilai to build altars for the various forces of Nature and to conduct the ceremonies seeking their assistance. The Altars of the Soil (Chin.: *she*) and Grain (*chi*), which were built in 1271, were probably the most significant. In the very first year of their construction, Khubilai ordered that annual sacrifices be conducted at these altars.[100] He himself participated in these offerings only infrequently. Instead, he often delegated Chinese officials to substitute for him. The symbolism at these two altars was clearly Chinese. The Altar of the Soil, for example, had patches of the five colors, green, red, white, black, and yellow, which were correlated with the five elements in Chinese cosmology.

The construction of a shrine for Confucius embodied even further the desire to attract the support of the scholar-official elite.[101] Representatives from the court made offerings to the Chinese sage and conducted ceremonies at the shrine. Khubilai himself had not adopted the Confucian system as his own; as we shall see later in this chapter, Buddhism and shamanism were still attractive to him. Yet he recognized the value of appearing to favor the Confucians.

The city of Ta-tu was, then, modeled on earlier Chinese cities in its major features. The Mongols had emerged only recently from their tent encampments and had not previously resided in fixed residences. They naturally turned for models to the civilization that was closest to them—China. And, although the design of their cities incorporated some Mongol elements, the predominant influence remained Chinese.

One striking example is the stone tortoises constructed at Khara Khorum. Steles placed on stone tortoises, with inscriptions ranging from copies of the Confucian classics to eulogies for revered ancestors or heroes, were commonplace in China. The Mongols simply borrowed this idea. In fact, a single stone tortoise is all that remains of the town of Khara Khorum, which was destroyed by a Chinese army in the fourteenth century.[102]

As Ta-tu became more of a Chinese-style city, Khubilai's original summer capital, Shang-tu, was converted to other uses. It became an outlet for the continuance of the Mongol rituals and lifestyles, and served increasingly as Khubilai's hunting park rather than as a real capital. By the time Marco Polo visited, Shang-tu had become, in large part, a hunting preserve, a means by which Khubilai could retain his connections with the traditional Mongol pursuits.[103] Shang-tu, more Mongol than Chinese in its lack of a settled government apparatus, also offered welcome relief from the Chinese style of life for the Mongol khan.

Yet Ta-tu, with its Chinese associations, remained the focus. Though the vast majority of the ordinary workers must have been Chinese, there were quite a few foreign artisans, including Yeh-hei-tieh-erh, the Muslim who was among its principal architects and is often credited with the plan of the city. Numerous other Muslims and other foreigners were accorded vital roles in the planning. The foreign craftsmen contributed enormously to the capital, but the overall responsibility, both for its design and its actual construction, lay with the Chinese.[104]

The city itself was built with striking rapidity. In the eighth moon of 1267, the workers broke ground for the city walls, and a year later the walls surrounding the Imperial City had been built. In March of 1271, they began in earnest to construct the Imperial City and were granted, by imperial orders, 28,000 laborers to work on the construction.[105] By the first moon in 1274, Khubilai convened his first audience in the main hall of the Imperial City.[106]

Khubilai wished to cultivate his image as a Confucian emperor in order to win over the Chinese. One way to do so was to follow patterns similar to those of the earlier dynastic founders in China. The very name of the dynasty was vital. Khubilai's selection of a name would yield clues on the orientation of his rule. By adopting a Chinese name rich in symbolism, Khubilai could indicate his wish to blend with Chinese tradition.[107] A Mongol name would certainly not win favor with the Chinese. In 1271, Khubilai, at Liu Ping-chung's suggestion, chose a Chinese name for his dynasty—the Yüan. *Yüan* had the meaning of "origin," but it had an even more significant connotation. In the *Book of Changes*, *yüan* referred to the "origins of the universe" or "the primal force." The name therefore had direct and close associations with one of the classic works in the Chinese tradition and with a central concept within that classical tradition.[108]

Another vital concern of traditional Chinese emperors was with the Confucian rituals. Khubilai had abided by the Confucian cults, creating tablets for his ancestors at the Great Temple and constructing a shrine for Confucius and altars for the soil, the mountains, and the rivers. Another duty of a Chinese emperor, and essential to an agricultural society, was the designation of a calendar. The emperor, who was perceived as Man's link to Nature, was to devise a precise calendar to aid in the age-old tasks of planting and harvesting. Khubilai had inherited a calendar used by the Chin dynasty since 1137. With the arrival of the Persian astronomer Jāmal al-Dīn to China in 1267, Khubilai began to have a group of astronomers who could work out an accurate calendar.[109]

Still another of the obligations of the Confucian emperor was to encourage the rituals of music and dance. The ancient Chinese believed that the proper performance of music and dance had magical powers over Nature and that the court's neglect or improper conduct of these rituals created an imbalance in Nature that led to floods, earthquakes, droughts, and other catastrophes. Confucius himself emphasized ritual "above all as an instrument of education. It promotes virtue; it is an intrinsic part of the Way that causes gentlemen to love other gentlemen and makes small men easy to rule."[110] The Confucian emperor was duty-bound to maintain and practice these rituals, but, with the defeat of the Chin in 1234, the rituals had been abandoned. The Chinese sources again credit Liu Ping-chung with the reinstitution or reinvigoration of the traditional rituals. In 1269, he proposed to Khubilai that the new Mongol rulers of China initiate court dance and music.[111] Another Chinese source insists that Yao Shu in 1262 urged the restoration of music and dance, but Liu is most often cited as the proponent of the proposal.[112] Khubilai responded enthusiastically and ordered Liu to conduct efforts to reestablish these court rituals. Liu, in turn, delegated several Confucian scholars to study the rituals followed by the preceding dynasty. Once this survey was concluded, they were to devise appropriate music and dance for the Mongol court. Probably most telling of all, they were ordered to teach the ceremonies to a selected group of over two hundred Mongols, who presumably would transmit these Chinese rituals to their fellow Mongols. By 1271, Confucian court music and dance were instituted in Khubilai's ceremonials. The establishment of the Office of Imperial Sacrifices and Rituals was another indication of Khubilai's support for these rituals.[113]

But again, this view of the reintroduction of court music and dance slights Khubilai's role. From these accounts, it appears that he simply listened to and was manipulated by his wise Confucian counselor. However, records of the Mongol dynasty indicate that even before Liu's proposal and before his accession as the Great Khan, Khubilai had designated a certain Sung Chou-ch'en to devise the proper music for the ceremonies at his just-established center at K'ai-p'ing.[114] When he became the Great Khan, it was only natural that he would seek to institute the rituals befitting his new august position. It seems hardly credible that he would require prompting from anyone. It would appear that Liu's proposal may have raised the question of ceremonies once again, but Khubilai had much earlier recognized the symbolic value of music and dance to the Chinese.

Further proof of Khubilai's knowledge of and sensitivity to things Chinese may be gleaned from his attitude toward his second son, whom he designated as his successor, and the training he prescribed for him. As early as 1243, the year of his birth, Khubilai had approved of a Chinese name for his son. Khubilai's Buddhist adviser Hai-yün had given him the name Chen-chin, or "True Gold."[115] Determined that Chen-chin receive a first-rate Chinese education, Khubilai assigned his advisers Yao Shu and Tou Mo to tutor the boy.[116] Later still, Khubilai appointed Wang Hsün (1235–81), a Confucian scholar, to instruct Chen-chin in the Chinese classics.[117] These learned men introduced him first to the *Hsiao ching* (Classic of filiality), a simple text which emphasized the virtues of filial piety.[118] Once he had mastered that work, he was encouraged to study the other more complex classics, and eventually to memorize the *Shih ching* (Book of odes). The government official Wang Yün also provided Chen-chin with an essay summarizing the views on government of some of the emperors and ministers of earlier dynasties in Chinese history.[119] Along with these textual studies, Chen-chin was repeatedly exposed to precepts and anecdotes that were supposed to cause him to reflect about the Confucian verities. Wang Hsün offered a typical homily:

"Man's heart is like a printing block. If the block does not err, then even if one copies ten million papers, there will not be errors. If the block errs, then if one repeatedly copies them on paper there will be none without errors."[120] It is said that Chen-chin reflected deeply on Wang Hsün's pithy observation.

Eventually, Chen-chin was also introduced to the other cults and religions in the Chinese realm. He became friendly with a leading Taoist master, who implored him to "explain the teachings of the Taoists ... to the khaghan [i.e., Khubilai]."[121] Later he received instruction from the ʿPhags-pa lama, and, like his mother Chabi, Chen-chin was deeply impressed by the teachings of the Tibetan Buddhist. The ʿPhags-pa lama wrote a brief work entitled *Ses-bya rab-gsal* (What one should know), which was specifically designed to offer Chen-chin a description of his Buddhist sect.[122] He referred to Khubilai's son as "Boddhisattva Imperial Prince," probably another indication of Chen-chin's developing involvement with the Buddhists. Khubilai, pleased with Chen-chin's growing acceptance by the Chinese, promoted his second son and offered him ever-increasing responsibilities. Early in 1263, Khubilai appointed him the Prince of Yen, with jurisdiction over the area where eventually Ta-tu would be located, clearly a major office.[123] In the very same year, Khubilai gave the twenty-year-old prince the vital task of supervising the Privy Council. And in 1273, he named Chen-chin, who was then thirty years old, the Heir Apparent.[124] Khubilai thus became the first Mongol ruler to designate his own successor.

Khubilai did not need to be induced to give his dynasty a Chinese name, however, or to restore Chinese court rituals. Neither did he need to be instructed on the grooming of Chen-chin for the imperial throne of China. Khubilai recognized almost instinctively that a Mongol well-rounded in the Chinese classics, knowledgeable about Chinese customs and etiquette, and imbued through his Chinese tutors with the teachings of Confucianism and the other cults and religions of China would be popular with the Chinese and would help Khubilai gain their loyalty. He deliberately educated Chen-chin in this way in order to attract the following of his Chinese subjects.

Another way that he attracted the Confucian scholars was by providing tangible support for them to propagate their views. For example, Khubilai promoted the translation of Chinese works into Mongol. Naturally he chose those texts that might prove helpful in governing, especially works on administration and history. His pragmatic bent is evident here; the sources for which he encouraged translation were of immediate and direct assistance to the Mongol elite.[125] If he was to gain influence among the Chinese scholars, however, he needed also to support the translation of Confucian texts. Such works as the *Classic of Filiality* and the *Book of History* were translated under Khubilai's patronage. One of the works translated by his Confucian advisers was the *Ta-hsüeh yen-i* by Chen Te-hsiu (1178–1235), which applied the teachings of the Sung Neo-Confucian Chu Hsi to questions of practical government.[126] By making these texts available to the Mongol elite, Khubilai showed the Chinese that he respected Confucian ideas and was not averse to their propagation. Other translations that he supported were histories of the reigns of Ögödei and Möngke, known as the *Veritable Records* (*Shih-lu*), in the Chinese style, as well as compilations of his own edicts and instructions. He sought to impress the Chinese by fostering the translation of some of their political and moral exhortations. In a more prosaic vein, he established a Mongolian Han-lin Academy to translate his own edicts and regulations from Mongolian to Chinese.[127]

Khubilai also recruited and patronized erudite scholars who were vigorous supporters of Neo-Confucianism, with the objective once again of ingratiating himself with this increasingly influential group. While many of them refused to serve the Mongols, some regarded the "civilizing" of the nomads from the North as their mission. Hsü Heng represented this new breed of Neo-Confucians, who were attracted to Khubilai's court and to whom Khubilai was drawn.[128] Hsü was to be universally recognized as one of the great scholars of his age. As a young man, he had been exposed, through Yao Shu and Tou Mo, to the main books and precepts of Neo-Confucianism.[129] Again through these two luminaries, he was introduced to Khubilai and by 1267 had been appointed the Chancellor of Education at the Imperial College. During his tenure at the college, Hsü taught many prominent Mongols and Central Asians and was able, in this way, to propagate his teachings among the foreigners who actually governed China. He developed a reputation as an outstanding teacher who emphasized dedication to one's state and society—quite naturally, attractive concepts to the Mongol rulers of the state. Even more pleasing to Khubilai and the Mongol court was Hsü's concentration on practical affairs. Unlike many other Neo-Confucians, he did not dwell on nonworldly matters in his writings or speeches. One reason for his success at the Mongol court was that he "did not go into speculative, metaphysical matters or 'things on the higher level.' " [130] Instead, he offered avuncular and useful advice to Khubilai.[131]

According to an anecdote in the Chinese histories, Khubilai insisted on candid advice from Hsü, even if such truthfulness required criticism of the emperor. When Hsü first entered Khubilai's service, the leading light at court was Wang Wen-t'ung, who was by no means a conventional scholar-official. Instead, Wang was a canny administrator with an expertise in finances. He tried, in fact, to reduce the power of the Confucians at court through a clever stratagem. He urged Khubilai to appoint Yao Shu Grand Preceptor, Tou Mo Grand Tutor, and Hsü Heng Grand Guardian to the Heir Apparent, thus effectively blocking them from holding positions in the administration.[132] All three, recognizing Wang's ploy, declined the appointments and temporarily retired from government service. In 1262, Wang was implicated in his son-in-law Li T'an's rebellion against the throne and was executed. Khubilai then recalled Hsü and admonished him for not speaking up against Wang, saying:

> At that time, you were . . . aware of [Wang's faults] why did you not speak up? Could it have been the teachings of Confucius that caused you to act like that? Would it rather not be your lack of obedience to the teachings of Confucius that caused you to act like that! What is past is past; do not repeat these mistakes in the future. Call what is right, right, what is wrong, wrong.[133]

Khubilai surely recognized that such an attitude would please his Chinese Confucian advisers.

Similarly, his positive reaction to the writing of a dynastic history in the traditional style must have met with the approval of the Confucians. Confucianism, with its emphasis on the past and the use of historical models as guides to behavior, offered an impetus to such officially endorsed historiographical projects. In August of 1261, Wang O, who had already (in 1234) written an account of the fall of the Chin court, proposed that the historical records of the extinguished Liao and Chin dynasties, as well as those of the early Mongol rulers, be collected.[134] He reiterated the traditional Chinese view that the study of history was useful in providing models for the present; both the virtues and the defects of the earlier dynasties served as valuable examples for that age. He implied that Khubilai ought to emulate the great emperors of the past.[135] To ensure the proper cataloging of records and administration of the archives, Wang suggested the establishment of a History Office, combined with the traditional Han-lin

Academy of Confucian erudites.[136] This new combination was "apparently aimed at utilizing the influence of the Han-lin academicians . . . to expedite the completion of the history projects." [137] The new office, known as the Han-lin kuo-shih yüan, would be responsible for assembling the records and then composing the histories of the Liao and Chin dynasties along with those of Khubilai's Mongol predecessors. Khubilai, who ostensibly did not share the Chinese enthusiasm for historical writing, nonetheless approved Wang's proposal and sanctioned the founding of a National History Office. His objective appears to have been to pacify the Chinese Confucians and to appear to follow their scholarly precedents. Khubilai's motivations aside, Wang O recruited editors, compilers, academicians, and so-called drafters for the History Office.[138] Though none of the histories of the Liao or Chin was completed or even drafted during Khubilai's reign, Wang O devised an organizational scheme for the *Chin History*. But credit for the conception and the initial work ought to be given to Khubilai and his advisers.

KHUBILAI AND RELIGION

Khubilai naturally had to appeal to more than the Confucian elite if he wished to be perceived as the ruler of China. Other religions and cults within China had to be placated. Khubilai pursued a policy designed to win over all the various religions in his realm. To the Chinese scholars, he assumed the pose of an upholder of the Confucian system; to Tibetan and Chinese monks, he portrayed himself as an ardent Buddhist; to European visitors such as Marco Polo, he predicted mass conversions to Christianity among his people; and to the Muslims, he acted as a protector. Such chameleon-like transformations proved invaluable for Khubilai in ruling his ethnically and religiously diverse domains.

One of the religious groups whom Khubilai was anxious to influence was the Muslims. From 1261 on, more and more Muslims were entrusted with positions of authority in government and were accorded special privileges. Muslims were, for example, exempt from regular taxation.[139] The court rarely impeded the Muslims' religious activities. References to Muslim communities abound in Chinese and Persian sources.[140] There were Muslims in Khubilai's summer capital at K'ai-p'ing as well as in his official capital at Ta-tu.[141] Some were craftsmen, merchants, and architects, occupations highly prized by Khubilai.

Khubilai tolerated and, on occasion, rewarded the Muslims, who in many areas formed virtually self-governing communities. An official known as the *Shaikh al-Islam* (in Chinese, *hui-hui t'ai-shih*) was often the leader of the community and served as an intermediary between it and the Mongol authorities. The *qadi* (in Chinese, *hui-chiao-t'u fa-kuan*) interpreted Muslim laws and principles. The Muslim quarters had their own bazaars, hospitals, and mosques.[142] Khubilai did not, except briefly, prevent the Muslims from following such dictates of Islam as circumcision and abstention from pork. Neither did he seek to impose the Mongol or Chinese languages on the Muslims. Arabic, Persian, and Turkish continued to be spoken by many members of the community. Khubilai pursued this benevolent policy toward the Muslims because they were useful to him in ruling China. They promoted trade with the rest of Asia and served as tax collectors and financial administrators, and they made Khubilai less dependent on Chinese advisers and officials. Because they were utterly dependent on the Yüan court for their position and power, the Muslims appeared more loyal than the Chinese.

Khubilai's efforts on their behalf proved fruitful. A number of influential Muslims served the court, the most renowned being Saiyid Ajall Shams al-Dīn (in Chinese, Sai-tien-ch'ih Shan-ssu-ting). Descended from a distinguished family in Bukhara, Saiyid Ajall had led one thousand of his cavalry in surrendering to the Mongols during Chinggis Khan's campaigns in Central Asia.[143] His Mongol captors were evidently impressed by his ability and loyalty, for shortly after his surrender they began to appoint him to increasingly responsible positions. Möngke selected him to be the chief administrator of the circuit of Yen-ching.[144] In 1260, Khubilai appointed him as Pacification Commissioner (*hsüan-fu shih*) in Yen-ching and within a year he was offered a position in the Central Secretariat.[145] He apparently performed well in these positions, because by 1264 Khubilai had commissioned him to be the virtual governor of much of modern Shensi, Kansu, and Szechwan. Here he was credited with conducting an accurate census, which brought more households on the tax rolls, and with effectively organizing his army.

Khubilai also appealed to the Buddhists, whom he had supported during their debates with the Taoists in 1258. By the time he succeeded his brother Möngke, Khubilai had been exposed to several schools of Chinese Buddhism, and particularly to Ch'an. But Ch'an was overly abstruse and lacked the tangible and practical benefits that

Khubilai sought. Tibetan Buddhism, on the other hand, was the ideal vehicle for his political purposes. It could offer ideological justification for the Mongol ruler's accession to power. Its emphasis on magic, its color, and its parades all appealed to Khubilai, but its most attractive feature was its involvement in politics. Many of the Tibetan Buddhist sects had traditionally played a role in secular affairs. Their religious hierarchs were also secular leaders, and the monasteries were often local centers of power. The Tibetan sects were not as divorced from politics as the Ch'an Buddhists appeared to be.

The Tibetan 'Phags-pa lama of the Sa-skya sect proved a useful figure to support Khubilai's aspiration to be perceived as the rightful ruler of China. He had, through his long association with the Mongols, imbibed many of their values. Yet he was, as the nephew of one of the principal leaders of the Sa-skya sect and as a Buddhist monk himself, respected, if not revered, by many Tibetan Buddhists. Since Khubilai's other prominent Tibetan ally, Karma Pakshi, had been accused of assisting Arigh Böke in his struggle against Khubilai, this so-called worker of miracles could not be counted upon.[146] The 'Phags-pa lama was much more reliable.

As soon as Khubilai took power, he began to woo the 'Phags-pa lama with honors and titles. In 1260, he appointed the Tibetan cleric to a new position as State Preceptor (Kuo-shih), and early the following year he placed him in charge of all the Buddhist clergy.[147] In 1264, the Mongol ruler presented the so-called pearl document, which granted tax exemptions to the Buddhist monasteries.[148] Khubilai did not need to offer many inducements to the 'Phags-pa lama, who had become so assimilated that he wore Mongol clothing, for which he was severely criticized by his own people. Yet Khubilai continued to try to win the 'Phags-pa lama's loyalty. In 1264, he founded the Tsung-chih yüan to administer Tibet and to supervise government relations with the Buddhists, and the 'Phags-pa lama became the first director of this new agency.[149] Simultaneously, Khubilai and the 'Phags-pa lama became even closer through marital alliances. The 'Phags-pa lama's younger brother married a Mongol princess, as did his nephew and, later, one of his grandnephews.[150]

The last step was to offer at least nominal jurisdiction over all Tibet to the 'Phags-pa lama and his fellow Sa-skya abbots. In 1264/65 Khubilai dispatched the Buddhist monk to Tibet to help in persuading the local people to accept Mongol rule. His younger brother the Phyag-na rdo-rje lama, who had also been reared at the Mongol court, arrived in Tibet with the Mongol-granted title of "Head of all Tibet" (in Tibetan, *Bod-spyi'i steng-du bkos*).[151] The division of responsibilities between the two brothers is not clear. Perhaps Khubilai meant the ʿPhags-pa lama, as the supervisor of the Buddhists throughout the empire, to reside in China while his younger brother would be stationed as his agent in Tibet. Whatever the rationale for granting the two brothers seemingly overlapping jurisdictions in Tibet, the plan quickly went awry, with the sudden, untimely death of the Phyag-na rdo-rje lama in 1267. The ʿBri-gung-pa order, the main opponents of the Sa-skya, capitalized on his demise to rebel against their rival Buddhist sect and against Mongol overlordship. Khubilai responded by sending a punitive force there, and by 1268 Mongol rule was restored. In that year Khubilai truly began to impose Mongol sovereignty over Tibet. He ordered a census conducted and a postal system developed.[152] Though the sources yield few details about additional duties imposed upon the Tibetans, it appears that Khubilai also devised a tax and militia system for them. The administrative structure Khubilai established in 1268 envisioned first a member of the Sa-skya sect as State Preceptor (at this time, the ʿPhags-pa lama), who would supervise the Buddhists throughout the empire as well as in the state of Tibet but would reside in China. The Mongols would, in addition, select a Tibetan official, known in Tibetan as a *dpon-chen*, to live in and to administer Tibet.[153]

Khubilai expected that the ʿPhags-pa lama and his fellow Buddhists would, in turn, provide him with the religious sanction he needed. The Tibetan Buddhist did indeed fulfill his side of the bargain. He devised a suitable relationship between the secular rulers and the religious hierarchs that demarcated the spheres of authority of Church and State. The ʿPhags-pa lama sought to differentiate their roles in the following way:

> Secular and spiritual salvation are . . . something that all human beings try to win. Spiritual salvation consists in complete deliverance from suffering, and worldly welfare is secular salvation. Both depend on a dual order, the order of religion and the order of the state. . . . The order of religion is presided over by the Lama, and the state by the King. The priest has to teach religion, and the king to guarantee a rule which enables everybody to live in peace. . . . The heads of the religion and of the state are equal, though with different functions.[154]

The ʿPhags-pa lama repaid his benefactor Khubilai by associating him with figures in the Buddhist pantheon. Khubilai became identified with Mañjuśrī, the Boddhisattva of Wisdom, and was perceived as an emanation or incarnation of that "enlightened one."[155] The Mongol sources, pursuing this same theme, referred to Khubilai as "Sechen Khan" (Wise Khan).[156] The 'Phags-pa lama and the other Tibetan Buddhists deified Khubilai and portrayed him as a Universal Emperor (*Cakravartin*, in Sanskrit) in the Buddhist tradition.[157] In a work written during that time, possibly by the 'Phags-pa lama, and then translated into Mongol as the *Chaghan Teüke* (White chronicle), Khubilai was depicted as both a Boddhisattva and a great ruler.[158]

To heighten still further the connections between his religious sect and the emperor, the 'Phags-pa lama proposed the initiation of court rituals associated with Buddhism. Annual processions and parades, which were designed to destroy the "demons" and to protect the state, were organized on the fifteenth day of the second month, and music, rituals, and parades also were mounted on the first and sixth months of the year.[159] For the 'Phags-pa lama, these ceremonies were meant to compete with or to offer an alternative to the Confucian court ceremonies; for Khubilai, they complemented but did not supplant the Confucian rituals. Yet Khubilai must have appeared to favor Buddhism, for a later source, which nonetheless reflects the attitudes of the times, offers this paean to him:

> Thus he [Khubilai] made to shine the sun of religion on the dark land of Mongolia and invited a Buddha image of veneration from India, relics of the Buddha, and patrabowls and a sandalwood *juu* presented by the Four Maharajas. He conducted a government of the ten meritorious doctrines, and stabilized the world, and owing to his having pacified and made happy those in the vast world, in this wise he became famous in all directions as the wise Cakravarti King who turns the thousand golden wheels. . . .[160]

In appearing to be attracted to their religion, Khubilai surely bolstered his prestige among the Buddhists. The 'Phags-pa lama's efforts on Khubilai's behalf bore fruit. Many in the Buddhist community began to perceive Khubilai both as a universal ruler and as the Emperor of China.

Khubilai attempted to strengthen his position by providing the Buddhists with special privileges and exemptions. He first granted the 'Phags-pa lama authority over the thirteen military myriarchies of Tibet, permitted the Tibetan cleric to instruct his son Chen-chin, and finally in 1270 awarded him the coveted title of Ti-shih (Imperial Preceptor).[161] He then offered Buddhist monks a tax-exempt status, though those who had families and farmed or traded would still be required to pay taxes.[162] Bona fide monks who did not seek profit through farming or trading, however, were accorded extraordinary favors. In 1261, Khubilai provided 500 *ch'ing* (each *ch'ing* was equivalent to about fifteen acres) of land to two Buddhist temples (one of them named for the monk Hai-yün), which were located near the future site of Ta-tu.[163] Five years later, he donated 15,000 *liang* of silver to assist a Buddhist temple to carry out seven days of religious ceremonies. He contributed funds for the construction of new temples and monasteries as well as for the repair of some that had been damaged during the Buddhist-Taoist disputes.[164] The government supplied artisans and slaves to some of the monasteries for their craft shops and their lands.[165] Government support, subsidies, or exemptions enabled the monasteries to become prosperous economic centers, often with their own inns, shops, ferries, and pawnshops. Khubilai's various benefactions to the Buddhist monasteries and temples thus served their purpose, providing him with tangible support from Buddhist advisers and officials.

Taoism was another of the religious orders from which Khubilai sought sanction and assistance. Khubilai's involvement in the Buddhist-Taoist debates of 1258 had, of course, not endeared him to the Taoist hierarchy.[166] Yet both Khubilai and the Taoists needed each other. The Mongol monarch was entranced by the Taoists' reputed magical powers, their alleged ability to call upon spirits and ghosts, and their experiments in alchemy and astrology. Moreover, he knew of the Taoists' strong appeal to the lower classes, a group he too needed to attract. A few of the Taoist leaders themselves recognized the need for an accommodation with the Confucians and Buddhists to avert the disastrous, often debilitating disputes that had wracked the Three Teachings (i.e., Confucianism, Buddhism, and Taoism) since the arrival of the Mongols in China. Several Taoists sought even to reconcile the Three Teachings. One prominent Taoist thinker devised a "Diagram of the One and the Same Origin of the Three Teachings," which offered the hope of some form of reconciliation among the three religions.[167] Such eclecticism did not prevent conflict between the Taoists and the other religious groups, in particular the Buddhists. Yet in the first decades of Khubilai's reign, these conflicts remained muted.

Khubilai offered inducements to the various Taoist sects in return for their support. He supplied funds for the construction of temples, in particular to those belonging to the Ch'üan-chen sect, the Taoist order favored by the Mongols since Chinggis Khan's time. The Ch'ang-ch'un temple, named for a Taoist master admired by Chinggis, was one of the main buildings subsidized by Khubilai. The Ch'üan-chen leader, Chang Chih-ching, received sums of money from the court to build other Taoist temples and to promote the interests of his sect.[168] The Taoists responded to these favors by providing ideological justification for Khubilai and by helping him to perform certain duties expected of a Chinese emperor. One of these tasks was the worship of T'ai-shan, one of the sacred mountains of China, which was a vital responsibility for a Chinese emperor. The Taoists were given jurisdiction over this cult, and Khubilai annually would dispatch Taoist leaders to perform the T'ai-shan ceremonies and sacrifices associated with it.[169] Their willingness to conduct these ceremonies for him signaled a kind of support that was transmitted to ordinary believers of Taoism.

KHUBILAI AND THE POLOS

Christinanity was the last of the religions that Khubilai sought to influence. Since Christianity was associated with the West, Khubilai had still another motivation for welcoming and seeking good relations with Christians. To bolster his claims to legitimacy and to demonstrate his "merit" to his Chinese Confucian subjects, he needed visitors from afar, who could be portrayed as foreign ambassadors, to bow down in his presence. He was thus delighted to welcome European Christians to his court.

Marco Polo was the most renowned Christian in the exchanges between East and West in Khubilai's time.[170] Some scholars have speculated that Marco may not have reached China and that some of the incidents he recounts may derive from conversations he had with Persian or Arab merchants or travelers. Marco's own words raise these doubts. He claims to have assisted the Mongols in their siege of the Sung base at Hsiang-yang, but that battle ended in 1273, two years before he allegedly arrived in China.[171] He also writes that he was governor of Yang-chou for three years, a claim that is not substantiated by Chinese or other sources, though one modern commentator ingeniously argues that Marco supervised the salt administration in the city.[172] Since the revenues derived from the salt trade were invaluable, Marco, according to this interpretation, may have perceived himself to be the true governor of Yang-chou. Whatever the validity of this viewpoint, there are, as well, curious omissions from his book. Marco fails to mention tea and teahouses, acupuncture, and footbinding among other unique features of Chinese culture. His supporters insist, however, that he associated primarily with the Mongols and would not have noticed these Chinese characteristics.[173] They respond in the same way to those critics who point to Marco's omission of any mention of Chinese writing as an indication that he did not reach China. Perhaps Herbert Franke has the best approach to Polo and his work when he writes: "Until definite proof has been adduced that the Polo book is a world description, where the chapters on China are taken from some other, perhaps Persian, source (some expressions he uses are Persian), we must give him the benefit of the doubt and assume that he was there after all."[174]

As Marco tells it, his travels to the East were preceded by the trip of his father Nicolo and his uncle Maffeo to the Mongol court.[175] Before the Polo brothers' arrival, relations between the Mongols and the West were decidedly cool. Missions led by John of Plano Carpini and by William of Rubruck had not been diplomatic successes, though the reports written by the two friars offered Europeans their first close and accurate glimpse of the Mongols. Their descriptions of the products of the East attracted such European merchants as the Polo brothers and stimulated them to travel to the Middle East and then farther east.

Nicolo and Maffeo Polo set forth on their journeys from Venice in 1252, not knowing that they would not return to their native city for almost two decades. They first stopped and traded in Constantinople, then passed through the territory of the Golden Horde before heading for Khubilai's court, which they reached in late 1265 or early 1266.[176] Khubilai was delighted with his visitors. According to Marco, Khubilai "beamed with the greatest kindness" and "received them with great honour and makes them great joy and very great festival."[177] Marco's descriptions of the meetings between his uncle and father and Khubilai reveal the Great Khan's almost insatiable curiosity. Khubilai determined the course of the conversations, inquiring about their kings, their system of justice, their methods in warfare, their customs, and, most important of all, their Christian religion. He asked the Polos to persuade the pope to send one hundred learned Christians with them when they returned to China. With his eclectic attitude toward religion, Khubilai probably was not as interested in recruiting learned

7.   The Polo Brothers Meeting Khubilai. From *Livre des merveilles*. Manuscript from the Bibliothèque Nationale, Paris.

clerics to convert his subjects to Christianity as he was in gathering
learned men to help him administer his domains in China. His request
to the Polos was a ploy to obtain such experts. As he recruited
Christians, he was not particularly eager that his own people convert
to Christianity. Yet he needed to persuade the Polos and the Christian
hierarchy that he wanted the learned Europeans to help in guiding his
people to Christianity.

When the Polos returned to the Christian world in 1269, they faced
disappointments. They learned that the pope had died in the previous
year and that the College of Cardinals could not settle on a successor.
Assuming that the deadlock would not be broken, the Polo brothers,
now accompanied by Marco, resolved to start on their journey without papal blessing. Nor could they obtain the requested hundred
learned Christians. They set forth nonetheless, and reached Khubilai's
court in 1275.

Khubilai must have been dismayed that the one hundred learned
men he had wanted had not arrived, but he still gave his three guests a
fine reception. Here was additional proof, after all, that foreigners
would travel great distances to pay tribute to the Great Khan. Marco
described their first meeting as one in which "they [the Polos] kneel
before him with great reverence and humble themselves the most that

8.   Portrait of Marco Polo. From *Marco Polo: The Description of the World*, by A. C. Moule and Paul Pelliot.

they are able stretching themselves out on the earth."[178] The Polos'
kowtow no doubt bolstered Khubilai's standing with his status-
conscious subjects. Though Khubilai did not obtain one hundred
learned men, in Marco he received a bonus: the services of a capable
and clever young man who was intelligent enough to have become
proficient in several languages, including Persian and possibly
Mongol, en route to China.

Marco asserts that he and Khubilai had numerous conversations,
and he offers a vivid, colorful verbal portrait of the Great Khan. He
saw Khubilai at the height of his powers and describes the Great Khan
in a flattering light. Marco's assessment was "as we say without
contradiction the greatest lord that ever was born in the world or that
now is."[179] His description of Khubilai's physical attributes is also
laudatory. Marco's depiction of Khubilai can be dated to the early
years of the young European's stay in China, for his description of the
Great Khan differs from the 1280 portrait painted by Liu Kuan-tao.[180]
Marco wrote that Khubilai was "neither too small nor too large"; Liu
pictured him as obese.[181] He had, according to Marco, black eyes and a
prominent and "well made nose." He was white faced, though occasionally his features (perhaps when he drank) became rose colored.[182]
Marco also described in loving detail the celebrations for Khubilai's

9. Khubilai on a Hunt. From *Livre des merveilles*. Manuscript from the
Bibliothèque Nationale, Paris.

birthday and for the New Year, the hunting and hawking forays led by the Great Khan, and Khubilai's wives and concubines.

Khubilai must have been pleased with the young European. He had at his court an intelligent Christian European and soon recognized that it was in his best interests to treat this young man well. If he wished to emphasize his legitimacy and at the same time to entice more Europeans to China, Khubilai needed to welcome with open arms the Europeans who ventured on this difficult trip.

Khubilai could further ingratiate himself to the Europeans through a tolerant policy toward Christianity. In his dialogues with Marco, Khubilai sought to give the impression that he favored Christianity above the other religions in his realm. Once one hundred learned Christians arrived in China, he told Marco, then the conversions to Christianity would start, and he himself would be baptized.[183] He employed quite a number of Christians in his court, including an astronomer and physician with the Chinese name Ai-hsüeh.[184]

Another indication of Khubilai's appeal to Christians was the dispatch of Nestorian Christian envoys to the West. The most prominent of these envoys was Rabban Sauma, who went on a pilgrimage to the Holy Land but also traveled farther west and had audiences with King Philip the Fair of France in Paris and King Edward I of England in Bordeaux.[185] Rabban Sauma's mission confirmed that Khubilai could maintain his contacts with the Christian West. Khubilai needed Western visitors both because of his desire for trade and because of his eagerness to impress his Chinese subjects with proof of his acceptance as the Great Khan in the wider world.

By 1279, Khubilai had established himself as the Emperor of China. He had appealed to a wide variety of occupational and social groups and to the various religions and cults in his domains. He had constructed a capital in China and reinstituted some of the rituals associated with Confucianism. All of these actions had garnered him a great deal of support from the Chinese populace.

CHAPTER SIX

The Cultural Patron

While Khubilai established himself as the ruler of China, he sought also to create and transmit his own identity. He could not readily abandon the trappings of Mongol culture. However, he could not appear to be a crude, unsophisticated "barbarian" if he wished to be accepted as the Chinese Son of Heaven. A Chinese emperor gained in stature by being a patron of literature and the arts. The Mongols did not have a similar tradition, though from earliest days they had prized the works of good craftsmen. Their appreciation of beautiful and utilitarian objects provided Khubilai with the opportunity he needed to support the arts, particularly handicrafts, in China. Even so, he struggled to maintain a balance between the highly developed culture of China and the less sophisticated expressions of his own people.

Further complications emerged because of Khubilai's aspiration to universal rule. As Khan of Khans, he naturally had a responsibility to promote the cultural expressions of diverse lands and ethnic groups and could not afford to be associated totally with Chinese culture. Such parochialism might damage his efforts to portray himself as the ruler of all the domains under Mongol control. He needed to sponsor cultural projects that did not favor any specific land within the Mongol-ruled territories. Too close an identification with Chinese culture could be as damaging as overly enthusiastic promotion of his native heritage. To maintain all of these various cultural strands in balance had important ramifications that Khubilai could not ignore and required constant shifts. The cultural choices he made were profoundly political questions, for they would either contribute to or undermine his acceptance in his realm.

THE WRITTEN LANGUAGE

Khubilai's characteristic response to cultural questions is revealed in his policy toward the written language in his domains. A serviceable written language was vital for the operation of the government of a great civilization. The fiscal, military, and welfare responsibilities of the government necessitated keeping proper written records, procedures to which the Mongols were not accustomed. The Mongols themselves had developed a written language only early in the thirteenth century. Thus they had had scant experience with the keeping and preservation of fiscal, military, and other kinds of records. Yet from Chinggis Khan's time on they wrote their fiscal and military accounts, their edicts, and their laws in the newly adopted Mongol script. Scribes or secretaries were brought in to the khan's court to record his decisions, commands, and edicts. Once the Mongols conquered China, they appointed Chinese or sinicized Jurchen or Khitan scribes to prepare a Chinese version of the khan's written documents.[1] Since the Chinese were, at various times, forbidden to learn Mongol, the scribe needed a translator or interpreter, either a Mongol or a Muslim or other Mongol subject, to translate the Mongol writings and to help him render them into colloquial Chinese (*pai-hua*). The Mongols decreed the use of colloquial Chinese rather than the previously official classical language of their subjects because "the adoption of the classical language would have implied yielding culturally to China."[2] Similarly, the employment of Muslim or other non-Chinese intermediaries in the process of translation was, in part, designed to serve as a check on the Chinese scribes and secretaries. This cautious policy persisted, as we have seen, into Khubilai's reign. The early Mongols, and even Khubilai, did not wish to be dependent upon or offer too much authority to the Chinese they employed. In short, court documents until the time of Khubilai were written in Mongol, and many were laboriously translated into Chinese. Mongol and Chinese were clearly the most important languages in the Mongols' eastern domains.

When Khubilai took power and deliberately chose to govern from China, the written language became more critical. The existing Mongol script was based on the Uighur script, which in turn derived from

Soghdian and ultimately from Aramaic. The Uighur script did not transcribe the sounds of the Mongol language with great precision, blurring distinctions between sounds and sometimes representing dissimilar sounds with the same symbol.[3] Certain Mongol sounds could not be accurately represented in the Uighur script, and some of the Uighur letters were hard to tell apart.[4] All of these characteristics of the Uighur script militated against its wider application.

And Khubilai planned much wider application for the official script. First, he needed a Mongol script that could be used to translate Chinese and to represent the Chinese sounds of the names, titles, and offices in China. The Uighur script was simply unsuitable for the accurate transcription of Chinese. It lacked some of the sounds of Chinese, so its transcription occasionally bore only the faintest resemblance to the original Chinese sounds. The scholars who had been assigned to translate the Chinese classics and histories as well as the more practical works on statecraft soon recognized its inadequacies.[5] They were occasionally stymied in conveying the meaning of the Chinese texts and in reproducing the sounds of the Chinese names and terms. Such an unwieldy script could prove a stumbling block in Khubilai's plans.

Khubilai planned to use the new official script to help unify his realm and to assert his claim to universal rule. He wanted to go beyond the two existing scripts, the Chinese characters and the Uighur script, which had been the official scripts under the earlier Mongol khans. Neither was satisfactory from the standpoint of phonology. Khubilai, however, objected to more than their technical inadequacies. As the ruler of a domain in which various ethnic groups resided and many languages were spoken, Khubilai wanted a script that could be employed to transcribe all these diverse languages. He aspired, in short, to developing nothing less than a universal script. Such a script would not only facilitate communication within his realm but also contribute to greater unity among its different language and ethnic groupings. He planned to have recourse to a new script for his own political purposes. What he failed to recognize, however, was people's reluctance to accept any artificially designed script, no matter how accurate or effective.

Khubilai was nonetheless determined to develop a better and more widely usable script. Within a few years after granting the ʿPhags-pa lama a state title and position, Khubilai assigned the Tibetan lama the task of creating the new script. Working with other monks and

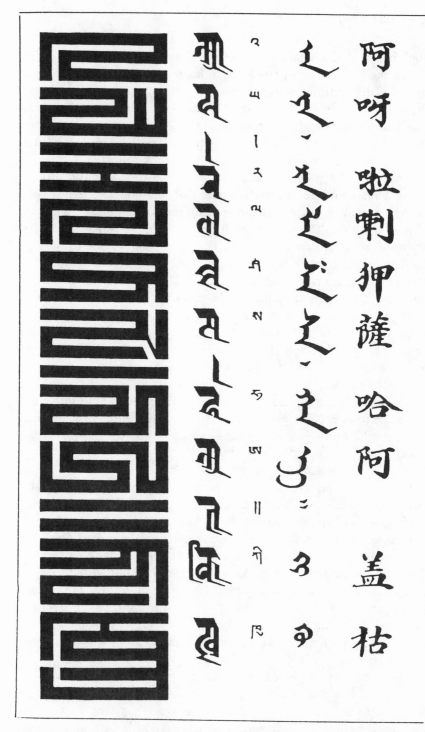

10.   A Comparison of Scripts. From a primer of ʿPhags-pa script found in manuscript collection of the Institute of Oriental Studies, Academy of Sciences of the U.S.S.R. *From right to left*: Chinese, Mongolian, Tibetan, Sanskrit, and ʿPhags-pa.

scholars, the ʿPhags-pa lama devised an alphabet that he presented to the Great Khan in 1269.[6] The alphabet, which was based upon Tibetan, consisted of forty-one letters, many of which were square in shape. Hence the alphabet is occasionally referred to as the "Square Script," though it is more often called the ʿPhags-pa script in honor of its creator.[7] It has been described as "a Tibetan alphabet adapted to the requirements of Mongol phonetics."[8] The new script did not differ markedly from the Tibetan alphabet, except that, like the older Uighur script, it was written vertically. It was much more precise than the Uighur script in its rendering of the sounds of the colloquial Mongol of the thirteenth century. Composed of many more symbols than the dominant Uighur script, it would appear to have had a decided advantage in its competition with the earlier alphabet. It could also more accurately reflect the sounds of other languages, including Chinese, in Khubilai's realm. Since it emphasized and was derived from the colloquial version of the Mongol language,[9] it blended well with Khubilai's endeavor to encourage the employment of the colloquial in writing—even, for example, the use of colloquial Chinese for official government documents in China. In short, the ʿPhags-pa alphabet appeared ideally suited to transcribe the languages, those with alphabets and those with characters, in Khubilai's domain, to serve as a universal script, and to contribute to the unification of the frequently antagonistic peoples under Mongol rule.

Khubilai was delighted with the alphabet and had great expectations for it. In 1269, he promulgated an edict displaying his hopes for this universal script. Seeking perhaps to justify his enthusiasm for and promotion of the ʿPhags-pa alphabet, he explained that the Jurchen and Khitan invaders and rulers of China (who founded, respectively, the Liao and Chin dynasties) had created their own scripts. Now the Mongol rulers could lay claim to the same achievement. Khubilai proudly designated the ʿPhags-pa alphabet as the Mongolian script (Chin.: *Meng-ku tzu*) and eventually referred to it as the "State Script" (*kuo-tzu*).[10] He ordered that it be used in court documents, but he was realistic enough to add that it should be employed in conjuction with Chinese. Khubilai surely hoped that ʿPhags-pa would eventually supersede though perhaps not replace the Chinese characters but conceded that a period of transition would be needed until the time when the Tibetan-based script became supreme. He apparently did entertain doubts about ʿPhags-pa's eventual adoption as the universal script but nonetheless actively encouraged its dissemination. Shortly after issuing his edict, he founded academies expressly for the propagation of the new script. In 1272 and again in 1273, he reiterated his order that court documents be written in the State Script.[11] Finally, in 1275, two of his most distinguished advisers proposed the establishment of a special Mongolian Academy (Meng-ku Han-lin yüan), on the same level as the Chinese Academy (Han-lin yüan), to study and teach the Mongol script and to translate the khan's pronouncements.[12]

Yet Khubilai's expectations remained unfulfilled, for the script was not readily adopted. He had been overly optimistic about its acceptance in his domain. Even his own officials evaded the regulations on its use in official documents, simply ignoring Khubilai's specific instructions. He responded by issuing repeated injunctions. In 1279, he required the Secretariat (Chung-shu sheng) to write all its official reports and documents in the Square Script, but in 1284 he was compelled to issue the same directive to the same government agency.[13] Obviously, his earlier pronouncement had been disregarded. Nor were the schools he had founded in 1269 as effective as he would have wished. A report in 1272 by one of his officials indicated that the children and relatives of his Chinese bureaucrats were not studying the new script.[14] Again he appealed to his officials to send their sons to the schools that taught the new Mongol script.

Despite his efforts and his repeated admonitions, the ʿPhags-pa alphabet never replaced the Uighur script or the Chinese characters. Few examples of ʿPhags-pa writing are extant. Several Chinese works, including the *Classic of Filiality* and the Chinese historical account, the *Tzu-chih t'ung-chien*, were translated, but they had limited circulations in their ʿPhags-pa versions.[15] Other ʿPhags-pa inscriptions comprised edicts and regulations written at the command of the Mongol royal family.[16] Chiseled out on stone slabs, they consisted of taboos and restrictions directed at the khan's officials and military. A few Buddhist texts, including two at the Chü-yung kuan, which was one of the gateways to North China, were also carved on stone in Square Script.[17] Still other ʿPhags-pa writings were found on *p'ai-tzu*, the metal tablets that served as passports or guarantees of safe passage through the Mongols' domains.[18] A potpourri of Square Script inscriptions, mostly cursory with the briefest kinds of identification, appeared on seals, coins, paper money, and porcelains.[19] Typical of these concise inscriptions was the message "*sayin darasun*" ("good wine") glazed on a Yüan dynasty wine jar that is now in the Oriental

11.   Ming Porcelain with ʿPhags-pa Writing. Freer Gallery of Art.

collections of the British Museum.[20] These carved, painted, and engraved writings, however, constitute but a tiny fraction of the total number of texts produced in the Yüan dynasty, most of which were written in Chinese or Uighur script.

The failures of the ʿPhags-pa script ought not to be attributed to its technical inadequacies, but to the method by which it was propa-

12.   *P'ai-tzu* (Passport) with ʿPhags-pa Writing. Kansu Provincial Museum.

gated. Despite its virtues, the ʿPhags-pa alphabet encountered strong opposition, in part because it was officially devised and sanctioned and imposed from above. And, despite the injunctions, pleas, and edicts of Khubilai and his top court officials, the resistance did not wane. Only official seals, steles, and coinage were affected by this attempted innovation in Mongol writing; ordinary literate Chinese and Mongols did not adopt the script. Khubilai's scheme can be judged a failure.[21] Yet it manifests his concern for a universal script and for a written language that reflected the colloquial language of his time.

YÜAN THEATER AND
OTHER LITERARY FORMS

The theater, in particular, blossomed during Khubilai's time and the reigns of his immediate successors. The growth of cities in the Sung and Yüan offered a fitting environment for the rise of the drama, providing the audience as well as the funds needed for performances. Without an urban culture and without patronage from the government and private citizens, theater would not have prospered.[22] The Yüan was indeed a period of flourishing cities, and for many Chinese the Yüan drama was the apogee of Chinese theater. At least one hundred and sixty Yüan plays are extant, and over five hundred additional ones were performed and written, but only their titles have been preserved.[23] Theatrical districts with dozens of theaters sprouted in many of the cities.[24] Actors and actresses, who had always been treated as social pariahs, found themselves in a more enviable position, at least during the early years of Mongol rule. The Yüan rulers "seemed to look upon entertainers as people who had some desirable function in their scheme of things."[25] The theatrical troupes, often composed of individual families, wandered from place to place, mounting performances of plays that included singing, dancing, pantomime, and acrobatics—spectacles that appealed to a mass audience. A leading Western scholar describes the Yüan dramas as "variety entertainment" because the genre was characterized by sketches, interspersed with songs and dances.[26] "Courtroom plays" (Chin.: *kung-an chü*) were among the most popular, but tragedies, comedies, and other kinds of drama were also produced.[27]

The traditional views of the social significance of the Yüan drama have of late been questioned. One traditional interpretation credited the abolition of the civil service examinations with the initial impetus for the rise of the Yüan theater. Having lost that vital avenue of social mobility, Chinese scholars turned to other cultural pursuits, including the writing of plays. Since their aspirations for official careers appeared to be blocked, they used their erudition and literary abilities in the drama.[28] It is important to remember, however, that professional playwrights, who in earlier times would not have qualified for office, also made their marks on the Yüan drama. The playwrights were no longer molded by the civil service examinations and Confucianism and therefore tackled different themes and subject matter.

The drama also used the colloquial. As one seventeenth-century critic remarked, "Yüan playwrights erred in this respect [i.e., using vulgar language too often], a shortcoming stemming from their overreaction against the artificial and elaborate style. . . . " [29] What the critic failed to recognize was that the colloquial language was increasingly the natural style of writing for the dramatist. The professional playwrights were more conversant with the vernacular, and even the officials used the colloquial. Since Khubilai and the Mongols required the officials to use the colloquial in their work, it was only natural that the playwrights who were also officials would be more familiar and comfortable with the vernacular. The Mongols' regulations, in that sense, facilitated the playwrights' tasks and contributed to the development of the Yüan theater.

Another way Khubilai and his Mongol court promoted the drama was their relative lack of interference. They were so eclectic in their views that playwrights could broach a variety of subjects without fear of government interference. [30] This led some later Chinese critics to suggest that "many *kung-an* playwrights delivered veiled attacks against their Mongol rulers by portraying the criminal as a member of some highly privileged class and invulnerable to punishment by ordinary process of law." But this interpretation appears doubtful, for "no concrete evidence has yet been offered to support this speculation." [31] Mongols did not usually figure as characters in the plays and were also not portrayed symbolically as the exploiters. Neither can the critics credibly represent the plays as dramas of social protest. There is no proof that the Mongols were portrayed as the oppressors.

Moreover, if traces of anti-Mongol sentiment had surfaced, Khubilai would not have patronized the theater, and he probably would not have adopted a policy of benign neglect. There is no evidence that he ever censored the theatrical productions performed during his reign. Though he probably did not read or write Chinese, he could understand and speak the language. He ordered the staging of a number of performances at court, attended several of them, and enjoyed the action without interfering or imposing restrictions on the playwrights. Officials continued to patronize the drama, and later in Khubilai's reign and the reigns of his immediate successors *tsa-chü* plays, farces which developed into serious dramas, were performed at court. [32] Another tangential indication of possible patronage by Khubilai involves the backgrounds of the most famous playwrights.

Khubilai's old appanage of Chen-ting was the birthplace of many of them. Seven of the forty-five renowned playwrights of the dynasty derived from that relatively small locality; only Ta-tu, with seventeen playwrights, could claim more of them as native sons.[33]

This is not to say that Khubilai and his Mongol underlings deserve credit for the development and successes of the Yüan theater. The Chinese playwrights and, to a small degree, their audiences were responsible for their own artistic creations. Yet Khubilai contributed to an environment that fostered, or at the very least did not undercut, the Yüan theater. He knew that a good emperor ought, in Chinese eyes, to be a patron of the country's culture, and that the theater, as a developing art form in China, ought to be supported. By emphasizing the colloquial language in writing, he, in a small sense perhaps, advanced the cause of a drama that attempted to employ the vernacular.

Khubilai also cannot be given credit for the development of the novel, nor for the larger number of printed texts available in China. Yet here again, as with the theater, his cultural and literary policies perhaps offered favorable circumstances for their growth. His emphasis on the colloquial was a boon to novelists, who often portrayed characters of a lower-class origin.[34] The use of the vernacular permitted novelists to reproduce the patterns of speech of the ordinary person and to present a broader range of characters and a freer expression of emotions. Few of the novels were actually written down during the Yüan period; in their final forms, most derive from the later Ming or Ch'ing dynasties.[35]

The texts that were produced under Khubilai and his immediate successors received wide circulation. Under the Yüan, "printing attained prominence from the standpoint of quantity if not quality and technique."[36] In 1269, Khubilai founded a special office to print books under official sponsorship, and by 1286, land was assigned to academies that used the income to print texts.[37] The growth in printed texts offered more access to books and initiated the rise in literacy characteristic of the Ming and Ch'ing dynasties.[38]

The Chinese did not cherish the drama and the novel, relatively new literary styles, as highly as such traditionally more prestigious literary forms as poetry and the essay, nor did they identify with them as intensely. Poetry in the Yüan did not reach the great heights of the T'ang and Sung dynasties. Whether the lack of distinguished achievement was due to the downgrading of the classical language, the ideal vehicle for poetry, is a matter of conjecture. The Mongols did not dismiss or seek to subvert the craft of poetry, but they faced difficult and, in most cases, insurmountable language problems in trying to understand Chinese poetry. The classical language of the Chinese poets was beyond Khubilai's limited familiarity with Chinese. Still, poets were well received at his court and the courts of his successors, and even Muslim poets such as A-li Yao-ch'ing and his son Li Hsi-ying were honored.[39] Like poetry, the essay form, at which the Chinese had excelled for centuries, languished during the Yüan, failing to attract the caliber of men that it had in earlier dynasties. To be sure, Khubilai recruited and subsidized such Confucian luminaries and scholars as Hsü Heng who might have been expected to and did produce fine essays. But the body of work produced by the Yüan essayists did not compare to the writings of the T'ang and Sung scholars. Here too the very different social status of scholars under the Mongols may have contributed to the relative scarcity of distinguished essays. Khubilai and his fellow Mongols did not understand, and might have been put off by, the refined language and the arcane references of the classical essay form. Nor did they provide the proper environment for the literary forms, the poetry and the essays, of the previously dominant scholar-elite.

PAINTING

But they did not inhibit painting in the same way. Painting, also traditionally the province of the scholar elite, was more accessible to Khubilai and his fellow Mongols, for they did not have to overcome a formidable language barrier to appreciate it. The khans' own vanity also made them responsive to visual representations. Khubilai himself had a formal portrait painted and then commissioned the artist Liu Kuan-tao to paint him in action on a hunt.[40] He became increasingly interested in painting once he had conquered the Southern Sung. He had the Sung's Imperial Painting Collection transported to Ta-tu, where it was catalogued by several Chinese connoisseurs. The Southern Sung paintings provided the foundation for his own collection, which grew as a result of his patronage of certain artists and his acquisition of some of their paintings for the court.[41] In short, Khubilai, and later some of his descendants, cherished Chinese painting and made a concerted effort to preserve its finest examples. And the Yüan produced a remarkable group of painters, causing one modern scholar to refer to a "revolution" in painting during this period.[42]

Yet some art historians have emphasized either the negative impact or the lack of influence of Khubilai and the Mongol rulers on Chinese painting. One writes that the "imperial family did not produce any noted writers or calligraphers or painters, and the artists whom they sponsored merely specialized in portrait or architectural painting."[43] Sherman Lee offers a more favorable interpretation of the Mongols' influence. Seeking to explain the scant attention devoted to Yüan art prior to 1968, when he and Wai-kam Ho mounted a major exhibition, he writes that "the ruling house of the Yüan Dynasty was a foreign one, Mongol, and this has always been a deterrent to proper and full Chinese appreciation. . . . The innate and expansive pride of the sons of Han hardly permits an objective, let alone a favorable, analysis and judgement of a time politically dominated by foreign barbarians."[44] This more balanced appraisal enables us to reconcile the adverse evaluations of the Mongols by some art historians with the simple fact that Khubilai sponsored and gave employment to a number of painters and initiated and bequeathed to his successors an outstanding collection of Chinese paintings of the Yüan and earlier dynasties. The denigration of the role of Khubilai and the Mongols as art patrons is at odds with the facts, and the implication that the Chinese painters' successes in the Yüan were, in part, a reaction against the Mongols merely appeals to nativist sentiments.

It is true that some of the great painters rejected employment or collaboration with the Mongols. As we have seen, some scholars who refused to accept positions with the foreign conquerors took up such occupations as medicine. Others became recluses (yin-shih), whose motives for abandoning the world were diverse. According to one art historian, "their self-imposed retirements were partly from a diffusive world-weariness, but more importantly an escape from the impossible burdens of taxes, from forced enlistment in public service, [and] from political persecution."[45] Still others may be classified as "leftover subjects" (i-min), who differed from other recluses in their political motivations. They remained loyal to the conquered Sung dynasty but concealed their antipathy for the Mongols. There were, in truth, no ways to express their dissent without endangering themselves.[46] One way of diverting themselves was to turn to private pursuits, by which they could occasionally display their bitterness toward the Mongol rulers. Painting was one such notable and natural pursuit for these discontented scholars. They constituted a group of so-called amateur painters, as distinct from the official Imperial Academy painters of Sung times. They lived as recluses and could not be said to form a school of painting.

Their art certainly cannot be said to have been encouraged by the Mongols. Instead, according to some art historians, these painters produced their greatest works in spite of the Mongols. Quite a few of them resided in the lakes region (Lake T'ai, West Lake) in the province of Chiang-nan, which eventually became a magnet for such dissident artists.[47] Cheng Ssu-hsiao (1241–1318), who was resolutely opposed to the Mongols and would have nothing to do with them, was typical of these *i-min* painters, who used art to lament the destruction of the Sung and to praise its virtues. The "literary-men's paintings" (*wen-jen hua*) that they evolved differed from the Sung Academy's paintings in its gradual shift from realism to a more pronounced emphasis on the emotional responses of the artist. This change naturally enabled the artists to express their hostility toward the Mongols in discreet ways. Cheng, for example, was renowned for his paintings of the Chinese orchid, and "asked why he depicted it without earth around its roots, he replied that the earth had been stolen by the barbarians."[48] Kung K'ai (1222–1307), Ch'ien Hsüan (ca. 1235–ca. 1301), and other *i-min* painters employed their art as a subtle means of social protest.[49]

However, when they vanquished the Southern Sung, Khubilai and the Mongols did not compel the painters to become recluses. Khubilai, in fact, offered several of them positions in the government, which they flatly rejected. He would have been eager to employ them and to provide them with the leisure for painting. The painters, for the understandable and praiseworthy notion of loyalty to a native dynasty, declined Khubilai's offers. Khubilai and his successors, on the other hand, were apprehensive about recruiting scholars who still had a strong attachment to the Sung. They suspected these recluses "—sometimes with good cause—of tenacious loyalty to the fallen dynasty."[50] It is unduly harsh, surely, to accuse Khubilai of deliberately discriminating against Chinese painters and impeding the development of Chinese painting.

To the contrary, Khubilai nurtured and supported some of the great Chinese painters of the Yüan. Chao Meng-fu (1254–1322), the most renowned painter of the dynasty, was granted a position in the Ministry of War and took up residence in Ta-tu. After Khubilai's death, Chao continued to receive official appointments, eventually becoming President of the Han-lin Academy, the most prestigious body of scholars in China, in 1316.[51] Kao K'o-kung (1248–1310), another distinguished painter, was appointed to the Ministry of Works in 1275.[52] He too continued to advance, even during the reigns of Khubilai's successors, and late in life held the title of Minister of Justice. Li K'an (1245–1310), the most famous painter of bamboo, became the Minister of Personnel.[53] Hsien-yü Shu (1257?–1302), a man from Northern China revered as one of the three most remarkable calligraphers of the Yüan, secured positions in the Censorate and in the Court of Imperial Sacrifices, among other offices.[54] These four artists were only the most prominent men to be granted positions at Khubilai's court; he subsidized many others through sinecures in his government. Khubilai did not wait for able scholars and artists to proffer their services, but sent emissaries to find them. In 1286, for instance, he dispatched the Confucian Ch'eng Chü-fu to Wu-hsing in Chiang-nan province to discover and recruit talented men for his government.[55] Ch'eng returned with the great, but as yet little known, painter Chao Meng-fu.

Chao was, without doubt, Khubilai's most important supporter among the painters. Since Chao was descended from the royal family of the Sung, his conversion to the Mongols boosted Khubilai's credibility and legitimacy among the Chinese. Here, after all, was an imperial clansman who renounced his own heritage to serve the "barbarians." For this, he was severely criticized by Chinese scholars of his and later dynasties. Chao had his own misgivings, but justified himself in a poem on one of his paintings. He explained that:

> Each person lives his life in this world according to his own
>   times;
> Whether to come forth and serve, or to retire in withdrawal,
>   is not a fortuitous decision.[56]

According to some accounts, his mother, who was ambitious for her son, saw possibilities for him to gain official rank under the Mongols and urged him to collaborate with Khubilai.[57] But his close association with Ch'ien Hsüan, an older painter who adamantly rejected Mongol overtures and remained a staunch Sung loyalist, made it difficult for him for a time to join in common cause with Khubilai. Both Chao and Ch'ien lived in Wu-hsing, and in their ultimately differing responses to the Mongols, they became models for other scholars and painters in that artistic center. As Li Chu-tsing observes:

> Ch'ien Hsüan's status as an *i-min* or Sung loyalist earned for him the
> respect of many intellectuals of that time who, having grown up and
> served under the Southern Sung, had no opportunity or desire to serve
> the foreign dynasty. Ch'ien thus became a symbol of their loyalty to the
> Sung and of their frustration under the new regime. Chao Meng-fu, on the
> other hand, having become the leading southerner among Yüan officials,
> was admired by those who aspired to serve in the Yüan government.[58]

They appeared to represent the responses of different generations to
Khubilai's rule, the older generation being perhaps less willing to
collaborate. Chao, in any case, did indeed serve the Mongols. When he
arrived in Ta-tu, however, there was considerable opposition to the
appointment of a descendant of the recently vanquished dynasty.[59]
Khubilai ignored such opposition and appointed Chao to the Ministry
of War. Chao responded by performing his tasks conscientiously. He
was especially concerned with reforming the postal service. He in-
veighed against the private, illegal use of the facilities of the postal
service and the abuse of these same facilities by foreign tribute
embassies. Later Chao also urged a reduction in taxes, particularly in
areas that had been devastated by a series of earthquakes. Chao, in
short, remained a valuable adviser to Khubilai until the Great Khan's
death.

Chao's painting, as well as that of some of his contemporaries,
attested to the new freedom offered by Khubilai. Chao repeatedly
repudiated Sung painting as superficial and proposed a return to a
classical model for painting. The Sung Imperial Academy's standards,
he argued, stifled and confined the imagination of artists.[60] Chao
found the Mongols, who did not interfere with the artistic creations of
the Chinese painters, to be less restricting.

But Khubilai and the Mongols did more than play a negative role in
developments in Chinese painting during the Yüan. They also influenced somewhat the themes and subjects that appeared in the painters' works, as painters who wished to appeal to Mongol taste chose
subjects that they thought would be popular among the Mongol elite.
Depiction of horses was an obvious example, for the Chinese painters
recognized how the Mongols valued and were devoted to their steeds.
The Mongols would, they reasoned, find paintings of horses attractive. Since Khubilai and the Mongols also found some subjects such as
birds, flowers, and humans that were portrayed in the Sung paintings
appealing, Yüan painters continued to treat some of these same

themes.[61] The Mongols' most important contribution, however, was to assist Chinese painters in breaking away from the formalism of Sung Academy style. Thus, Khubilai and the other Mongols' contributions to painting and their patronage of artists ought not to be dismissed.

CRAFTS

The Mongols' influence on crafts was even more pronounced. From earliest times, the Mongols had valued artisans and made special provisions to protect and support them. When Khubilai took power in China, he followed the policies of his Mongol predecessors in ensuring a good supply of artisans who could produce the articles that he and his people prized and needed. He devised organizations under the Ministry of Works to supervise and control the artisans in China. The Directorate-General for the Management of Artisan-serfs and All Classes of Civil Artisans, with thirty branch offices, was the main administrative organ.[62] Within these agencies were specialized departments, each one regulating a specific craft such as metals, leather, textiles, and ceramics. The Bureau for Imperial Manufactures had its own craftsmen, who created goods for the needs of the khan and his retinue. Both Chinese and non-Chinese craftsmen were recruited by Khubilai's officials. The court designated certain families as hereditary artisan households, circumscribing the vocational opportunities of the young. Yet craftsmen had numerous privileges, including exemptions from most taxes, and they enjoyed a higher status than in any other previous Chinese dynasty. It is thus no accident that the Mongols influenced and at least indirectly contributed to the technical and aesthetic advances during this era.[63]

Khubilai valued Chinese ceramics both for use at court and for foreign trade. Yet a noted student of Chinese ceramics has observed that "in the history of Chinese ceramics, the Yüan period has been regarded in the past as an ugly duckling. . . . It has also been held that the Mongols had no real interest in the arts, that they did not find Chinese taste congenial, and that in consequence they neglected the creative arts." [64] She asserts, however, that "nothing could be farther from the truth" than this judgment. Khubilai, seeing the potential for revenue in the export of ceramics, began to regulate ceramics production. He ordered that all kilns be registered and that taxes be levied on them.[65] The court obtained the porcelains it required, and for the rest it promoted an extensive and lively trade with foreigners, particularly in Southeast Asia and the Middle East. The various societies southeast of China, as well as the Persian and Arab Muslims, admired Chinese ceramics and imported substantial quantities, primarily for their monarchs and their elites.[66] Most of the Chinese kiln sites were ideally situated for foreign trade. They were located in the Southeast, not far from the fine harbors of that region. Te-hsing, An-fu, Te-hua, and, the most famous of them all, Ching-te-chen constituted the leading sites, and all had access to the southern ports stretching from Hangchow through Wen-chou to Ch'üan-chou.

The main contribution of Khubilai and his immediate successors to ceramics was the freedom they granted to the potters. Instead of being bound by the dictates of the Sung court and the Chinese scholar elite, the potters were permitted to experiment with forms and decorations. The Sung standards had led to the production of outstanding ceramics, but slavish adherence to them impeded creativity and resulted in the manufacture of some rather ordinary wares.[67] The Yüan potters, who were not inhibited by the Sung canon of taste, could innovate, and such experimentation resulted in the creation of some new and beautiful porcelains. The blue-and-white porcelains often associated with the Ming dynasty actually originated in the Mongol period, when the Chinese first had access to the cobalt blue they needed to produce fine blue glazes.[68] White porcelains, rather than the white stonewares of the Sung, and new kinds of celadons were also introduced during this time.

The Mongols' influence, direct and indirect, extended to other crafts as well. They monopolized textile manufactures and produced textiles for foreign trade. Chinese craftsmen fashioned beautiful robes and vestments, some of which were designed for European prelates. Some lacquer ware previously attributed to the Ming dynasty may, in fact, have stemmed from the Mongol period.[69] Stone sculpture, particularly with Buddhist themes, continued to flourish, as it had under previous dynasties. The most impressive products of Yüan stone sculpture were the rock carvings in Chü-yung kuan, the gateway to North China, and the Fei-lai Feng in Hangchow, both of which derive from the later years of the dynasty.[70] Though Khubilai had little to do specifically with these two projects, he supported Buddhist art and employed Tibetan monks and artisans, the groups who would supervise the creation of the rock carvings.

Khubilai's impact on Chinese architecture derived, in large part, from an invitation extended to a Nepalese craftsman whom the ʿPhags-pa lama had brought to the attention of the Great Khan. During one of his periodic visits to his native land, the Tibetan monk was greatly impressed by a newly constructed Buddhist temple designed by the Nepalese craftsman A-ni-ko (1244–1306).[71] Despite A-ni-ko's protestations and his desire to return to Nepal, the ʿPhags-pa lama took the Nepalese artisan with him to China in 1265. He soon arranged an imperial audience for A-ni-ko, and the Great Khan and the Nepalese craftsman formed favorable impressions of each other. Khubilai first tested A-ni-ko's abilities by ordering him to repair a damaged copper image of a man, which was used for acupuncture. The test turned out to be a great success, as A-ni-ko performed a remarkable restoration.[72] Overwhelmed by A-ni-ko's talents, Khubilai assigned him a number of construction projects. A-ni-ko designed and built a Buddhist temple, the Ta-hu-kuo-jen-wang ssu, and a pavilion in a park in Ta-tu, an ancestral temple in Cho-chou, and a temple in Shang-tu among others.[73] He also fashioned some beautiful gold and jade jewelry. Clearly delighted with A-ni-ko, Khubilai offered lavish rewards to the young Nepalese. In 1273, he was named the head of the Directorate General for the Management of Artisans, making him the supervisor of all the craftsmen in China. Later he was granted an elegant home, together with land, in the Hsien-i-li section of Ta-tu. Khubilai's wife Chabi, who also was enchanted with the young Nepalese, arranged his marriage to a high-born woman, a descendant of the Sung royal family.[74] Khubilai and his family thus recognized a great craftsman and welcomed and rewarded him for his efforts. The non-Chinese craftsmen were given the same opportunities for success and patronage as the Chinese.

It would be erroneous to suggest that Khubilai himself or his people made a major direct contribution to China's arts and crafts. Yet their patronage of the arts is undeniable. By such support, Khubilai, in particular, promoted advances in the arts. Similarly, by allowing artists and artisans much freedom and flexibility, he inspired greater innovation and experimentation in the arts. He had no vested interest in imposing classical or traditional forms on artists and allowed them leeway to be imaginative; under this policy, painters, dramatists, and potters flourished. As a foreigner himself, Khubilai was not averse to the introduction of non-Chinese forms and ideas into Chinese art. His support and patronage of A-ni-ko, for example, led to the appearance of Tibetan and Nepalese forms in Chinese architecture. Moreover, his sponsorship of Chinese and non-Chinese alike boosted his claims to universal rule.

PRESERVING THE MONGOL HERITAGE

Khubilai needed to be the sovereign of China as well as the khan of the Mongols and the ruler of the non-Chinese domains under Mongol control. To the Chinese, he had to seem somewhat sinicized. Yet he could not adopt too many Chinese customs and beliefs for fear of offending conservative Mongols. Khubilai had to walk a thin line in his approach and attitude to Chinese culture. As the khan of the Mongols, he needed to practice the rituals and to abide by the regulations of his nomadic forebears. As an aspirant to universal rule, he could not confine himself to the attractions of one culture (i.e., the Chinese) within his lands, but had to be ecumenical in his acceptance of traits and practices from the different territories he, in theory, controlled.

Khubilai attempted to avoid being engulfed by Chinese civilization. One way he sought to prevent such assimilation was to distinguish between the Mongols and the Chinese. His policies aimed at preserving the Mongols' uniqueness and identity. He forbade intermarriage between the two peoples; the Mongols were to remain pure and unsullied. As far as possible, he tried to keep the Chinese from learning the Mongol language.[75] He also attempted to discourage fraternization between the Mongols and Chinese. As an emperor of China, he continued to carry out the Confucian rituals, festivals, and sacrifices and, in fact, assigned An-t'ung, one of his closest Mongol confidants, and other top advisers to examine and select Chinese canons and rituals that could be employed at his court.[76] But he repeatedly sought to limit expenditures on such ceremonies.

In governmental matters, he distinguished between his own practices and those of the Chinese. The civil service exams were abolished, thus dispensing with the most common traditional means of entering the bureaucracy.[77] Chinese could not generally be appointed as local commissioners (Mong.: *darughachi*). The financial administration of China was in the hands of non-Chinese.[78] Some scholars have interpreted these changes in government as evidence that the system introduced by Khubilai and his successors was more autocratic. They have asserted that the Yüan witnessed an increased use of force and physical violence in resolving problems. The emperor, in this view, acquired more power, as there was no independent civil service to restrain him. A rougher, more brutal military atmosphere was found at court.[79] Censors were stationed as spies on officials throughout the empire. Some of the emperors, including Khubilai's immediate successors, flogged their leading officials, a humiliation that bureaucrats in earlier dynasties had not endured. However, the scholars who have made these accusations have not offered sufficient documentation to prove that the Mongols inaugurated a more despotic and more violent era in Chinese history. Instead, preliminary research and evidence appears to contradict their views. The central government seems not to have been more dominant than in previous dynasties. Local authorities in some areas appear to have been virtually autonomous.[80] The question of Yüan despotism is, at the very least, controversial. Similarly, the attribution of increased violence to Mongol rule is difficult to substantiate and open to challenge. Earlier (i.e., Chinese) emperors mistreated their officials. Flogging and brutalization of officials did not suddenly emerge in the Mongol era. Some of the criticism may stem from Khubilai's efforts to distinguish between the Mongols and the Chinese, thus preserving Mongol customs while simultaneously preventing Chinese officials from dominating government.

Khubilai also took some positive initiatives to preserve Mongol rituals and customs, for instance by performing the traditional Mongol ceremonies. Every August, before leaving Shang-tu to spend the fall and winter in Ta-tu, he conducted the ritual of the scattering of mare's milk.[81] This ceremony, in which four shamans also participated, reputedly ensured a year of good luck. It consisted of the sacrifice of a horse and a few sheep, bowing toward Heaven, calling out Chinggis Khan's name, and the scattering of mare's milk from specially bred horses.[82] Khubilai, in this way, honored his ancestors and sought their blessings for another winter of good fortune. Another Mongol ceremony performed toward the end of the year was designed to rid them of bad luck. The celebrants shot arrows at straw and grass models of a man, representing the Mongols' enemies, and a dog, an auspicious symbol; then the shamans prayed for prosperity and for the elimination of the afflictions that could beset the people. When a member of the imperial family was ill, he or she was placed in a yurt and two sheep were sacrificed daily until the ailing one had recovered.[83] Before Khubilai went to battle, he poured out a libation of *koumiss*, invoking the assistance of Heaven against his enemies. Shamans also recited incantations to assure the support of Heaven. Khubilai and his successors continued to conduct Mongol-style sacrifices to mountains, rivers, and trees. Khubilai's frequent employment of shamans shows his persistent support of the Mongol tradition.[84] At the same time, he encouraged the practice of the Buddhist and Confucian rituals, and on at least one occasion he consulted a shamaness from Korea.[85]

Khubilai asserted Mongol practices in other tangible ways. Mongol women retained their rights; they did not adopt the Chinese practice of footbinding. Many Mongols continued to wear their native costume of furs and leathers, though Khubilai himself frequently donned the clothing of a typical Chinese emperor.[86] Elaborate, extravagant feasts, more reminiscent of the nomads' celebrations, with almost uncontrolled eating and drinking, were held on Khubilai's birthday and at the start of the New Year. According to Marco Polo, thousands of guests attended these marathon celebrations. All of the foods mentioned by Marco were meats, again another legacy of the Mongols' pastoral nomadism.[87] Judging by the enormous quantities of liquor drunk by the guests, the alcoholism that was so much a part of early Mongol history apparently persisted into Khubilai's reign.

The fascination with the hunt was perhaps the most telling signal of the retention of Mongol ways. Khubilai changed the season of the hunts from fall to spring. According to Marco, Khubilai was accompanied on hunts by trained lions, leopards, and lynxes who chased and often captured boars, oxen, bears, and wild asses. He also took five hundred gerfalcons with him to snatch other birds from the sky. A huge retinue of falconers, hunters, and soldiers accompanied Khubilai on these hunts. Khubilai himself

> always goes on four elephants, on which he has a very beautiful wooden room, which is all covered inside with cloth of beaten gold and outside it is wrapped round & covered with lion skins, in which room the great Kaan always stays when he goes hawking because he is troubled with the gout. . . . And he sees [the hunt] always sitting in his room lying on his couch, and it is a very great amusement and great delight to him.[88]

In his private life, he also asserted his native heritage. All four of his wives were Mongols. But his sexual relationships were not limited to his wives. He had a sizable harem, of which Marco Polo offered this memorable description:

> It is true that there is a province in which dwells a race of Tatars who are called Ungrat who are very handsome and fair-skinned people; and these

13.   Khubilai on a Hunt. Painted by Liu Kuan-tao. National Palace Museum, Taipei.

women are very beautiful and adorned with excellent manners. And every second year a hundred maidens, the most beautiful to be found in that race, are chosen and are brought to the great Kaan as he may wish. The great Kaan sends his messengers to the said province that they may find him the most beautiful girls according to the standard of beauty. . . . And when they are come to his presence he has them valued again by other judges. . . . And he had them kept by the elder ladies of the palace . . . and makes them lie with them in one bed to know if [one] has good breath and sweet, and is clean, and sleeps quietly without snoring, and has no unpleasant scent anywhere, & to know if she is a virgin.[89]

In short, even in selecting sexual partners he decided to remain with Mongol concubines.

Khubilai succeeded admirably in charting a cultural policy that affirmed the Mongol heritage, accepted certain Chinese practices, and strove for universalism. As with his religious policy, Khubilai presented himself in different guises to the different audiences he faced. To the Mongols, he was a staunch defender of his native traditions. He took part in hunts, married and took as concubines Mongol women exclusively, and sought to preserve the Mongols' marital values. To the Chinese, he assumed the role of patron of the arts. He subsidized some Chinese painters, potters, and other craftsmen and provided the freedom for Chinese dramatists and novelists to undertake experiments within their traditions. He often compared himself to one of the greatest emperors in the Chinese tradition, T'ai-tsung of the T'ang dynasty, knowing full well that such an association would improve his image with the Chinese.[90] To the rest of his domains, he was a cosmopolitan, espousing a universal script and encouraging foreign craftsmen in China. The cosmopolitanism that he inspired in Yüan culture no doubt added to his luster as a ruler of a realm much larger than China.

CHAPTER SEVEN

Mismanagement and the Chinese Response

The year 1279 proved to be a watershed in Khubilai's reign. Until that time, he had scarcely experienced any failures in his undertakings. Though he had not met with an unbroken series of triumphs, neither had he encountered a serious reversal. Before his accession to the throne, he had organized his appanage so smoothly that he had garnered the support of his Chinese subjects and had readily secured the taxes and other obligations he demanded from them. His campaign against Tai-li in Southwest China had been a resounding success. Having attracted to his domain a distinguished and dedicated group of advisers who helped design an appropriate government for his territory, he was prepared to rule an even larger realm. He had presided over and resolved an important Buddhist-Taoist debate. Thus, even before he became the Great Khan, he had met with successes as an administrator, as a military commander, and as a cultural arbiter, all of which would serve him well.

When he took the throne, he was relentless in pursuing his objectives. He crushed all opposition, including that of his younger brother. His advisers and he established a government based on Chinese models but not dominated by Chinese ideals and forms. His two capitals at Shang-tu and Ta-tu were well-planned, functional, and beautiful. He had, through a carefully considered policy, gained favor with most of the religious leaders in his realm. His armies had succeeded in asserting Mongol control over Korea and Mongolia, had somewhat dissipated the military threat of his chief enemy in Central

Asia, and had conquered the rest of China. He had encouraged the creative arts and had recruited some of the ablest artisans in the land to produce exquisite craft articles for the court and the elite and for use in foreign trade. Khubilai's most conspicuous failure was the abortive invasion of Japan, but he could rationalize this defeat by blaming it on the natural disaster, the terrible storm, that devastated his forces. Moreover, he intended to avenge himself on the Japanese for what he perceived to be a temporary setback. The fiasco along the Japanese coast was, he believed, merely bad luck. All else in the first two decades of his reign seemed to be proceeding smoothly.

But appearances, in this case, were deceptive. Some difficult problems lay beneath the surface. They could erupt if the occasion arose, particularly if Khubilai suffered a significant setback in any of his domestic or foreign policies. Some Confucian scholars, whose previously prestigious positions had been downgraded by Khubilai's policies, were not reconciled to this change in status. The dissatisfaction with Khubilai became even more pronounced with the amalgamation of the Southern Sung into the Yüan domains. The Confucian scholars in the North had adjusted to cooperation with foreign rulers because the Liao and Chin, both dynasties governed by foreigners, had dominated part or all of North China from the tenth century on and had employed Chinese bureaucrats to help them administer their domains. The scholars in the South, however, had not experienced foreign rule, and many refused to collaborate with the Mongols. They pursued nonpolitical interests and awaited the development of failures and weaknesses in the Mongol system that might lead to its downfall.

Khubilai himself began to slow down after 1279. Now in his late sixties, he was afflicted with health problems. Gout plagued him and made it difficult for him to walk. He grew heavier and was drinking heavily. These personal problems contributed to his political problems.

AHMAD AND FINANCIAL DIFFICULTIES

The most pressing problem he faced was finances. Khubilai's policies in the first two decades of his rule entailed great expenditures. The building projects he initiated, the construction of capitals at Shang-tu and Ta-tu, required vast outlays. Khubilai's patronage of the arts and his even more lavish entertainments, feasts, and hunts consumed a

growing share of the court's and country's income.[1] The establishment of postal stations, the building of roads, the promotion of
agriculture, and the maintenance of public work projects added to the
court's expenditures.

Yet the cost of Khubilai's military campaigns was probably more
worrisome. His sorties against his younger brother Arigh Böke and
the rebel Li T'an were essential to his survival as the ruler of China. His
military support for the Korean king and his dispatch of his son
Nomukhan to combat the threat posed by Khaidu in Central Asia were
vital to the defense of his borders. His conquest of the Southern Sung,
which stubbornly resisted all his peace overtures and his demand to
accept his authority, offered control over a vital region. These expeditions were expensive, but the political gains compensated for their
costliness. The planned invasion of Japan was not as critical. And the
expenses for this overseas campaign were not as easy to justify. Yet
Khubilai, as a Mongol leader, had to avenge himself against Japan's
blow to his prestige—its unwillingness to accept him as its nominal
ruler. The combination of public works, construction projects, and
military expeditions could not be sustained without additional
revenues.

To obtain the needed funds, Khubilai sought assistance from the
infamous Muslim finance minister, Aḥmad.[2] Khubilai here simply
adopted the same policies as his predecessors Ögödei and Möngke,
who had employed Muslims as financial administrators and governors. Little is known of Aḥmad's early life and career except that he
was a native of Central Asia, having been born in a town not far from
modern Tashkent.[3] The Yüan dynastic history classifies him as one of
the "three villainous ministers" (the others were Sangha and Lu Shih-
jung), and Chinese and Western sources alike revile him for exploiting
and oppressing the Chinese.[4] Marco Polo believed that Aḥmad had
"bewitched" Khubilai with his "spells." According to Marco,
Khubilai's support allowed Aḥmad to acquire a fortune and to indulge
his sexual appetite. He tells us that

> there was no fair lady whom if he [Aḥmad] wanted her, he did not have at
> his will, taking her for wife if she was not married, or otherwise making
> her consent. And when he knew that anyone had some pretty daughter,
> he had his ruffians who went to the father of the girl saying to him, What
> wilt thou do? Thou hast this daughter of thine. Give her for wife to the
> Bailo [Aḥmad] and we will make him give thee such a governorship or
> such an office for three years.[5]

In his defense, it must be said that Aḥmad knew that he would be judged by the amount of revenue he collected for the court. The more funds he raised, the greater his power, prestige, and income. According to the Chinese accounts, he abused his power and imposed an inordinate tax burden on the Chinese. He profited from his position, to be sure, but it must be remembered that his accusers (i.e., those who wrote the Chinese accounts) were officials unsympathetic to his policies.

Aḥmad's main financial goals, simply stated, were to register all eligible taxpayers, to impose state monopolies on certain products, and to increase tax revenues. From 1262, when he was appointed to the Central Secretariat, until his death in 1282, he directed the state financial administration.[6] One of his first tasks was to enroll taxable households that had not been included in earlier tax lists. In 1261, some 1,418,499 households in North China were listed in tax registers; by 1274, the number had been increased to 1,967,898 households.[7] A regular system of land taxation was instituted. In addition, the revenue from the taxes on merchants grew from 4,500 ingots of silver in 1271 to 450,000 ingots by 1286 (the first figure leaves out revenues from merchants in South China that the second figure includes; however, there was a significant increase in both the North and the South).[8] Aḥmad also attempted to use the state monopolies for additional revenue. He established quotas for the monopolized goods that were to be turned over to the government. Chun-hsü chou in Honan, for example, had a quota of 1,037,070 catties (*chin*) of iron, 200,000 of which would be fashioned into farm tools and sold to farmers in return for grain.[9] Revenues from the salt monopoly grew from 30,000 *ting* in 1271 to 180,000 *ting* by 1286.[10] In 1276, Aḥmad forbade private production of copper tools, reserving that privilege for the government.[11] Even earlier, he had instituted state monopolies on tea, liquor, vinegar, gold, and silver, all of which were profitable. Control bureaus (*t'i-chü ssu*) were founded to supervise the laborers and merchants who worked on the monopolies and to prevent private trade in these products.[12] In short, Aḥmad's policies were lucrative for the state treasury.

However, the Chinese sources repeatedly accuse him of garnering handsome profits from these policies and of countenancing, if not actively encouraging, abuses. He had, according to these accounts, such awesome power that he could take advantage of his position for his own gain. Since there was no fixed price for gold and silver, he could manipulate the rates paid for the two metals for his own profit.[13] He relinquished little in private transactions but received hoards of precious metals. His policies, including the repeated issuance of paper money, prompted many Chinese, as well as many foreigners in China, to hoard their gold and silver, provoking a loss of faith in the value of paper money.[14] Such loss of faith inevitably led to inflation, as did the increased government printing of paper money. Prices for goods monopolized by the government rose throughout the 1270s, and Aḥmad capitalized on these fluctuations to enrich himself. Such abuses of the tea, salt, iron, and other monopolies were often blamed on Aḥmad. It is difficult in the present state of research to evaluate these accusations against the Muslim finance minister. It may, in fact, be almost impossible to verify these charges. Even though these accusations were probably exaggerated, Khubilai's continued support of his finance minister harmed his standing among his Chinese subjects.

The Chinese sources also denounce Aḥmad for cronyism. Of the eleven men he chose to direct the state monopolies, four were definitely Muslims and one other may have been.[15] Muslims and other non-Chinese dominated the major financial positions in government. Some Chinese were recruited into the financial administration, but they generally received low-ranking positions. One of the most damning accusations leveled at Aḥmad was that he attempted to place his inexperienced and perhaps unqualified and incapable sons in influential posts in the bureaucracy. He succeeded in having his son Mas'ūd appointed the *darughachi* of the commercial center of Hangchow, a political plum that offered numerous opportunities for personal profit. But Aḥmad encountered opposition in naming his son Ḥusain as intendant in Ta-tu. The Minister of the Right, An-t'ung, objected that Ḥusain had no training for the position.[16] This argument apparently failed to sway the court, and Ḥusain continued his climb in the bureaucracy, becoming an important official in Kiangsi by 1279. In 1270, Aḥmad sought to wangle a position as a military commander for another of his sons. The Confucian luminary Hsü Heng opposed this nomination, but Aḥmad succeeded in securing the appointment.[17]

Opposition to his policies provoked Aḥmad's vengefulness and resentment. He despised most of Khubilai's Confucian and Buddhist advisers, who had sharply divergent views on government policy. Shih T'ien-tse, Lien Hsi-hsien, and others among Khubilai's closest counselors repeatedly objected to Aḥmad's tax policies, arguing that the new levies were an intolerable burden on the Chinese populace. They accused him of profiteering and of having a "sycophantic character and treacherous designs."[18] He, in turn, accused some of them of embezzling state funds and of unbecoming personal conduct. The Chinese sources assert that Aḥmad falsely accused one of his opponents named Ts'ui Pin, an official in Chiang-huai, of pilfering government grain and had the emperor order Ts'ui to be executed.[19] Whether the source on this particular case is accurate or not, it is true that many of Aḥmad's opponents left government service in the 1270s. Unlike Ts'ui Pin, most were neither executed nor imprisoned; some retired of their own accord. Unable to limit Aḥmad's power, the Confucian scholar Hsü Heng retired from active involvement in court politics to become Director of the National College (Kuo-tzu chien). The Uighur Confucian Lien Hsi-hsien retired after Aḥmad accused him of embezzlement, adultery, and other improprieties.[20] Fortunately for Aḥmad, a number of Khubilai's advisers died of natural causes in the 1270s: Liu Ping-chung in 1274, Shih T'ien-tse in 1275, Chao Pi in 1276, Yao Shu in 1279, and Tou Mo in 1280. With the death of these opponents, Aḥmad became even more powerful at court. Aḥmad was hostile to Khubilai's non-Confucian advisers as well. He was not on good terms with the Buddhist and Taoist leaders at Khubilai's court. The death of the ʿPhags-pa lama in 1280 thus rid him of still another opponent. Khubilai's edicts of 1281 circumscribing the power of the Taoists (which we shall discuss later) further bolstered Aḥmad's status.

The Persian accounts of Aḥmad's career and personality differ from the Chinese assessments. Rashīd al-Dīn writes that "Ahmad held the vizierate with honor for nearly 25 years."[21] He is praised for promoting Chinese trade with the Muslim world and presumably for protecting Muslims within China. The Muslim records omit mention of the charges of nepotism, exploitation, and profiteering leveled at Aḥmad in the Chinese sources. Viewed from a different perspective, however, the Chinese accusations appear less serious. Bringing relatives and like-minded associates into the government was perfectly sensible. In order for Aḥmad to overcome opposition and implement his policies, he needed to place his supporters in influential positions. The creation of such cliques was condemned by traditional Chinese thinkers, but Aḥmad recognized that he could not succeed without sympathizers, most of whom would be Muslims, in the bureaucracy. He may, in fact, have exploited the Chinese, as their historians assert,

by imposing heavy taxes and high prices on essential goods monopolized by the government. But his position at court, not to mention
possible promotions and rewards, depended on his ability to satisfy
the seemingly insatiable revenue requirements of the Mongols. In his
defense, one might say that he was merely an agent, albeit a dedicated
and effective one, of the Mongol court, which had a considerable need
for income.

This is not to say that he lacked interest in his own advancement
and rewards. He tried, on several occasions, to increase his power and
elevate his position. In 1262, he had been appointed to the Secretariat,
and two years later he became a Vice Chancellor in that office. The
Confucian scholars, who were apprehensive of Aḥmad's opportunity
for his own aggrandizement, lobbied successfully with Khubilai to
place an important figure in charge of the Secretariat. Finally
Khubilai's son Chen-chin was granted jurisdiction over the Secretariat, in an attempt to prevent Aḥmad from using this agency as a
power base. In 1271, Aḥmad again tried to expand his authority. He
succeeded in being appointed Administrator of the Supreme Secretariat (Shang-shu sheng), but considerable opposition developed over
the creation of this office.[22] Within two years, the office was abolished, and the Secretariat was reinstated as the most important administrative agency in the government. Aḥmad no doubt sought,
through his position, to increase his wealth. Many Chinese surely
attempted to enrich themselves in the same way. Should Aḥmad alone
be singled out for blame?

Aḥmad's financial policies had, in any case, aroused the opposition
of some leading Chinese at court. Perhaps as critical, Chen-chin, who
despised Aḥmad and objected to the prominent positions in government accorded to his sons and relatives, had joined the opposition.
Others in the Mongol ruling elite who feared Aḥmad swelled the
opposition to the Muslim financial administrator.[23] On the night of
April 10, 1282, while Khubilai was in his secondary capital at Shang-
tu and conveniently out of Ta-tu, a group of Chinese conspirators
lured Aḥmad out of his house and assassinated him.[24] Shortly thereafter, Khubilai returned to the capital and executed the conspirators.
Within a few months, however, Khubilai's Chinese advisers persuaded him of Aḥmad's treachery and corruption. Their charges
rested partly on evidence uncovered after Aḥmad's death. A jewel
that had originally been given to Khubilai for his crown was found in
Aḥmad's house.[25] Was the precious stone planted there by Aḥmad's

enemies? If not, why did his wife and son not transfer the jewel to a less conspicuous location? Why was it so easy for government officials to find it in his house? Why should Aḥmad have kept it in such an obvious place? The evidence against Aḥmad here is suspect. He may indeed have stolen government and imperial goods, but it is worth remembering that his accusers were the Chinese officials who had opposed his financial policies.[26] The evidence, nonetheless, impressed Khubilai, and the Great Khan had Aḥmad's corpse exhumed and hung in a bazaar at the capital; it was then placed on the ground and carts were driven over the head; finally, Khubilai's dogs were allowed to attack the corpse. Several of Aḥmad's sons were executed, his property was confiscated, and most of the officials specifically appointed by Aḥmad were dismissed.

Yet the elimination of Aḥmad did not resolve Khubilai's financial problems. His revenue requirements became even more pressing after Aḥmad's death. Khubilai initiated several disastrous expeditions to Japan and Southeast Asia. He needed vast sums for these military campaigns, as well as for other public works projects that he began at the same time. The financial problems therefore persisted, and shortly thereafter Khubilai resorted once again to non-Chinese for help in fiscal matters. Simultaneously, by the early 1280s, Khubilai had experienced the great loss of his most faithful Chinese advisers, who died in alarming and rapid succession in the 1270s. Nearly all of the Chinese scholars whom he had so assiduously courted and recruited had died. Though the Chinese historical accounts undoubtedly overemphasize their roles and their influence on Khubilai, the advisers had clearly had intimate contact with the Great Khan prior to and during his reign. Their deaths left him bereft of reliable Chinese advisers. There were now few restraints on his non-Chinese counselors and on his own more capricious actions. Perhaps his advisers' demise also brought to mind intimations of his own mortality. Many of them were part of his generation, and quite a few were younger than he. His own death must surely have intruded on his thoughts. The sources agree that Khubilai became increasingly remote around this time. He began to lose interest in government, as he had fewer reliable counselors with whom to discuss policy matters. Particularly in the late 1280s he abdicated more and more of his responsibilities as a ruler. Officials, some of whom were not always scrupulously honest or capable, and members of Khubilai's family and retinue routinely made important decisions.[27]

INTEGRATION OF THE SOUTHERN SUNG

Before he slowly started to relinquish his authority, Khubilai did attempt to deal with one of his most serious problems—incorporating the Southern Sung territories into the political and economic system he had organized in North China. Here, too, financial problems plagued him. The wars between the Mongols and the Southern Sung had damaged both lands and property in South China. The existing economic institutions of the Sung differed from those of the North and needed to be integrated into the Yüan structure. A truly unified and centralized China was essential if Khubilai wished to fulfill his other political and economic objectives.

Khubilai first sought to ingratiate himself with the Chinese in the South. He released many of the Sung soldiers and civilians whom his armies had captured. Several tens of thousands or perhaps as many as several hundred thousand prisoners received their freedom.[28] Khubilai was determined that the Sung Chinese perceive themselves not as a conquered people but simply as almost equal citizens or subjects to the Mongols of a unified China under Mongol rule. Reprisals against the Southern Chinese for opposing him would merely alienate them, without leading to the unification of the two divisions of China. His edicts and pronouncements aimed therefore at recovery of South China and at preservation of many of the traditional features of the Southern economy.[29] He prohibited, for example, his own people from hunting on the farmlands of the Southern Chinese.[30] He also established granaries in the South to store surplus grain and to ensure sufficient supplies in times of agricultural distress due to natural disaster, drought, or other unpredictable forces.[31] Here again he offered an indication to the Chinese of the South that he would not overturn their agrarian-based economy.

His most significant signal to the Chinese was that he did not tamper with the existing network of obligations and responsibilities. The new system he established did not, as one scholar has observed, "introduce fundamental social changes analogous to those in the North into South China."[32] He did not generally confiscate land from the large estates of the dominant Southern landowners, and he confirmed those Chinese in their landholdings and in their authority on the local level. In return, he anticipated and generally received the cooperation of these landlords in maintaining order and collecting taxes. Khubilai and his government did not undermine the power of the landowners and the officials in the South; they simply added another layer—themselves—at the top of the hierarchy. The Mongols thus imposed fewer changes in the South than in the North. Large landowners were more prevalent in the South, and Khubilai found it to be in his best interests to prevent the alienation of this previously powerful group. He did expropriate some land, but much of it belonged to Chinese who remained truculently opposed to Mongol rule. Moreover, the land that was confiscated in this way was often used to benefit the entire population. On some of this land, the government founded military colonies (*t'un-t'ien*) as a means of protecting the South's borders.[33] Finally, Khubilai used part of the income from this land to pay the salaries of Southern officials.[34]

The Mongols' economic demands on the population were also not onerous. The land taxes imposed on the Chinese were relatively mild and in times of distress were waived. As was true of their policy in the North, the Mongols emphasized the founding of *she* to promote the agrarian recovery of the South. The *she* of the South, like the ones in the North, operated charity granaries to protect the indigent—still another example of the Mongols' continuing efforts to win over all levels of Southern society.[35] Khubilai imposed monopolies in the South, as he had in the North. Salt, tea, and liquor, among other commodities, were monopolized by the government, but the resulting prices for these products were not burdensome.[36]

A principal indication of Khubilai's desire to assist rather than to subvert the economy of the South emerged from his policy toward the paper money of the South. Sung China had its own system of paper money, which now needed to be integrated into the Yüan system. The conquest of the Southern Sung had undermined its paper currency, and, without some Mongol support for it, it would be virtually worthless. Yet the unification of the country necessitated one standard currency. The *hui-tzu* currency of the South could not coexist with the Chung-t'ung currency devised by Khubilai and his advisers for the North. Some of Khubilai's advisers and cohorts recommended that he simply declare the Sung currency invalid. Such a policy would have caused havoc in the Sung economy and ruined many merchants and landowners, however, and Khubilai chose a course that did not damage the economic interests of the South. He allowed the Chinese of the Southern Sung to convert the *hui-tzu* for the currency of the North over a period of years.[37] The Northern currency would gradually supersede the *hui-tzu*. If the Mongols had refused to accept the *hui-tzu* or had demanded that it be taken out of circulation immediately, the Sung economy would surely have been disrupted. Khubilai prevented the economic chaos that might have engulfed the Sung.

Another indication of Khubilai's concern for the South's prosperity was his support for maritime commerce. His policy here did not diverge from his oft-expressed desire for expansion of foreign trade. As noted earlier, Khubilai increased the number of Maritime Trade Superintendencies. He permitted the merchants of many overseas nations to come to the South China ports for trade. Trade developed rapidly and a variety of products reached China, contributing to the prosperity of the South.[38] Khubilai's and the Mongols' efforts were not altogether altruistic, for the government reaped substantial taxes from foreign trade as well as collecting useful and rare products for the court. Its support for the agrarian recovery of the South and its integration of the *hui-tzu* into the Yüan system of currency would eventually mean greater profits.

Despite Khubilai's efforts, the hostile feelings of some Chinese in the South toward the Mongols did not subside. Rebellions flared up in a number of Southern regions. Some Sung forces refused to surrender. In 1279, Ch'en Kuei-lung led remnants of the Sung troops, amounting to "several ten thousand men" according to the Chinese accounts, in Chiang-nan in a revolt against the Mongol forces. Two years elapsed before Khubilai and his soldiers crushed the rebellion, captured Ch'en, and beheaded (if we trust the Chinese histories) 20,000 of the rebel troops.[39] In 1284, a minor rebellion erupted in Kuang-tung, but only 10,000 or so men took part in the outbreak, which was quickly quelled. The next disturbance was not so easily suppressed. A rebel from Fukien led a more serious challenge to Khubilai's control in that region. One hundred thousand Mongol troops were needed to overwhelm these rebels and to assert Khubilai's domination over this area. This pacification of the rebels did not last long, for troublesome insurrections continued throughout Khubilai's reign. Many in the South were not reconciled to Mongol domination and persisted in resisting the foreigners. These continuing outbreaks compelled Khubilai in 1289 to prohibit ordinary people from Chiang-nan from possessing bows and arrows.[40] A decade after the submission of the South, Khubilai still found it necessary to eliminate as many weapons as possible from this so-called conquered territory. He was also forced to station garrison troops in the South, particularly in the cities.[41] Despite all this opposition, Khubilai is cited as lenient to his enemies.

According to the Chinese sources, he periodically released many of the captured rebel forces from his jails.

The Confucian scholar elite in the South was, as we have noted, ambivalent in its attitude toward cooperation with the Mongols. The intellectuals had the option of joining the Mongols and seeking to transform the so-called barbarians. Or, as loyalists, they could express their protonationalism by refusing to cooperate with Khubilai and his court. Opposing the Mongols on cultural or national grounds, they had a number of practical choices. Some retreated into their private activities, including painting, drama, and other pursuits. A few refused to serve the Mongols, feeling that the "barbarians" were uninterested in Chinese civilization and thought.[42] Others founded special academies to pursue their own intellectual interests while simply avoiding involvement with the Mongols.[43] Still others actively resisted the Mongols. In sum, though a few Southern Sung intellectuals served in responsible official positions for the Mongols, Khubilai was unable to gain the allegiance of some influential, notable scholars in the South.[44] Though he permitted the Southern Chinese intellectuals great leeway as long as they fulfilled their tax obligations, he did not have mastery over and loyalty from them to the degree that he had it in North China.[45]

THE GRAND CANAL

His efforts in the South having been partially stymied, Khubilai set about to fulfill the needs of his core territories. His most important concern was food supplies for the North, a perennial issue from the Sui dynasty (589–617) on. The North needed to import grain from the more fertile areas in the South. Having established his capital in Ta-tu and having organized an administration in that region, Khubilai was required to ensure a ready supply of grain for his new city. Boat transport from south to north was the best option, but two alternatives were possible. He could either transfer the grain along the eastern seacoast or he could send it via the Grand Canal, a time-honored route to the North. Each route had its proponents, and their differing proposals reveal some of the pressures on Khubilai and how he responded to these tensions in the last years of his reign.

With Khubilai's increased naval power and his support for foreign commerce, he would surely show interest in the sea route. Chu Ch'ing and Chang Hsüan, two Chinese pirates who had cooperated with Bayan in his campaigns against the Southern Sung, advocated the dispatch of rice by sea to the North.[46] In the winter of 1282, they were assigned the task of transporting substantial quantities of rice along the coast.[47] They departed from Yang-chou with one hundred and forty ships loaded with rice and sailed around the Shantung peninsula, arriving at their destination in the Northern port of Chih-ku by the spring of 1283.[48] Over 90 percent of the rice reached the North and only six ships were lost in the treacherous waters along the coast. Such a resounding success naturally improved the chances of securing Khubilai's support for the sea route. By 1284, Khubilai was calling for either the abolition of the government's Directorate-General of Grain Transportation (Ts'ao-yün ssu) he had established to explore the inland north-south routes or at the very least the reassignment to other positions of some of its officials.[49] Numerous court debates raged and intrigues of Byzantine complexity repeatedly surfaced before Khubilai issued an edict in which he relegated the inland waterways route to a lesser position. Khubilai was present at a few of the debates and asked some questions, but he does not seem to have played an active role in the discussions.

The sea route appeared thus to have emerged as the preferred means of transportation. In 1285, the two pirates Chu and Chang were granted a lucrative contract to bring the grain north from the South. They exploited their positions to obtain substantial profits, becoming "two of the wealthiest and most influential men in southeast China."[50] The court would probably not have objected to a degree of profiteering if sufficient grain had been received for the North, and in particular for the region around Ta-tu.[51] However, bad luck in the form of a typhoon that wrecked part of the two pirates' fleet and flooding in the North that contributed to poor harvests plagued Chu and Chang and provoked the court's temporary dissatisfaction with the maritime route.

Khubilai's chief minister, Sangha, later classified as a "villainous minister," was ultimately responsible for the emphasis on the inland waterways. He proposed the lengthening of the Grand Canal almost as far as Ta-tu. This project entailed the construction of a 135-mile-long canal from Ch'ing-ning to Lin-ch'ing in Shantung province; from Lin-ch'ing, goods could be transshipped on the Wei river to Chih-ku, which was a short distance from Ta-tu. With such a project, grain could be transported from the Yangtze directly to Khubilai's capital. Sangha's support meant that the project would be initiated and concluded expeditiously. By February of 1289, the extension was completed and the new canal, known as the Hui-t'ung, was opened to boat traffic.[52] But the expenses were enormous. With about three million laborers taking part, the construction entailed a government expenditure of vast sums of money. Even so, once the canal was built, maintenance was costly; it was, in fact, not done properly, and large vessels could not employ the route. The downfall and execution of Sangha (which shall be described later), the principal patron of the inland waterway, in August of 1291 was an additional blow. Without a strong advocate at court, the resources needed for proper maintenance would simply not be provided. Khubilai, as we shall note, was by this time in failing health and scarcely able to take part in court deliberations. Only a decisive and powerful minister could see to it that his projects were implemented. In any event, the staggering costs no doubt contributed to the fiscal problems plaguing the Mongol court in the 1280s.

The two routes for grain transportation were thus extremely expensive. On the one hand, the sea route entailed large payments to Chu Ch'ing and Chang Hsüan for the purchase of grain in the South and for the use of their ships. The extension of the Grand Canal, on the other hand, required huge initial expenses for construction and additional heavy costs for maintenance. Such expenses naturally exacerbated the financial tensions of the Mongol court and made Khubilai ever more dependent on his financial advisers.

THE FISCAL POLICIES OF LU SHIH-JUNG

One of these advisers was Lu Shih-jung, who is reviled in the Chinese accounts. As one of the "three villainous ministers," Lu was associated in the Yüan dynastic history with the despised financial administrator Aḥmad. The hated Muslim is credited with offering Lu a position in the tea administration of Kiangsi.[53] Lu did survive after Aḥmad's death and disgrace. In fact, he received a promotion rather than being punished for his association with Aḥmad. Aḥmad's old position in the Secretariat would now be shared by two men so as to prevent the reputed abuses associated with the Muslim financial administrator. The Mongol An-t'ung was appointed the head of the Office of the Right in the Secretariat, and Lu became the head of the Office of the Left, with jurisdiction over much of the fiscal administration in Khubilai's domain.[54] In this capacity, his principal concern was to increase the government's revenues in order to meet the mounting costs at court. One way was to augment the government's income from monopolies. Lu proposed that the licenses to salt merchants be made more expensive.[55] Similarly, he protested that rich households were evading the government's liquor monopoly and brewing their own wines.[56] He demanded that the government monopoly on liquor be reimposed, assuring the court a larger share of the profits. Foreign trade, he believed, was another lucrative source of income, and he wanted the Maritime Trade Superintendencies to secure a larger share of the profits of this seaborne commerce.[57] Together with the monopolies on goods, Lu imposed government control on copper coinage and on silver, confiscating the copper coinage of the Southern Sung, for example. He also encouraged the issuance of paper money, a policy that the Chinese accounts claim fueled the inflation that characterized Khubilai's last years.[58]

Lu had innumerable schemes to increase government revenues. One of them entailed the recruitment of idle Mongols into pastoral pursuits. Twenty percent of the products from the animals they cared for they would keep, and 80 percent would be used to clothe and feed the army. Lu also began to staff the tax offices of the government with merchants, but many of them were accused of exploiting the populace and profiting from their positions.[59]

Lu's economic programs engendered the same hostility as those of Aḥmad, his predecessor as financial administrator, and he received the same criticism that had earlier been directed at the feared and despised Central Asian Muslim. The Chinese sources accuse Lu of developing cliques within the government to support his policies. Like Aḥmad, he was accused of persecuting, hounding to death, and even executing his rivals and potential enemies. The accuracy of many of these charges is subject to dispute because the sources never give Lu's own version of events, only that of his opponents. In his defense it could be argued that like Aḥmad he simply attempted to raise funds desperately needed at court. Like Aḥmad, he was lambasted in the Chinese sources for his financial policies, and his efforts earned him the enmity of many of his fellow Chinese. His fate was sealed when Khubilai's son Chen-chin turned against him. Chen-chin, who had been one of Aḥmad's principal opponents, objected to Lu for the same reason that he opposed Aḥmad—he appeared to be exploiting the Chinese.[60] With Chen-chin's backing, the opposition to Lu swelled considerably until Khubilai had to dismiss him and then arrest him in May of 1285. His accusers charged him with profiteering, extorting funds from the people, and murdering some of his opponents. No one could save him at this point, and by the end of the year Khubilai had him executed.[61] His removal from office and his death may have eliminated what the Chinese perceived to be an exploiter. Unfortunately, however, they did nothing to alleviate the mounting fiscal problems of the court.

SANGHA AND BUDDHIST ABUSES

Sangha (in Chinese, Sang-ko), the last of the triumvirate of "villainous ministers," was also granted great authority by Khubilai.[62] Like Aḥmad, he derived from non-Chinese stock. His foreign origins did not endear him to the Chinese. Lu Shih-jung could at least seek to capitalize on his affinity with the people of China, but Sangha did not have the same option. He was thus in a more vulnerable position than Lu, whom he had supported. His ethnic origins are obscure. Historians have long assumed that he was a Uighur, though his biography in the Yüan dynastic history does not explicitly describe him as such.[63] The history does mention that he served as an interpreter of a variety of languages, including Tibetan. He may, in fact, have been, as a recent scholarly article by Luciano Petech suggests, a Tibetan whose family had assimilated some Uighur traits.

What is known of his early life and career also suggests a Tibetan origin. He was a student of Dam-pa Kun-dgaʿ-grags (1230–1303), a learned Tibetan who had been granted the title of State Preceptor.[64] After the completion of his studies with the Tibetan erudite, he joined the staff of the ʿPhags-pa lama as an interpreter. His talents were quickly recognized by the revered and influential lama, who repeatedly sent him on delicate missions to Khubilai. His successes enabled Sangha again and again to receive rewards and promotions. Khubilai apparently found Sangha to be capable and resourceful and decided to recruit him into government. Since the ʿPhags-pa lama wished to return to Tibet, Khubilai had an opportunity to appoint a new official, who would be stationed in Ta-tu and would oversee the areas formerly under the lama's sole jurisdiction. Some time before 1275, he assigned Sangha to be the head of the Tsung-chih yüan, the office in charge of Tibetan and Buddhist affairs.[65] Until the 1280s, Sangha appears to have been involved in Chinese matters only nominally. Aḥmad administered the financial affairs of China until his death in 1282, and Sangha confined himself to the limited areas under his jurisdiction. In 1280, for example, he left Ta-tu to lead an expedition to crush a rebellion in Tibet. The campaign was successful, and Sangha set about to consolidate Mongol control over Tibet. He stationed garrisons at various strategic locations in the capital and along the borders, and established an effective postal system to bring Tibet in closer touch with the rest of China.[66] Khubilai was no doubt impressed with Sangha's accomplishment in Tibet. When Sangha returned to China, Khubilai granted him ever-greater responsibilities.

With Aḥmad's death in 1282, a political vacuum was created, and Khubilai moved to fill it with Sangha. From 1282 to 1291, Sangha was the dominant figure in the government. As a result, he attracted much criticism from numerous officials and court advisers who resented his power. Even the Persian sources portray him in a harsh light. The Persian historian Rashīd al-Dīn, for example, accuses him of theft and of accepting bribes.[67] The Koreans accused Sangha of demanding Korean slave girls or concubines for his own household.[68] Numerous other aspersions on his character appear in the Chinese sources. Corruption, theft of Khubilai's and the state's property, and repeated efforts to satisfy his "disgusting" carnal appetites were the main criticisms of his private life. As with Aḥmad, it is difficult to judge the reliability of many of these accusations. Most were made some time after his downfall and execution, and some may have been later fabrications by his enemies. The incident that led to his downfall, the discovery of some purloined pearls, appears to be suspicious. The same anecdote was also used against Aḥmad. In the attack against each man, a search of the residence after the leader's disgrace and fall was an integral component. In Sangha's case, pearls were found; in Aḥmad's, it was stolen jewelry. Both incidents are highly improbable. In any case, why would a canny man like Sangha or Aḥmad leave incriminating evidence lying around his house?

Some of the most prominent men of the 1280s hurled damning accusations against Sangha. The renowned painter and official Chao Meng-fu opposed him and warned Khubilai of his nefarious intentions.[69] His fiercest opponent was the Minister of the Right, An-t'ung, who had also fervently battled against Sangha's ally and protégé Lu Shih-jung. An-t'ung, descended from one of the oldest and most distinguished Mongol families, resented Sangha's ascendancy in the government; as Minister of the Right he continually sought to undermine his authority. The tensions between the two officials intensified as Sangha proposed new ideas and pressed for their implementation. Sangha could not, however, assert his supremacy without having a more imposing title than director of the Tsung-chih yüan (Bureau of General Regulation), which in 1288 had a change of name to Hsüan-cheng yüan (Bureau of Buddhist and Tibetan Affairs). Khubilai now revived the title that Aḥmad had earlier attempted to claim as his own, but doing so drew so much opposition that he was forced to abandon the effort. In March of 1287, Khubilai appointed Sangha as Vice Minister of the Supreme Secretariat, and by December had promoted him to the Minister of the Right of that same body.[70] With this new position, Sangha would no longer need to abase himself in front of An-t'ung. He had his own secure post and could not be intimidated. This new position also enabled him to exercise more authority over all the ministries in the government.

Which of Sangha's policies attracted such hostility? One was his active support for men of the so-called Western Regions in China. He vowed to protect and advance the interests of the non-Chinese at court and throughout China. He promoted, for example, the founding of an academy for the teaching of the Muslim languages, and in 1289 Khubilai decreed the establishment of the National College for the Study of Muslim Script.[71] Sangha repeatedly served as a patron to Uighur scholars and protected them from hostile Chinese. He is credited, in particular, with sheltering a number of Uighur painters at court.[72] As we shall note later, he also convinced Khubilai to halt a temporary and hastily organized anti-Muslim campaign in the early 1280s.[73] Again he appeared as the protector of the foreigners in China, a policy that did not endear him to the Chinese.

His financial policies, however, drew the sharpest reactions. Like his predecessors Aḥmad and Lu Shih-jung, he was constantly under pressure to raise additional funds for the court. Its revenue needs continued to be great, particularly with its military invasions in Southeast Asia and with a campaign against the rebellious Mongol prince Nayan in Manchuria. One way of increasing government income was to promote commerce and to tax some of the profits collected by the merchants.[74] He precipitated hostility by his call for higher taxes. He wished to increase taxes on salt, tea, and liquor among other goods, and a dramatic increase in the prices of these products surely generated even more antagonism against Sangha and his policies and led to accusations of his exploitativeness and prof-iteering. He was charged with seeking private profit rather than additional income for the state.[75] But his most notorious economic program entailed a reform of the paper currency. The system of paper money that was introduced at the beginning of Khubilai's reign was not in balance in the 1280s. The amount of paper money issued annually from 1260 to the mid-1270s remained relatively stable, but then, with the wars against the Sung and with the Japanese invasions, court expenditures rose dramatically, compelling a proportional growth in the printing of paper currency. A catastrophic inflation threatened to engulf the economy.[76] In April of 1287, to cope with this potentially devastating fiscal crisis, Sangha persuaded Khubilai to replace the existing paper money with an entirely new unit known as the *Chih-yüan ch'ao*, which was named after Khubilai's reign title, Chih-yüan. The old currency was converted on a five-to-one basis with the Chih-yüan notes, temporarily curbing the inflation afflicting the economy.[77] In the initial stage, the number of paper notes in circulation declined substantially, from 4,770,000 *ting* to 1,345,000 *ting*. Yet those Chinese who were forced to exchange their now less valuable old notes at less than satisfactory rates were incensed by what they perceived to be a decline in their net worth.

Like Aḥmad and Lu Shih-jung, Sangha was accused of cronyism and of persecution of his opponents. He gave many like-minded supporters promotions in their government positions, a not unnatural strategy for an official facing such relentless opposition. He executed a Censor named Wang Liang-pi, who, he claimed, had conspired against him. He intimidated and persecuted an official named Mai-shu-ting into committing suicide. Then he tried to replace these and other men whom he hounded or dismissed or executed with his own allies. Nearly all of his candidates for positions of authority were non-Chinese. He wanted the Persian Sha-pu-ting to be a prominent official in the province of Chiang-che, to supervise the coastal trade.[78] Later the Chinese sources would insinuate that he demanded and received bribes from these men to promote their careers. There is no independent way of verifying these accusations against Sangha, which blackened his reputation among the Chinese and diverted Chinese animosity from the Mongols and Khubilai to the khan's (literally) foreign ministers.[79]

Sangha's reputation among the Chinese was damaged particularly by his apparent sanction for the pillaging of the tombs of the Southern Sung emperors. Khubilai had welcomed and protected the royal family and ensured that his subordinates did not harm these former enemies. He wished in this way to ingratiate himself with the Chinese of the South. A repressive policy against them or harsh treatment of their rulers would not lead to amicable relations. The actions of a Buddhist monk named Yang Lien-chen-chia, supported by his superior Sangha, were not conducive to the improvement of relations between the khan and his officials and his Chinese subjects.

Yang, who derived from the Western Regions and may have been of Tibetan origin, had been appointed Supervisor of the Buddhist Teachings in Chiang-nan (Chiang-nan tsung-she chang shih-chiao)—or really in South China—almost as soon as the Sung dynasty had been toppled. In this office, he served under the jurisdiction of Sangha, who headed the Office of Buddhist and Tibetan Affairs for all of China. Yang could not have committed the outrageous deeds that he did without the support, or at least the acquiescence, of Sangha. Yang was interested in the aggrandizement of the Buddhists' wealth and power. With Sangha's sanction, he set about enriching the Buddhists by any means at his disposal. Since he had jurisdiction over a recently subjugated territory, he had considerable leeway to do as he chose.

Yang's first projects were the construction and renovation of Buddhist monasteries and temples in South China. Buddhist temples, formerly converted into Taoist monasteries by staunch Taoists, now reverted to their original functions, and Yang provided funds for their restoration. He also supplied the financial support for the renovations of the T'ien-i temple and the Lung-hua temple in the old Southern Sung capital.[80] The Sung rulers had used the Lung-hua temple for the ritual sacrifices to Heaven and Earth, and the Confucian Chinese in the South were naturally offended by its conversion to a Buddhist establishment. All in all, Yang is credited with restoring over thirty temples in the period from 1285 to 1287. Since many of the temples had been employed by other religions or cults, their conversion to Buddhist temples generated hostility.

Even more upsetting to the Chinese were the methods Yang used to raise funds for the construction and repair of these buildings. In 1285, he ordered his men to ransack the tombs of the Sung royal family for the valuables buried with the emperors and empresses.[81] His subordinates plundered 101 temples and eventually extracted 1,700 ounces of gold, 6,800 ounces of silver, 111 jade vessels, 9 jade belts, 152 miscellaneous shells, and 50 ounces of big pearls.[82] Yang used these precious goods to pay for the erection and restoration of the Buddhist temples. Some of the buildings in the tombs were razed, and in their place were erected Buddhist temples such as the T'ai-ning. The government even provided the building materials, including the wood. Yang then attended to the Sung palaces, which he quickly renovated and made available to the Buddhists. Some of the Sung buildings were turned into Buddhist temples and stupas. Yang justified what appeared to be desecration of the Sung tombs and palaces by pointing out that the Sung rulers had originated the practice. The Sung court had, for example, torn down the original T'ai-ning temple in the town of Shao-hsing and on its ruins had built a mausoleum for the Ning-tsung emperor. Yang was, in his view, simply restoring the site to its pre-Sung conditions. The Sung, not he, had caused the real damage.

Yang devised new economic arrangements for the construction and maintenance of the temples. To build the temples, he employed forced laborers. To provide revenues for maintenance Yang expropriated land and laborers from landowners and turned them over to the temples. The land was removed from the tax rolls, and the tenants who farmed the land on behalf of the Buddhist establishments also received tax exemptions.[83] The Southern land-owners were infuriated by what seemed to them to be the high-handed expropriation of their land; they were similarly galled by the tax exemption granted to the temples. There were accusations that Yang himself benefited enormously from these policies. One account written after his downfall asserted that he commandeered or accepted as bribes 116,200 *ting* of paper money and 23,000 *mou* of land.[84] The same source reveals that Yang removed many individuals from the tax rolls; then, in return for a bribe, he registered them as tenants on the lands of the Buddhist temples. However, since his detractors and enemies were responsible for these accusations, their credibility is suspect.

Similarly, some of the other aspersions on his character must be evaluated with caution. He is reported to have demanded that the Chinese in the South provide him with beautiful young women in payment for whatever service they wished from him. The evidence for this claim is that he had several wives and concubines. Again, the case against him is not impressive, as it derives from the official histories.[85] A more serious transgression, also somewhat suspect, was the desecration of the corpses of the Sung royal family. The body of one of the last emperors, which was still well preserved, was allegedly exhumed and hung from a tree for three days. The decapitated body was then burned, and, as a final indignity, the bones were buried once

again but amidst the bones of horses and cows. The Chinese condemned such disrespect.[86] The whole incident could not have provided a more perfect pretext for the Southern Chinese, who despised
the intrusions of such foreigners as the Buddhist lamas, to vent their
spleen. Similarly, Yang offered a perfect target for their aggression. It
is difficult to determine how much credence should be given to these
allegations. Yang clearly approved of the conversion of the Sung
palaces and tombs into Buddhist sites, and he doubtless sanctioned
the pillaging of some of the tombs, but there is no direct proof that he
supported and participated in the desecration of the corpse of the
Sung emperor. Why deliberately and needlessly provoke the wrath of
the Southern Chinese with an act that violated Chinese sensibilities?
Such a gratuitous deed seems senseless and scarcely credible. It seems
likelier that the desecration was attributed to Yang after his downfall
and served to justify the campaign of vilification leveled against him.

Yang's more positive traits and accomplishments can be gleaned
only through inference. He was a devout Buddhist who tried to
promote the interests of his religion in what he perceived to be the
hostile environment of South China. There can hardly be any doubt
about the sincerity of his religious views. Even his detractors acknowledge that "Yang might have seen himself as a missionary and a
faithful follower of his creed, according to which the building of
temples and stupas were acts of religious merit. But, being unfamiliar
with Chinese ways and with Chinese ideas of loyalty and piety, he
inevitably and inadvertently antagonized the population in Chiang-
nan." [87] Buddhism did indeed flourish in the South during his era. For
example, he provided the resources for the Fei-lai Feng rock carvings
in Hangchow, one of the most impressive Buddhist sites in China. By
1291, there were 213,148 Buddhist monks and nuns and 42,318
temples and monasteries in the country, due partly to his patronage.[88]

Yet his abuses, of which there were no doubt some but not as many
as the Chinese accounts would lead us to believe, rankled on the
Southern Chinese and reflected on his patron Sangha. Both men were,
from the standpoint of the Chinese, exploitative and oppressive. The
Chinese sources repeatedly reviled them for their financial and personal misdeeds, and the accusations against Sangha by both Chinese
and Mongol officials finally compelled action. On March 16, 1291,
Khubilai relieved Sangha, his most important official, of his responsibilities, stripped him of his ranks and privileges, and placed him
under arrest. Khubilai delayed a judgment on his previously trust-

worthy minister while court officials debated Sangha's fate. They did so and quickly imposed a death sentence. Sangha was executed on August 17.[89] Some scholars have suggested that Khubilai tried to delay or even prevent the execution of his long-time minister and associate. A later Tibetan source asserts that he had grave misgivings about the death of Sangha: "The emperor [Khubilai] said: 'Now that my Sang-ko has gone this causes me great sorrow.'"[90]

Though the Chinese sources overstate the case against the "three villainous ministers"—Aḥmad, Lu Shih-jung, and Sangha— Khubilai's standing with his Chinese subjects was damaged by his choice of these officials. In the early years of his reign, he had recruited numerous Chinese advisers, and some of the top officials at court and thus those with whom he had frequent dealings were Confucians. But by the 1280s the deaths of some of his leading Confucian counselors and his more pressing financial problems made him turn primarily to non-Chinese ministers. Even the Chinese officials, such as Lu Shih-jung, met with a hostile reception. The tasks these ministers faced in the 1280s were difficult and thankless, for they had to raise additional revenues for the state's needs. Whatever they did would have alienated the Chinese because they needed to impose stiff taxes on the populace. It appeared that the dynasty was careening out of control. One minister after another took charge, and each became the virtual ruler of the country. Yet within a few years each was challenged, accused of serious crimes, and eventually either executed or murdered.[91] Was Khubilai, in fact, in charge? Was he aware of the empire's affairs and of his subordinates' actions? He seemed less and less in touch with the politics of his domains, pursuing policies that were on occasion diametrically opposed to those he had upheld earlier.

KHUBILAI'S PROBLEMS WITH RELIGIONS

The religious toleration that had been a cornerstone of his policies and a vital factor in the Mongols' success appeared to be abandoned. Problems with the religions of China intensified. It may seem surprising, for example, that Khubilai began in the late 1270s to issue anti-Muslim regulations. There were some justifications for these new policies. The Muslim Khaidu repeatedly threatened China's northwestern frontier lands. Farther to the west, Muslim states had thwarted Khubilai's Mongol allies and constantly challenged the

Mongol governors of Persia. The Muslims had also generated hostility in China itself. Khubilai's Chinese advisers had repeatedly denounced the ambition and ruthlessness of the leading Muslim officials. Essays and popular anecdotes satirizing Muslim avarice, vulgarity, and "strangeness" started to appear at this time.[92] Khubilai himself may have been concerned about the growing power of the Muslims in government. His own grandson, Prince Ananda, had been raised in a Muslim household, and as an adult had, according to Rashīd al-Dīn, converted most of the 150,000 troops under his command to Islam.[93]

The Christian official known in the Chinese texts as Ai-hsüeh instigated additional anti-Muslim sentiment. Having held positions in the bureaus of astronomy and medicine, he had some influence in the Yüan government.[94] Rashīd al-Dīn accused him of inciting slaves and laborers in Muslim households to bring false charges against their masters. And, according to Rashīd, Ai-hsüeh himself falsely accused Maulānā Burhān al-Dīn Bukhārī, one of the leaders of the Muslims in China, of a crime (unspecified by Rashīd) and had him exiled.[95]

Rashīd also asserts that Khubilai, abetted by Ai-hsüeh and by his Chinese advisers, began in 1279 to adopt a harsher policy toward the Muslims. Late in that year, Muslim merchants from Central Asia arrived in court to offer gerfalcons and an eagle as tribute. Khubilai invited them to a banquet, but because the animals had not been slaughtered in the Muslim fashion they refused to eat the meat. Incensed by this refusal, Khubilai issued an edict in January of 1280 prohibiting the Muslim method of slaughtering sheep and imposing the death penalty on transgressors.[96] Khubilai demanded strict adherence to the *Jasagh* regulations on slaughtering. With encouragement from Ai-hsüeh and his followers, Khubilai also forbade the practice of circumcision. Finally, Rashīd concludes his list of accusations by noting that Ai-hsüeh and other Christians "sought to attack them [Muslims] by representing to the Qa'an that there was a verse in the Qur'an which ran: 'Kill the polytheists, all of them.'" Obviously disturbed by this quotation from the Muslim Holy Book, Khubilai asked his Muslim advisers whether they considered him a polytheist. A Muslim sage from Samarkand finally calmed Khubilai by responding, "Thou art not a polytheist since thou writest the name of the Great God at the head of thy *yarlighs* [edicts]. Such a one is a polytheist who does not recognize God, and attributes companions to Him, and rejects the great God."[97] Khubilai was apparently satisfied with this response, but, according to Rashīd, he was not deterred from his policy of restricting the Muslims.

Whether all the specific incidents recounted by Rashīd actually took place is difficult to tell, but the Chinese sources confirm that the court issued a series of anti-Muslim edicts. On January 27, 1280, it imposed the death penalty for anyone slaughtering an animal in the Muslim way.[98] Earlier it had levied taxes and demanded corvée labor from the Muslims.[99] Khubilai was apparently concerned about an overly powerful Muslim presence in the government and about a possible rebellion precipitated by the exactions of the Muslims. Khubilai's repressive edicts thus were inspired more by political considerations than by hatred of Islam.

The anti-Muslim policy persisted until 1287. In that year, Sangha pleaded with Khubilai to reverse his policy toward the Muslims. He argued that "all the Muslim merchants have departed from hence [i.e. China] and no merchants are coming from the Muslim countries; . . . and all this because for the past seven years they have not slaughtered sheep. If it be so commanded, the merchants will come and go."[100] If the court changed its policies, the revenues derived from Muslim merchants would increase. Rashīd asserts that several Muslim leaders bribed Sangha to champion their cause. Whatever Sangha's motivation, Khubilai relented and dispensed with the anti-Muslim regulations; however, one incident recounted in the Chinese histories illustrates Khubilai's less than welcoming attitude toward some Muslim traders. In 1293, a Muslim merchant sought to sell pearls to Khubilai, but the Great Khan declined this offer, noting that his money could be better spent to "relieve the people."[101]

Yet Khubilai was not wholly consistent, for he did not forswear the recruitment of Muslims for his government. Undogmatic Muslims with administrative or fiscal skills were not ignored or discriminated against. Khubilai did, for example, select the Central Asian Muslim, Saiyid Ajall Shams al-Dīn, to govern the newly conquered territory of Yünnan. This region, now a province in Southwest China, was the only land in China to be ruled by a Muslim. The motives underlying this appointment are puzzling. Perhaps Khubilai looked upon Yünnan as an important thoroughfare in trade with Burma and India, and, since the Muslims were the most significant merchants in the Mongol dominions, a Muslim governor for Yünnan appeared logical. Or he may have perceived of Yünnan as a fine territory in which to settle some of the Muslims whom the Mongols had moved eastward from Central Asia and Persia. Yünnan was still sparsely inhabited, and its inhabitants were primarily illiterate non-Chinese peoples. Khubilai may have decided that it was more sensible to encourage the Muslims to colonize the region than to try to colonize with Chinese, who were more hostile to Mongol rule. Or the court may have simply delegated governing power to Saiyid Ajall because it considered him a loyal, trustworthy subject.

When he was appointed governor of Yünnan in 1274, Saiyid's first objectives were to strengthen the military and economic control of the Yüan dynasty in the region. Before taking up his post, he studied Yünnan's topography, economy, and customs. Once he reached the region, he sought to gain the confidence of the native non-Chinese peoples. Though he established guards and garrisons throughout the region, he instructed his soldiers not to provoke the "barbarians." When several of his officers deliberately attacked some native people, he executed them.[102] With such fair and even-handed policies, he quickly won over much of the non-Chinese population. He also moved rapidly to create a postal system for communications, defense, and commerce. Yünnan prospered under his policies. He encouraged the growth of agriculture, ordering his men to teach farming and forestry to the local people. Before his arrival, the people of Yünnan "had no rice of any variety, no mulberry trees, and no hemp."[103] Probably Saiyid's most significant contribution to the economy was his promotion of irrigation projects in the Kun-ming region, some of which were still used in the twentieth century. He built reservoirs and dams, so that floods and droughts would not impair the farming season.[104] His Muslim subjects improved conditions of trade, and he permitted the use of the traditional cowry shells as a medium of exchange in order to inspire the local people to engage in commerce. Finally, he lightened the tax and corvée burdens on the population, making it easier for them to accept Mongol rule.

Despite his own background, Saiyid did not impose Islam on Yünnan. Had Saiyid been a militant Muslim, Khubilai would surely not have entrusted him with the responsibility of governing. Saiyid introduced Chinese customs and culture in Yünnan. He promoted the use of Chinese marital and funeral ceremonies, built Confucian schools, and made available copies of the Confucian classics. Though he constructed two mosques, he also built a Confucian temple and a Buddhist monastery.[105] In short, he intended to sinicize, not to Islamicize, Yünnan, and the same was true for those of his sons who resided and became officials in Yünnan. Saiyid died in 1279 (and in 1297 was posthumously awarded the title of Hsien-yang wang, or Prince of Hsien-yang). Two of his sons, Nāṣir al-Dīn and Mas'ūd, succeeded him as governors of Yünnan,[106] and they continued their father's policies in the area. Nāṣir al-Dīn, in addition, participated in military campaigns in Burma and Annam and served as an official in Shensi and at the capital.[107] In April of 1292, however, he was accused of stealing 130,000 *ting* of paper money and then executed.[108] His four brothers were not implicated and continued to hold influential positions in Yünnan, Kwangtung, and Kiangsi, where they received numerous honors and rewards.

Despite Saiyid's accomplishments and the trust Khubilai showed in him and his sons, the Great Khan's relations with the Muslims remained unsettled and somewhat hostile throughout the 1280s. The earlier, balanced relationship was rendered askew. In former times, Khubilai had taken great pains to ensure no officially sanctioned discrimination against the Muslims because he realized that serious difficulties would ensue if he alienated the small but influential Muslim minority in China. In the 1280s this tolerant and more balanced view was suddenly overturned, as Khubilai temporarily subverted one of his cardinal precepts.

Similarly, a crisis bedeviled his relations with the Buddhists and Taoists. The Buddhist-Taoist debates of 1258, over which Khubilai had presided, had presumably concluded the strife that had plagued the leadership of these religions. However, the underlying hostility repeatedly surfaced, and the incorporation of the Southern Sung intensified the animosity. The Taoists, instead of abiding by the decisions made at the 1258 debates, challenged the Buddhists at every opportunity.

A series of incidents involving the two groups culminated in a major confrontation in 1281. As early as 1276 Khubilai's son Manggala had cautioned the Taoists not to "commit unlawful deeds, saying they have a writ." [109] The Taoists apparently ignored this warning, for late in 1280 they, according to the Chinese accounts, deliberately started a fire at the Ch'ang-ch'un Taoist temple in Ta-tu and tried to place the blame on a Buddhist monk named Kuang Yüan.[110] Khubilai assigned several officials to investigate this suspicious fire, and they reputedly uncovered the Taoists' scheme. The Great Khan did not show any mercy toward the guilty. Two of the Taoists were executed; one had his nose and ears chopped off; and six others were exiled.[111] This incident prompted the Buddhists to seek government investigations of other Taoist abuses and excesses. The court discovered, according to the Buddhist sources, that the Taoist texts that had been banned since 1258 were still circulating and that the printing blocks for these works had been preserved. Khubilai was enraged by this evidence of gross insubordination and illegality. Late in 1281, he ordered that all Taoist texts, other than Lao Tzu's *Tao te ching*, be burned and that the printing blocks be totally and irrevocably smashed and obliterated.[112] Similarly, he imposed restrictions on Taoist charms, incantations, and magic. The Taoists sold charms and amulets that promised enormous profits for merchants, longevity for men, happy marriages for men and women, and a bountiful posterity for all families.[113] Khubilai, who disapproved of these claims, forbade the sale of the charms. Simultaneously, he forced some of the Taoist monks to convert to Buddhism. Finally, he dispatched emissaries from among the Buddhists to enforce these regulations.

Khubilai's policies did resolve his difficulties with the Taoists, though the Buddhists, who were now dominant, continued, as we have already noted and will document even further, to create problems for him and for the dynasty. Khubilai had not meant to suppress Taoism: his principal objective was to curb Taoist abuses. To manifest his support for the more responsible and less belligerent Taoists, he had deliberately recruited their leaders to participate in the investigation of their co-religionists. Chang Tsung-yen, the T'ien-shih or "Celestial Master" (often inaccurately referred to in the West as the "Taoist Pope"), was part of the delegation that pored over the Taoist books and decided which were forged and ought to be destroyed. Khubilai appointed Chang as the supervisor of Taoist affairs in South China.[114] On several occasions, Khubilai sent gifts of silk and incense to the Taoist master in order to keep on good terms with this important leader. In return, Chang offered sacrifices for the dead, prayed for an end to a particularly severe drought, and practiced magic to change the weather or to cure illnesses.[115]

The Buddhists, who had gained a smashing victory in 1281, gloated over their defeat of their religious rivals. Apparently they also abused their power. They had been favored by Khubilai from the early days of his reign, and after 1281 the Buddhist monks became increasingly assertive, even brazen. The Chinese sources offer detailed descriptions of the abuses of such Buddhists as Sangha and Yang Lien-chen-chia. Throughout the 1280s, the Buddhists acquired more and more wealth, land, and authority.[116] As they persisted in their acquisitiveness, they began to alienate the Chinese, who saw them as foreigners. The Mongols, as foreigners, also were tarnished by their deference toward and support of the Buddhists, particularly those from Tibet or from outside of China.[117]

The conquest of the Southern Sung in 1279 was the high point of Khubilai's reign. But there was considerable hostility toward him in the South. Despite his solicitousness and his economic support, some Chinese scholar-officials in the South refused to cooperate with him. The 1280s witnessed a series of domestic disasters. Khubilai's need for additional revenues caused him to depend on three chief ministers—Ahmad, Lu Shih-jung, and Sangha—who alienated the Chinese through their exactions. Khubilai, in each case, recognized the opposition of the scholar-officials and eventually dismissed, became disenchanted with, or executed all three ministers. Chinese hostility also contributed to a short-lived and damaging anti-Muslim policy. Khubilai's support of the Buddhists apparently gave rise to some haughty and exploitative behavior by its leadership. Moreover, none of the new leaders—the three ministers or the Buddhists—were able to resolve Khubilai's fiscal problems. Also by the 1280s, the most influential of the Chinese Confucians who had served as his advisers since the 1250s had died, making him ever more dependent on non-Chinese for counsel and creating more tension between him and the Southern Chinese in particular.

CHAPTER EIGHT

Decline of an Emperor

In the last years of his reign, Khubilai was afflicted with personal losses. His favorite wife, Chabi, died in 1281, and his favorite son and designated successor, Chen-chin, five years later. Perhaps as a reaction to these personal tragedies, he began to drink heavily and to eat voraciously. He grew obese and suffered from ailments associated with alcoholism. His personal difficulties were compounded by failures in some of his policies.

Khubilai's most conspicuous failures in this period centered on his foreign expeditions. He had suffered defeats before on foreign campaigns, but the 1280s and early 1290s were replete with disasters. Though his forces had been stymied earlier in Japan in 1274, this could be explained away as an isolated incident, brought about by an unforeseen natural catastrophe. The later defeats reflected a change in policy that could not so readily be justified. The new policy reversed traditional Mongol views of expansionism. The Mongol military had never attempted overseas expansion. The Mongols lacked expertise in naval warfare. Moreover, they had no experience in fighting in lands in the southern regions of Asia. Fighting in this unfamiliar terrain, they were confronted with tremendous difficulties.

Khubilai's sudden outbursts against foreign territories make sense only in the context of the domestic failures of the 1280s. His difficulties within China presaged similar catastrophes abroad. A lack of control characterized both domestic and foreign policies. The sure executive authority that Khubilai had exercised seems to have dissipated. It became increasingly difficult to achieve stability as the court careened from one reckless policy to another. Ill-considered decisions tended to be the rule rather than the exception. The justification for some of these dramatic turn-arounds lacks credibility. The sources imply that the extraordinary naval expeditions were mounted simply to punish foreigners who harmed Mongol envoys. There was clearly much more at stake in these expeditions. Khubilai's need to assert his legitimacy after his unorthodox accession to the throne prompted him, on occasion, to initiate foolhardy foreign ventures. His insecurity inspired repeated attempts to coerce foreign potentates to acknowledge his superiority, a means by which he could impress his own subjects. As both the Emperor of China and the Khan of Khans, he encountered relentless pressure to prove his worth, his virtue, and his acumen by the incorporation of additional territory into his domains. Finally, the crass desire for tangible economic benefits from conquest was certainly a motive. Yet with all of this, the ill-conceived campaigns of the 1280s and 1290s hardly added to Khubilai's luster as Khan of Khans.

KAMIKAZE

The most prominent of these expeditions was directed at Japan. The Regent for the Japanese Shōgun Hōjō Tokimune, acting for his Emperor, had repeatedly spurned Khubilai's overtures for the creation of a sound relationship as defined by the Mongols. The Mongol invasion of 1274, which was a response to these rebuffs, had failed abysmally. In 1275, trying to avoid the necessity of organizing another assault on Japan, Khubilai sent another embassy demanding the Emperor's and the Shōgun's peaceful submission. The Japanese responded by executing the unfortunate envoys and by preparing their defenses for an anticipated Mongol attack.[1] The Shōgun transferred a large contingent of samurai south to the island of Kyūshū, where the Mongols would have to land, and furnished them with the supplies they needed to repel the invaders. Probably their major defense effort was to erect a stone wall along Hakata Bay, stretching from the coastal town of Hakozaki through Hakata and somewhat past Imazu, a construction project that took five years to complete yet would afford valuable protection against the first waves of an assault. On the other hand, as one historian of Japan has remarked, the building of the wall was "certain to come to the knowledge of the invaders and cause them to look for other landing places along the coast, from which they could turn Japanese positions behind the wall."[2] But at least the central points along Hakata Bay were well defended. Moreover, the Japanese warriors were mobile, allowing their leaders to shift them quickly to whatever region the Mongol troops landed. Having received a seven-year respite after the first Mongol invasion, the Japanese used the time to design a formidable, though not impregnable, defense.

Khubilai had not deliberately granted them seven years to prepare for an invasion. He was at first diverted by his campaign against the Southern Sung. Only after the drowning of the last pretender to the Sung throne in 1279 could Khubilai focus his attention on the subjugation of the Japanese. Moreover, the Koreans, who were vital in any planned campaign against the Japanese, needed to recuperate from the 1274 expedition, which had devastated the Korean economy. Not only had the Mongols commandeered vast quantities of grain, reducing the supply for the native inhabitants, but they had also conscripted many adult Korean males for service in the expedition, leaving few able-bodied men to till the soil. Thus, grain was in short supply, and Khubilai needed to send periodic supplies of food to Korea; even as late as 1280 he offered relief supplies of grain to his neighbors.[3] But despite these problems, Khubilai was determined to attack Japan, an act that proved to be a disastrous miscalculation.

By 1280, Khubilai was ready to launch his invasion. He began to recruit the troops and gather the supplies he needed for the campaign. In 1279, he had sent a final embassy to persuade the Japanese to relent. Instead, the Shōgun, claiming that the embassy was composed of spies, beheaded the hapless envoys.[4] Khubilai responded by mounting a massive retaliatory expedition. By the early spring of 1280, plans for the invasion were well under way. The leadership of the expedition was carefully balanced—with one Mongol, one Chinese, and one Korean. The Korean, Hong Tagu, would serve as the admiral of the campaign because the king of Korea insisted on indigenous leadership for the Korean sailors in the navy. Khubilai selected Fan Wen-hu, the Southern Sung general who had earlier submitted, as the Chinese leader for the expedition, and Hsin-tu as Fan's Mongol co-leader.[5] By the end of the year, Khubilai had assigned 100,000 troops to be placed under Fan's and Hsin-tu's command. He also supplied them with the paper money and the armor needed for the expedition. The Korean king provided 10,000 troops, 15,000 sailors, 900 boats, and reserves of grain.[6] In gratitude for this assistance, Khubilai specifically instructed his own soldiers not to harass the Koreans while traversing their lands en route to the seacoast to embark for the attack. In the following year, Khubilai had supplemented his earlier supplies to the troops with lavish donations including paper money, armor, and bows and arrows.[7] The Fukien Maritime Trade Superintendent, P'u Shou-keng, provided the single discordant note. He remarked that the Mongols had demanded that he and his people build two hundred ships. In fact, only fifty boats were constructed. Two hundred ships, he averred, was simply beyond their means.[8] His implied criticism of the Mongols' immoderate demands for ships was the first of many such complaints about planned invasions of Japan.

The Yüan military leaders had organized a two-pronged assault on the Japanese islands. 40,000 troops from North China, transported in Korean ships, were to link up on the island of Iki with 100,000 forces who had departed from Ch'üan-chou. From there, they would jointly attack the rest of Japan. According to the Chinese accounts, there were premonitions that the expedition would not go well. The omens included the sighting of a serpent at sea and the smell of sulphur that emanated from the sea water.[9] And indeed the plans for the expedition went awry from the start. The various commanders apparently argued among themselves. The troops from the South, in Chinese ships, were delayed because their larger numbers required more sophisticated logistical support. The ships from the North, which had Korean commanders, waited for a time, but finally, despairing of "the arrival of the main body of the Chinese fleet," they attacked and occupied Iki on June 10.[10] Within two weeks, they headed for the main island of Kyūshū. They landed near Manakata, just north of the wall the Japanese had laboriously constructed as their defense perimeter. Meanwhile the Southern Chinese forces had concluded their preparations, and, having learned of their compatriots' landing, they decided to link up with the smaller force on Kyūshū. They landed on the southern part of Kyūshū and intended to fight their way northward to rendezvous with the other Yüan forces. With such a powerful military machine and with such momentum, success ought to have been within their grasp.

Yet the expedition failed miserably. Through August, the Japanese soldiers were able to prevent the Mongol-led forces, both from the South and from the North, from breaching the defenses afforded by the wall. The Yüan troops' own deficiencies contributed to the surprisingly stiff resistance the Japanese mounted against them. Ten-

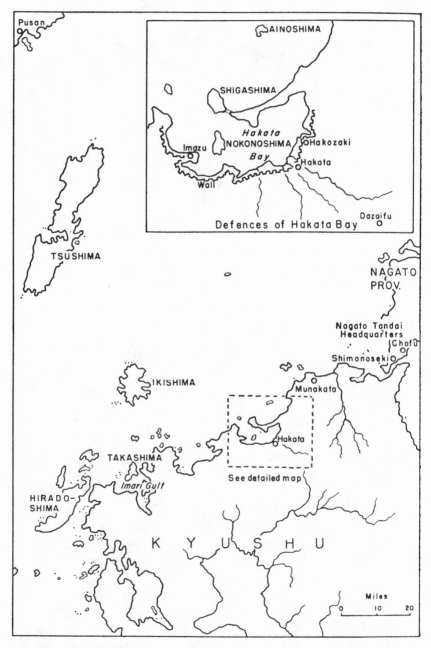

3.   Mongol Invasions of Japan. From George Sansom, *A History of Japan to 1336*, 446. Courtesy of Stanford University Press.

14.   Mongol Invasion of Japan. Painting from Japanese Imperial Collection.

sions between the Mongol commanders and the Chinese leaders weakened the expeditionary force. The Chinese troops, who comprised the vast majority of the soldiers, had little stake in the combat and did not try to put up a strong fight. And, from the time that they landed on Kyūshū, they found themselves vulnerable, without protection from their enemies or from the elements. They were out in the open without a castle, a stronghold, or a town to provide adequate defense and from which they could make forays against the enemy.[11] Thus, they made little headway against the Japanese. The two armies fought for almost two months, but no victor emerged.

A natural catastrophe interceded to dash the Mongol hopes for victory. On August 15 and 16, a typhoon, a typical occurrence of late summer in East Asia, struck the coast of Kyūshū. The Korean sailors, who sensed that a storm was in the offing, tried to head for the open seas and away from danger, but their efforts were futile. One-third of the 40,000 Northern soldiers perished, and more than half of the 100,000 Southern troops died while trying to escape. The soldiers who were stranded on Kyūshū were slaughtered or captured or drowned when they sought to flee on the small vessels that remained near the shore.[12]

To the Japanese, the typhoon was no accident. It was a divine wind (kamikaze) sent by the gods to save Japan, for their land was divinely protected. The failure of the invasion gave rise to exaggerated Japanese ethnocentric views. To the Japanese, the lesson was that the gods would never allow Japan's enemies to conquer and occupy their territory. For the Mongols and for Khubilai, the defeat was a devastating shock. Khubilai had never suffered such a disastrous loss.

Khubilai did not learn his lesson, however; angered by this humiliating loss, he doggedly proceeded with plans for a third campaign against the Japanese. In 1283, he ordered merchants in Southern China to build ships for the expedition.[13] By 1285, he was recruiting the Jurchens of Manchuria to contribute to the campaign by building two hundred vessels.[14] Later in the same year, Khubilai demanded that the Koreans provide large quantities of rice for the attack.[15] Almost as soon as he started to exact supplies and ships, he encountered opposition. In 1283, the Southern Chinese merchants objected to the burden of having to build five hundred boats for the expedition. In 1285 and early 1286, Khubilai received several reports from his advisers, who sought to dissuade him from attacks on Japan.[16] Finally, in 1286, he yielded to overwhelming opposition, and the planned campaign was aborted.[17]

Yet the campaign had caused considerable damage. The failures shattered the Mongols' mantle of invincibility in East Asia. Khubilai's subjects noticed that the Mongols were vulnerable. One of the principal underpinnings of their power—the psychological edge of terror they held over their opponents—was badly shaken, if not dislodged. Most damaging of all was the tremendous expense incurred in these expeditions. The construction of the ships and the provisioning of supplies were costly and precipitated some of the revenue problems that compelled Khubilai to turn to such financial administrators as Aḥmad and Lu Shih-jung, whom the Chinese despised. Khubilai's prestige and finances were squandered in these campaigns. His efforts here once again reveal the same lack of control we saw in his financial policies of the 1280s.

MILITARY EXPEDITIONS IN SOUTHEAST ASIA

Similarly, his campaigns in Southeast Asia were, for the most part, ill conceived and resulted in some devastating reversals. Khubilai wished to assert his control over the lands bordering Southern China. Once his troops had subjugated the rest of China in 1279, he conceived of expansion farther south. Here again his principal objective was to secure the *pro forma* acquiescence of the kings and leaders of Southeast Asia to his rule. When they rejected such submission to the Mongols, Khubilai initiated expeditions against them. There were no real or even perceived threats from Southeast Asia. Khubilai's campaigns must be considered expansionist rather than defensive, with different motives from those of the campaigns against Khaidu in Central Asia and the Sung in Southern China. The Southeast Asian campaigns were inspired by the Mongols' traditional expansionist ambitions and policy as well as Khubilai's personal need for legitimacy. Yet the difficulties and obstacles the Mongols encountered here were as cumbersome as any they had faced in their abortive invasion of Japan. The tropical heat and rain, the forests, and the diseases of the South were conditions with which the Mongols had dealt before, in the campaigns against Southern Sung, but always with difficulty. To crush the resistance of the natives of Southeast Asia, the Mongol troops needed to hack their way through the forest, an arduous and unappealing prospect. Since horses were unsuited to such terrain, the strength of the Mongols' army—their cavalry—was rendered ineffective. Khubilai surely knew of the difficulties, particularly after his troops experienced a few initial losses. Yet he resolutely persisted in his efforts to subjugate the Southeast Asian lands.

Initially, before the hostilities erupted, Khubilai had promoted commerce with Southeast Asia. Even while he was dispatching punitive expeditions to some Southeast Asian lands, he still maintained, and even encouraged, commercial relations with others. For example, in 1281 he dispatched envoys to Ceylon (modern Sri Lanka), in 1285 and 1290 to Malabar, and in 1279 to Annam (the northern region of modern Vietnam) to seek tribute and trade.[18] He sought and occasionally received spices, medicines, pearls, and rare and exotic animals.[19]

From Ceylon, he was eager to obtain Buddhist relics, such items as the presumed teeth, hair, or purple porphyry dish belonging to the historical Buddha.[20] In his relations with Southeast Asia, as with other lands, he attempted to recruit experts—doctors, craftsmen, and interpreters, for example. In the early years of his reign, the rulers of Southeast Asia did, in fact, offer tribute. In 1265, the King of Annam sent an envoy to present tribute and, in return, received a calendar from the Great Khan, which he was expected to use for his own land.[21] As late as 1279, Annam dispatched embassies, which were probably trade missions in the guise of tribute, to Khubilai's court.[22]

Yet even in the 1270s there were conflicts. In 1273, Khubilai had sent three emissaries to the Kingdom of Pagan in Burma to request the dispatch of tribute to China. King Narathihapate (r. 1256–87), a vain despot who described himself as "supreme commander of 36 million soldiers, swallower of 300 dishes of curry daily," and sexual mate of 3,000 concubines, executed three Yüan envoys for daring to suggest that he humble himself to the Great Khan.[23] He also incurred the Mongols' wrath by attacking the small border state of Kaungai, north of Pagan, which had accepted the Great Khan's authority. Khubilai's reaction was predictable. He did not take the deliberate killing of peaceful envoys—a grave crime from the traditional Mongol standpoint—and the raids against one of his tributaries lightly. In 1277, he ordered Nāṣir al-Dīn, the son of his trusted Muslim retainer Saiyid Ajall, to lead an expedition to Pagan to avenge the murder of the three envoys.[24]

This mission has been colorfully described by Marco Polo, who offers a vivid and detailed, though perhaps not entirely accurate, account of the battle. According to his description, the first engagement was a near-disaster for the Mongols. The battle was fought on a plain along the Yünnanese-Burmese border. In preparation for his assault, Narathihapate had placed two thousand of his war elephants at the head of his detachments and had spaced his cavalry and foot soldiers behind the elephants. Meanwhile, Nāṣir al-Dīn had stationed his troops with the forest at their rear. This position offered them the option of seeking sanctuary in the forest in case they needed to retreat,[25] and it soon became clear that they would have to do so. Their horses panicked at the sight of the elephants and headed into the forest, refusing to advance against the elephants. Quickly devising a new strategy, Nāṣir al-Dīn had his troops tether their horses in the forest and line up with bows and arrows poised for the arrival of the enemy. Knowing that his 10,000-man army was vastly outnumbered, Nāṣir al-Dīn decided on an imaginative but hazardous plan: as Narathihapate's forces advanced ever closer, the archers were to take aim at the elephants, which were totally unprotected. Marco Polo presents a graphic description of the ensuing battle:

> You may know that so great was the number of arrows in this beginning, and all at the mark of the elephants . . . that they were wounded on every side of the body. And when the elephants were so wounded as I have told you . . . and felt the pain of the wounds of the pellets which came in such numbers like rain, and were frightened by the great noise of the shouting, I tell you that they all turn themselves in rout & in flight towards the people of the king with so great an uproar that it seemed that the whole world must be rent, putting the army of the king of Mien [Burma] into the greatest confusion.[26]

The battle was nonetheless hard fought, and for some time no clear-cut victor emerged. Finally, the tide turned to the Mongols' advantage. The Burmese "were beginning to turn the back . . . and when the Tartars saw that those were turned in flight they go beating and chasing and killing them so evilly that it was a pity to see." In short, the battle became a rout. Marco criticizes Narathihapate's battle tactics:

> The said king ought not to have gone to attack the Tartars in that position which had the wood on the flanks, but to have waited for them in a wide plain where they would not have been able to bear the charge of the first armed elephants; and then with the two wings of horse and foot he would have surrounded them and put them from the midst.[27]

He concludes by writing that Nāṣir al-Dīn captured two hundred elephants and returned with them to Khubilai's court, but this version is contradicted by the Chinese dynastic history, which states that Nāṣir al-Dīn arrived at the court in July of 1279 with only twelve elephants.[28] Moreover, the latter source also notes that Nāṣir al-Dīn established Mongol authority (that is, the registration of the population for tax purposes and the building of postal stations) over only 110,200 households along the Burmese border. He had clearly not subjugated the Kingdom of Pagan, for in March of the following year Khubilai again ordered him to prepare for a campaign against Narathihapate. Marco's description may thus have been overstated. Whatever the explanation, the Yüan had not subdued Burma in Nāṣir al-Dīn's first expedition.

Perhaps equally troublesome to Khubilai was the repeated defiance of the kingdoms of Annam and Champa (the latter roughly equivalent to the southern part of modern Vietnam). Khubilai had on a number of occasions implored the King of Annam, Tran Thanh-Ton, and the King of Champa, Jaya Indravarman VI, to come in person to the court in Ta-tu, but neither monarch made the journey. Khubilai also requested that they send population registers essential for the levying of taxes and the imposition of corvée labor.[29] Finally, Khubilai demanded that each ruler deliver one of his younger brothers to Khubilai's court, presumably to serve as hostages.[30] Tran Thanh-Ton dispatched tribute but never came personally on a tribute-bearing mission. Some of the tribute was quite valuable, including golden statues of men, which were meant to substitute for the king, who declined to come to China.[31] The king probably regarded these tribute embassies as commercial ventures, but, knowing that the court in China was more receptive to merchants if they were members of tribute missions, he disguised these essentially mercantile undertakings as official embassies. Champa, however, was less compliant. Jaya Indravarman VI dispatched a few tribute missions, but he and his successors remained implacably hostile to China throughout Khubilai's thirty-four-year reign.

Khubilai chose to deal with Champa first. In August of 1279, envoys from Champa, it is true, had arrived at court with tribute consisting of an elephant, a rhinoceros, and precious jewelry. Khubilai accepted the tribute goods but demanded that Jaya Indravarman VI personally accompany the next mission.[32] A second embassy from Champa reached Ta-tu in 1280, with tribute but without the king. Khubilai rebuked the envoys and ordered them to deliver a message to their monarch, commanding him to send his brothers or sons as hostages to the court.[33] When there was no response, Khubilai decided on a sterner approach. In 1281, he instructed Sodu (Mong.: Sodu), his highest official in Canton and a Maritime Trade Superintendent, to lead a punitive expedition against the defiant and recalcitrant monarch of Champa.[34] With an army of 5,000 men, a hundred ships, and a crew of able-bodied sailors, Sodu set out for the coast of Champa, a relatively short distance.[35] Landing in the port of Vijaya, Sodu and his troops quickly occupied the town, but they found that Jaya Indravarman VI had retreated inland to the mountains. Though Sodu advanced into the interior, he could not engage the enemy. Instead, guerrillas harassed him, entrapping and either killing or capturing some of his soldiers. Early in the following year, Khubilai sent reinforcements of

15,000 soldiers under the command of a certain A-t'a-hai, but they too were mired and could make little headway.[36] A few months later, he ordered Arigh Khaya, one of his ablest commanders, to support Sodu.[37] Nothing, however, seemed to work.

With such scant success, the Yüan needed a different strategy, and Khubilai decided to dispatch his troops by land. By this route, they would have to cross through Annam to reach their destination in Champa. Having received tribute from Annam's king, Khubilai assumed that Tran Thanh-Ton would cooperate and permit his troops direct access to Champa through his lands. So he dispatched his son Toghon with a contingent of Mongol and Chinese soldiers to carry out his new strategy. He invested Toghon as the Prince of Chen-nan and ordered him to collaborate with Sodu in pacifying the unruly King of Champa.[38]

But Khubilai's assumption proved to be erroneous. Before Toghon could get to Champa, he found himself at war with Annam. Tran Thanh-Ton had refused to permit him to use Annamese territory as a staging area for an invasion of Champa. Toghon and Sodu were compelled to mount an assault on the uncooperative Annamese potentate. Gathering an army from Fukien and the other southern provinces of China, they headed south toward Annam.[39] They seemed at first to be unbeatable, advancing to the Hanoi region without much opposition as their troops repeatedly defeated and pushed back the Annamese soldiers.[40] They had, however, been drawn into the enemy's lair. Taking advantage of their knowledge of the terrain, the Annamese had concealed themselves in the forests and the mountains and unleashed periodic guerrilla raids whenever they sensed that they had a tactical advantage over the invaders. Guerrilla warfare, heat, and disease began to take their toll on the interlopers. The Mongol-led armies were increasingly demoralized by the elusive enemy and the mounting losses of life and supplies. They were experienced in pitched battles, not in small-scale, unexpected engagements.[41] In the summer of 1285, Toghon, who commanded one of the two Mongol detachments, decided to withdraw his troops. But he failed to inform Sodu, the other leader, of his intentions, and Sodu found himself isolated and on the defensive. Prince Tran Nhat-Canh concentrated his forces against the remaining Mongol army, and defeated them in the central part of the country.[42] Realizing that he was in great trouble, Sodu tried to escape to the north. He reached Ssu-ming along the Annamese-Chinese border, but there the enemy

caught up with him. They surrounded Sodu's army, and, in one of
the few real battles of the Annamese campaign, they trounced the
Mongols and killed Sodu.[43] The first expedition against Annam thus
ended as a fiasco.

Khubilai could not permit this embarrassing defeat to go un-
avenged. In March of 1286, he assigned his grandson Esen Temür, the
son of his son Hügechi, to assist the commander Arigh Khaya, whose
troops had remained along the Annamese border.[44] Within a few
months, Nāṣir al-Dīn was also dispatched to the same region.[45] In
1287, they were joined by a much larger army, led once again by
Toghon. The Mongol forces reached Hanoi, only to find that the king
and his son had already fled.[46] Hanoi was eventually recovered,
however, because the heat and the unfavorable environment compelled Toghon to withdraw. When he learned of Toghon's lack of
success, Khubilai would not permit his son to come to court. And, in
a display of disappointment and anger, he transferred Toghon to a
sinecure in Yang-chou and would not allow him to return to Ta-tu.[47]
But these failures were not, after all, solely Toghon's fault. None of the
competent or, in some cases, brilliant commanders sent by Khubilai
was able to defeat the kingdoms of Annam and Champa.

The Annamese king recognized, however, that he would continue
to be plagued by the Mongols unless he formally acquiesced to their
hegemony in Asia. To avert further incursions, he pretended to offer
his submission, sending an envoy to present tribute and to pledge his
loyalty to Khubilai's court. Khubilai accepted this "submission" and
dispatched no further expeditions against Annam. In turn, Annam
began to send tribute on a regular basis.[48] For similar reasons, Jaya
Indravarman VI of Champa also started to dispatch missions to
Khubilai's court.

Meanwhile, Khubilai was determined to punish the arrogant King
of Pagan, Narathihapate. In 1283, he sent an army to compel the king
to submit, but Narathihapate merely fled to the surrounding mountains. Only in 1287 did Khubilai dispatch another force to subjugate
the Burmese. This contingent, under the leadership of his grandson
Esen Temür, fought its way to the capital city of Pagan and occupied it
for some months.[49] The dejected and humbled Narathihapate was
forced to send tribute to the Mongol court in order to recover his
capital.[50] His inglorious defeat at the hands of the Mongols undermined his stature with his own people, and his son took advantage of

his loss in popularity to have him poisoned. The Mongols had gained little from this campaign, however. Burma offered tribute, but the financial cost of these expeditions was burdensome and difficult to justify.

It is even more difficult to justify the more renowned and spectacular campaigns against Java. Like the attacks on Japan, Khubilai's expedition against Java had to be sent across the seas and thus relied on the navy. Also like the Japanese campaigns, it was provoked by the mistreatment of one of Khubilai's envoys. The King Kertanagara of Java was just as unyielding as Hōjō Tokimune of Japan. He had succeeded in unifying much of his land, had himself converted to Tantric Buddhism, and had formed a marital alliance with Champa.[51] He sought to control the lucrative spice trade based in the Moluccas and to have the Javanese serve as the middlemen in this commerce.[52] He may have feared that Khubilai intended to dislodge his grasp over this trade.

Not surprisingly, then, his reaction to Khubilai's embassy to his territory was not cordial. Khubilai's ambassador, Meng Ch'i, arrived in Java in 1289 and asked for Java's submission. Kertanagara's response to what seemed to him a haughty demand was to brand the face of the unfortunate envoy.[53] This incident provided a pretext for Khubilai to initiate a military expedition against the King of Java. To a Mongol, the mutilation or killing of an envoy was one of the most heinous crimes. Therefore, Khubilai instructed a Mongol named Shih-pi, a Chinese named Kao Hsing, and a Uighur named I-k'o-mu-ssu to gather forces and supplies from the provinces of Fukien, Kiangsi, and Hu-kuang for the expedition.[54] Shih-pi was granted overall direction of the campaign while Kao was the general in the field and I-k'o-mu-ssu provided the ships and the naval expertise. Late in 1292, the expedition set forth from Ch'üan-chou with a 20,000-man army, 1,000 boats, a year's supply of grain, and 40,000 ounces of silver for the purchase of additional provisions.[55] By early in 1293, Kao Hsing's troops had landed; I-k'o-mu-ssu with his ships remained offshore. Kertanagara, who had been apprised of this impending attack, had already dispatched a sizable military force to Champa and to the Malay Peninsula, where he assumed that the enemy would land first before heading toward Java. With the bulk of his army far distant from Java, he was peculiarly vulnerable to fellow Javanese whom he had not been able to pacify and bring under his flag. One of these leaders, Jayakatwang of the unpacified state of Kediri, did, in fact, rebel against him, defeating his troops and killing Kertanagara himself.[56]

Kertanagara's mantle fell to the treacherous Prince Vijaya, his son-in-law. Seeking to avenge his father-in-law's defeat, Vijaya offered his submission to the Mongol forces in return for help in crushing the unruly rebel. His underlings provided the Yüan troops with detailed information about the ports, rivers, and topography of Kediri, to-gether with a carefully drawn map of the province. The Mongol troops were pleased with the offer and decided to cooperate in defeating the rebel Jayakatwang. The Sino-Mongol fleet sailed for Kediri and en route overwhelmed a naval force sent to halt their progress. Kao Hsing landed in Kediri, and within a week his forces had crushed the opposition and killed 5,000 of the Kediri troops. Jayakatwang finally surrendered and was apparently executed. But, although it appeared that the Mongol expedition had been a resounding success, the leaders of the campaign had been too trusting. Vijaya requested that he be provided with two hundred unarmed men from the Sino-Mongol expedition to escort him to the town of Madjapahit, where he would prepare to submit officially to the Great Khan's representa-tives. The Mongol leaders agreed, not suspecting Vijaya's duplicity. En route to Madjapahit, the prince's troops ambushed the Chinese and Mongol escorts and began surreptitiously to surround the other Mongol contingent. So successful was his ploy that General Shih-pi, the leader of the Mongol expedition, barely escaped with his life. Shih-pi had to travel quite a distance before reaching his ships, and he lost three thousand men on his retreat to his vessels.[57] Once he and the other leaders of the expedition were back on board, they disagreed about whether to return to Java to punish the double-dealing Prince Vijaya. Unable to reach an agreement, they withdrew and set sail for China.

Thus, yet another costly expedition had resulted in failure. Though the expenses incurred in the Java expedition were not as great as the ones for the naval campaigns against Japan, the loss in prestige and the lack of any material gains were just as devastating. The Yüan forces did bring back with them incense, perfumes, rhinoceros horns, ivory, a map of Java, a register of its population, and a letter in gold characters from Bali.[58] But the value of these goods hardly com-pensated for the planning and expenses, both in supplies and man-power, of the expedition.

REBELLIONS IN KHUBILAI'S DOMAINS

Perhaps a more damaging confirmation of Khubilai's lack of control was rebellions in regions theoretically under his jurisdiction—the first in Tibet, the second in Manchuria. Such tangible evidence of disloyalty was a blow to Khubilai's claims as Khan of Khans and Emperor of China. True, these challenges to his authority were based in outlying regions, not in the core of his domains. Nonetheless, if the peripheral areas rebelled, what would prevent the central part of his domain from doing so? Therefore, Khubilai acted decisively to crush both insurrections, clearly determined to prevent the infection of rebellion from spreading to China. But its very eruption along the borderlands in the 1280s underlines the difficulties Khubilai was encountering.

The first outbreak occurred in Tibet. Since the early years of his reign, Khubilai had maintained close relations with the land of the lamas. The Tibetan Buddhist 'Phags-pa lama was one of his closest advisers, and there were many Tibetan lamas in his court in Ta-tu. Khubilai had founded a special agency, the Tsung-chih yüan, to administer Buddhist affairs and had appointed a Tibetan *dpon-chen* (Civilian Administrator) to govern Tibet when the 'Phags-pa lama was in China. Nevertheless, there was great turbulence in the land, provoked partly by Khubilai but also by domestic problems and disputes among the Buddhist sects. Khubilai's creation of both an Imperial Preceptor (i.e., the 'Phags-pa lama) and a *dpon-chen* gave rise to hostilities. The *dpon-chen* Kun-dga '-bzang-po and the 'Phags-pa lama were often in conflict: as one scholar has written, "there was no love lost between the abbot and the *dpon-chen* Kun-dga'-bzang-po."[59] Khubilai also appointed a Tibetan Office of Pacification (Hsüan-wei ssu), which was staffed by military men. This office further complicated the organization of the country and added another layer of officials competing for power. In 1280, the 'Phags-pa lama died at the relatively young age of forty-five, from no discernible cause. The leaders of the Sa-skya sect accused the *dpon-chen* of poisoning the lama, first imprisoned him, and then had him executed.[60] Khubilai provided the expenses for the burial of his loyal lama, and built a stupa in his honor.[61] In 1281, he appointed the 'Phags-pa lama's thirteen-year-old nephew Dharmapalaraksita as the Imperial Preceptor, and peace temporarily reigned over the land.

Yet the animosity toward the Mongols would resurface. Some of the

Buddhist sects had been highly critical of the ʿPhags-pa lama's close relationship with the Mongols. Dharmapalaraksita, who, since infancy had resided at the Mongol court, was even more offensive to them because of his intimate involvement with Khubilai and his people.[62] Khubilai's choice of a boy who had been brought up at the Mongol court as the ruler of Tibet showed poor political judgment. Dharmapalaraksita would be a visible and intrusive presence in a land that he hardly knew. The Sa-skya orders to which Dharmapalaraksita belonged had rivals in Tibet, in any case, and the ʿBri-gung, one of these hostile sects, capitalized on the animosity toward the new "alien" Imperial Preceptor to rebel. In 1285, troops from ʿBri-gung started to lay siege to the monasteries of other sects. Shortly thereafter, they clashed with both the Sa-skya sect and the Mongol troops who supported them. According to the Tibetan sources, they received assistance from the "King of sTod Hor Hu-la." sTod Hor is the Tibetan name for Eastern Turkestan, and King Hu-la has been identified as the Chaghadai Khan Duʿa, the puppet ruler supported by Khubilai's nemesis, Khaidu.[63] Thus, the ʿBri-gung insurrection now assumed a more serious, international dimension. Khubilai recognized that he needed to act decisively to crush the rebellion before it seriously challenged his authority in Tibet. A punitive force led by his grandson Temür Bukha arrived in Tibet, and by 1290 had destroyed the ʿBri-gung monastery, killing 10,000 men in the process, and collapsing the ʿBri-gung threat.[64] No further violence erupted in Tibet during the remaining years of Khubilai's reign.[65] Tibet was more or less pacified, and the Hsüan-cheng yüan, founded in 1288 to replace the Tsung-chih yüan, managed to maintain the peace.[66]

The second rebellion erupted in Manchuria. It, too, had international implications. The rebel leader Nayan, who was a descendant of one of Chinggis Khan's half-brothers, was a Nestorian Christian who reacted with horror at Khubilai's growing closeness to the agricultural world and increasing estrangement from his nomadic heritage.[67] His concerns and interests thus coincided with those of Khubilai's Central Asian adversary Khaidu, and the two leaders appear to have coordinated their movements in their attack against the Great Khan. Marco Polo, who offers an intimate and detailed portrait of Nayan's rebellion, writes that the Mongol chief "sent his messengers very secretly to Caidu [Khaidu] who was a very great lord and strong in the region towards the great Turquie, and was nephew to the great Kaan, but was also a rebel against him and wished him great ill, because he was always afraid that the great Kaan would chastise him." [68] Khubilai at first dispatched Bayan, his most renowned general, to investigate the situation in Manchuria. In March of 1287, Bayan set forth for Nayan's camp. The Chinese sources accuse Nayan of seeking to entrap Bayan: "Upon his [Bayan's] arrival, Nai-yen [Nayan] had a banquet for him with a prearranged plot to seize him. Po-yen [Bayan], apprehending [it], hurried out with his attendants and [they] escaped by three separate routes." [69] It is unclear how much of this account is credible. Was the story fabricated later to prove Nayan's duplicity? It is unlikely that Nayan would permit the enemy's leading general to slip through his fingers so easily.

Khubilai must have thought that the threat posed by Nayan was serious, for he personally led the punitive campaign against the dissident leader. He sent one detachment westward to harass Khaidu and to prevent his troops from helping Nayan, and he dispatched another contingent to Liao-tung, in southern Manchuria, to forestall assistance from the Mongol chieftain Khadan, still another dissident. [70] Before setting forth, he consulted his diviners, who assured him, "Thou shalt return victorious over thine enemies." [71] Khubilai himself gathered his troops and marched toward the mouth of the Liao River. Marco Polo claims that his force consisted of 460,000 men, 360,000 cavalry and 100,000 foot soldiers. Surely these were inflated figures, for a huge number of men and horses could not be fed and supplied on the scant resources of Manchuria. The grass for their horses, for example, would have been insufficient. Khubilai could have had no more than several tens of thousands of soldiers.

Moving quickly, his troops reached Nayan's campgrounds and totally surprised the rebel leader. Khubilai was carried on a palanquin mounted on the backs of four elephants. [72] He was by this time seventy-two years old and afflicted by gout and rheumatism and other ailments, but, despite these physical difficulties, he insisted on going to the battlefield. The two armies faced each other, and the Mongols sounded their drums, their horns, and their voices "in so great numbers that the air seemed to tremble." [73] The Great Khan's drums rolled, and his troops advanced. First came the arrows released by the archers, then as the armies drew closer, lances and swords and iron clubs were produced. The battle lasted from morning until midday, and finally the tide turned against Nayan. His troops started to flee, and the pursuing Mongol armies caught and killed many of them. Nayan himself was captured and then was executed as a prince in a traditional bloodless Mongol manner:

> He [Nayan] was wrapped very tightly and bound in a carpet and there was
> dragged so much hither and thither and tossed up and down so rigorously
> that he died; & then they left him inside it; so that Naian ended his life in
> this way. And for this reason he made him die in such a way, for the Tartar
> said that he did not wish the blood of the lineage of the emperor be spilt on
> the ground.[74]

Though Nayan was a Nestorian, his rebellion did not result in an
attack on the Christians within Khubilai's domains.[75] Khubilai
showed more balance and rationality here than in some of his other
policies.

Yet he could not crush the Mongol opposition to his reign. Khadan
remained a threat throughout Khubilai's life. Khaidu continued to
harass Khubilai's troops in 1288 and 1289.[76] Khubilai at first sent
Bayan to pacify Khaidu, but he soon found the great but aging Mongol
general too dilatory and so recalled him. Bayan was replaced by one of
Khubilai's grandsons, who had greater success.[77] In 1289, Khaidu
reached almost to Khara Khorum before being driven back by Khubilai's
forces. Though he withdrew from the region of Khara Khorum, he continued to plague the Yüan borders until his death in 1301, seven years
after Khubilai's own demise.[78]

In short, frustration was Khubilai's lot in his dealings with foreign
lands in the 1280s. The naval expeditions against Japan and Java,
which were to cause him such grief, are inexplicable except in the
context of his grandiose ambitions and his concern for his legitimacy
or possibly his longevity. Both expeditions turned out disastrously
and simultaneously precipitated financial problems for the dynasty
that could not be readily resolved. The outbreaks challenging Mongol
rule in Tibet and Manchuria exacerbated these fiscal difficulties.
These failures were devastating, but this is not to say that there were
failures in every area in the 1280s and early 1290s. On the positive side,
a new legal code was instituted; the source of the Yellow River was
explored under government auspices; and new schools and institutes
were founded and developed. Yet the overwhelming impression of the
1280s and early 1290s is one of loss and despondency.

KHUBILAI'S PERSONAL LOSSES

These years also witnessed personal frustrations and grief for Khubilai. The death of Chabi, whom the emperor had prized more than any
of his other wives, in 1281 left Khubilai wretched and alone. Her son

Chen-chin had been named Crown Prince. She was the only one of Khubilai's wives to be accorded a memorial tablet in his temple.[79] She had been an indispensable helpmate in the early years of his reign. It may be pure coincidence, but there is no doubt that after her death Khubilai personally, and China as a whole, suffered a series of drastic reversals. Perhaps Chabi could not have prevented these calamities, but she might have served as a restraining influence on some of the more outlandish decisions made during that period.

Nambi, Chabi's successor as principal wife, was a distant relative of Chabi's. It seems likely that Chabi, knowing that she was in failing health, selected her own successor. Unfortunately, we do not know as much about her successor as we do about Chabi. As Khubilai grew older and his own health declined, Nambi reportedly made important political decisions on her own initiative. Khubilai saw few people in the later years of his reign, perhaps because of his despondency over the deaths of Chabi and some of his other relatives. His ministers transmitted reports and memorials through Nambi, and she, in turn, handed down his decisions and edicts. The Chinese sources suggest that, as he weakened, Khubilai permitted her to issue edicts in his name, but they do not cite any specific decisions made by Nambi.[80] Like many of the other Mongol empresses and noble ladies of the period, she was personally assertive and politically influential.

Information about Khubilai's other wives is meager. Mongol khans traditionally had four *ordo*s, or wifely households, and Khubilai was no exception. His first wife, Tegülün, died sometime before he became the Great Khan in 1260. Chabi and Nambi, the most prominent and influential of his wives, both belonged to the second *ordo*. Chabi bore him four sons, and Nambi gave him one son. Chabi's son Chen-chin had been designated as Khubilai's successor; another son, Dorji, died before his father. The two younger sons, Manggala (d. 1280), who was named the Prince of An-hsi (in the modern province of Shansi), and Nomukhan (d. 1301), the Prince of Pei-an, were not considered as successors to their father, but, as we have seen, Khubilai had enough confidence in them to dispatch them on several vital military expeditions.[81] His other sons, including Toghon, were given important military assignments, but they were also exposed to the cultures of the populations whom they ruled. Prince Ananda, Manggala's son and successor, for example, was raised in a Muslim household, and as an adult, according to Rashīd al-Dīn, had converted most of the 150,000 troops under his command to Islam.[82] Nothing is known of Nambi's son. Similarly, nothing is known of Khubilai's wives in the third and fourth *ordo*s except that they bore him another seven sons.

Chabi was clearly his favorite wife, and her death, along with that of Crown Prince Chen-chin in 1285, were not only heart-breaking but also undermined his plans for the succession. Chabi's prominence is attested by the fact that she is the only one of his wives whose portrait, jointly executed by Chinese and Turkish-Mongolian artists, has survived.[83] Undoubtedly a partial explanation for the capricious decision-making at the end of his reign lies in his despondency after her death.

Perhaps as devastating was the loss of his favorite son and designated successor, Chen-chin, who had been carefully groomed to be the next Great Khan and the next Emperor of China. He had been tutored by some of the leading figures of the time in subjects ranging from Chinese history to Buddhism, and was as well prepared to assume the khanate as any Mongol ruler in history. His early death, when he was still in his forties, must thus have shattered Khubilai and contributed to the gloom at court. Chen-chin's son Temür was eventually designated as the successor to Khubilai and became the Ch'eng-tsung emperor of China in 1294.

Only two of Khubilai's daughters are mentioned in the histories in any detail, and it is not known how many there were in all. This younger generation of Mongol court ladies exerted little political influence. Unlike the powerful Mongol women starting with Chinggis's mother, Hö'elün, all the way down to Chabi, Khubilai's daughters played no role in political decisions. Perhaps they were influenced by Chinese cultural standards, which imposed severe restrictions on women and limited their political influence. On the other hand, it may simply be that Khubilai's daughters lacked any interest in politics. Whatever the explanation, the Chinese historians give the names of only two. Miao-yen is noted for her ardent devotion to Buddhism. She became a Buddhist nun and lived and was finally buried in T'an-che ssu, a monastery in the Western Hills of Peking. She worshiped Kuan-yin, the Goddess of Mercy, "day and night with such fervour that the marks of her forehead and her feet may be traced on the flagstone where she devoutly 'k'otowed.'"[84] Her portrait was hung in one of the halls of the monastery, and a 1935 guide to Peking reported that the portrait was still intact at that time.[85] Hu-tu-lu Chieh-li-mi-shih, the other daughter who is mentioned by name, was used, as we have noted earlier, by her father for his own political purposes. He arranged her marriage to the Korean king, a marriage that strengthened the bonds between the Yüan court and its Korean subjects.[86] We know nothing more about Khubilai's daughters, but they surely could not compare with the assertive and colorful women of Khubilai's own and earlier generations.

With personal sorrows and the failures in his foreign and domestic policies weighing heavily on Khubilai, he turned more and more to drink and food for comfort. The court banquets became increasingly lavish. The food served at these affairs was Mongol fare, heavily laden with meats. Even ordinary meals were elaborate, sumptuous repasts, and served as Khubilai's consolation. Boiled mutton, cooked whole, was the standard fare, and other rich and fatty foods supplemented the meat diet. And a typical meal might include cooked breast of lamb, eggs, raw vegetables seasoned with saffron and wrapped in pancakes, tea with sugar, koumiss, and a kind of beer made of millet.[87] Banquets naturally were even more elaborate. The Mongols did not frown upon excess, and over-eating, particularly on ceremonial occasions, tended to be the rule rather than the exception. Mongol khans had tradition-ally been heavy drinkers, and now Khubilai joined them in their vice. He drank vast quantities of koumiss and wine, making it more difficult for him to cope with the political crises he faced.

His drinking and eating habits also contributed to his health prob-lems. Obesity and the physical consequences that ensued plagued him for the last decades of his life. Liu Kuan-tao's portrait of him in 1280 already reveals his corpulence, but in the later 1280s his diet truly caught up with him. He became grotesquely fat and began to suffer from gout and other ailments. His physical difficulties were exacerbated by his alcoholism. Marco Polo was but one of several witnesses to the exceptional drinking at the Mongol court. Khubilai among many Mongols was unable to control his liquor intake, partic-ularly as grief and old age took hold of him. He sought a variety of remedies to his physical suffering—everything from drugs and doc-tors from Southeast Asia to shamans from Korea. Nothing produced relief, and his eating and drinking binges continued.

Old age, weariness, disappointments, and excessive drinking fin-ally took their toll. The Chinese sources reveal that, by early 1294, he was extremely dispirited and depressed. He even spurned those who traditionally offered New Year greetings to the Great Khan. His old comrade-in-arms Bayan arrived at court for a visit to cheer him up, but was unsuccessful.[88] Khubilai rapidly weakened, and on February

18, in his eightieth year, he died in the Tzu-t'an hall in his palace.[89] The imperial princes and the high officials arrived to offer condolences to Khubilai's grandson and successor Temür, who eventually came to be known as the Ch'eng-tsung emperor. A *khuriltai* was convened to choose a successor, but it, in fact, ratified Khubilai's choice. The *khuriltai* was beginning to give way to the Chinese method of designating a successor as emperor, another indication of Khubilai's attempts to accommodate himself to Chinese practices.

Within a few days after Khubilai's death, a solemn caravan began to wind its way to the Kentei Mountains, where Khubilai was to be buried. The precise site of his burial is not recorded and has still not been discovered. The elaborateness or lack thereof of his burial site is also not noted in the sources. No grandiose tomb for one of the greatest figures in Asian, not to say world, history has survived. In the fourth month of the year, his grandson did ask the leading officials to decide upon an appropriate posthumous title and an appropriate location for an altar in Khubilai's honor. They built an altar for the deceased emperor seven *li* south of Ta-tu and gave him the temple or posthumous name of Shih-tsu ("founder of a dynasty").[90]

A proper, orderly, and unchallenged succession to the throne, a vital consideration for the founder of a dynasty, eluded Khubilai's successors. Khubilai successfully arranged the first transfer of authority from himself to his grandson, but struggles for power surfaced later. Political infighting continued to plague the Mongol royal family. In 1328–29, for example, Khoshila and Tugh Temür, two brothers, battled for the throne. On February 27, 1329, Tugh Temür stepped aside and let his older brother assume the throne, with the reign title of T'ien-li. By August 30, Khoshila had been killed, probably poisoned by his brother's agents, and Tugh Temür took power with the reign title of Chih-shun. The conflict between the two brothers mirrored the struggle of Khubilai and Arigh Böke. The same issues separated the two combatants, with Khoshila representing the interests of the nomadic steppe Mongols and Tugh Temür reflecting the policies of their more sinicized or Confucianized brothers based in China.[91] Such dynastic struggles weakened the court and were at least one factor in the eventual collapse of the Yüan in 1368. Khubilai's dynasty thus survived him for less than seventy-five years.

Yet Khubilai's achievements ought not to be slighted. His legacy was short-lived, but his successes during his own lifetime have earned him lasting renown. Contemporary historians and travelers from Europe and Asia wrote of his deeds, often lavishing great praise on him. Marco Polo's report familiarized Europeans with the splendid court and the huge empire governed by the Great Khan, while Rashīd al-Dīn spread his fame in the Islamic world. Simultaneously, the Chinese court chroniclers, the Korean authors of the *Koryŏ-sa*, and the Hebrew physician Bar Hebraeus wrote enthusiastic accounts of his policies.

Praise from these diverse sources furthered Khubilai's plan to portray himself as a universal ruler who was appealing to the wide variety of peoples in his domain. To the Confucians, he appeared broad-minded and a good judge of men. The Chinese dynastic history writes that he employed Confucians in government, made the Chinese classics available, and by means of Chinese civilization "pacified" the "barbarians." In short, he was portrayed as an ideal Confucian ruler.[92] The Buddhists thought of him as Mañjuśrī, the Boddhisattva of Wisdom. The Islamic historians, Rashīd al-Dīn in particular, depicted him as a patron of the Muslims. Marco Polo implied that Khubilai was about to convert to Christianity. These differing images demonstrate his ability to ingratiate himself to disparate groups who each believed itself favored by the Great Khan. Yet Khubilai remained a Mongol and never abandoned his native identity.

Like the other Mongol Khans, he embarked upon numerous military campaigns. His most stunning victory was his conquest of Southern Sung China, a territory that had over 50 million people and vast resources at its command. This engagement, which required more sophisticated planning and logistics than many earlier Mongol campaigns, ensured his status as a great commander among the Mongols. The leaders of the expedition could not rely solely upon their superb cavalry, as so many Mongols had in the past. Instead, they needed to coordinate their infantry along with their naval forces, not to mention their supply lines, in a massive operation that lasted for at least a decade. Khubilai's smashing success over the Sung was the crowning military achievement of the first two decades of his reign.

Yet his policies ultimately gave rise to disunity among the Mongols. To rule the sedentary civilizations he had helped to conquer, he needed to settle down, and to accept some of the political, economic, and cultural ideals of his sedentary subjects. If he took this course, he would arouse the opposition of many of the Mongols whom he had led. When he, in fact, moved his residence to Ta-tu, in China, some of his nomadic brethren began to resist him. First his younger brother, then his cousins Khaidu and Nayan challenged his authority to rule. They did not topple him, but their actions pointed to the splits within the Mongol world, an alarming lack of unity that would subvert and ultimately lead to the collapse of the Mongol empire. Khubilai did have another option. He could have remained a steppe leader and could have abandoned his attempts to govern China and the sedentary world. His nomadic opposition would perhaps not have developed. But he would have been unable to gain the loyalty and support of his sedentary subjects and to rule rather than simply to exploit China.

Throughout his reign as Emperor of China and founder of the Yüan dynasty, he attempted to maintain his Mongol credentials. He chose Mongol generals to lead the army, and even in the civilian administration he did not rely exclusively on Chinese advisers and officials; he recruited foreigners to help him govern. Though he himself was attracted by Buddhism and other foreign religions, he continued to carry out the practices associated with shamanism and to abide by Mongol customs. Finally, he persisted in the Mongols' traditional expansionist policies.

In the last decade or so of his life, however, he initiated costly military expeditions that turned out to be disastrous. These campaigns in Japan and Southeast Asia were risky and unrewarding. Building a capital, developing public works projects to promote the Chinese economy, and obtaining the luxuries that Khubilai and the Mongol court craved added to their fiscal difficulties. To cope with these fiscal problems, Khubilai relied principally on non-Chinese officials, who counted on increased taxes, additional state monopolies, and an inflated paper currency to raise the needed revenues. Such policies alienated many Chinese.

Earlier Khubilai had sought to ingratiate himself with the Chinese. He had established a government that resembled those of the Chinese dynasties, and, by reinstating Confucian rituals, he won over many Chinese. He also recruited a number of Chinese for important positions in the government. Though he did not rely on the traditional Chinese civil service examinations for the selection of his officials, he still employed many Chinese at court. Finally, he patronized Chinese painters, craftsmen, and playwrights. But his military expeditions and the consequent financial demands doomed his efforts and lost him much of his influence with and support from the Chinese.

Similarly, he was compelled to abandon his desire for rule over all the Mongol domains. The Golden Horde in Russia had pursued an independent policy long before Khubilai's accession as the Great Khan. The hostile Chaghadai khanate in Central Asia sought to topple Khubilai. The Il-Khans of Persia were the only Mongol group that remained loyal to the Great Khan, but, since communications between Persia and Khubilai's capital in Ta-tu were poor, the Il-Khans were autonomous. They eventually became entranced with the Muslim civilization of their subjects, distancing them even further from the Mongols in East Asia. Even areas traditionally part of the Chinese cultural sphere, such as Manchuria, rebelled against Khubilai's rule. These difficulties were heightened by personal crises in the last decade of his life.

Yet Khubilai had numerous accomplishments to his credit. He sought to govern, not simply exploit, the largest and most populous empire in the history of the world until that time. With a vision unique for one with a nomadic heritage, he endeavored to protect the welfare and promote the interests of his diverse subjects in a time when such consideration was rare. Through his political and economic policies, through his support and patronage of culture and commerce, and through his toleration for different religions, he attempted to unify the lands in Asia under Mongol hegemony. Like those of many great rulers, his empire did not survive for long after his death. Even within his own lifetime, its weaknesses were apparent. Khubilai's disastrous foreign expeditions, his excessive financial demands, and his own personal decline undermined his great vision. His Mongol predecessors, including his grandfather Chinggis Khan, did not have his dream of unifying and administering the known world. Nor did his successors implement this vision. Khubilai's dream for a world empire was not fulfilled, but his glory remains untarnished.

Notes

CHAPTER ONE

1. See Morris Rossabi, "Trade Routes in Inner Asia."

2. Herbert Franke, in "Sino-Western Contacts under the Mongol Empire," 50, writes in this context that "there remains some doubt whether it was easier to get from, say, Venice or the Black Sea region or Persia to China under the Mongols than some centuries earlier." But he also notes that "there can be no doubt that there *was* a certain amount of cultural contact between China and the non-Chinese West under the rule of the Mongol emperors." And he concludes his article with the following thought: "When Columbus left Spain to discover a sea route to the East Indies and to Cathay, land of the Great Khan, he had a copy of Marco Polo's book on board his ship. And so it came that instead of achieving a renewed contact between the Far East and the West a new world was discovered" (p. 71).

3. ʿAlā-ad-Dīn ʿAta-Malik Juvainī, *The History of the World Conqueror* (trans. John Andrew Boyle), 1:152 (hereafter, Boyle, *History*).

4. F. W. Mote, "The Growth of Chinese Despotism: A Critique of Wittfogel's Theory of Oriental Despotism as Applied to China," 17.

5. Sechin Jagchid and Paul Hyer, *Mongolia's Culture and Society*, 9.

6. Sung Lien et al., *Yüan shih*, p. 2553 (hereafter, *Yüan shih*); S. Jagchid and C. R. Bawden, "Some Notes on the Horse Policy of the Yüan Dynasty," 246.

7. On Chinggis, see *The Life of Chingis Khan*, by B. Vladimirtsov, and *Conqueror of the World: The Life of Chingis Khan*, by René Grousset, among other works. The Mongols and the Chinese celebrated his eighth centenary in 1962. For a popular work on Soviet and Chinese Communist views of Chinggis, see John Joseph Saunders, "Genghis Khan and the Communists," 390–96.

8. Owen Lattimore, "Chingis Khan and the Mongol Conquests," 57.

9. Gareth Jenkins, "A Note on Climatic Cycles and the Rise of Chinggis Khan," 222.

10. The *Secret History of the Mongols* is the principal Mongolian source on Chinggis's early life and career. For this work, see Erich Haenisch's translation, entitled *Die geheime Geschichte der Mongolen*, as well as his transcription of the text, found in *Manghol und Niuca Tobca'an* (*Yüan-ch'ao pi-shi*), and his glossary *Wörterbuch zu Manghol un Niuca Tobca'an* (*Yüan-ch'ao pi-shi*). F. W. Cleaves's review of Haenisch's translation (in *Harvard Journal of Asiatic Studies* 12 [1949]: 497–534) and Cleaves's own translation are indispensable. The dating of the *Secret History* has become embroiled in scholarly controversy. The dates 1228, 1242, and 1252 have all been proposed. Several useful articles on this debate include William Hung, "The Transmission of the Book Known as *The Secret History of the Mongols*," 433–92; Gari Ledyard, "The Mongol Campaigns in Korea and the Dating of the *Secret History of the Mongols*," 1–22; and Igor de Rachewiltz, "Some Remarks on the Dating of the *Secret History of the Mongols*," 185–205. Thomas T. Allsen, *The Mongols in East Asia, Twelfth–Fourteenth Centuries: A Preliminary Bibliography of Books and Articles in Western Languages*, 7–10, and Henry G. Schwarz, *Bibliotheca Mongolica, Part 1*, 166–69, cite additional sources on the *Secret History*.

11. Hsiao Ch'i-ch'ing, *The Military Establishment of the Yüan Dynasty*, 34–35.

12. Vladimirtsov, *Chingis Khan*, 24–25; for more on the Kereyid, see Paul Pelliot and Louis Hambis, *Histoire des campagnes de Gengis Khan: Cheng-wou ts'in-tcheng lou*, 207–12. It might be well at this point to caution the reader about some of the biographies of Chinggis. Harold Lamb's *Genghis Khan: Emperor of All Men* and Peter Brent's *Genghis Khan: The Rise, Authority, and Decline of Mongol Power* are two cases in point. These books, written for the general reader, misleadingly emphasize the exotic. They are written in an overdramatic prose style and also contain many errors and inaccurate transcriptions.

13. Herbert Franz Schurmann, *Economic Structure of the Yüan Dynasty*, 3.

14. Thomas T. Allsen, "The Yüan Dynasty and the Uighurs of Turfan in the 13th Century," in *China among Equals: The Middle Kingdom and Its Neighbors, 10th–14th Centuries*, ed. Morris Rossabi, 244–45.

15. E. I. Kychanov's *Ocherk istorii tangutskogo gosudartsva* is the standard source on the Hsi Hsia.

16. Secondary studies on the Chin include several by Tao Jing-shen: *The Jurchen in Twelfth-Century China: A Study of Sinicization*; "The Influence of Jurchen Rule on Chinese Political Institutions," 121–30; "Political Recruitment in the Chin Dynasty," 24–34; and "The Horse and the Rise of the Chin Dynasty," 183–89. Other important studies include Hok-lam Chan, *The Historiography of the Chin Dynasty: Three Studies*; idem, "Tea Production and Tea Trade under the Jurchen Dynasty," in *Studia Mongolica: Festschrift für Herbert Franke*, ed. W. Bauer, 109–25; Herbert Franke, "Treaties Between Sung and Chin," *Études Song in memoriam Étienne Balázs*, ed. Françoise Aubin, 1:1, 55–84; idem, "Chinese Texts on the Jurchen,"

119–86; Ho Ping-ti, "An Estimate of the Total Population of Sung-Chin China," 3–53; the essays by Herbert Franke, Charles Peterson, and Michael Rogers in *China among Equals*, ed. Rossabi; and the dated book by Charles de Harlez, *Histoire de l'empire du Kin ou empire d'or*. Tao's *The Jurchen*, 177–99, has a good listing of the principal Oriental sources on the Chin dynasty.

17. These events are described in detail by T'o T'o et al., *Chin shih*, 306–16 (the *pen-chi* of the Emperor Hsüan-tsung), and the biographical sections in the work.

18. V. V. Barthold, *Turkestan down to the Mongol Invasion*, 399.

19. Boyle, *History*, 106. Juvainī is an invaluable source on Chinggis's conquests in Central Asia.

20. This raid came to the attention of the Russian chroniclers. See Robert Michell and Nevill Forbes, trans., *The Chronicle of Novgorod, 1016–1471*, 64. E. Bretschneider, *Mediaeval Researches from Eastern Asiatic Sources*, 1: 294–99, and Boyle, *History*, 142–49.

21. Erich Haenisch, "Die letzten Feldzüge Čingis Khans und sein Tod: Nach der ostasiatischen Überlieferung," 503–51. Juvainī asserts that all of Chinggis's sons were with him at his death, while Rashīd al-Dīn tells us that only Ögödei and Tolui were present. Later, Rashīd describes the Great Khan Güyüg as sickly, but Juvainī treats him as a vigorous ruler. On discrepancies in the works of the two historians, see John A. Boyle, "Juvainī and Rashīd al-Dīn as Sources on the History of the Mongols," in *Historians of the Middle East*, ed. B. Lewis and P. M. Holt, 133–37; Paul Pelliot, *Notes on Marco Polo*, 1: 353; V. V. Barthold, "The Burial Rites of the Turks and the Mongols," 204–05; John A. Boyle, "The Thirteenth-Century Mongols' Conception of the After Life: The Evidence of Their Funerary Practices," 8–10; Henry Serruys, "Mongol 'Qori': Reservation," 76–91; John A. Boyle, "The Burial Place of the Great Khan Ögedei," 46. Felt was often used in funerals of the Great Khans—on this, see Leonardo Olschki, *The Myth of Felt*, 16.

22. A concise description of the language problems faced by the Mongols is found in Igor de Rachewiltz, "Some Remarks on the Language Problem in Yüan China," 65–80.

23. Valentin A. Riasanovsky, *Fundamental Principles of Mongol Law*, 83. See also A. N. Poliak, "The Influence of Chingiz-Khān's Yāsa upon the General Organization of the Mamlūk State," 862–76; Curt Alinge's *Mongolische Gesetze* offers a brief study of the development of Mongol law.

24. Joseph Fletcher, "Turco-Mongolian Monarchic Tradition in the Ottoman Empire," 242.

25. Erich Haenisch, "Die Ehreninschrift für den Rebellengeneral Ts'ui Lih," *Abhandlungen der Preussischen Akademie Wissenschaften Phil.-Hist. Klasse 4*.

26. Yanai Wataru, *Yüan-tai ching-lüeh tung-pei k'ao*, 82–91; see also Morris Rossabi, *The Jurchens in the Yüan and Ming*; William Henthorn, *A History of Korea*, 117–18.

27. W. E. Allen, *A History of the Georgian People*, 109–12; Kirakos Gandzaketski, *Istoriia Armenii*, 137–38; Sechin Jagchid, "Meng-ku yü Hsi-tsang li-shih shang ti hsiang-hu kuan-hsi ho t'a tui chung-yüan ti ying-

hsiang," 25–28; idem, "Meng-ku ti-kuo shih-tai tui T'u-fan ti ching-lüeh," 125–34; Luciano Petech, "Tibetan Relations with Sung China and with the Mongols," in *China among Equals*, ed. Rossabi, 181.

28. See the works of Grekov and Iakoubovski, Vernadsky, and Spuler on the Golden Horde and the campaigns against Russia.

29. Iwamura Shinobu, "Mongol Invasion of Poland in the Thirteenth Century," 110; one of the Polish chronicles noted that the Mongols had "poured so much blood of ... innocent people as the streams of blood descended into the river Vistula and caused its inundation" (p. 121).

30. Aritaka Iwao, "Gendai no nōmin seikatsu ni tsuite," in *Kuwabara hakushi kanreki kinen tōyōshi ronsō*, 94. On Yeh-lü, see Igor de Rachewiltz, "Yeh-lü Ch'u-ts'ai (1189–1243): Buddhist Idealist and Confucian Statesman," in *Confucian Personalities*, ed. Arthur F. Wright and Denis Twitchett, 189–216.

31. *Yüan shih*, 3458.

32. For greater detail on these Muslims, see Morris Rossabi, "The Muslims in the Early Yüan Dynasty," in *China under Mongol Rule*, ed. John D. Langlois, 264–66.

33. A report on the Soviet Union's excavation of the town of Khara Khorum is found in S. V. Kiselev, ed., *Drevnemongol'skie goroda*.

34. Murakami Masatsugu, "Genchō ni okeru senfushi to kandatsu," 161.

35. John A. Boyle, *The Successors of Genghis Khan*, 82.

36. Brief Chinese biographies of Sorghaghtani are found in *Yüan shih*, 2897–98, and T'u Chi, *Meng-wu-erh shih-chi*, 19, 6b–7a.

37. Christopher Dawson, ed., *Mission to Asia*, 26.

38. Boyle, *Successors*, 168.

39. E. A. Wallis Budge, trans., *The Chronography of Gregory Abû'l Faraj: The Son of Aaron, the Hebrew Physician Commonly Known as Bar Hebraeus*, 1:398.

40. Boyle, *History*, 2:549–50. Pétis de la Crois, *Histoire du Grand Genghizcan: Premier empereur des anciens Mongols et Tartares*, 513–17, offers some dated though generally useful information about the house of Tolui.

41. Boyle, *Successors*, 164; some of his Central Asian campaigns are described in J. A. Boyle, ed., *The Cambridge History of Iran: Volume 5, The Saljuq and Mongol Periods* (hereafter Boyle, *Cambridge History*), 313–15.

42. *Yüan shih*, 2885–87.

43. Boyle, *Successors*, 167. The same story is preserved in *Yüan shih*, 2887. On the problems concerning this anecdote, see Pavel Poucha, *Die geheime Geschichte der Mongolen als Geschichtsquelle und Literaturdenkmal*, 10, and Antoine Mostaert, *Sur quelques passages de l'Histoire secrète des Mongols*, 233.

44. Boyle, *History*, 2:549–50; Igor de Rachewiltz, in *Papal Envoys to the Great Khans*, 82, asserts, without reservation, that Tolui died of alcoholism. The *Secret History* notes that he died in China in 1231, while the *Yüan shih* gives the date as 1232 and the location as Mongolia. See Francis W. Cleaves, "The Expression Jöb Ese Bol in the *Secret History of the Mongols*," 311–20, for a brief discussion of these discrepancies.

45. L. A. Khetagurov et al., *Rashīd ad-Dīn, Sbornik letopisei*, 2:111–12.

46. Otagi Matsuo, *Fubirai Kan*, 78.

47. Boyle, *Successors*, 199–200.

48. Ibid., p. 200; V. V. Barthold, *Turkestan down to the Mongol Invasion*, 473.

49. A. C. Moule and P. Pelliot, *Marco Polo: The Description of the World*, 1:81.

50. John R. Krueger, trans., "Sagang Sechen, *History of the Eastern Mongols to 1662 (Erdeni-yin Tobči)*," 70, and C. R. Bawden, trans., *The Mongol Chronicle Altan Tobči*, 143, offer an incredible story about Khubilai's relationship to Chinggis. On his deathbed, Chinggis reputedly said to those assembled around him: "The words of the boy Qubilai [Khubilai] have emerged most remarkably. Act all of ye in accordance with his word in all regards." These two Mongol chronicles were compiled centuries after the events described, and the authenticity of these remarks is questionable. They reflected the outcome of the struggle for power among Chinggis's descendants. After surmounting many obstacles, Khubilai had gained the throne. It was only natural that the chroniclers would seek to justify the victor's assumption of power. Thus they devised a touching but highly improbable deathbed scene.

51. "Kublai Khan Hunting," by Liu Kuan-tao, reproduced in *Masterpieces of Chinese Figure Painting in the National Palace Museum*, plate 30 and pp. 86, 146. It is a hanging scroll on silk and measures 182.9 by 104.1 centimeters.

52. Igor de Rachewiltz, "Turks in China under the Mongols," in *China among Equals*, ed. Rossabi, 286–87.

53. On her views, see T'u, *Meng-wu-erh shih-chi*, 19, 6b–7a.

54. Otagi, *Fubirai Kan*, 85–87.

55. Katsufuji Takeshi, *Fubirai Kan*, 87–90.

56. *Yüan shih*, 57–58.

57. The *Yüan shih* does not accord Hai-yün a biography. The principal source on his life and career is Nien-ch'ang, *Fo-tsu li-tai t'ung-tsai*.

58. *Ch'en Yüan hsien-sheng chin nien-nien shih-hsüeh lun-chi*, 24.

59. Kunishita Hirosato, "Gensho ni okeru teishitsu to Zensō to no kankei ni tsuite," 107–09.

60. For additional sources on Chao, see Harvard Yenching Institute Sinological Index Series, *Combined Indices to Thirty Collections of Liao, Chin, and Yüan Biographies* (hereafter *CILCY*), 35d; and Igor de Rachewiltz and May Wang, *Index to Biographical Material in Chin and Yüan Literary Works, Second Series* (hereafter *IBCY* 2), 14. On Tou, see *CILCY*, 66c; *IBCY* 2, 73; and K'o Shao-min, *Hsin Yüan shih*, in *Erh-shih-wu shih*, 6921 (hereafter, *Hsin Yüan shih*).

61. On this "kitchen cabinet" of Confucian advisers, see Hsiao Ch'i-ch'ing, "Hu-pi-lieh shih-tai 'ch'ien-ti chiu-lü' k'ao," 18–20.

62. A good discussion of their motives is found in Dietlinde Schlegel, *Hao Ching (1222–1275): ein chinesischer Berater des Kaisers Kublai Khan*, 28–32.

63. *Yüan shih*, 3823; *CILCY*, 135c–d.

64. *Yüan shih*, 3824; T'u, *Meng-wu-erh shih-chi*, 85, 3a.

65. Walter Fuchs, "Analecta zur mongolischen Übersetzungsliteratur der Yüan-Zeit," 38—39.

66. Herbert Franke, "Could the Mongol Emperors Read and Write Chinese?" 29.

67. On the Uighurs' influence on the Mongols, see Thomas T. Allsen, "The Yüan Dynasty and the Uighurs of Turfan in the 13th Century," in *China among Equals,* ed. Rossabi; and Li Fu-t'ung, "Wei-wu-erh jen tui-yü Yüan-ch'ao chien-kuo chih kung-hsien," 334—37.

68. *Yüan shih,* 3246; Paul Pelliot, *Recherches sur les Chrétiens d'Asie centrale et d'Extrême-Orient,* 247; on Mungsuz, see also A. von Gabain, "Ein chinesisch-uigurischer Blockdruck," in *Tractata Altaica: Festschrift für Denis Sinor,* 203—10; and Herbert Franke, "A Sino-Uighur Family Portrait: Notes on a Woodcut from Turfan," 33—40.

69. On the Muslims, see Rossabi, "The Muslims," 257—95.

70. On his Confucian advisers, see Yao Ts'ung-wu, "Hu-pi-lieh han tui-yü Han-hua t'ai-tu ti fen-hsi," 22—32; and Sun K'o-k'uan, *Yüan-ch'u ju-hsüeh.*

71. She is accorded a brief biography in *Yüan shih,* 2871—72. For portraits of Chabi, see *Masterpieces of Chinese Portrait Painting in the National Palace Museum,* plate 34; and E. Esin, "A Pair of Miniatures from the Miscellany Collections of Topkapi," 3—35.

72. Shao Hsün-cheng, "*Yüan-shih La-t'e-chi-shih Meng-ku ti-shih* shih-hsi so-chi Shih-tsu hou-fei k'ao," 969—75; Pelliot, *Notes on Marco Polo,* 1 : 567—68.

73. There is a discrepancy in the Chinese, the Mongolian, and the Persian listing of her sons. Rashīd al-Dīn credits her with three sons—Dorji, Nomu-khan, and Manggala (Boyle, *Successors,* 242—43). But the *Yüan shih* (2871, 2888) adds Chen-chin to the list. T'u, *Meng-wu-erh shih-chi,* 19, 7b, omits Dorji from his list but includes Chen-chin, Nomukhan, and Manggala. The *Erdeni-yin Tobči,* a Mongolian chronicle, indicates that she had four sons (I. J. Schmidt, trans., *Geschichte der Ost-Mongolen und ihres Fürstenhauses verfasst von Ssanang Ssetsen Chungtaidschi,* 118). For a discussion of her sons and their gifts from the court, see Isenbike Togan, "The Chapter on Annual Grants in the *Yüan shih,*" 165ff.

74. *Yüan shih,* 353; T'ao Hsi-sheng, "Yüan-tai fo-ssu t'ien-yüan chi shang-tien," 109.

75. There is a brief notice of her in the Chinese dynastic history. See *Yüan shih,* 2870. For inquiries into her background, see Igor de Rachewiltz, "The Secret History of the Mongols: Chapter Eight," 33; and Paul Pelliot, *Les Mongols et la Papauté,* 193—95.

76. H. G. Raverty, trans., *Jūzjānī: Ṭabaḳāt-i-Nāṣirī: A General History of the Muhammadan Dynasties of Asia,* 1144; Boyle, *Successors,* 176.

77. Boyle, *History,* 243—45; Hsiao Ch'i-ch'ing, *Hsi-yü-jen yü Yüan-ch'u cheng-chih,* 40—44; Fāṭima was reputed to cast a hypnotic spell on Töregene. On sorceresses among the Mongols, see John Boyle, "Kirakos of Ganjak on the Mongols," 208.

78. Fāṭima was accused and convicted of sorcery and then "her upper and lower orifices were sewn up, and she was rolled up in a sheet of felt and thrown into the river" (Boyle, *History,* 246).

79. Turrell V. Wylie, "The First Mongol Conquest of Tibet Reinterpreted," 113; James E. Bosson, *A Treasury of Aphoristic Jewels: The Subhāṣitarananidhi of Sa Skya Paṇḍita in Tibetan and Mongolian*, 5; Guiseppi Tucci, *Tibetan Painted Scrolls*, 1 : 10–12. See also D. Schuh, "Wie ist die Einladung des fünften Karma-pa an den chinesischen Kaiserhof als Fortführung der Tibet-Politik der Mongolen-Khane zu verstehen," in *Altaica Collecta*, ed. Walther Heissig, 230–33; George Huth, *Geschichte des Buddhismus in der Mongolei*, 130–35; Luciano Petech, "Tibetan Relations with Sung China and with the Mongols," in *China among Equals*, ed. Rossabi, 182; Helmut Hoffman, *The Religions of Tibet*, 135–37; George N. Roerich, trans., *The Blue Annals*, 582; R. A. Stein, *Tibetan Civilization*, 77–78; Li Tieh-tseng, *Tibet: Today and Yesterday*, 18–19. Luc Herman M. Kwanten's doctoral dissertation, "Tibetan-Mongol Relations during the Yüan Dynasty, 1207–1368," which deals with this period, is marred by a number of errors.

80. Sirarpie Der Nersessian, *The Armenians*, 41–43; Kirakos Gandzaketsi, *Istoriia Armenii*, 175–92; see also the dated but somewhat useful works of E. Dulaurier, "Les Mongols d'après les historiens arméniens," 192–255, 426–73, 481–508; M. Klaproth, "Des entreprises des Mongols en Géorgie et en Arménie dans le xiiie siècle," 193–214; on Lajazzo, see W. Heyd, *Histoire du commerce du Levant au moyen-âge*, 75; see also the translation of the account of Armenia by one of Het'um I's nephews in *Recueil des historiens des croisades: Documents arméniens II*, and for another travel account, see Sirarpie Der Nersessian, "The Armenian Chronicle of the Constable Smpad or of the 'Royal Historians,'" 141–68; Herbert Duda, *Die Seltschukengeschichte des Ibn Bībī*.

81. The best editions of the original Latin are found in Wyngaert.

82. Boyle, *Successors*, 180–88; for more on Güyüg, see the dated and less reliable work of E. Blochet, "La mort du Khaghan Kouyouk," 160–71.

83. Boyle, *Successors*, 201.

84. *Yüan shih*, 826; Louis Hambis, "Le voyage de Marco Polo en Haute Asie," in *Oriente Poliano*, 178.

85. Boyle, *Successors*, 212–13.

86. Ibid., 218; Budge, trans., *Chronography*, 420–24; Bertold Spuler, *Die Mongolen in Iran: Politik, Verwaltung, und Kultur der Ilchanzeit, 1220–1350*, 238.

87. A useful secondary account of Möngke's reign is Thomas T. Allsen, "Politics of Mongol Imperialism: Centralization and Resource Mobilization in the Reign of the Grand Qan Möngke, 1251–59." Allsen's evaluation of Möngke's policies is perhaps too rosy. He attributes overly great success to Möngke's efforts and often credits Möngke as the originator of policies that were devised by others; Möngke's *pen-chi* in the *Yüan shih* has a good though brief description of his early policies.

88. Hsiao, *Military Establishment*, 13.

89. On the orders of submission, see Eric Voegelin, "The Mongol Orders of Submission to European Powers, 1245–1255," 405–09.

90. The most important study of the Ismā 'īlī order is Marshall G. S. Hodgson, *The Order of Assassins: The Struggle of the Early Nizârî Ismâ'îlîs against the Islamic World*. King Het'um I of Armenia was a valuable ally

during Hülegü's western campaigns. On Het'um, see M. J. Brosset, *Deux historiens arméniens, Kirakos de Gantzag, Oukhtanes d'Ourha*; John Boyle, "The Journey of Het'um I, King of Little Armenia to the Court of the Great Khan Möngke," 175–89; Bretschneider, *Mediaeval Researches*, 1:164–72; and Der Nersessian, "Armenian Chronicle," 141–68.

91. Marshall G. S. Hodgson, "The Ismāʿīlī State," in Boyle, *Cambridge History*, 431.

92. Étienne Marc Quatremère, *Raschid-Eldin: Histoire des Mongols de la Perse* 1:283–99; Bertold Spuler, *The Muslim World, a Historical Survey: Part II, The Mongol Period*, 18–21; and John Boyle, "The Death of the Last 'Abbāsid Caliph: A Contemporary Muslim Account," 145–61.

CHAPTER TWO

1. *Yüan shih*, 3712–13; see also Hok-lam Chan's useful biography, "Yao Shu (1201–1278)"; *Hsin Yüan shih*, 6922; and Li Chieh, *Yüan shih*, 48. Chan's biography offers a comprehensive bibliography on Yao. The index of the *Yüan shih* prepared by Tamura et al. in Japan, entitled *Genshi goi shūsei*, has proved an invaluable guide for this incident as well as for nearly everything in this book.

2. *Yüan shih*, 48; Ch'en Pang-chan et al., *Sung-shih chi-shih pen-mo*, 858–59. The Chin lasted from 1115 to 1234.

3. Li Chieh, *Yüan shih*, 48–49; *Yüan shih*, 3713.

4. Hok-lam Chan, "Yao Shu," 26.

5. On Uriyangkhadai, see *Yüan shih*, 2979. In a rather garbled passage, Rashīd al-Dīn credits Uriyangkhadai with the real success of the campaign (see Boyle, *Successors*, 227); Pelliot, *Notes on Marco Polo*, 170, concurs in Rashīd al-Dīn's assessment.

6. Katsufuji, *Fubirai Kan*, 101–06.

7. *Yüan shih*, 59; Joseph F. Rock, *The Ancient Na-khi Kingdom of Southwest China*, 1:392; Hsia Kuang-nan, *Yüan-tai Yün-nan shih-ti ts'ung-k'ao mu-lu*, 107; and Lü Shih-p'eng, "Yüan-tai chih Chung-Yüeh kuan-hsi," 11–12.

8. For Ts'ao Pin, see T'o T'o et al., *Sung shih*, 8977–83. Also see Herbert A. Giles, *A Chinese Biographical Dictionary*, 759–60. For additional sources, see Wang Te-i et al., *Sung-jen chuan-chi tzu-liao so-yin* (hereafter, *SJCC*), 2190–91; *Yüan shih*, 3713.

9. The names of his envoys are mentioned in *Yüan shih*, 59; C. d'Ohsson, *Histoire des Mongols, depuis Tchinguiz-Khan jusqu'à Timour-Bey ou Tamerlan*, 2:310–14, recounts the same story.

10. *Yüan shih*, 59–60.

11. Ibid.

12. On these events, see also Édouard Chavannes, "Inscriptions et pièces de chancellerie chinoises de l'époque mongole," 1–5; Charles P. FitzGerald, *The Southern Expansion of the Chinese People*, 65, says of Khubilai's campaign in Ta-li that "their coming was wholly unexpected, for they had made a march of more than six hundred miles through wild country almost un-

known to travelers." René Grousset, *L'empire des steppes*, 350–51, a standard source, erroneously writes that the campaign started in 1252.

13. *Yüan shih*, 59; Yao Ts'ung-wu, "Hu-pi-lieh han tui-yü Han-hua t'ai-tu ti fen-hsi," 23–24.

14. *Yüan shih*, 59–60. I have been unable to discover any information about Liu Shih-chung.

15. Lü Shih-p'eng, "Yüan-tai chih Chung-Yüeh kuan-hsi," 11–13; *Yüan shih*, 2979–80; for the Annamese viewpoint, see D. G. E. Hall, *A History of South-East Asia*, 186–87; the Tibetans were also concerned about Uri-yangkhadai's campaigns; for this, see Liu Kuang-i, "T'u-lu-fan Fo-chiao yü Yüan Shih-tsu," in *Ta-lu tsa-chih shih-hsüeh ts'ung-shu*, 239–41.

16. *Yüan shih*, 3085.

17. Ch'en Yüan, *Western and Central Asians in China under the Mongols*, 22.

18. Hok-lam Chan, "Liu Ping-chung (1216–1274): A Buddhist-Taoist Statesman at the Court of Khubilai Khan," 102–03, 113; see also his biography in *Yüan shih*, 3687–94.

19. *Yüan shih*, 3688–90.

20. Wang O was later to persuade Khubilai to initiate just such a compilation. See Hok-lam Chan's studies, "Wang O (1190–1273)," 43–70, and "The Compilation and Sources of the *Chin-shih*," 125–63, later reprinted in his *The Historiography of the Chin Dynasty: Three Studies*, 1–65. Finally, Hok-lam Chan's "Chinese Official Historiography at the Yüan Court: The Composition of the Liao, Chin, and Sung Histories" in *China under Mongol Rule*, ed. by John Langlois, 56–106, is also a useful source.

21. Pelliot, *Notes on Marco Polo*, 256.

22. *Yüan shih*, 60.

23. Ibid., 92. On the city's importance as a source of legitimation for Khubilai, see Herbert Franke, *From Tribal Chieftain to Universal Emperor and God: The Legitimation of the Yüan Dynasty*, 39.

24. Harada Yoshito, *Shang-tu: The Summer Capital of the Yüan Dynasty in Dolon Nor, Mongolia*, 11. On Ch'ang-an, the T'ang dynasty capital, see Arthur F. Wright, "Symbolism and Function: Reflections on Changan and Other Great Cities," 667–79; on geomancy, see the introductory study by Andrew L. March, "An Appreciation of Chinese Geomancy," 253–67.

25. Good sketches of the plan of the city are found in Komai Kazuchika, "Gen no Jōto narabi ni Daito no heimen ni tsuite," 131–32.

26. Harada, *Shang-tu*, 6–7, 14–16; see also Ishida Mikinosuke, "Gen no Jōto ni tsuite," 271–319.

27. James Legge, *The I Ching: The Book of Changes*, 32–33.

28. S. W. Bushell, "Notes on the Old Mongolian Capital of Shangtu," 329–38; see also Lawrence Impey's useful report, "Shang-tu, Summer Capital of Khubilai Khan," 584–604.

29. Harada, *Shang-tu*, 9.

30. Boyle, *Successors*, 277.

31. Moule and Pelliot, *Marco Polo*, 1:185; Henry Yule, *The Book of Ser Marco Polo, the Venetian, Concerning the Kingdoms and Marvels of the East*,

298–99, does not offer as many details about Shang-tu as does Moule and Pelliot's edition and translation of Marco's travel account.

32. Harada, *Shang-tu*, 17–19.

33. Moule and Pelliot, *Marco Polo*, 187.

34. Coleridge's poem "Kubla Khan" may be conveniently consulted in Oscar Williams's *F. T. Palgrave's The Golden Treasury*, 267–68.

35. Yao Ts'ung-wu, "Hu-pi-lieh han yü Meng-ko han chih-li Han-ti ti ch'i-chien," 225–26.

36. *Yüan shih*, 3713; Tamura Jitsuzō, "Ari Buka no ran ni tsuite," 4–7.

37. *Yüan shih*, 3660.

38. Katsufuji, *Fubirai Kan*, 109–11.

39. *Yüan shih*, 3075; Yao Ts'ung-wu, "Hu-pi-lieh han yü Meng-ko han," 223–25.

40. Yao Ts'ung-wu, "Hu-pi-lieh han yü Meng-ko han," 227.

41. Hok-lam Chan, "Yao Shu," 28; *Yüan shih*, 3713.

42. Lucid descriptions of both philosophical and popular Taoism may be found in Holmes Welch, *Taoism: The Parting of the Way*; and Herrlee G. Creel, *What Is Taoism? and Other Studies in Chinese Cultural History*.

43. On the Ch'üan-chen, see the brief exposition in Arthur Waley, *The Travels of an Alchemist*, 21–26; and for more detail about the various Taoist sects in the Yüan, see Sun K'o-k'uan, "Yü Chi and Southern Taoism during the Yüan Period," in *China under Mongol Rule*, ed. by John Langlois, 214–220. See also Professor Sun's work in Chinese, *Yüan-tai Tao-chiao chih fa-chan*.

44. For comprehensive descriptions of the role of Buddhism in China, see Arthur F. Wright's *Buddhism in Chinese History* as well as Kenneth Ch'en's *Buddhism in China: A Historical Survey*.

45. See Hoffman, *The Religions of Tibet*, for additional details on Tibetan religions.

46. On the *hua-hu* controversy, see Paul Pelliot, "Les Mo-ni et le *Houahou king*," 318–27; Joseph Thiel, "Der Streit der Buddhisten und Taoisten zur Mongolenzeit," 1–81; Noritada Kubo, "Prolegomena on the Study of the Controversies between Buddhists and Taoists in the Yüan Period," 39–61; Nogami Shunjō, "Gendai Dō Butsu nikyō no kakushitsu," 213–75; Feng Ch'eng-chün, *Yüan-tai pai-hua pei*, 16–20; Wang Wei-ch'eng, "Lao-tzu hua-hu-shuo k'ao-cheng," 44–55.

47. The Taoists were referred to as *hsien-sheng*, which Marco Polo romanized as *sensin* (see Moule and Pelliot, *Marco Polo*, 191). On the *Hua-hu ching*, see Kuwabara Jitsuzō, "Rōshi Kekukyō," 1–14; and Chavannes, "Inscriptions et pièces," *T'oung Pao* 5 (1904): 375–85 and 6 (1905): 1–42.

48. Kenneth Ch'en, "Buddhist-Taoist Mixtures in the *Pa-shih-i-hua t'u*," 1–12.

49. On Mahākāśyapa, see William Edward Soothill and Lewis Hodous, comps., *A Dictionary of Chinese Buddhist Terms*, 316b.

50. Kenneth Ch'en, *Buddhism in China*, 185–86.

51. Paul Demiéville, "La situation religieuse en Chine au temps de Marco Polo" in *Oriente Poliano*, 207–08.

52. For both, see the *Taishō shinshū daizōkyō* editions.

53. Moule and Pelliot, *Marco Polo*, 201.

54. Translated from the *Fo-tsu li-tai t'ung-tsai* in Sechin Jagchid, "Chinese Buddhism and Taoism during the Mongolian Rule of China," 77.

55. See Bosson, *A Treasury*, for more on Sa-skya Paṇḍita.

56. Wylie, "First Mongol Conquest," 119. There is no good biography of this important Tibetan lama. The *Yüan shih* (4517—18) offers only the skimpiest details about his life and career. Useful bibliographical citations may be found in Nakano Miyoko, *A Phonological Study on the ʿPhags-pa Script and the Meng-ku Tzu-yün*. On his cultural significance, see Nicholas Poppe, *The Mongolian Monuments in ḥP'ags-pa Script*.

57. Roerich, *The Blue Annals*, 486; on the appeal of Tibetan Buddhism, as opposed to the Ch'an Buddhism of China, see Demiéville, "La situation religieuse," in *Oriente Poliano*, 206.

58. Nakano, *A Phonological Study*, 33—34; Schmidt, *Geschichte der Ost-Mongolen*, 114—17; Tsepon W. D. Shakabpa, *Tibet: A Political History*, 64—65; Hoffmann, *The Religions of Tibet*, 137—38.

59. The most important participants are listed in Hsiang-mai, *Pien-wei lu*, 4:20b—21a.

60. Yú. N. Rerikh, "Mongol-Tibetan Relations in the 13th and 14th Centuries," 47—48. For Ssu-ma Ch'ien's *Shih-chi*, see the partial translation by Burton Watson in *Records of the Grand Historian of China*.

61. Chavannes, "Inscriptions et pièces," 382—84.

62. In 1259, as he set forth for his campaigns against the Southern Sung, Khubilai even asked the Taoists for a prophecy, and one of them replied, "Within twenty years all below heaven will be united." See Janet Rinacker Ten Broeck and Yiu Tung, "A Taoist Inscription of the Yüan Dynasty: The Tao-chiao pei," 10.

63. Katsufuji, *Fubirai Kan*, 118.

64. Shiba Yoshinobu, "Urbanization and the Development of Markets in the Lower Yangtze Valley," in *Crisis and Prosperity in Sung China*, ed. by John W. Haeger, 22.

65. Grousset, *L'empire des steppes*, 380; see also Grousset, *The Empire of the Steppes: A History of Central Asia*, 283.

66. *Yüan shih*, 50.

67. On the practice of scattering mare's milk and its significance, see Paul Ratchnevsky, "Über den mongolischen Kult am Hofe der Grosskhane in China," in *Mongolian Studies*, ed. Louis Ligeti, 426; Marco Polo also mentions the practice; see Moule and Pelliot, *Marco Polo*, 234.

68. Spuler, *Die Mongolen in Iran*, 48—51; Boyle, *Successors*, 247—48.

69. Yao Ts'ung-wu, "Yüan Hsien-tsung (Meng-ko Han) ti ta-chü cheng-Shu yü t'a-tsai Ho-chou Tiao-yü Ch'eng ti chan-ssu," 66—67.

70. Katsufuji, *Fubirai Kan*, 120.

71. Yao Ts'ung-wu, "Yüan Hsien-tsung," 63. Particularly reliable is the account of the expedition by a participant in the campaigns, Yeh-lü Chu, the son of the great Khitan adviser to the Mongols, Yeh-lü Ch'u-ts'ai.

72. Katsufuji, *Fubirai Kan*, 116—18.

73. See Yao Ts'ung-wu's analysis of the difficulties involved in this campaign; "Yüan Hsien-tsung."

74. *Yüan shih*, 50–51.

75. Ibid., 53.

76. Katsufuji, *Fubirai Kan*, 118–19.

77. Li Chieh, *Yüan shih*, 50.

78. *Yüan shih*, 54.

79. Boyle, *Successors*, 228.

80. *Yüan shih*, 63.

81. Ibid., 61.

82. Ibid.

83. Boyle, *Successors*, 248.

84. *Yüan shih*, 62. For a later pictorial representation of the siege of O-chou, see J. Marek and H. Knížková, *The Jenghiz Khan Miniatures from the Court of Akbar the Great*, plate 20.

85. For a recent interpretation of Chia Ssu-tao's role in this campaign, see Herbert Franke, "Chia Ssu-tao (1213–1275): A 'Bad Last Minister,'" in *Confucian Personalities*, ed. Arthur F. Wright and Denis Twitchett, 225–29.

86. *Yüan shih*, 62; for additional citations on Lü, see *SJCC*, 1192–93.

87. On Shan-yüan, see C. Schwarz-Schilling, *Der Friede von Shan-yüan (1005 n. Chr.)*, and the articles by Wang Gungwu and Tao Jing-shen in *China among Equals*, ed. Rossabi.

88. Translated by Franke in "Chia Ssu-tao," 227.

89. Togan, "Annual Grants," 160–65.

90. *Yüan shih*, 62–63.

91. Ibid., 63.

92. Boyle, *Successors*, 249.

93. Ibid., 250.

94. Ibid., 251.

CHAPTER THREE

1. Marco Polo erroneously asserted that Khubilai was enthroned in 1256. The reasons for his confusion are discussed in Pelliot, *Notes on Marco Polo*, 566–67.

2. *Yüan shih*, 65.

3. See H. G. Raverty, trans., *Ṭabaḳāt-i-Nāṣirī: A General History of the Muhammadan Dynasties of Asia*, 1252.

4. *Recueil des historiens des Croisades*, 2:13; Der Nersessian, "Armenian Chronicle," 159–60.

5. Quatremère, *Histoire des Mongols*, 341–45.

6. P. M. Holt, Ann K. S. Lambton, and Bernard Lewis, eds., *The Cambridge History of Islam*.

7. For more on Baibars, who was to become the fourth Mamlūk sultan, see Syedah Fatima Sadeque, *Baybars I of Egypt*.

8. Holt, Lambton, and Lewis, *Cambridge History of Islam*, 212–13; for the

most recent scholarship on the battle, see J. M. Smith, "'Ayn Jālūt: Mamlūk Success or Mongol Failure," 307–45.

9. Quatremère, *Histoire des Mongols*, 353.

10. See George Vernadsky, *The Mongols and Russia*, 162–63; Bertold Spuler, *Die Goldene Horde: Die Mongolen in Russland, 1223–1502*, 40–42; Grekov and Iakoubovski, *La Horde d'Or*, 76–77.

11. *Yüan shih*, 64–65.

12. Ibid., 65; for Khubilai's effort to legitimize himself as a Chinese emperor, see Franke, *From Tribal Chieftain*, 25–52. As Franke points out, Khubilai deviated from the traditional pattern: he chose a reign title a decade before adopting a Chinese name for his dynasty; usually the names were chosen at the same time. Wang O wrote the edict proclaiming the reign title, which probably derives from the *Book of Changes* (*I ching*). Franke writes (p. 27) that "the reference to the Book of Changes [in Wang's edict] alludes possibly to the Commentaries to hexagram *Ch'ien* (The Creative) where the text speaks of a man emerging like 'a dragon in the field' and who has the quality of a ruler, being correct and moderate (*chung*). If this interpretation is correct we would have to translate the reign-name of Chung-t'ung as 'Moderate Rule.'" John Langlois translates it as "Pivotal Succession." See his introduction to *China under Mongol Rule*, 5. On Wang O, see Hok-lam Chan, "Wang O," 43–70; and *CILCY*, 22c.

13. *Yüan shih*, 63; see *CILCY*, 18b, for references on Wang Wen-t'ung.

14. T'o T'o, *Sung shih*, 13781; Herbert Franke, ed., *Sung Biographies*, 206, for a somewhat abbreviated biography.

15. Schlegel, *Hao Ching*, 116–222.

16. For a recent study of the Uighurs and the early Yüan, see Thomas Allsen, "The Yüan Dynasty and the Uighurs of Turfan in the 13th Century," in *China among Equals*, ed. Rossabi, 243–80.

17. John W. Dardess, "From Mongol Empire to Yüan Dynasty: Changing Forms of Imperial Rule in Mongolia and Central Asia," 122–23.

18. Kiselev, *Drevnemongol' skie goroda*, 117–25.

19. See Tamura Jitsuzō, "Ari Buka no ran ni tsuite," 1–16, and Ch'en Pang-chan, *Sung-shih chi-shih pen-mo*, for useful details about Arigh Böke's rebellion. The *Yüan shih* and Rashīd al-Dīn offer the most detailed versions of events in the rebellion.

20. Boyle, *Successors*, 255; Peter Jackson, "The Accession of Qubilai Qa'an: A Re-examination," 2–6, discusses Rashīd al-Dīn's biases against Arigh Böke.

21. *Yüan shih*, 66.

22. Ibid., 66–67.

23. Katsufuji, *Fubirai Kan*, 148–49; d'Ohsson, *Histoire des Mongols*, 2:344–48; on Liu T'ai-p'ing, see *CILCY*, 189c.

24. Katsufuji, *Fubirai Kan*, 49–150.

25. *Yüan shih*, 68–69.

26. Ibid., 68.

27. For a Chinese view of Arigh Böke, see *Hsin Yüan shih*, 6849. Arigh Böke is not accorded a biography in the *Yüan shih*; see also *CILCY*, 182a.

28. Barthold, *Turkestan*, 488, also discusses Alghu's efforts to dislodge Berke's troops from Central Asia.

29. Boyle, *Successors*, 256.

30. *Yüan shih*, 76; Boyle, *Successors*, 256–57; Grousset, *L'empire des steppes*, 353.

31. Joseph Hammer-Purgstall, trans., *Geschichte Wassaf's*, 25–26.

32. Boyle, *Successors*, 259.

33. See Marek and Knížková, *Miniatures*, plate 19, for a portrayal of the battles between Alghu and Arigh Böke.

34. Boyle, *Successors*, 261.

35. Ibid., 262–65.

36. For more about his family background, see Charles A. Peterson, "Old Illusions and New Realities: Sung Foreign Policy, 1217–1234," in *China among Equals*, ed. Rossabi, 218.

37. *Yüan shih*, 4591; on Li T'an, see also *CILCY*, 90b.

38. *Yüan shih*, 66; on Sung, see *CILCY*, 64a.

39. For a good secondary study of Li's rebellion, see Otagi Matsuo, "Ri Dan no hanran to sono seijiteki igi," 253–55. See also Sun K'o-k'uan, "Yüan-ch'u Li T'an shih-pien ti fen-hsi," 7–15.

40. *Yüan shih*, p. 69.

41. Ibid., 4593.

42. Ibid., 82.

43. Ibid., 4593.

44. Ibid., 86. On Shih Ch'u, see *CILCY*, 13a.

45. On Wang in the early days of Khubilai's reign, see Yan-shuan Lao, "The *Chung-t'ang shih-chi* of Wang Yün: An Annotated Translation with an Introduction."

46. *Yüan shih*, 4595; see also *CILCY*, 18b.

47. *Yüan shih*, 4596.

48. The portrait is found in the National Palace Museum in Taipei.

49. *Yüan shih*, 2871; "Gen no Sei So no kōgo," 681.

50. *Yüan shih*, 2871.

51. *Hsin Yüan shih*, 6837; on T'ang T'ai-tsung, see Charles Patrick FitzGerald, *Son of Heaven*.

52. Schlegel, *Hao Ching*, 38–43.

53. For an interesting study of these exams, see Ichisada Miyazaki, *China's Examination Hell*.

54. A useful account of these distinctions is found in Meng Ssu-ming, *Yüan-tai she-hui chieh-chi chih-tu*.

55. See, for example, Schlegel, *Hao Ching*, 13–27.

56. Schurmann, *Economic Structure*, 3–7, offers a succinct account of these appanages.

57. For more on the importance of the *khuriltai*, see Elizabeth Endicott-West, "Aspects of Decision-Making and Personnel Management in the Early Yüan," 8–19. I wish to thank Professor Charles Peterson of Cornell University for making this paper available to me.

58. *Yüan shih*, 63.

59. David M. Farquhar, "Structure and Function in the Yüan Imperial Government," in *China under Mongol Rule*, ed. Langlois, 27–29; *Yüan shih*, 2200, 2220, 2294, and 2296.

60. Farquhar, "Structure and Function," 36.

61. Paul Ratchnevsky, *Un code des Yüan*, 1:127–32.

62. The ten provinces were Ho-nan Chiang-pei, Chiang-che, Chiang-hsi, Hu-kuang, Shan-hsi, Ssu-ch'uan, Liao-yang, Yün-nan, Kan-su, and Fu-li (i.e., the Metropolitan Province). Ling-pei (the modern Mongolian People's Republic) and Cheng-tung (modern Korea) were two other provinces that were often lumped together with the ten others in China proper.

63. Charles O. Hucker, *The Censorial System of Ming China*, 27.

64. See Ratchnevsky, *Code*, 1:57–83, for some of these regulations.

65. Farquhar, "Structure and Function," 51; Endicott-West, "Aspects," 26–27, concurs in this assessment.

CHAPTER FOUR

1. This view is best set forth in John K. Fairbank, *Trade and Diplomacy on the China Coast: The Opening of the Treaty Ports, 1842–1854*, 23–38.

2. Jagchid and Bawden, in "Some Notes," 264, point to the difficulties the Mongols encountered in raising the horses they needed even after they conquered Southern China.

3. William H. McNeill, *Plagues and Peoples*, 132–75, develops a hypothesis about the Mongols and the rodents of the steppes as carriers of the bubonic plague starting in the middle of the fourteenth century.

4. Jacques Gernet, *Daily Life in China on the Eve of the Mongol Invasion 1250–1276*, 84.

5. Ibid., p. 137; for more on the Sung and food, see Michael Freeman, "Sung," in *Food in Chinese Culture: Anthropological and Historical Perspectives*, ed. K. C. Chang, 141–93.

6. See Friedrich Hirth and W. W. Rockhill, trans., *Chau Ju-kua: His Work on the Chinese and Arab Trade in the Twelfth and Thirteenth Centuries Entitled Chu-fan-chi*, for a contemporary view of this trade; for a glimpse of the scope of this trade, see Thomas H. C. Lee, "A Report on the Recently Excavated Song Ship at Quanzhou and a Consideration of Its True Capacity," 4–9.

7. Laurence J. C. Ma, *Commercial Development and Urban Change in Sung China (960–1279)*, 29–48.

8. Shiba Yoshinobu, *Commerce and Society in Sung China*, 126–40, for a study of these new cities; Gustav Ecke and Paul Demiéville's *The Twin Pagodas of Zayton* shows the cultural impact of the prosperity of the city of Ch'üan-chou.

9. Lo Jung-pang, "The Emergence of China as a Sea Power during the Late Sung and Early Yüan Periods," 500–501; see also Joseph Needham, *Science and Civilisation in China*, 4:3,656–95, for more on Chinese developments in naval warfare.

10. Lo Jung-pang, "Maritime Commerce and Its Relation to the Sung Navy," 81.

11. Ibid., p. 92.

12. On the role of eunuchs in an earlier dynasty, see J. K. Rideout, "The Rise of the Eunuchs during the T'ang Dynasty"; Taisuke Mitamura's *Chinese Eunuchs: The Structure of Intimate Politics* must be used with care.

13. On the influence of the relatives of empresses, see Priscilla Ching Chung, *Palace Women in the Northern Sung*, 69–77.

14. On the difficulties encountered by earlier reformers, see Hans Bielenstein, "The Restoration of the Han Dynasty"; and James T. C. Liu, *Reform in Sung China: Wang An-shih (1021–1086) and His New Policies*.

15. Franke, "Chia Ssu-tao," in *Confucian Personalities*, ed. Wright and Twitchett, 217–34, and idem, "Die Agrarreformen des Chia Ssu-tao," 345–69.

16. Franke, "Chia Ssu-tao," 223.

17. Schlegel, *Hao Ching*, 120–24.

18. *Yüan shih*, 70, 82.

19. Ibid., 74, 83, 97.

20. Ibid., 122.

21. Ibid., 87, 96, 100.

22. Ibid., 71.

23. Ibid., 68, 75, 82–84.

24. Ibid., 69, 85.

25. Ibid., 106.

26. Lo, "The Emergence of China," 492.

27. Grousset, *L'empire des steppes*, 353–56; d'Ohsson, *Histoire des Mongols*, 2 : 387–89; both emphasize the importance of this battle. For the location of Hsiang-yang, see Albert Herrmann, *An Historical Atlas of China*, 41.

28. Boyle, *Successors*, 290.

29. See the overly brief biography of Lü in Franke, *Sung Biographies*, 2 : 749–51; for additional sources on Lü, see *Combined Indices to Forty-Seven Collections of Sung Dynasty Biographies*, 131b (hereafter, *CIS*).

30. On Arigh Khaya, see *CILCY*, 182c; *IBCY* 1, p. 1; *IBCY* 2, p. 9; and *Yüan shih*, 3124–28.

31. On A-chu, see *CILCY*, 181d, and *Yüan shih*, 3119–24.

32. On ʿAlā al-Dīn, see *CILCY*, 184a; on Ismāʿīl, see *CILCY*, 50a; for partial translations of the *Yüan shih* biographies of these men, see A. C. Moule, *Quinsai, with Other Notes on Marco Polo*, 74–76.

33. *Yüan shih*, 119.

34. Ibid., 120.

35. Moule, *Quinsai*, 73.

36. *Yüan shih*, 122; Franke, *Sung Biographies*, 1 : 395–97; *CIS*, 127b.

37. *Yüan shih*, 122.

38. Ibid., 128.

39. Franke, "Chia Ssu-tao," 226.

40. *Yüan shih*, 128.

41. Ibid., 122.

42. Ibid., 131; *CIS*, 102c.

43. *Yüan shih*, 142–43.

44. For their Chinese biographies, see ibid., 4544–45.

45. L. C. Goodrich and Feng Chia-sheng, "The Early Development of Firearms in China," 118; see also L. C. Goodrich, "Firearms among the Chinese: A Supplementary Note," 63–64.

46. Moule, *Quinsai*, 76.

47. *Yüan shih*, 147. On the battles at Hsiang-yang, see also Ch'en Pang-chan, *Sung-shih chi-shih pen-mo*, 892–900.

48. For Shih's involvement in the southern campaigns, see *Yüan shih*, 3662.

49. Francis W, Cleaves, "The Biography of Bayan of the Barin in the *Yüan shih*," 206.

50. Ibid., 220.

51. Chia was forced to leave office on March 26, 1275. For later popular criticisms of Chia, see Franke, "Chia Ssu-tao," 231–34.

52. For a brief biography of Ch'en, see Franke, *Sung Biographies*, 134–36; see also *CIS*, 180d; for Ch'en I-chung, see Franke, *Sung Biographies*, 138–46, and *CIS*, 181b; and for Fang, see Franke, *Sung Biographies*, 349–55, and *CIS*, 91b.

53. Cleaves, "Bayan," 232.

54. *Yüan shih*, 170–71; Bayan divided his army into three divisions, each to follow a different route to Hangchow.

55. Pelliot, *Notes on Marco Polo*, 2:658–59; for brief sketches of each of these emperors, see Franke, *Sung Biographies*, 1010–19.

56. T'o T'o, *Sung shih*, 12533–40, for his biography; see also William A. Brown, "The Biography of Wen T'ien-hsiang in the *Sung shih*," and *CIS*, 92c; on Chang Shih-chieh, see *CIS*, 149c.

57. Cleaves, "Bayan," 238.

58. *Yüan shih*, 171.

59. Ibid., 176.

60. Ibid., 177.

61. Cleaves, "Bayan," 256.

62. *Yüan shih*, 178–79.

63. Ibid., 179.

64. Franke, *Sung Biographies*, 1010; Hsien committed suicide in 1323.

65. *Yüan shih*, 179.

66. T'u Chi, *Meng-wu-erh shih-chi*, 19, 8b.

67. Pelliot, *Notes on Marco Polo*, 2:659; Leonardo Olschki, *Marco Polo's Asia*, 340.

68. Franke, *Sung Biographies*, 679–86; *CIS*, 179b; on the chronology of the last years of Sung rule, see Aoyama Sadao, ed., *Sōdai shi nenpyō*, 267–76.

69. Franke, *Sung Biographies*, 397.

70. *Yüan shih*, 183.

71. Ibid., 190.

72. On Sodu, see *CILCY*, 195b.

73. *Yüan shih*, 3151.

74. Kuwabara Jitsuzō, "On P'u Shou-keng," 34–40.

75. For an inclusive study of P'u's career, see Maejima Shinji, "Senshū no Perushiyajin to Ho Jukō," 256–321.

76. Kuwabara, "On P'u Shou-keng," 57.

77. *Yüan shih*, 189.

78. Ibid., 191–92.

79. A brief description of Sodu's activities is in William W. Rockhill, "Notes on the Relations and Trade of China with the Eastern Archipelago and the Coast of the Indian Ocean during the Fourteenth Century," 428; a more complete narrative of his career is found in *Yüan shih*, 3150–55.

80. *Yüan shih*, 3152.

81. Ibid., 198.

82. Franke, *Sung Biographies*, 34.

83. On the Sung leaders who fled to Annam and Champa, see Hok-lam Chan, "Chinese Refugees in Annam and Champa at the End of the Sung Dynasty," 1–10.

84. Franke, *Sung Biographies*, 36.

85. Ibid., 145.

86. *Yüan shih*, 203–04.

87. Ibid., 46–47, 51; *chüan* 208 of the *Yüan shih* (pp. 4607–24) offers a detailed Chinese view of Sino-Korean relations during the period of Mongol rule of China.

88. Henthorn, *A History of Korea*, 119.

89. Takashi Hatada, *A History of Korea*, 53.

90. *Yüan shih*, 63; Li T'ang, *Yüan Shih-tsu*, 52.

91. *Yüan Kao-li chi-shih*, 15.

92. Katsufuji, *Fubirai Kan*, 215–17; *Yüan shih*, 72, 81, 91–92, 109.

93. *Yüan shih*, 64, 93.

94. Ibid., 85; see also William E. Henthorn, *Korea: The Mongol Invasions*, 106–07, 111–12; and Rossabi, *The Jurchens*, 10.

95. *Yüan shih*, 112.

96. Henthorn, *Korea: The Mongol*, 154–60; *Yüan shih*, 122.

97. *Yüan shih*, 123, 127–28.

98. Chŏng In-ji, *Koryŏ-sa*, 1:570; *Yüan shih*, 155; Louis Hambis, "Notes sur l'histoire de Corée à l'époque mongole," 179–83. During the course of the Yüan dynasty, seven Mongol princesses were married into the Korean royal family.

99. Henthorn, *Korea: The Mongol*, 202–05; for the importance of falconry at the traditional Chinese court, see Edward Schafer, "Falconry in T'ang Times," 293–338; and for the medicinal uses of falcons, see Bernard E. Read, *Chinese Materia Medica: 6, Avian Drugs*, nos. 311 and 314. The sources make no mention of the importation of Korean ginseng into Yüan China—a curious omission, for it was a highly prized commodity in the Middle Kingdom. For the uses of ginseng, see Emil Bretschneider, *Botanicon Sinicum*, 3:18–25; Maurice Kains, *Ginseng*, 130–31; and M. Pomet, *A Complete History of Drugs*, 194–95. For the import of Manchurian and Korean ginseng during the succeeding dynasty, see Ma Wen-sheng, *Fu-an tung-i chi*, 2b.

100. Henthorn, *History of Korea*, 127; on Korean ceramics of the Koryŏ period, see Gregory Henderson, *Korean Ceramics: An Art's Variety*; Robert Griffing, Jr., *The Art of the Korean Potter*; and, in particular, G. M. Gompertz, *Korean Celadon and Other Wares of the Koryŏ Period*.

101. Translated from the *Koryŏ-sa*, 3:257, in Chewon Kim, "Random Notes on Literary References to Koryŏ Ceramics," 32; see also Gregory Henderson, "Koryŏ Ceramics: Problems and Sources of Information," 5–28.

102. *Yüan shih*, 4610–22.

103. *Koryŏ-sa*, 3:519.

104. Henthorn, *Korea: The Mongol*, 194–97.

105. Lao Yen-hsüan, "Lun Yüan-tai ti Kao-li nu-li yü ying-ch'ieh," 1005–08.

106. Henthorn, *History of Korea*, 122.

107. On the earlier history of the Korean Office of Interpreters, known as the T'ongmun kwan, see the sources cited in Herbert Franke, "Sung Embassies: Some General Observations," in *China among Equals*, ed. Rossabi, 127 and 144, n. 65.

108. *Koryŏ-sa*, 3:757.

109. On this persecution, see Wright, *Buddhism in Chinese History*, 83–93, and Kenneth Ch'en, *Buddhism in China*, 225–33; for the limited contact betwen China and Japan from the ninth to thirteenth centuries, see Edmund H. Worthy, Jr., "Diplomacy for Survival: Domestic and Foreign Relations of Wu Yüeh, 907–978," and Shiba Yoshinobu, "Sung Foreign Trade: Its Scope and Organization," both in *China among Equals*, ed. Rossabi, 34–36, 104–08. Zen monks traded with the Chinese dynasties during the twelfth century.

110. Bejamin H. Hazard, "The Formative Years of the Wakō, 1223–63," 260–77.

111. *Yüan shih*, 111–12 and 4626; see also Nabaka Yamada's outdated but still somewhat useful *Ghenkō: The Mongol Invasion of Japan*.

112. *Hsin Yüan shih*, 7072; the section on Japan is translated and summarized in Ryūsaku Tsunoda and Luther Carrington Goodrich, *Japan in the Chinese Dynastic Histories*, 74–75; *Yüan Kao-li chi-shih*, 17–18. Some Koreans were willing to serve the Mongols, but feared that they might be involved in a full-scale war between the Mongols and the Japanese. On a few Koreans who cooperated with Khubilai and the Mongols, see *Koryŏ-sa*, 3:212.

113. *Yüan shih*, 115.

114. Ibid., 119; Tsunoda and Goodrich, *Japan*, 75.

115. Kyotsu Hori, "The Mongol Invasions and the Kamakura Bakufu," 94–97.

116. George Sansom, *A History of Japan to 1334*, 440.

117. Tsunoda and Goodrich, *Japan*, 76–79.

118. *Yüan shih*, 132; Wu Chung-han, "Yüan Ming Wo-tsei ju-k'ou yü Chung-kuo chiao-tsei ta-shih piao," 12–14.

119. *Yüan shih*, 3746; for additional biographical details about Chao, see his biography in the *Yüan shih*, 3743–46; and for additional sources about him, see *CILCY*, 36a; *IBCY* 2, p. 14; Wang Te-i, ed., *Yüan-jen chuan-chi tzu-liao so-yin* (hereafter, *YJCC*) 1732–33; *Hsin Yüan shih*, 7072.

120. Sansom, *History*, 441–42.

121. *Yüan shih*, 150.

122. Hori, "Mongol Invasions," 107–11.

123. *Yüan shih*, 154; Tsunoda and Goodrich, *Japan*, 81–82.

124. Joseph Needham, *Science*, 4:3, 477, asserts that a quarter of a million soldiers took part in the Mongol attack. His figure is grossly inflated.

125. Hori, "Mongol Invasions," 121; Yamada, *Ghenkō*, 107–37.

126. Sansom, *History*, 443–44.

127. Hori, "Mongol Invasions," 123–26.

128. Wu, "Yüan Ming Wo-tsei," 15–16; *Yüan shih*, 161.

129. On the Chinese and Mongol perception of Japan, as filtered through the descriptions of Marco Polo, see Enoki Kazuo, "Marco Polo and Japan," in *Oriente Poliano*, 23–26.

130. See a description of this process in the biography of the Mongol Arughtai in L. C. Goodrich and Chaoying Fang, eds., *A Dictionary of Ming Biography*, 12–14.

131. On Khaidu, see *CILCY*, 124d, and Pelliot, *Notes on Marco Polo*, 1:124–29.

132. Olschki, *Marco Polo's Asia*, 357, asserts that the story of Khutulun, whom he refers to as "Aigiaruc" (as does Marco Polo), "has the characteristics of a popular legend or historical fable." Yet the same account appears in the works of two disparate contemporaries—Marco Polo and Rashīd al-Dīn. For Rashīd al-Dīn's version, see Boyle, *Successors*, 26–27. Moreover, Khutulun is only one of a number of self-confident, independent, and assertive Mongol noblewomen of the thirteenth century. For this, see Morris Rossabi, "Khubilai Khan and the Women in His Family," 158–80. The story is, to my mind, authentic.

133. Yule, *The Book of Ser Marco Polo*, 2:463.

134. Ibid., 464.

135. Ibid., 465.

136. Boyle, *Successors*, 266.

137. The hostile Chinese views of Khaidu may be found in *Hsin Yüan shih*, 6850; T'u Chi, *Meng-wu-erh shih-chi*, 74, 6a–7b; Shao Yüan-p'ing, *Yüan shih lei-pien*, 1595–97.

138. V. V. Barthold, *Four Studies on the History of Central Asia*, 1:50; H. A. R. Gibb et al., *Encyclopedia of Islam*, 1:504–05.

139. Barthold, *Four Studies*, 2:4–7.

140. Dardess, "From Mongol Empire," 134; Barthold, *Four Studies*, 1:126, writes that "Khaydu, even though he possessed an excellent army, never undertook expeditions of conquest."

141. Louis Hambis, *Le chapitre cvii du Yüan che*, 114–15; idem, *Le chapitre cviii du Yüan che*, 94–95.

142. T'u Chi, *Meng-wu-erh shih-chi*, 76, 8b; *Yüan shih*, 265; Pelliot, *Notes on Marco Polo*, 2:795.

143. Pelliot, *Notes on Marco Polo*, 1:127.

144. T'u Chi, *Meng-wu-erh shih-chi*, 76, 8b–9a.

145. *Yüan shih*, 144.

146. Igor de Rachewiltz, "Muqali, Böl, Tas, and An-t'ung," 56–57; *CILCY*, 63c; for his career, see *Yüan shih*, 3081–84.

147. Pelliot, *Notes on Marco Polo*, 1:127.

148. Rachewiltz "Muqali," 57, identifies him as Tolui's son, but Pelliot, *Notes on Marco Polo*, 2:796, and Boyle, *Successors*, 162, correctly identify him as Tolui's grandson. Rashīd al-Dīn describes him as "extremely brave and a good archer.... Because of his great bravery his brain was full of rebellion" (Boyle, *Successors*, 162); T'u Chi, *Meng-wu-erh shih-chi*, 102, 2a; Pelliot, *Notes on Marco Polo*, 2:796, mistakenly identifies Yobukhur as the man offended by An-t'ung.

149. On Togh Temür, see Hambis, *Le chapitre cvii*, 104; on Melik Temür, see Boyle, *Successors*, 161; the Yüan dynastic history does not mention this son—see Hambis, *Le chapitre cvii*, 99, for a table of Arigh Böke's sons based on the *Yüan shih*. Both Rashīd al-Dīn (Boyle, *Successors*, 161) and the *Yüan shih* (Hambis, *Le chapitre cvii*, 94) agree that Yobukhur was Arigh Böke's oldest son; on Shiregi's descendants, see Hambis, *Le chapitre cvii*, 111–14.

150. Boyle, *Successors*, 266.

151. Ibid., 267; Pelliot, *Notes on Marco Polo*, 2:796; Yanai Wataru, *Mōkoshi kenkyū*, 515–16.

152. Dardess, "From Mongol Empire," 136.

153. *Yüan shih*, 270; interestingly enough, his reinstatement is not mentioned in his biography in the *Yüan shih*.

154. Boyle, *Successors*, 160.

155. Hambis, *Le chapitre cviii*, 94.

156. See Cleaves, "Bayan," for a comprehensive study of the earlier life and career of this renowned general.

157. Pelliot, *Notes on Marco Polo*, 2:796.

158. Rachewiltz, "Muqali," 57.

159. See repeated examples of such remissions and relief in Khubilai's *pen-chi* in the *Yüan shih* from the years 1270 on.

160. Dardess, "From Mongol Empire," 138; *CILCY*, 191b; *YJCC*, 1784–85.

161. *Yüan shih*, 221; *CILCY*, 92d; *YJCC*, 1674.

162. *Yüan shih*, 232.

163. Tōru Saguchi, "Mongoru-jin shihai jidai no Uiguristan."

164. Allsen, "The Yüan Dynasty and the Uighurs," in *China among Equals*, ed. Rossabi, 257.

165. Abe Takeo, "Where Was the Capital of the West Uighurs?" 437–38.

166. *Hsin Yüan shih*, 6937.

167. On the difficulties involved in maintaining control over one of the more important oases, see Morris Rossabi, "Ming China and Turfan, 1406–1517," 206–10.

168. Dardess, "From Mongol Empire," 143–60, offers a more detailed study of Khubilai's policies in Mongolia and the Upper Yenisei.

169. Based upon a study of Khubilai's *pen-chi* in the *Yüan shih*.

170. See Francis W. Cleaves, "Qabqanas ∼ Qamqanas," 402–03.

171. Boyle, *Successors*, 267–69.

172. Ibid., 268.

173. Ibid., 269.

CHAPTER FIVE

1. For more on these divisions, see Huang Ch'ing-lien, *Yüan-tai hu-chi chih-tu yen-chiu.*

2. T'o T'o, *Chin shih*, 1036; for an analysis of these Chin figures, see Ho Ping-ti, "Estimate," 3–53. The precise figure for the population given in the *Chin History* for 1195 is 48,490,400; see also Tao, *The Jurchen*, 51.

3. Ho Ping-ti, *Studies on the Population of China, 1368–1953*, 258; see also John Langlois's brief remarks on this demographic problem in the introduction to his *China under Mongol Rule*, 20. Robert Hartwell in "A Cycle of Economic Change in Imperial China: Coal and Iron in Northeast China, 750–1350," 150–53, writes that the population of the province of Honan in Northern China declined from 6,426,000 in 1208 to 908,235 in 1330. He attributes the decline to wars, pestilence, and floods of the Yellow River that occurred in 1234, 1286, 1288, 1290, and from 1296 to 1298.

4. On censuses during Ögödei's reign, see *Yüan shih*, 32, 34. See the helpful comments and translation by Waltraut Abramowski, "Die chinesischen Annalen von Ögödei und Güyük—Übersetzung des 2. Kapitels des Yüan-shih," 145, as well as Otagi Matsuo, "Mōkojin seiken-chika no Kanchi ni okeru hanseki no mondai," 390–402.

5. *Yüan shih*, 159.

6. Ibid., 70–71.

7. Ibid., 84.

8. Lao, "The *Chung-t'ang shih-chi*," 38.

9. *Yüan shih*, 86. Such relief efforts apparently continued throughout Khubilai's reign. Marco Polo wrote extensively about them. See Moule and Pelliot, *Marco Polo*, 247–48. Marco writes, "Now you may know about the truth that the great lord sends his trusty messengers and inspectors always every year . . . through all his lands and realms and provinces to know of his men, if any wrong has been done them and if they have had loss of their corn either through failure of weather, that is by storms or by great rains and winds as often happens, or through locusts, caterpillars, or through other pestilence that year. And if he finds that any of his people have had . . . such loss and that they have no corn he does not take the tax from them . . . but he gives of his own corn from his granaries as much as they need."

10. *Yüan shih*, 84.

11. Ibid., 83, 85, 87–88.

12. Ibid., 71.

13. Lao, "The *Chung-t'ang shih-chi*," 24.

14. Ibid., 113–14.

15. *Yüan shih*, 68.

16. See Igor de Rachewiltz, "Turks in China under the Mongols: A Preliminary Investigation of Turco-Mongol Relations in the 13th and 14th Centuries," in *China among Equals*, ed. Rossabi, 281–308.

17. *Yüan shih*, 2354.

18. Ibid., 73.

19. Ratchnevsky, *Code*, 1 : 189–90; Farquhar, "Structure and Function," in *China under Mongol Rule*, ed. Langlois, 41.

20. *Ta Yüan ts'ang-k'u chi*, in *Kuo-hsüeh wen-k'u* 37, 1.

21. *Yüan shih*, 81.

22. Ibid., 2354–55; Farquhar, "Structure and Function," in *China under Mongol Rule*, ed. Langlois, 41.

23. Inosaki Takaoki, "Gendai shasei no seijiteki kōsatsu," 6–10. See also Yang Na, "Yüan-tai nung-ts'un she-chih yen-chiu," 117–34.

24. Schurmann, *Economic Structure*, 44.

25. Matsumoto Yoshimi, "Gendai ni okeru shasei no sōritsu," 332–34.

26. See S. Kuczera's "The Influence of the Mongol Conquest on the Chinese System of Education and Selection of Officials."

27. Aritaka Iwao, "Gendai no nōmin seikatsu ni tsuite," in *Kuwabara hakushi kanreki kinen tōyōshi ronsō*, 951–57.

28. Schurmann, *Economic Structure*, 44–45; Lao, "The *Chung-t'ang shih-chi*," 40–42.

29. *Yüan shih*, 2357–58; see also Schurmann, *Economic Structure*, 75–77.

30. Schurmann, *Economic Structure*, 95–96.

31. See Farquhar, "Structure and Function," in *China under Mongol Rule*, ed. Langlois, 27–30, 45, for these agencies. On the later significance of the porcelains, see John A. Pope, *Chinese Porcelains from the Ardebil Shrine*.

32. Chü Ch'ing-yüan, "Government Artisans of the Yüan Dynasty," 245.

33. Farquhar, "Structure and Function," in *China under Mongol Rule*, ed. Langlois, 33.

34. See Chü, "Government Artisans," 242–44.

35. Morris Rossabi, *China and Inner Asia from 1368 to the Present Day*, 21.

36. Lo, "Maritime Commerce," 96.

37. On the camel's importance, see Edward Schafer, "The Camel in China Down to the Mongol Invasion," 190.

38. Kuwabara, "On P'u Shou-keng," 25; see also Ma, *Commercial Development*, 39–43.

39. Margaret Medley, *Yüan Porcelain and Stoneware*, 6; the production of ceramics for Muslims in China and in foreign countries continued into the Ming dynasty. See, for example, Kamer Aga-Oglu, "Blue-and-White Porcelain Plates Made for Moslem Patrons," 12–16.

40. Yang Lien-sheng, *Money and Credit in China: A Short History*, 46; for paper currency in the Yüan, the standard work is Herbert Franke, *Geld und Wirtschaft in China unter der Mongolenherrschaft*.

41. Murakami Masatsugu, "Genchō," 164.

42. Yang Lien-sheng, *Money and Credit*, 97.

43. Schurmann, *Economic Structure*, 215.

44. Weng Tu-chien, "Wo-t'o tsa-k'ao," 207.

45. Gordon Tullock, "Paper Money—A Cycle in Cathay," 401; Yang Lien-sheng, *Money and Credit*, 2.

46. *Yüan shih*, 68; Franke, *Geld*, 38–39.

47. Moule and Pelliot, *Marco Polo*, 238–40.

48. *Yüan shih*, 2371–72.

49. See Maeda Naonori, "Gendai no kahei tan-i," for more on paper money and the units involved; even the annual grants given to the Mongol nobles were now to be offered in paper money instead of in silk and silver. See Togan, "Annual Grants," lii–lx. On silver, see Robert F. Blake, "The Circulation of Silver in the Moslem East Down to the Mongol Epoch,' 291–328.

50. Boyle, *Successors*, 276.

51. Peter Olbricht, *Das Postwesen in China unter der Mongolenherrschaft im 13. und 14. Jahrhundert*, 40–42; Haneda Tōru, *Genchō ekiden zakko*, 30; Fang Hao, *Chung-hsi chiao-t'ung shih*, 12.

52. Yüan Chi, *Yüan-shih yen-chiu lun-chi*, 243; in the border province of Liao-yang, "a typical postal station might have twenty horses, twenty oxen and carts, and depending on its location, perhaps a few mules or camels" (Rossabi, *The Jurchens*, 4); on Liao-yang, see also Wada Sei, *Tōashi kenkyū: Manshū hen*, 230–31.

53. Yüan Chi, *Yüan-shih*, 244–45.

54. Moule and Pelliot, *Marco Polo*, 246.

55. Ibid., 235–37.

56. Sherman Lee and Wai-kam Ho, *Chinese Art under the Mongols: The Yüan Dynasty (1279–1368)*, 83; see also Lao "The *Chung-t'ang shih-chi*," 15.

57. Rockhill, "Notes," 438–40; Khubilai also sought to obtain medicines from Korea. For this, see *Koryŏ-sa*, 3:519.

58. Jutta Rall, *Die vier grossen Medizinschulen der Mongolenzeit*, 30–31; on Persian borrowings from Chinese medicine, see idem, "Zur persischen Übersetzung eines Mo-chüeh, eines chinesischen medizinischen Textes," 150–57.

59. Fang Hao, *Chung-hsi chiao-t'ung shih*, 3:149.

60. Ratchnevsky, *Code*, 2:46–48; *Yüan shih*, 2220–22.

61. See Robert P. Hymes, "Doctors in Sung and Yüan: A Local Case Study," for an interpretation of the change in status of doctors.

62. Haenisch, "Steuergerechtsame," 17.

63. Joseph Needham, "Medicine and Chinese Culture," in his *Clerks and Craftsmen in China and the West*, 265.

64. Needham, *Science*, 3:372–74; Chang Kuei-sheng, "The Maritime Scene in China at the Dawn of Great European Discoveries," 350; Alexander Wylie, "The Mongol Astronomical Instruments in Peking," in *Chinese Researches*, 16.

65. Boyle, *Cambridge History*, 668–73; Karl Jahn, "Wissenschaftliche Kontakte zwischen Iran und China in der Mongolenzeit," 199–200.

66. *Yüan shih*, 136; see Juliet Bredon, *Peking: A Historical and Intimate Description of Its Chief Places of Interest*, for a twentieth-century description of the Peking observatory. For Kuo Shou-ching, see *Yüan shih*, 3845–52.

67. Franke, "Sino-Western Contacts," 59.

68. For the world map, see W. Fuchs, *The Mongol Atlas of China by Chu Ssu-pen*.

69. Farquhar, "Structure and Function," in *China under Mongol Rule*, ed. Langlois, 29.

70. Hsiao, *Military Establishment*, 16.

71. Ibid., 25; Hsiao offers additional details on the financial obligations of the soldiers.

72. Farquhar, "Structure and Function," in *China under Mongol Rule*, ed. Langlois, 49.

73. Hsiao, *Military Establishment*, 39–44.

74. Inosaki Takaoki, "Gendai no take no senbai to sono shikō igi," 29–47.

75. *Yüan shih*, 2288.

76. *Ta-Yüan ma-cheng chi*, 1–3, 18; Jagchid and Bawden, "Some Notes," 261–62.

77. *Ta-Yüan ma-cheng chi*, 19.

78. *Yüan shih*, 82.

79. Ibid., 95, 109, 124.

80. Paul Heng-chao Ch'en, *Chinese Legal Tradition under the Mongols*, 46.

81. Liu's biography in the *Yüan shih* does not mention his involvement in the decision to build Peking, but later texts, including the *Hsü Tzu-chih t'ung-chien*, 4847, cite Liu as the main proponent for the construction of a new capital in China.

82. Two fourteenth-century sources, the *Cho-keng lu* of T'ao Tsung-i and the *Ku-kung i-lu* of Hsiao Hsün, offer useful descriptions of the layout and the actual buildings of Peking at that time. Nancy Schatzman Steinhardt has used these two texts in her "Imperial Architecture under Mongolian Patronage: Khubilai's Imperial City of Dadu," which she kindly allowed me to consult. Chinese archeologists have also begun to explore and discover some of the remains of the Mongols' capital of Ta-tu. For examples of their recent discoveries, see *K'ao-ku* 1 (1972): 19–28; 4 (1972): 54–57, on some inscriptions of the time; and 6 (1972): 2–15, 25–34.

83. Henry Serruys, "Ta-tu, Tai-tu, Dayidu," 73–81; and Pelliot, *Notes on Marco Polo*, 2:843–44.

84. For descriptions of geomancy, see Paul Wheatley, *The Pivot of the Four Quarters: A Preliminary Inquiry into the Origins and Character of the Ancient Chinese City*, 411–51; March, "Chinese Geomancy," 253–67; and Arthur F. Wright, "The Cosmology of the Chinese City," in *The City in Late Imperial China*, ed. G. William Skinner, 33–73.

85. Wai-kam Ho, "Government Adminstration and Supervision of Crafts in the Yüan Dynasty."

86. On this Muslim, see *chüan* 9 of Ou-yang Hsüan, *Kuei-chai wen-chi*, which is partially translated in Ch'en Yüan, *Western and Central Asians*, 219–20; see also George Kates, "A New Date for the Origins of the Forbidden City," 197.

87. For studies of these cities in earlier times, see Hans Bielenstein, "Loyang in Later Han Times," 1–142; and E. A. Kracke, Jr., "Sung K'ai-feng: Pragmatic Metropolis and Formalistic Capital," in *Crisis and Prosperity*, ed. Haeger, 49–77.

88. The Ming eventually chose this area for its capital at least in part for the same reasons. See Edward L. Farmer, *Early Ming Government: The Evolution of Dual Capitals*, 137.

89. F. W. Mote, "The Transformation of Nanking, 1350–1400," in *City,* ed. Skinner, 110; Wright, "Symbolism and Function," 668–71.

90. Ku Yen-wen, "Ta-tu, the Yüan Capital," in *New Archaeological Finds in China: Discoveries during the Cultural Revolution,* 21–25; E. Bretschneider, *Recherches archéologiques et historiques sur Pékin et ses environs,* 46–52; Andrew Boyd, *Chinese Architecture and Town Planning, 1500 B.C.–A.D. 1911,* 60–72; Lin Yutang, *Imperial Peking: Seven Centuries of China,* 33–41; Bredon, *Peking,* 8–30; L. C. Arlington and William Lewisohn, *In Search of Old Peking,* 77, 155, 243; Chu Hsieh, *Yüan Ta-tu kung-tien t'u-k'ao,* 8–54; and Jeffrey F. Meyer, *Peking as a Sacred City,* 28–32, all have useful sections on Ta-tu during the Yüan dynasty.

91. Steinhardt, "Imperial Architecture," 14.

92. Lin, *Imperial Peking,* 35; Osvald Siren, *The Imperial Palaces of Peking,* 1–2.

93. Bredon, *Peking,* 8.

94. A. Favier, *Pékin: Histoire et description,* plate 3; Marie Luise Gothein, "Die Stadtanlage von Peking," 10, offers a good map of the city; the observatory was damaged after a storm on August 17, 1979, but after some restoration it was reopened to the public in late March of 1983—see "Ancient Observatory Reopens," *China Daily,* April 1, 1983, p. 1.

95. Steinhardt, "Imperial Architecture," 21, translated from the *Ku-kung-i-lu* of Hsiao Hsün.

96. Paul Ratchnevsky, "Über den mongolischen Kult am Hofe der Grosskhane in China," in *Mongolian Studies,* ed. Ligeti, 435–41; *Yüan shih,* 1925.

97. Emil Bretschneider, *Recherches archéologiques et historiques sur Pékin et ses environs,* 57.

98. Arlington and Lewisohn, *Search,* 184–96, offers a fine description of the temple. Lao, "The *Chung-t'ang shih-chi,*" 216, reveals that Khubilai demanded that the temple be kept clean and in good repair and prohibited drinking and banqueting on the premises. See also Demiéville, "La situation religieuse," in *Oriente Poliano,* 217–18.

99. *Yüan shih,* 91, 1832. E. Blochet, *Introduction à l'histoire des Mongols de Fadl Allāh Rashīd Ed-Dīn,* 3.

100. *Yüan shih,* 1879. The cults are described in great detail in Ratchnevsky, *Code,* 2:1–20.

101. *Yüan shih,* 1892–1902.

102. Morris Rossabi, "Kublai Khan," 2, has a photo of this tortoise.

103. Moule and Pelliot, *Marco Polo,* 185–88.

104. The foreigners included Muslims, Khitans, Jurchens, and Nepalese.

105. *Yüan shih,* 133.

106. Ibid., 153.

107. For a study of the naming of the dynasty, see "Sull'adozione del nome dinastico Yüan" by Maurizia Dinacci Saccheti, 553–58.

108. *Yüan shih,* 138; the edict written to accompany the naming of the dynasty is translated in Langlois, *China under Mongol Rule,* 3–4; for the meaning of the term and its use in the *Book of Changes,* see Hellmut Wilhelm,

Eight Lectures on the I Ching, 51; for one view of Liu Ping-chung's role, see Hok-lam Chan, "Liu Ping-chung," 133.

109. For Kuo, see *Yüan shih*, 3847–52.

110. Arthur Waley, *The Analects of Confucius*, 69.

111. Chan, "Liu Ping-chung," 132; *Yüan shih*, 1665.

112. Hok-lam Chan, "Yao Shu," 31.

113. *Yüan shih*, 1665–66, 2217; Ratchnevsky, *Code*, 2:1–3.

114. *Yüan shih*, 1692.

115. For his name, see Pelliot, *Notes on Marco Polo*, 278–80; his biography is found in *Yüan shih*, 2888–93; see also *CILCY*, 102b.

116. *Yüan shih*, 2888; T'u Chi, *Meng-wu-erh shih-chi*, 76, 1a–1b; see also John D. Langlois, "Chin-hua Confucianism under the Mongols," 220; Chao Yi, *Nien-erh shih cha-chi*, 431–32.

117. On Wang, see *CILCY*, 22a; *IBCY*, 2:80

118. For a translation of this work, see Mary Lelia Makra, trans., *The Hsiao Ching; Yüan shih*, 2888.

119. Lao, "The *Chung-t'ang shih-chi*," 31.

120. *Yüan shih*, 3844.

121. Sun K'o-k'uan, "Yü Chi and Southern Taoism during the Yüan Period," in *China under Mongol Rule*, ed. Langlois, 222–23.

122. Herbert Franke, "Tibetans in Yüan China," in *China under Mongol Rule*, ed. Langlois, 307; a partial translation of the work is found in Prabodh Chandra Bagchi, *Sino-Indian Studies* 2:136–56, and a complete translation is in Constance Hoog, trans., *Prince Jin-gim's Textbook of Tibetan Buddhism*.

123. Hambis, *Le chapitre cvii*, 114–15; Hambis, *Le chapitre cviii*, 1–2.

124. *Yüan shih*, 92; Hambis, *Le chapitre cviii*, 1–2.

125. Fuchs, "Analecta," 33–64, describes some of the texts that were translated, as does Herbert Franke in "Wang Yün (1227–1304): A Transmitter of Chinese Values," in *Yüan Thought: Chinese Thought and Religion under the Mongols*, ed. Hok-lam Chan and William Theodore de Bary, 153–54.

126. See William Theodore de Bary, *Neo-Confucian Orthodoxy and the Learning of the Mind-and-Heart*, 91–126.

127. Fuchs, *Analecta*, 53; *Yüan shih*, 2190; Ratchnevsky, *Code*, 1:149–51.

128. *CILCY*, 129c; *IBCY* 1:23; *IBCY* 2:37; a brief account of Hsü's career appears in Alfred Forke, *Geschichte der neueren chinesischen Philosophie*, 286–90; see also Julia Ching, "Hsü Heng (1209–81): A Confucian under the Mongols"; on the recruitment of Confucians, see Abe Takeo, "Gendai chishikijin to kakyo," 136–45.

129. *Yüan shih*, 3717.

130. Wing-tsit Chan, "Chu Hsi and Yüan Neo-Confucianism," in *Yuan Thought*, ed. Chan and de Bary, 209. For a useful compilation of Yüan sources on the Imperial College, see Yüan Chi, *Yüan-shih yen-chiu lun-chi*, 203–35.

131. Wing-tsit Chan, "Chu Hsi," 211–12.

132. *Yüan shih*, 3717–18.

133. Translated in Julia Ching, "Hsü Heng," 4.

134. See Hok-lam Chan, "Wang O," 43–70, and idem, "Prolegomena to

the *Ju-nan i-shih*: A Memoir on the Last Chin Court under the Mongol Siege of 1234," 2–19.

135. *Yüan shih*, 3757; Khubilai had asked Wang earlier to explain the views expressed in the *Classic of Filiality* and other texts on family organization.

136. Farquhar, "Structure and Function," in *China under Mongol Rule*, ed. Langlois, 29; *Yüan shih*, 2180; Ratchnevsky, *Code*, 1 : 148–49.

137. Hok-lam Chan, "Chinese Official Historiography at the Yüan Court: The Composition of the Liao, Chin, and Sung Histories," in *China under Mongol Rule*, ed. Langlois, 63. See also the same author's "Wang O's Contribution to the History of the Chin Dynasty (1115–1234)," in *Essays in Commemoration of the Golden Jubilee of the Fung Ping Shan Library (1932–1982)*, ed. Chan Ping-Leung, 345–75.

138. Abramowski, "Annalen," 117–24.

139. Erich Haenisch, "Steuergerechtsame der chinesischen Klöster unter der Mongolenherrschaft," 15.

140. Tazaka Kōdō, *Chūgoku ni okeru kaikyō no denrai to sono kōtsū*, 613.

141. Harada, *Shang-tu*, 16; on the Muslims during the early years of Mongol rule, see Morris Rossabi, "The Muslims in the Early Yüan Dynasty," in *China under Mongol Rule*, ed. Langlois, 257–95.

142. Tazaka, *Chūgoku*, is to date the most comprehensive study of the Muslims in Chinese history.

143. For a study of his ancestors, see Omeljan Pritsak, "Āli-Burhān," 81–96.

144. Shimazaki Akira, "Gendai no kaikyōjin Saitenseki Tanshitei," 13–15; A. Vissière, *Études sino-mahométanes*, 1 : 6–7.

145. *Yüan shih*, 3063.

146. Luciano Petech, "Tibetan Relations with Sung China and with the Mongols," in *China among Equals*, ed. Rossabi, 184; his biography in Roerich, *The Blue Annals*, 485–86, does not mention his break with Khubilai.

147. *Yüan shih*, 4518; for more on ʿPhags-pa, the following, among numerous other sources, are helpful: Wylie, "First Mongol Conquest," 117–21; Paul Ratchnevsky, "Die mongolischen Grosskhane und die buddhistische Kirche," in *Asiatica: Festschrift Friedrich Weller zum 65. Geburtstag gewidmet*, ed. Johannes Schubert, 489–504; Tucci, *Scrolls*, 1 : 7–17; Shakabpa, *Tibet*, 61–72; and Jagchid Sechin, *Meng-ku yü Hsi-tsang li-shih kuan-hsi chih yen-chiu*, 64–88.

148. Dieter Schuh, *Erlasse und Sendschreiben mongolischen Herrscher für tibetische Geistliche*, 118–24.

149. *Yüan shih*, 2193, which has been translated in Francis W. Cleaves, "The Sino-Mongolian Inscription of 1346," 41, n. 39; on the Hsüan-cheng yüan, see also Nogami Shunjō, "Gen no senseiin ni tsuite," 779–95; on the various government agencies involved with Tibet, see Petech, "Tibetan Relations," in *China among Equals*, ed. Rossabi, 190–94; Liu Kuang-i, "T'u-fan fo-chiao yü Yüan Shih-tsu," in *Ta-lu tsa-chih shih-hsüeh ts'ung-shu: Liao Chin Yüan shih yen-chiu lun-chi*, 240–42; Jagchid, *Meng-ku*, 209–40 and *Yüan tien-chang*, 465.

150. Shōju Inaba, trans., "The Lineage of the Sa skya pa: A Chapter of the Red Annals," 109–10; two valuable paintings of ʿPhags-pa meeting with Khubilai are reproduced in An Shou-jen, "Pa-ssu-pa ch'ao-chien Hu-pi-lieh pi-hua," 12–13.

151. Petech, "Tibetan Relations," in *China among Equals*, ed. Rossabi, 185.

152. Luciano Petech, "The Mongol Census in Tibet," in *Tibetan Studies in Honour of Hugh Richardson*, ed. Michael Aris and Aung San Ssu Kyi, 233–37.

153. Josef Kolmas, *Tibet and Imperial China*, 21–23; Wylie, "First Mongol Conquest," 124–25.

154. Franke, *From Tribal Chieftain*, 61; Klaus Sagaster, "Herrschafts-ideologie und Friedensgedanke bei den Mongolen," 227–30.

155. Klaus Sagaster, trans., *Die weisse Geschichte*, 264; on Mañjuśrī, see Soothill and Hodous, *Dictionary*, 153–54.

156. Schmidt, *Geschichte der Ost-Mongolen*, 113.

157. On Cakravartin, see Soothill and Hodous, *Dictionary*, 445, for a brief identification.

158. Sagaster, *Die weisse*, 109.

159. *Yüan shih*, 1926–27; see also the discussion in Franke, *From Tribal Chieftain*, 60–61.

160. Krueger, "Sagang Sechen," 77; it is interesting to compare these words with the words uttered by a fictional Khubilai in a later novel. The fictional Khubilai says: "Buddhism pacifies human character and Confucian-ism regulates human conduct. They are both noble ideologies. Yet those who do not know how to regulate these principles will favor one against the other and often violate the equilibrium of the Way of the World." John Hangin, trans., *Köke sudur (The Blue Chronicle): A Study of the First Mongolian Historical Novel by Injannasi*, 49–50.

161. Petech, "Tibetan Relations," in *China among Equals*, ed. Rossabi, 187.

162. *Yüan shih*, 95; Ratchnevsky, *Code*, 1:lxxx–lxxxiv, describes some of the abuses of the monasteries.

163. Nogami Shunjō, "Gendai Dō Butsu nikyō no kakushitsu," 250–51.

164. On some products of this restoration and construction, see Lee and Ho, *Art*, 3–5.

165. T'ao Hsi-sheng, "Yüan-tai fo-ssu t'ien-yüan chi shang-tien," 0111–13.

166. For useful sources on Taoism in the Yüan, see Sun K'o-k'uan, *Sung Yüan Tao-chiao chih fa-chan*; and idem, *Yüan-tai Tao-chiao*.

167. Liu Ts'un-yuan and Judith Berling, "The 'Three Teachings' in the Mongol-Yüan Period," in *Yuan Thought*, ed. Chan and de Bary, 495.

168. Broeck and Tung, "Taoist Inscription," 7–8; Sun, *Yüan-tai Tao-chiao*, 197–202; on Chang, see *CILCY*, 113; *IBCY*, 10.

169. Broeck and Tung, "Taoist Inscription," 16–18; Édouard Chavannes, *Le T'ai Chan*.

170. The literature on Marco and his book is voluminous; here I shall only mention some of the sources I found most useful. The best translation is the

oft-cited work of A. C. Moule and Paul Pelliot, *Marco Polo: The Description of the World* (2 vols.), a composite of the various Polo texts, which should be consulted together with Pelliot's *Notes on Marco Polo* (2 vols.). Henry Yule's *The Book of Ser Marco Polo* (2 vols.), though dated, is still useful and should be supplemented by Henri Cordier, *Ser Marco Polo: Notes and Addenda to Sir Henry Yule's Edition*. Other translations include A. J. H. Charignon, *Le livre de Marco Polo*, and Louis Hambis, *Marco Polo: La description du monde*. A useful popular biography, though not always entirely reliable, is Henry H. Hart, *Marco Polo: Venetian Adventurer*, and the finest study of Polo's book is Leonardo Olschki, *Marco Polo's Asia*. In addition to Samuel Taylor Coleridge's poem "Kubla Khan," numerous imaginative works in the West deal with Marco and Khubilai. Two of the most interesting are *Marco Millions*, by Eugene O'Neill (see the text of the play in Eugene O'Neill, *Nine Plays*, 211–304) and *Invisible Cities* by Italo Calvino. A well-illustrated, popular account of Marco's life and career is found in Richard Humble, *Marco Polo*. The written and visual material on Marco is so vast that I once taught a course entitled "Marco Polo in Fact and Fiction," which at various times included the screening of such long-forgotten (with good reason) films as *The Adventures of Marco Polo* (United Artists, 1938), with Gary Cooper in the title role, *Marco Polo* (American International, 1962) with Rory Calhoun as Marco and Camillo Pilotto as Khubilai, and *Marco the Magnificent* (Metro Goldwyn Mayer, 1966), with Horst Buchholz in the leading role and Anthony Quinn as Khubilai.

171. Franke, "Sino-Western Contacts," 53.

172. Pelliot, *Notes on Marco Polo*, 2:834; Moule and Pelliot, *Marco Polo*, 316; see also R. Almagia et al., *Nel VII Centenario Della Nascita di Marco Polo*, 19.

173. Olschki, *Marco Polo's Asia*, 100; Francis W. Cleaves, "A Chinese Source Bearing on Marco Polo's Departure from China and a Persian Source on His Arrival in Persia," 181–203, asserts that Marco was indeed in China and that he departed from the Middle Kingdom to escort the Mongol princess Kökejin, who was promised in marriage to Arghun, the Il-Khan of Persia. Neither the Chinese nor the Persian sources mention Marco by name, but Cleaves believes that they both allude to the Venetian traveler and merchant.

174. Franke, "Sino-Western Contacts," 54.

175. On his family, see Rodolfo Gallo, "Marco Polo: La Sua famiglia e il suo libro," in *Nel VII Centenario*, ed. Almagia, 65–86, and Moule and Pelliot, *Marco Polo*, 15–21.

176. A. A. Vasiliev, *History of the Byzantine Empire, 324–1453*, 532–40; Marco was somewhat vague on dates. On occasion, therefore, precision in dating particular events is impossible. Even the precise date of Marco's birth is unknown. The errors and imprecise dates may be the result of the lack of a definitive early recension of his book. The available editions, consisting of about 120 manuscripts, differ in many particulars, making the translator's work very difficult indeed.

177. Moule and Pelliot, *Marco Polo*, 77.

178. Ibid., 85.

179. Ibid., 192.

180. *Masterpieces of Chinese Figure Painting*, no. 30. For more on him, see James Cahill, *An Index of Early Chinese Painters and Paintings, T'ang, Sung, and Yüan*, 303, and idem, *Hills beyond a River: Chinese Painting of the Yüan Dynasty, 1279–1368*, 153; Liu received the title of Keeper of the Imperial Wardrobe for his services.

181. Moule and Pelliot, *Marco Polo*, 204.

182. Ibid., 204–05.

183. Ibid., 202.

184. *Yüan shih*, 3249.

185. E. A. Wallis Budge, *The Monks of Kublai Khan, Emperor of China*, 45. Budge offers a complete translation of the Syriac text of the travels of Rabban Sauma and his companion Rabban Marcos.

CHAPTER SIX

1. For a detailed study of these scribes, see Jagchid Sechin, "Shuo *Yüan-shih* chung ti 'Pi-she-ch'ih' ping chien-lun Yüan-ch'u ti 'Chung-shu ling,'" 19–113.

2. Rachewiltz, "Some Remarks on Language," 68.

3. Gerard Clauson, "The hP'ags-pa Alphabet," 300–303.

4. For the letters, see Nicholas Poppe, *Grammar of Written Mongolian*, 17; for brief surveys of the early history of the Mongol languages and written scripts and their general characteristics, see Paul Pelliot, "Les systèmes d'écriture en usage chez les anciens Mongols," 284–89; and Nicholas Poppe, *Introduction to Altaic Linguistics*; for more sources on the Mongol languages, see Schwarz, *Bibliotheca Mongolica, Part I*, 48–55.

5. Nicholas Poppe, *The Mongolian Monuments in ḥP'ags-pa Script*, 2.

6. *Yüan shih*, 121.

7. Nakano, *Phonological Study*, 41–45, describes the script, and the work has an extensive bibliography though it does not include the Russian sources.

8. Poppe, *Mongolian Monuments*, 4.

9. On the use of the pai-hua in Yüan dynasty writings, see Ts'ai Mei-piao, *Yüan-tai pai-hua-pei chi-lu*, which discusses the use of the colloquial in the Yüan dynasty.

10. *Yüan shih*, 4518.

11. Ibid., 139, 147.

12. Ibid., 165; Farquhar, "Structure and Function," 29; Ratchnevsky, *Code*, 149–51.

13. *Yüan shih*, 209, 266.

14. Ibid., 142.

15. Poppe, *Mongolian Monuments*, 8–9; Rachewiltz, "Some Remarks on Language," 72–74.

16. Chavannes, "Inscriptions et pièces," 376–81, 407–10, and 413, for some examples of these steles; see also Marian Lewicki, "Les inscriptions mongoles inédites en écriture carrée," 1–72.

17. Roland Bonaparte, *Documents de l'époque mongole des xiii et xiv siècles*, plate 8, nos. 61—62, 65—66, offer translations of the two steles.

18. Louis Ligeti, *Monuments en écriture ʿPhags-pa: Pièces de chancellerie en transcription chinoise*, 109—16, for some transcriptions of these inscriptions on the *p'ai-tzu*. Examples of *p'ai-tzu* are found throughout China. I came across one in the Kansu Provincial Museum in Lan-chou in 1980.

19. David M. Farquhar, "The Official Seals and Ciphers of the Yüan Period," 362—93; Richard Schlösser, "Die Münzen der beiden Epochen Chi Yüan," 38—46; E. Drouin, "Notices sur les monnaies mongoles," 486—544; *K'ao-ku*, no. 4 (1972): 54—56; M. Aurel Stein, *Innermost Asia*, 1 : 441—55; and An Shou-jen, "Pa-ssu-pa ch'ao-chien Hu-pi-lieh pi-hua," 13.

20. Ligeti, *Monuments*, 121—22; John Ayers, "Some Characteristic Wares of the Yüan Dynasty," 69—86; see also Koyama Fujio, " 'Pa-ssu-pa' moji aru Shina kotōji," 23—31, and Basil Gray, "Art under the Mongol Dynasties of China and Persia," 166.

21. Yet it has proved invaluable for philologists and phonologists. See, for example, Paul B. Denlinger, "Chinese in hP'ags-pa Script," 407—33.

22. Perng Ching-hsi, *Double Jeopardy: A Critique of Seven Courtroom Dramas*, 11; on the question of patronage, see also Stephen H. West, "Mongol Influence on the Development of Northern Drama," in *China under Mongol Rule*, ed. Langlois, 457—62; John K. Fairbank and Edwin O. Reischauer (*East Asia: The Great Tradition*, 286) write of its appeal to the "less highly educated urban audiences of the day."

23. Perng, *Double Jeopardy*, 2.

24. Liu Jung-en, *Six Yüan Plays*, 18.

25. J. I. Crump, *Chinese Theater in the Days of Kublai Khan*, 22.

26. Ibid., 178.

27. Translations of some of these dramas may be found in the following works: Liu Jung-en's above-cited book; Gladys Yang and Yang Xianyi, *Selected Plays of Guan Hanqing*; Shih Chung-wen, *Injustice to Tou O (Tou O Yüan)*; and S. I. Hsiung, *The Romance of the Western Chamber*. The courtroom plays are discussed in Perng, *Double Jeopardy*, and George A. Hayden, "The Courtroom Plays of the Yüan and Early Ming Periods," 192—220.

28. Richard F. S. Yang, "The Social Background of the Yüan Drama," 332—333.

29. Perng, *Double Jeopardy*, 8.

30. Richard F. S. Yang, "Social Background," 332.

31. Both quotes from Hayden, "Courtroom Plays," 202.

32. West, "Mongol Influence," in *China under Mongol Rule*, ed. Langlois, 460.

33. Crump, *Chinese Theater*, 6—7.

34. For more detail, see W. L. Idema, *Chinese Vernacular Fiction: The Formative Period*.

35. C. T. Hsia, *The Classic Chinese Novel: A Critical Introduction*, 8, but see his entire introduction, 1—33; West, "Mongol Influence," 464.

36. K. T. Wu, "Chinese Printing under Four Alien Dynasties," 459.

37. Ibid., 463; *Yüan shih*, 287.

38. For this later period, see Evelyn Sakakida Rawski, *Education and Popular Literacy in Ch'ing China*, and Tadao Sakai, "Confucianism and Popular Educational Works," in *Self and Society in Ming Thought*, ed. William Theodore de Bary, 331–66.

39. Liu Ming-shu, "Yüan Hsi-yü ch'ü-chia A-li Yao-ch'ing fu-tzu," 105–09; Ch'en Yüan, *Western and Central Asians*, 180.

40. Antoine Mostaert, "À propos de quelques portraits d'empereurs mongols," 147–56.

41. His great granddaughter Princess Sengge (ca. 1328–1332) embraced Chinese culture, became one of its great champions, and continued to add to the collection of Chinese paintings to which he had contributed. Fu Shen, "Nü-ts'ang chia huang-tzu ta-chang kung-chu: Yüan-tai huang-shih shu-hua shou-ts'ang shih-lüeh," 25–52.

42. On Wen-tsung, see Kanda Kiichirō, "Gen no Bunshū no fūryū ni tsuite," 477–88; Cahill, *Hills beyond a River*, 3–4.

43. Susan Bush, *The Chinese Literati on Painting: Su Shih (1037–1101) to Tung Ch'i-ch'ang (1555–1636)*, 118.

44. Lee and Ho, *Art*, 1.

45. Ibid., 91.

46. Cahill, *Hills beyond a River*, 15–16.

47. For more on Yüan paintings, see the following works by Li Chu-tsing: "The Development of Painting in Soochow during the Yüan Dynasty," 483–500; "Stages of Development in Yüan Landscape Painting"; and "The Uses of the Past in Yüan Landscape Painting," 73–88.

48. Cahill, *Hills beyond a River*, 17; for more on Cheng's hatred of the Mongols, see Frederick W. Mote, "Confucian Eremitism in the Yüan Period," in *The Confucian Persuasion*, ed. Arthur F. Wright, 234–36; on Cheng, see *CILCY*, 206c.

49. On Kung, see Cahill, *Hills beyond a River*, 17–19, and *CILCY*, 50c; on Ch'ien, see Cahill, *Hills beyond a River*, 19–37; Li Chu-tsing, "The Role of Wu-hsing in Early Yüan Artistic Development under Mongol Rule," in *China under Mongol Rule*, ed. Langlois, 344–48; and *CILCY*, 205.

50. Cahill, *Hills beyond a River*, 15.

51. See Herbert Franke, "Dschau Mong-fu: Das Leben eines chinesischen Staatsmannes, Gelehrten und Künstlers unter der Mongolenherrschaft," 48, and *CILCY*, 35b–c; *IBCY* 1 : 6; *IBCY* 2 : 14.

52. Cahill, *Hills beyond a River*, 47–49; *CILCY*, 53b.

53. Cahill, *Hills beyond a River*, 159–60; *IBCY* 1 : 33.

54. Marilyn Wong Fu, "The Impact of the Reunification: Northern Elements in the Life and Art of Hsien-yü Shu (1257?–1302) and Their Relation to Early Yüan Literati Culture," in *China under Mongol Rule*, ed. Langlois, 383.

55. On Ch'eng, see Yao Ts'ung-wu, "Ch'eng Chü-fu yü Hu-pi-lieh p'ing-Sung i-hou ti an-ting nan-jen wen-t'i," 353–79, and *Yüan shih*, 4015–18.

56. Mote, "Confucian Eremitism," in *The Confucian Persuasion*, ed. Wright, 236.

57. Franke, "Dschau Mong-fu," 28.

58. Li Chu-tsing, "The Role of Wu-hsing," in *China under Mongol Rule*, ed. Langlois, 344.

59. *Yüan shih*, 4018.

60. Bush, *Chinese Literati*, 119; for some of Chao's own views on art and political matters, see his *Sung-hsüeh-chai wen-chi*, 10a–15a.

61. Li Chu-tsing, "The Role of Wu-hsing," in *China under Mongol Rule*, ed. Langlois, 348. For a study of a later Yüan dynasty painter, see Konrad Wegmann, *Kuo Pi: Ein Beamter und Literaten-Maler der Mongolenzeit*.

62. Farquhar, "Structure and Function," in *China under Mongol Rule*, ed. Langlois, 32; *Yüan shih*, 2258.

63. See Wai-kam Ho, "Government Administration and Supervision of Crafts in the Yüan Dynasty," 5–6.

64. Medley, *Yüan Porcelain and Stoneware*, 1.

65. *Yüan shih*, 2227.

66. For discoveries of Chinese porcelains in other lands, see G. T. Scanlon, "Egypt and China: Trade and Imitation," in *Islam and the Trade of Asia*, ed. D. S. Richards, 81–95; Friedrich Sarre, *Die Keramik von Samarra*; T. Harrison, "Trade Porcelain and Stoneware in South-east Asia," 222–26; Paul Kahle, "Chinese Porcelain in the Lands of Islam," 27–46.

67. Medley, *Yuan Porcelain and Stoneware*, 10–11.

68. On the blue-and-whites, see John Alexander Pope, *Fourteenth-Century Blue-and-White: A Group of Chinese Porcelains in the Topkapu Sarayi Müzesi, Istanbul*.

69. Lee and Ho, *Art*, 63–70, 72.

70. Ho, unpublished paper; for a present-day description of Fei-lai Feng, see *Nagel's Encyclopedia-Guide: China*, 1084–85; see also Huang Yung-ch'üan, *Hang-chou Yüan-tai shih-k'u i-shu*.

71. On A-ni-ko, see *CILCY*, 184a; see also *Hsin Yüan shih*, 7058–59, and Chang Hsing-lang, *Chung-hsi chiao-t'ung shih-liao hui-pien*, 6:471–72.

72. *Yüan shih*, 4545–46.

73. Ishida Mikinosuke, "Gendai no kōgeika Nepāru no ōzoku 'A-ni-ko' no den ni tsuite," 250–51.

74. Ibid., 251–55; his son A-seng-ko, following in his father's footsteps, sculpted five images of the Buddha for the Kao Liang-ho temple in Ta-tu.

75. Rachewiltz, "Some Remarks on Language," 57–68.

76. Rachewiltz, "Muqali," 57.

77. Ratchnevsky, 1:137–38.

78. H. F. Schurmann, "Problems of Political Organization during the Yüan Dynasty," 5:26–31.

79. Mote, "Chinese Despotism," 17–18.

80. Farquhar, "Structure and Function," in *China under Mongol Rule*, ed. Langlois, 54–55.

81. Henry Serruys, *Kumiss Ceremonies and Horse Racing: Three Mongolian Texts*, 1–5.

82. Paul Ratchnevsky, "Über den mongolischen Kult am Hofe der Grosskhane in China," *Mongolian Studies*, ed. Ligeti, 426–28.

83. Ibid., 434–42.

84. Ratchnevsky, Code, 2:2–4.

85. Jean-Paul Roux, "Le chaman gengiskhanide," 407.

86. See Schuyler Cammann, "Mongol Costume: Historical and Recent," in Aspects of Altaic Civilization, ed. Denis Sinor, 157–66.

87. Moule and Pelliot, Marco Polo, 220; Polo claims that more than forty thousand guests could be accommodated at these celebrations.

88. Ibid., 231.

89. Ibid., 205; see also Morris Rossabi, "Khubilai Khan and the Women in His Family," Studia Sino-Mongolica, ed. Bauer, 171–72.

90. On Khubilai's efforts to associate himself with T'ang T'ai-tsung, see Yanai, Mōkoshi kenkyū, 977–89.

CHAPTER SEVEN

1. Moule and Pelliot, Marco Polo, 220–36.

2. See Herbert Franke, "Ahmed: Ein Beitrag zur Wirtschaftsgeschichte Chinas unter Qubilai," 222–23.

3. Pelliot, Notes on Marco Polo, 1:10.

4. See his biography in Yüan shih, 4458–64.

5. Moule and Pelliot, Marco Polo, 214.

6. Yüan shih, 4558–59.

7. Franke, "Ahmed," 232.

8. Tamura Jitsuzō et al., Ajia-shi kōza, 282.

9. Ch'en Pang-chan, Yüan-shih chi-shih pen-mo, 30.

10. Tamura, Ajia-shi kōza, 282.

11. Franke, "Ahmed," 229.

12. Schurmann, Economic Structure, 147–48.

13. Franke, Geld, 43.

14. Yang Lien-sheng, Money and Credit, 7.

15. Yüan shih, 4560–61.

16. Hsiao Ch'i-ch'ing, Hsi-yü-jen yü Yüan-ch'u cheng-chih, 67; Rachewiltz, "Muqali," 56–58.

17. Yüan shih, 4559–60.

18. Hok-lam Chan, "Wang O," 53; see also Chan's "Wang O's Contribution to the History of the Chin Dynasty (1115–1234)," in Essays, ed. Chan Ping-leung, 355.

19. Li Chieh, Yüan shih, 64; Ch'en Pang-chan, Yüan-shih chi-shih pen-mo, 30.

20. J. Deguignes, Histoire générale des Huns, des Turcs, des Mongols, et des autres Tartares occidentaux, 3:152.

21. Boyle, History, 291.

22. Yüan shih, 4560–61.

23. Franke, "Ahmed," 235.

24. Moule, Quinsai, 79–88, for a full account of this cabal and its plot to kill Ahmad.

25. Ibid., 80.

26. Olschki, *Marco Polo's Asia*, 411, offers a different, harsher assessment of Aḥmad's influence on government.

27. See, for example, *Yüan shih*, 2873.

28. Ibid., 221–22, on one such release of prisoners; on Sung officials, merchants and soldiers who sold their women into prostitution, see Ratchnevsky, *Code*, 1:136.

29. Schurmann, *Economic Structure*, 9–10.

30. *Yüan shih*, 210; Aritaka Iwao, "Gendai no nōmin seikatsu ni tsuite," 957.

31. See *Ta Yüan ts'ang-k'u chi*, 1.

32. Schurmann, *Economic Structure*, 10.

33. *Yüan shih*, 213.

34. Schurmann, *Economic Structure*, 29–31.

35. Matsumoto Yoshimi, "Gendai ni okeru shasei no sōritsu," 329.

36. Schurmann, *Economic Structure*, 146–212, for a more detailed analysis of these monopolies.

37. Franke, *Geld*, 53–55.

38. Schurmann, *Economic Structure*, 223–28.

39. Ch'en Pang-chan, *Sung-shih chi-shih pen-mo*, 1–3.

40. Ibid., 3.

41. Hsiao, *Military Establishment*, 56.

42. On this, see the oft-cited work by Mote, "Confucian Eremitism," in *Confucian Persuasion*, ed. Wright, and Fu Lo-shu, "Teng Mu: A Forgotten Chinese Philosopher," among other works on these dissidents.

43. See Lao Yan-shuan, "Southern Chinese Scholars and Educational Institutions in Early Yüan: Some Preliminary Remarks," in *China under Mongol Rule*, ed. Langlois, 107–33.

44. See the essays by Tu Wei-ming and John Langlois in *Yuan Thought*, ed. Chan and de Bary.

45. Chou Tsu-mo, "Sung-wang hou-shih Yüan chih ju-hsüeh chiaoshou," 191–214.

46. On Chu and Chang, see *CILCY*, 4d and 136c, respectively.

47. *Hsin Yüan shih*, 6964–65.

48. A useful map of these sites is found in Lo Jung-pang, "The Controversy over Grain Conveyance during the Reign of Qubilai Qaqan (1260–94)," 262.

49. That office had been founded in 1282, according to *Yüan shih*, 247. The debate over the routes is recounted throughout Khubilai's annals in the Yüan dynastic history.

50. Lo, "Controversy," 277.

51. For more on the sea route, see *Ta Yüan hai-yün chi*, 35–50.

52. *Yüan shih*, 319.

53. Ibid., 4564.

54. Ibid., 4564–65; see also Luciano Petech, "Sang-ko, a Tibetan Statesman in Yüan China," 201.

55. Schurmann, *Economic Structure*, 170.

56. For his comprehensive program, see Ch'en Pang-chan, *Yüan-shih chishih pen-mo*, 45–46.

57. Ibid., 46.

58. Franke, *Geld*, 72–74.

59. Ch'en Pang-ch'an, 47; Li Chieh, *Yüan shih*, 65.

60. *Yüan shih*, 271; Ch'en T'ien-hsiang was another of the officials who was not intimidated by Lu and continued to criticize him and his policies— see ibid., 4569.

61. Ibid., 276, 281.

62. Petech, "Sang-ko," 194, presents his view that Sang-ko, not transcribed Sengge as traditionally believed, was a Tibetan, and he uses Tibetan sources to provide the most comprehensive view of this man to date.

63. *Yüan shih*, 4570.

64. For a brief biography, see ibid., 4519; see also Tucci, *Scrolls*, 1:55.

65. Nogami Shunjō, "Gen no senseiin ni tsuite," 770–95.

66. Petech, "Sang-ko," 198–200; Herbert Franke, "Sen-ge: Das Leben eines uigurischen Staatsbeamten zur Zeit Chubilai's dargestellt nach Kapitel 205 der Yüan-Annalen," 90–92.

67. Boyle, *Successors*, 295–96.

68. Kuwabara, "On P'u Shou-keng," 63.

69. See Franke, "Dschau Mong-fu," 34–35.

70. *Yüan shih*, 301–02.

71. Ibid., 2028; Otagi Matsuo, "Gendai shikimokujin ni kansuru ikkōsatsu," 44; Paul Ratchnevsky, "Rašīd al-Dīn über die Mohammedaner Verfolgungen in China unter Qubilai," 180, and Ratchnevsky, *Code*, 2:21.

72. See Esin, "Miniatures," 14, 34.

73. Boyle, *Successors*, 294.

74. Uematsu Tadashi, "Gensho kōnan ni okeru chōzei taisei ni tsuite," 28–32.

75. See, for example, Franke, "Sen-ge," 94–100, for some of these accusations.

76. Schurmann, *Economic Structure*, 135; Franke, *Geld*, 57–59.

77. *Yüan shih*, 297.

78. Ibid., 4572.

79. This was the same policy that Khubilai and the Mongols adopted in employing other foreigners in ruling China: "By serving as intermediaries between the Mongol rulers and their Chinese subjects, the Muslims performed valuable services but simultaneously provoked the wrath of the conquerors and the conquered.... The Mongols, consciously or not, used the Muslims as scapegoats, thereby diverting Chinese animosity from themselves.... By employing the Muslims as tax collectors and moneylenders, the Mongols ensured that the Chinese and the Muslims would frequently be at odds" (Rossabi, "The Muslims," 258–59).

80. Liu Kuang-i, "T'u-fan Fo-chiao yü Yüan Shih-tsu," in *Ta-lu tsa-chih shih-hsüeh ts'ung-shu*, 241–43.

81. Li Chieh, *Yüan shih*, 60–70.

82. Yen Chien-pi, "Nan-Sung liu-ling i-shih cheng-ming chi-chu ts'uan-kung fa-hui nien-tai k'ao," 28–36.

83. Herbert Franke, "Tibetans in Yüan China," in *China under Mongol Rule*, ed. Langlois, 324–25.

84. *Yüan shih*, 362.

85. Ibid., 352.

86. On this incident, see Paul Demiéville, "Les tombeaux des Song méridionaux," 458–567, and his "La situation religieuse en Chine au temps de Marco Polo," in *Oriente Poliano*, 214.

87. Franke, "Tibetans," in *China under Mongol Rule*, ed. Langlois, 325.

88. *Yüan shih*, 354; Paul Ratchnevsky, "Die mongolischen Grosskhane und die buddhistische Kirche," 497.

89. *Yüan shih*, 344.

90. Petech, "Sang-ko," 207.

91. As we shall note, Khubilai was not, in fact, the guiding figure he had been in the past. He had abdicated many of his duties, and some sources suggest that one of his wives screened the affairs that were brought to his attention and often made decisions in his name.

92. One of the more interesting such satires, written in the late Yüan, is translated by Herbert Franke in "Eine Mittelalterliche chinesische Satire auf die Mohammedaner," 202–08.

93. Boyle, *Successors*, 323–28.

94. For more on Ai-hsüeh, see A. C. Moule, *Christians in China before the Year 1550*, 228–29.

95. Boyle, *Successors*, 294.

96. *Yüan shih*, 217–18; Heyd, *Histoire*, 2:245.

97. Boyle, *Successors*, 295.

98. *Yüan tien-chang*, 763–64.

99. *Yüan shih*, 183, 3266; Erich Haenisch, *Die Geheime Geschichte der Mongolen*, 17.

100. Boyle, *Successors*, 294.

101. Joseph-Anne-Marie de Moyriac deMailla, *Histoire générale de la Chine, ou annales de cet empire: traduites du Tong-kien-kang-mou*, 10:456.

102. H. M. G. d'Ollone, *Recherches sur les Musulmans chinois*, 68.

103. Ch'en Pang-chan, *Yüan-shih chi-shih pen-mo*, 58.

104. Fang Kuo-yü, "Kuan-yü Sai-tien-ch'ih fu-Tien kung-chi," 48–49.

105. L. C. Goodrich, "Westerners and Central Asians in Yüan China," in *Oriente Poliano*, 8.

106. Hambis, *Le chapitre cviii*, 126, n. 4.

107. Olschki, *Marco Polo's Asia*, 333.

108. *Yüan shih*, 361; T'u Chi, *Meng-wu-erh shih-chi*, 80, 4b.

109. Poppe, *Mongolian Monuments*, 47.

110. Chavannes, "Inscriptions et pièces," 394; Kubo, "Prolegomena," 51–61.

111. Kenneth Ch'en, *Buddhism in China*, 425.

112. *Yüan shih*, 234; see also Igor de Rachewiltz, "The *Hsi-yu-lu* by Yeh-lü Ch'u-ts'ai," 1–3, for a useful summary.

113. Chavannes, "Inscriptions et pièces," 400–401.

114. Broeck and Tung, "Taoist Inscription," 12–13; Nogami, "Gendai Dō Butsu nikyō no kakushitsu," 258–59, takes a less sanguine view of Khubilai's policy toward Taoism.

115. *Yüan shih*, 232; Sun, *Yüan-tai Tao-chiao*, 43–46, 132, 181; for a more detailed English summary of Khubilai's patronage of the Taoists, see Sun's "Yü Chi and Southern Taoism during the Yüan Period," *China under Mongol Rule*, ed. Langlois, 212–53.

116. T'ao, "Yüan-tai fo-ssu," 0108–14.

117. On the influence of the Central Asian Buddhists, see Şinasi Tekin, *Buddhistische Uigurica aus der Yüan-Zeit.*

CHAPTER EIGHT

1. *Yüan shih*, 161; Tsunoda and Goodrich, *Japan*, 83–84.

2. Sansom, *History*, 448.

3. *Yüan shih*, 224.

4. Ibid., 215, 222; Hori, "Mongol Invasions," 137.

5. *Yüan shih*, 226.

6. Ibid., 228.

7. Ibid., 230.

8. Ibid., 230; see also Lo, "Maritime Commerce," 99.

9. Tsunoda and Goodrich, *Japan*, 88.

10. Sansom, *History*, 449; Wu, "Yüan Ming Wo-tsei," 16–17; a useful summary of the Japan campaign is in Ch'en Pang-chan, *Yüan-shih chi-shih pen-mo*, 25–31.

11. Olschki, *Marco Polo's Asia*, 345, makes this point most effectively.

12. Wu, "Yüan Ming Wo-tsei," 17–18; *Yüan shih*, 233; on the Koreans involved in the campaign, see *Yüan Kao-li chi-shih*, 30; for one view of Marco Polo's description of the Japanese campaigns, see Enoki Kazuo, "Marco Polo and Japan," in *Oriente Poliano*, 32–33. Enoki writes that Marco "attributes the reason for the invasion to the 'nobility and wealth' of the island of Japan, which Khubilai wanted to obtain."

13. *Yüan shih*, 256.

14. Ibid., 277; see also *Hsin Yüan shih*, 2222; Tsunoda and Goodrich, *Japan*, 85; Rossabi, *Jurchens*, 7–8.

15. *Yüan shih*, 281.

16. Ibid., 4629–30; see also, Lo, "Maritime Commerce," 99.

17. Recent underwater excavations off the coast of Japan, led by Professor Torao Mozai, have uncovered a number of artifacts from these sunken ships. For a brief, popular account, see John Saar, "Japanese Divers Discover Wreckage of Mongol Fleet," 118–29.

18. *Yüan shih*, 217; Rockhill, "Notes," 431, 438.

19. Rockhill, "Notes," 438–40.

20. See the paintings reflecting these expeditions to Ceylon in Esin, "Miniatures," 16–19, 31.

21. *Yüan shih*, 108.

22. Ibid., 207.

23. Shelley Mydans and Carl Mydans, "A Shrine City, Golden and White: The Seldom-Visited Pagan in Burma," 79.

24. Hall, *History*, 145; K. G. Tregonning, "Kublai Khan and South-East

Asia," 166–67; for more on Nāṣir al-Dīn, see T'u Chi, *Meng-wu-erh shih-chi*, 80, 4b; Hambis, *Le chapitre cviii*, 126–27.

25. Cordier, *Ser Marco Polo*, 87; Pelliot, *Notes on Marco Polo*, 2:793–94; Olschki, *Marco Polo's Asia*, 332–35.

26. Moule and Pelliot, *Marco Polo*, 289–90.

27. Ibid., 291.

28. *Yüan shih*, 213.

29. Ibid., 116.

30. For the role of hostages in Chinese history, see Lien-sheng Yang, "Hostages in Chinese History," in his *Studies in Chinese Institutional History*, 43–57.

31. Liu Ming-shu, "Yüan-tai An-nan chin-kung chih tai-shen chin-jen," 93–98.

32. *Yüan shih*, 232, 3152.

33. See Paul Pelliot, trans., *Mémoires sur les coutumes du Cambodge de Tcheou Ta-kouan (version nouvelle)*, 105–07, who also provides a narrative account of So-tu's expedition to Champa.

34. *Yüan shih*, 232, 3152.

35. Ch'en Pang-chan, *Sung-shih chi-shih pen-mo*, 31.

36. For A-t'a-hai's biography, see *Yüan shih*, 3149–50.

37. Ibid., 268.

38. Ibid., 267; Boyle, *Successors*, 245; Hambis, *Le chapitre cviii*, 89.

39. Li Chieh, *Yüan shih*, 71–72.

40. *Yüan shih*, 272–73, 275.

41. For more on these campaigns, see Lü, "Yüan-tai chih Chung-Yüeh kuan-hsi," 22–30.

42. Hok-lam Chan, "Chinese Refugees," 4–6.

43. *Yüan shih*, 277–88.

44. Ibid., 286; Boyle, *Successors*, 244; for more on Khubilai's descendants, see Shao Hsün-cheng, "*Yüan shih La-t'e-chi shih Meng-ku ti-shih* shih-hsi so-chi Shih-tsu hou-fei k'ao," 969–75.

45. *Yüan shih*, 289.

46. Ibid., 303.

47. Pelliot, *Notes on Marco Polo*, 875, for more on Toghon's banishment.

48. *Yüan shih*, 311, 333, 350.

49. Ibid., 299–300; Hall, *History*, 147.

50. *Yüan shih*, 326–27.

51. C. C. Berg, "The Javanese Picture of the Past," in *Introduction to Indonesian Historiography*, ed. Soedjatmoko, 115; G. Coèdes, *The Indianized States of Southeast Asia*, 199.

52. John F. Cady, *The Southeast Asian World*, 15–16.

53. On this incident as well as the expedition as a whole, see the dated but still not wholly superseded "The Expedition of the Mongols against Java in 1293 A.D.," by W. P. Groeneveldt, 246–54.

54. For biographies of Shih-pi and Kao Hsing, see *Yüan shih*, 3799–3806.

55. Niwa Tomosaburō, " 'Gen Sei So Jaba ensei zakkō—toku ni gunshi narabi ni kaisen sū ni tsuite," 57–63, for the exact number of ships and men on the expedition.

56. For an abbreviated version of events, see Chang Hsing-lang, *Chung-hsi chiao-t'ung*, 3 : 26–27; for a more complete account, see Hall, *History*, 75ff.

57. Georges Maspero, *Le royaume de Champa*, 244.

58. *Yüan shih*, 372.

59. Petech, "Tibetan Relations," in *China among Equals*, ed. Rossabi, 188; Rerikh, "Mongol-Tibetan Relations," 47–50.

60. Roerich, *The Blue Annals*, 2 : 582.

61. Franke, "Tibetans," in *China under Mongol Rule*, ed. Langlois, 310; *Yüan shih*, 240; Ratchnevsky, "Die mongolischen Grosskhane," 494–95.

62. Tucci, *Scrolls*, 1 : 15.

63. Petech, "Tibetan Relations," in *China among Equals*, ed. Rossabi, 189; see also Wylie, "First Mongol Conquest," 131–32.

64. Boyle, *Successors*, 244; Rashīd al-Dīn writes that "the province of Tibet was given to this Temür-Buga." Temür Bukha was presumably granted nominal jurisdiction over Tibet after this campaign.

65. Shakabpa, *Tibet*, 70–71, asserts that Khubilai contemplated the continuance of the campaign into India and Nepal.

66. On the Hsüan-cheng yüan, see Nogami, "Gen no senseiin ni tsuite," 779–95, and Liu Kuang-i, "T'u-fan fo-chiao yü Yüan Shih-tsu," in *Ta-lu tsa-shih hsüeh ts'ung-shu*, 240–42.

67. I have been unable to consult E. P. J. Mullie, *De Mongoolse Prins Nayan*. On this work, see Herbert Franke's review in *Asia Major*, n.s. 12, pt. 1 (1966): 130–31.

68. Moule and Pelliot, *Marco Polo*, 193–94.

69. Cleaves, "Bayan," 265.

70. For an interpretation of Nayan's rebellion, by a scholar from the People's Republic of China, see Yao Ta-li, "Nai-yen chih luan tsa-k'ao," 74–82; and for Nayan's rebellion in the context of the Mongols' relations with the Jurchens of Manchuria, see Rossabi, *The Jurchens*, 3–11.

71. Moule and Pelliot, *Marco Polo*, 196.

72. Boyle, *Successors*, 298–99.

73. Moule and Pelliot, *Marco Polo*, 198.

74. Ibid., 199.

75. Moule, *Christians*, 224–29, indicates that Khubilai continued to employ Nestorians even after Nayan's rebellion, which appears not to have poisoned his view of Christians.

76. *Yüan shih*, 313, 323–25.

77. D'Ohsson, *Histoire des Mongols*, 2 : 466.

78. For more on Khaidu, see Pelliot, *Notes on Marco Polo*, 124–29, and Bertold Spuler, ed., *Handbuch der Orientalistik, 5, 5: Geschichte Mittelasiens*, 212–17.

79. *Yüan shih*, 2871; Rashīd al-Dīn writes that Chabi died in 1284; Boyle, *Successors*, 242.

80. *Yüan shih*, 2873.

81. There are some discrepancies in the various Persian and Chinese lists of Khubilai's sons. It appears that he had twelve sons (though Marco Polo credits him with twenty-two sons), and the most likely order of birth is Dorji, Chen-chin, Manggala, Nomukhan, Khoridai, Hügechi, A'urugchi, Ayachi,

Kököchü, Khudlugh Temür, Toghon, and Temechi. See Pelliot's discussion of these lists in his *Notes on Marco Polo*, 569. See also Shao Hsün-cheng, "*Yüan shih*," 969–75, and Togan, "Annual Grants," for more on these sons.

82. Boyle, *Successors*, 324.

83. Esin, "Miniatures," 26.

84. Bredon, *Peking*, 358.

85. Arlington and Lewisohn, *Search*, 315.

86. *Koryŏ-sa*, 570.

87. Lao Yan-shuan, "Notes on Non-Chinese Terms in the Yüan Imperial Dietary Compendium *Yin-shan Cheng-yao*," 399–416, offers descriptions of some typical recipes and meals.

88. *Yüan shih*, 376.

89. Nancy Schatzman Steinhardt, "The Plan of Khubilai Khan's Imperial City," 156.

90. *Yüan shih*, 376–77.

91. John W. Dardess, *Conquerors and Confucians: Aspects of Political Change in Late Yuan China*, 26–27.

92. *Yüan shih*, 377.

Glossary of Chinese Characters

A-li Yao-ch'ing　阿里耀卿

A-ni-ko　阿尼哥

A-t'a-hai　阿塔海

Ai-hsüeh　愛薛

an-ch'a shih　按察使

An-fu　安撫

An-t'ung　安童

Cha-la-erh-tai　札剌兒帶

Chang Chih-ching　張志敬

Chang Hsüan　張瑄

Chang Shih-chieh　張世傑

Chang Shun　張順

Chang Te-hui　張德輝

Chang Tsung-yen　張宗演

Chang Wen-ch'ien　張文謙

Ch'ang-ch'un　長春

Ch'ang-sha　長沙

Chao Liang-pi　趙良弼

Chao Meng-fu　趙孟頫

Chao Pi　趙璧

Ch'ao-chou　潮州

Chen-chin　眞金

Chen-nan　鎭南

Chen Te-hsiu　眞德秀

Chen-ting fu　眞定府

Ch'en　陳

Ch'en I-chung　陳宜中

Ch'en Kuei-lung　陳桂龍

Ch'en Wen-lung　陳文龍

Cheng-i　正一

Cheng Ssu-hsiao　鄭思肖

Cheng-wu-lun　正誣論

Ch'eng Chü-fu　程鉅夫

Ch'eng-hsiang　丞相

Ch'eng-tu　成都

chi　稷

Chi-nan　濟南

Chi Kung-tz'u　基公次

Ch'i Kung-chih　綦公直

Chia Ssu-tao　賈似道

Chiang-hsi　江西

Chiang-nan tsung-she chang shih-
　chiao　江南總攝掌釋教

Ch'ien Hsüan　錢選

Ch'ien-yüan　乾元

Chih-ku　直沽

Chih-yüan ch'ao　至元鈔

Chin-sha chiang　金沙江

Chin-shui　金水

Ching-chao　京兆

Ching-lüeh ssu　經略司

Ching-te-chen　景德鎮

ch'ing　頃

Ch'ing-ching fa-hsing ching
　清淨法行經

Ch'ing-ning　清寧

Cho-chou　涿州

Ch'oe　崔

Ch'oe Ǔi　崔竩

Chǒn　全

Chou-li　周禮

Chu Ch'ing　朱清

Ch'u-chou　處州

Chü-yung kuan　居庸關

Ch'üan　全

Ch'üan-chen　全眞

Ch'üan-chou　泉州

Ch'üan-nung ssu　勸農司

Chung-shu ling　中書令

Chung-shu sheng　中書省

Chung-tu　中都

Chung-t'ung　中統

Chung-t'ung yin-huo　中統銀貨

Chung-t'ung yüan-pao-ch'ao
　中統元寶鈔

Ch'ung-ch'ing　重慶

Fan-ch'eng　樊城

Fan Wen-hu　范文虎

Fang Hui　方回

Fei-lai Feng　飛來峯

fen-ti　分地

feng-shui　風水

Fu-chou　福州

Fu-yü　福裕

Hai-chou　海州

Hai-yün　海雲

Han-jen　漢人

Han-k'ou　漢口

Han-lin yüan　翰林院

Hangchow　杭州

Hao Ching　郝經

Ho-chou　合州

Ho-hsi　河西

Ho Wen-chu　何文著

Ho Yüan　何源

Hōjō Masamura　北條政村

Hōjō Tokimune　北條時宗

Hsi-an　西安

Hsi-liang　西涼

Hsia Kuei　夏貴

Hsiang-yang　襄陽

Hsiao ching　孝經

Hsieh Huang-hou　謝皇后

Hsien-i-li　咸宜里

Hsien-tsung　憲宗

Hsien-yang wang　咸陽王

Hsien-yü Shu　鮮于樞

hsing　行

Hsing-chou　邢州

Hsü Heng　許衡

Hsüan-cheng yüan　宣政院

Hsüan-fu shih　宣撫使

Hsüan-fu ssu　宣撫司

Hsüan-wei ssu　宣慰司

Hsüeh-shih yüan　學士院

Hu-tu-lu Chieh-li-mi-shih　忽都魯
揭里迷失

hua-hu　化胡

Hua-yen　華嚴

Huai (river)　淮

Huai-meng　懷孟

Hui-chiao-t'u fa-kuan　回教徒
法官

Hui-chou　徽州

Hui-hui ssu-t'ien chien　回回司
天監

hui-hui t'ai-shih　回回太師

Hui-t'ung　會通

hui-tzu　會子

i　義

I ching　易經

I-k'o-mu-su　伊克穆蘇

i-min　遺民

I-tu　益都

i-ts'ang　義倉

Jui-tsung　睿宗

K'ai-feng　開封

K'ai-p'ing fu　開平府

Kan-chou　甘州

Kanghwa　江華

Kao Hsing　高興

Kao K'o-kung　高克恭

Kao-liang　高涼

Kao T'ai-hsiang　高泰祥

Kou-k'ao chü　鉤考局

Ku-yüan　固原

Kua-chou　瓜州

Kuan-chung　關中

Kuan-hsi　關西

Kuan-yin　觀音

Kuang-chou　廣州

Kuang-hui ssu　廣惠司

Kuang-ning　廣寧

Kuang Yüan　廣淵

kung-an chü　公案劇

Kung K'ai　龔開

Kuo-shih   國師

Kuo Shou-ching   郭守敬

kuo-tzu   國字

Kuo-tzu hsüeh   國子學

K'uo-k'uo   闊闊

Lan-ts'ang chiang   蘭滄江

Lao Tzu   老子

Lei-chou   雷州

Li Ch'üan-i   李全義

Li K'an   李衎

Li T'an   李璮

Li Yen-chien   李彥簡

liang   兩

Liang-chou   涼州

Liao-yang   遼陽

Lien-chou   連州

Lien Hsi-hsien   廉希憲

Lin-an   臨安

Lin-ch'ing   臨清

Lin-t'ao   臨洮

Liu Cheng   劉整

Liu En   劉恩

Liu Jen-chieh   劉人傑

Liu Kuan-tao   劉貫道

Liu-p'an shan   六盤山

Liu Ping-chung   劉秉中

Liu Shih-chung   劉時中

Liu T'ai-p'ing   劉太平

lu   路

Lu Hsiu-fu   陸秀夫

Lu-men shan   鹿門山

Lu Shih-jung   盧世榮

Lü Wen-huan   呂文煥

Lü Wen-te   呂文德

Luan   灤

Lung-hua   龍華

Mai-shu-ting   麥術丁

Meng Ch'i   孟琪

Meng-ku chün   蒙古軍

Meng-ku Han-lin yüan   蒙古翰林院

Meng-ku tzu   蒙古字

Meng-su-ssu   孟速思

Miao-yen   妙嚴

Min   閩

Ming-chou   明州

Na-mo   那摩

Nan-ching   南京

Nan-jen   南人

Ning-hsia   寧夏

Nu-chiang   怒江

O-chou   鄂州

Pa-shih-i hua-t'u   八十一化圖

pai-hua   白話

p'ai-tzu   牌子

Pei-an   北安

Pei-p'ing wang   北平王

Pien-ching   汴京

Ping (Emperor) 昺

P'ing-chang cheng-shih
平章政事

Po-ho-k'ou 白河口

P'u Shou-keng 蒲壽庚

Sai-tien-ch'ih Shan-ssu-ting
賽典赤瞻思丁

Sang-ko 桑哥

Se-mu jen 色目人

Sha-chou 沙州

Sha-pu-ting 沙不丁

Shan-yüan 澶淵

Shang-shu sheng 尚書省

Shang-tu 上都

Shao-hsing 紹興

she 社

she-chang 社長

she-li-pieh 舍利別

shih 石

Shih (Emperor) 是

Shih ching 詩經

Shih Ch'u 史樞

Shih-lu 實錄

Shih-pi 史弼

Shih T'ien-tse 史天澤

Shih-tsu 世祖

Shou-shih li 授時曆

Shu-mi yüan 樞密院

So-tu 唆都

ssu-ch'ao 絲鈔

Ssu-ming 思明

Su-chou 肅州

Sung Ching 宋京

Sung Chou-ch'en 宋周臣

Sung Tzu-chen 宋子貞

Ta-an ko 大安閣

Ta-hsüeh yen-i 大學衍義

Ta-hu-kuo-jen-wang ssu 大護國
仁王寺

Ta-li 大理

Ta-ming 大名

Ta-tu 大都

Ta tu-tu 大都督

T'a-t'a T'ung-a 塔塔統阿

T'ai-miao 太廟

T'ai-ning 泰寧

T'ai-shan 泰山

T'ai-tsu 太祖

T'an-che ssu 潭柘寺

T'an Ch'eng 覃澄

Tao te ching 道德經

Ti-shih 帝師

T'i-chü shih-po shih 提舉市舶使

t'i-chü ssu 提舉司

Tiao-yü shan 釣魚山

T'ieh-ku-lun 帖古倫

T'ien-i 天衣

T'ien Shan 天山

T'ien-shih 天師

ting 錠

Ting-chia chou   定家州

Ting-tsung   定宗

Tou Mo   竇默

tsa-chü   雜劇

Ts'ao Pin   曹彬

Ts'ao-yün ssu   曹運司

Tso ch'eng-hsiang   左丞相

Ts'ui Ming-tao   崔明道

Ts'ui Pin   崔斌

Tsung-chih yüan   總制院

tsung-kuan   總管

Tsung-miao   宗廟

Tu Shih-chung   杜世忠

Tu-tsung   度宗

Tuan Hsing-chih   段興智

tuan-shih kuan   斷事官

t'un-t'ien   屯田

Tung-Hsia   東夏

T'ung-hui   通惠

Wan-an kung   萬安宮

Wan-nien li   萬年曆

Wang Chien   王堅

Wang Fu   王浮

Wang Hsün   王恂

Wang Liang-pi   王艮弼

Wang O   王鶚

Wang Te-ch'en   汪德臣

Wang Wen-t'ung   王文統

Wang Yün   王惲

Wen-chou   溫州

wen-jen hua   文人畫

Wen T'ien-hsiang   文天祥

wo-k'ou   倭寇

wo-t'o-ch'ien   斡脫錢

Wŏnjong   元宗

Wu-ch'ang   武昌

Wu-hsing   吳興

Yai-shan   崖山

Yang-chou   揚州

Yang Lien-chen-chia   楊璉眞加

Yao Shu   姚樞

Yeh-hei tieh-erh   也黑迭兒

Yeh-lü Chu   耶律鑄

Yeh-lü Ch'u-ts'ai   耶律楚材

Yen-chiang chih-chih shih   沿江
制置使

Yen-ching   燕京

Yen-hai chih-chih shih   沿海制
置使

yin-shih   隱士

Yu ch'eng-hsiang   右丞相

Yü-shih-t'ai   御史臺

Yüan   元

Yünnan   雲南

Yung-ch'ang   永昌

Yung-ning   永寧

Bibliography of Works in Western Languages

Abe Takeo. "Where Was the Capital of the West Uighurs?" In *Silver Jubilee Volume of the Zinbun Kagaku Kenkyusyo, Kyoto University*, pp. 435–50. Kyoto: Zinbun Kagaku Kenkyusyo, Kyoto University, 1954.

Abel-Rémusat, Jean Pierre. *Nouveaux mélanges asiatiques, ou recueil de morceaux de critique et de mémoires*. Paris: Schubart et Heideloff, 1829.

Abramowski, Waltraut. "Die chinesischen Annalen von Ögödei und Güyük— Übersetzung des 2. Kapitels des Yüan shih." *Zentralasiatische Studien* 10 (1976): 117–67.

Aga-Oglu, Kamer. "Blue-and-White Porcelain Plates Made for Moslem Patrons." *Far Eastern Ceramic Bulletin* 3:3 (September 1951) 12–16.

Alinge, Curt. *Mongolische Gesetze*. Leipzig: T. Weicher Verlag, 1934.

Allen, W. E. D. *A History of the Georgian People*. London: Kegan Paul, Trench, Trubner, & Co., Ltd., 1932.

Allsen, Thomas T. "Mongol Rule in East Asia, Twelfth to Fourteenth Centuries: A Bibliography of Recent Soviet Scholarship." *Mongolian Studies* 3 (1976): 5–27.

———. *The Mongols in East Asia, Twelfth–Fourteenth Centuries: A Preliminary Bibliography of Books and Articles in Western Languages*. Philadelphia: Sung Studies Newsletter, 1976.

———. "Politics of Mongol Imperialism: Centralization and Resource Mobilization in the Reign of the Grand Qan Möngke, 1251–59." Ph.D. diss., University of Minnesota, 1979.

Almagia, R., et al. *Nel VII Centenario Della Nascita di Marco Polo*. Venice: Istituto Veneto di Scienze, Lettere ed Arti, 1955.

"Ancient Observatory Reopens." *China Daily*, April 1, 1983, p. 1.

Aris, Michael, and Kyi, Aung San Ssu, eds. *Tibetan Studies in Honour of Hugh Richardson*. Warminster: Aris & Phillips, Ltd., 1981.

Arlington, L. C., and Lewisohn, William. *In Search of Old Peking*. Peking: Henri Vetch, 1935.

Ayalon, David. "The Great Yasa of Chingiz Khan: A Reexamination." *Studia Islamica* 33 (1971): 97–140; 34 (1971): 151–80; 36 (1972): 113–58; 38 (1973): 107–56.

Ayers, John. "Some Characteristic Wares of the Yüan Dynasty." *Transactions of the Oriental Ceramic Society* 29 (1957): 69–86.

Bagchi, Prabodh Chandra. *Sino-Indian Studies*. Vol. 2. Calcutta, 1947.

Barthold, V. V. *Four Studies on the History of Central Asia*. 4 vols. Trans. by V. and T. Minorsky. Leiden: E. J. Brill, 1962.

————. *Turkestan down to the Mongol Invasion*. Trans. by T. Minorsky. 3rd ed. London: Luzac & Co., Ltd., 1968.

————. "The Burial Rites of the Turks and the Mongols." Trans. by J. M. Rogers. *Central Asiatic Journal* 14:1–3 (1970): 195–227.

Bauer, W., ed. *Studia Mongolica: Festschrift für Herbert Franke*. Wiesbaden: Franz Steiner, 1979.

Bawden, Charles R., trans. *The Mongol Chronicle Altan Tobči*. Wiesbaden: Otto Harrassowitz, 1955.

Beazley, C. R. *The Dawn of Modern Geography*. London, 1901.

Bielenstein, Hans. "The Restoration of the Han Dynasty." *Bulletin of the Museum of Far Eastern Antiquities* 27 (1954): 1–209.

————. "Lo-yang in Later Han Times." *Bulletin of the Museum of Far Eastern Antiquities* 48 (1976): 1–142.

Blake, Robert F. "The Circulation of Silver in the Moslem East Down to the Mongol Epoch." *Harvard Journal of Asiatic Studies* 2 (1937): 291–328.

Blake, Robert F., and Frye, Richard, trans. and eds. "History of the Nation of the Archers (The Mongols) by Grigor of Akanc." *Harvard Journal of Asiatic Studies* 12:3–4 (December 1949): 269–399.

Blochet, E. *Introduction à l'histoire des Mongols de Fadl Allāh Rashīd Ed-Dīn*. Leiden: E. J. Brill, 1910.

————. "La mort du Khaghan Kouyouk." *Revue de l'orient chrétien* ser. 3; 23 (1922–23): 160–71.

Bonaparte, Roland. *Documents de l'époque mongole des xiii et xiv siècles*, Paris, 1895.

Bosson, J. E. *A Treasury of Aphoristic Jewels: The Subhāṣitarananidhi of Sa Skya Paṇḍita in Tibetan and Mongolian*. Bloomington: Indiana University Press, 1969.

Boyd, Andrew. *Chinese Architecture and Town Planning, 1500 B.C.–A.D. 1911*. London: Alec Tiranti, 1962.

Boyer, Martha. *Mongol Jewellery*. Copenhagen: I Kommission Hos, Guyldenda Boghandel, Nordisk Forlag, 1952.

Boyle, John Andrew. "The Death of the Last 'Abbāsid Caliph: A Contemporary Muslim Account." *Journal of Semitic Studies* 6:2 (Autumn 1961): 145–61.

————. "Kirakos of Ganjak on the Mongols." *Central Asiatic Journal* 8:3 (September 1963): 199–214.

————. "The Journey of Het'um, King of Little Armenia, to the Court of the Great Khan Möngke." *Central Asiatic Journal* 9:3 (1964): 175–89.

————. "The Burial Place of the Great Khan Ögedei." *Acta Orientalia:*

Societates Orientales Danica Norvegica Svevica 32 (1970): 45–50.

———. "The Seasonal Residences of the Great Khan Ogedei." *Central Asiatic Journal* 16 (1972): 125–31.

———. "The Thirteenth-Century Mongols' Conception of the After Life: The Evidence of Their Funerary Practices." *Mongolian Studies* 1 (1974): 5–14.

———. *The Mongol World Empire, 1206–1370*. London: Variorum Reprints, 1977.

Boyle, John Andrew, ed. *The Cambridge History of Iran, Volume 5: The Saljuq and Mongol Periods*. Cambridge: Cambridge University Press, 1968.

Boyle, John Andrew, trans. *The History of the World Conqueror*. See ʿAlā-ad-Dīn ʿAta-Malik Juvaini.

———. *The Successors of Genghis Khan*. New York: Columbia University Press, 1971.

Bredon, Juliet. *Peking: A Historical and Intimate Description of Its Chief Places of Interest*. 3rd ed. Shanghai: Kelly & Walsh, Ltd., 1931.

Brent, Peter. *Genghis Khan: The Rise, Authority, and Decline of Mongol Power*. New York: McGraw-Hill, 1976.

Bretschneider, Emil. *Recherches archéologiques et historiques sur Pékin et ses environs*. Trans. by Collin de Plancey. Paris: Ernest Leroux, 1879.

———. *Botanicon Sinicum*. Vol. 3. London: Trubner, 1895.

———. *Mediaeval Researches from Eastern Asiatic Sources*. 2 vols. Reprint. New York: Barnes & Noble, 1967.

Broeck, Janet Rinaker Ten, and Yiu Tung. "A Taoist Inscription of the Yüan Dynasty: The Tao-chiao pei." *T'oung Pao* 40 (1950): 4–66.

Brosset, M. *Histoire de la Géorgie depuis l'antiquité jusqu'au xixe siècle*. St. Petersburg: L'imprimerie de l'académie impériale des sciences, 1858.

———. *Deux historiens arméniens, Kirakos de Gantzag, Oukhtanes d'Ourha*. St. Petersburg, 1870–71.

Brown, William A. "The Biography of Wen T'ien-hsiang in the *Sung shih*." Ph.D. diss., Harvard University, 1962.

Browne, Edward G. *A Literary History of Persia*. 4 vols. Reprint. London: Cambridge University Press, 1969.

Brunel, C. "David d'Ashby, auteur méconnu des *Faits des Tartares*." *Romania* 84 (1958): 39–46.

Budge, E. A. Wallis, trans. *The Monks of Kublai Khan, Emperor of China*. London: The Religious Tract Society, 1928.

———. *The Chronography of Gregory Ab'ûl Faraj: The Son of Aaron, the Hebrew Physician Commonly Known as Bar Hebraeus*. 2 vols. London: Oxford University Press, 1932.

Buell, Paul D. "Sino-Khitan Administration in Mongol Bukhara." *Journal of Asian History* 13 (1979): 121–51.

Bulliet, Richard. *The Camel and the Wheel*. Cambridge: Harvard University Press, 1975.

Bush, Susan. *The Chinese Literati on Painting: Su Shih (1037–1101) to Tung Ch'i-ch'ang (1555–1636)*. Cambridge: Harvard University Press, 1971.

Bushell, S. W. "Notes on the Old Mongolian Capital of Shangtu." *Journal of* the Royal Asiatic Society of Great Britain and Ireland 7 (1875): 329–38.

Cady, John. *The Southeast Asian World*. St. Louis: Forum Press, 1977.

Cahill, James. *Hills beyond a River: Chinese Painting of the Yüan Dynasty, 1279–1368*. New York: John Weatherhill, Inc., 1976.

———. *An Index of Early Chinese Painters and Painting, T'ang, Sung, and Yüan*. Berkeley: University of California Press, 1980.

Calvino, Italo. *Invisible Cities*. Trans. by William Weaver. New York: Harcourt Brace Jovanovich, 1974.

Chan Hok-lam. "The Compilation and Sources of the *Chin-shih*." *Journal of Oriental Studies* 1–2 (1961–64): 125–63.

———. "Chinese Refugees in Annam and Champa at the End of the Sung Dynasty." *Journal of Southeast Asian History* 7 : 2 (September 1966): 1–10.

———. "Liu Ping-chung (1216–1274): A Buddhist-Taoist Statesman at the Court of Khubilai Khan." *T'oung Pao* 53 (1967): 98–146.

———. *The Historiography of the Chin Dynasty: Three Studies*. Wiesbaden: Franz Steiner Verlag, 1970.

———. "Prolegomena to the *Ju-nan i-shih*: A Memoir on the Last Chin Court under the Mongol Siege of 1234." *Sung Studies Newsletter* 10 (1974): 2–19.

———. "Wang O (1190–1273)." *Papers on Far Eastern History* 12 (September 1975): 43–70.

———. "Yang Huan (1186–1255)." *Papers on Far Eastern History* 14 (September 1976): 37–59.

———. "Yao Shu (1201–1278)." *Papers on Far Eastern History* 22 (September 1980): 17–50.

Chan Hok-lam and de Bary, William Theodore, eds. *Yuan Thought: Chinese Thought and Religion under the Mongols*. New York: Columbia University Press, 1982.

Chan Ping-leung, ed. *Essays in Commemoration of the Golden Jubilee of the Fung Ping Shan Library (1932–1982)*. Hong Kong: Hong Kong University Press, 1982.

Chang Kuei-sheng. "The Maritime Scene at the Dawn of Great European Discoveries." *Journal of the American Oriental Society* 94 : 3 (July–September 1974): 347–59.

Chang Kwang-chih, ed. *Food in Chinese Culture: Anthropological and Historical Perspectives*. New Haven: Yale University Press, 1977.

Chapman, Walker [pseud.]. *Kublai Khan: Lord of Xanadu*. Indianapolis: Bobbs-Merrill Co., Inc., 1966.

Charignon, A. J. H. *Le livre de Marco Polo*. 2 vols. Peking: Albert Nachbaur, 1924–26.

Chavannes, Édouard. "Inscriptions et pièces de chancellerie chinoises de l'époque mongole." *T'oung Pao* 5 (1904): 357–447; 6 (1905): 1–42; 9 (1908): 297–428.

———. *Le T'ai Chan*. Reprint. Taipei: Ch'eng-wen Publishing Co., 1970.

Ch'en, Kenneth K. S. "Buddhist-Taoist Mixtures in the *Pa-shih-i-hua t'u*." *Harvard Journal of Asiatic Studies* 9 (1945–47): 1–12.

———. *Buddhism in China: A Historical Survey*. Princeton: Princeton University Press, 1964.

Ch'en, Paul Heng-chao. "Chih-yüan hsin-ko: The Yüan Code of 1291 as Reconstructed and a Survey of Yüan Legal Institutions." Ph.D. diss., Harvard University, 1973.

———. *Chinese Legal Tradition under the Mongols*. Princeton: Princeton University Press, 1979.

Ch'en Yüan. *Western and Central Asians in China under the Mongols*. Trans. by Ch'ien Hsing-hai and L. C. Goodrich. Los Angeles: Monumenta Serica Institute, 1966.

Ching, Julia. "Hsü Heng (1209–81): A Confucian under the Mongols." Paper for the Conference on Yüan Thought. Issaquah, Washington. January 1978.

Chung, Priscilla Ching. *Palace Women in the Northern Sung*. Leiden: E. J. Brill, 1981.

Ch'ü Ch'ing-yüan. "Government Artisans of the Yüan Dynasty." In *Chinese Social History: Translations of Selected Studies*, trans. and ed. by E-tu Zen Sun and John DeFrancis, pp. 234–46. Washington: American Council of Learned Societies, 1956.

Clauson, Gerard. "The hP'ags-pa Alphabet." *Bulletin of the School of Oriental and African Studies, London University* 22 (1959): 300–323.

Cleaves, Francis Woodman. "The Expression *Jöb Ese Bol* in the *Secret History of the Mongols*." *Harvard Journal of Asiatic Studies* 11 (1948): 311–20.

———. "Review of E. Haenisch, *Die geheime Geschichte der Mongolen*." *Harvard Journal of Asiatic Studies* 12 (1949): 497–534.

———. "A Chancellery Practice of the Mongols in the Thirteenth and Fourteenth Centuries." *Harvard Journal of Asiatic Studies* 14 (1951): 493–526.

———. "The Sino-Mongolian Inscription of 1346." *Harvard Journal of Asiatic Studies* 15 (1952): 1–123.

———. "The Historicity of the Baljuna Covenant." *Harvard Journal of Asiatic Studies* 18:2 (1955): 357–421.

———. "The Biography of Bayan of the Bārin in the *Yuan shih*." *Harvard Journal of Asiatic Studies* 19:3–4 (1956): 185–301.

———. "Qabqanas ~ Qamqanas." *Harvard Journal of Asiatic Studies* 19:3–4 (1956): 390–406.

———. "The 'Fifteen Palace Poems' by K'o Chiu-ssu." *Harvard Journal of Asiatic Studies* 20 (1957): 391–479.

———. "A Chinese Source Bearing on Marco Polo's Departure and a Persian Source on His Arrival in Persia." *Harvard Journal of Asiatic Studies* 36 (1976): 181–203.

Cleaves, Francis Woodman, trans. *The Secret History of the Mongols*. Cambridge: Harvard University Press, 1982.

Cleaves, Francis Woodman, and Mostaert, Antoine. "Trois documents mongols des archives secrètes vaticanes," *Harvard Journal of Asiatic Studies* 15 (1952): 419–506.

Coèdes, G. *The Indianized States of Southeast Asia*. Honolulu: East-West Center Press, 1968.

Combined Indices to Forty-Seven Collections of Sung Dynasty Biographies. 2nd

ed. Tokyo: Harvard Yenching Institute Sinological Index Series No. 34.
Japan Council for East Asian Studies, 1959.

Commeaux, C. *La vie quotidienne chez les Mongols de la conquête (xiiie siècle)*.
Paris: Librairie Hachette, 1972.

Cordier, Henri. *Les voyages en Asie au xive siècle du bienheureux frère Odoric de
Pordenone*. Paris: Ernest Leroux, 1891.

————. *Ser Marco Polo: Notes and Addenda to Sir Henry Yule's Edition*.
London: John Murray, 1920.

Creel, Herrlee G. *What Is Taoism? and Other Studies in Chinese Cultural
History*. Chicago: University of Chicago Press, 1970.

Crump, James I. *Chinese Theater in the Days of Kublai Khan*. Tucson: University of Arizona Press, 1980.

Dardess, John W. "From Mongol Empire to Yüan Dynasty: Changing Forms
of Imperial Rule in Mongolia and Central Asia." *Monumenta Serica* 30
(1972–73): 117–65.

————. *Conquerors and Confucians: Aspects of Political Change in Late Yuan
China*. New York: Columbia University Press, 1973.

Dauvillier, Jean. "Les provinces chaldéenes de l'extérieur au moyen-âge." In
Mélanges offerts au R. P. Ferdinand Cavallera. Toulouse: Bibliothèque de
L'Institut Catholique, 1948.

Davidovich, E. *Deneznoe khozjajstvo Srednei Azii v xiii veke* [The money
economy of Central Asia in the thirteenth century]. Moscow: Nauka,
1972.

Dawson, Christopher, ed. *Mission to Asia*. New York: Harper & Row, 1966.

de Bary, William Theodore. "The Rise of Neo-Confucian Orthodoxy in Yüan
China." Paper for the University Seminar on Traditional China. Columbia
University. December 1979.

————. *Neo-Confucian Orthodoxy and the Learning of the Mind-and-Heart*.
New York: Columbia University Press, 1981.

de Bary, William Theodore, ed. *Sources of Japanese Tradition*. New York:
Columbia University Press, 1958.

————. *Self and Society in Ming Thought*. New York: Columbia University
Press, 1970.

Deguignes, J. *Histoire générale des Huns, des Turcs, des Mongols, et des autres
Tartares occidentaux*. Paris: Desaint & Saillant, 1756–58.

deMailla, Joseph-Anne-Marie de Moyriac. *Histoire générale de la Chine, ou
annales de cet empire: traduites du Tong-kien-kang-mou*. Paris, 1779.

Demiéville, Paul. "Les tombeaux des Song méridionaux." *Bulletin de l'École
Française d'Extrême-Orient* 25 (1925): 458–67.

DeWeese, Devin. "The Influence of the Mongols on the Religious Consciousness of Thirteenth-Century Europe." *Mongolian Studies* 5 (1978–
79): 47–53.

Denlinger, Paul. "Chinese in hP'ags-pa Script." *Monumenta Serica* 22:2
(1963): 407–33.

Der Nersessian, Sirarpie. "The Armenian Chronicle of the Constable Smpad
or of the 'Royal Historians.'" *Dumbarton Oaks Papers* 13 (1959): 141–68.

————. *The Armenians*. London: Thames & Hudson, Ltd., 1969.

Desmaisons, Petr I., trans. *Histoire des Mogols et des Tatares par Aboul-Ghâzi Béhâdour Khân: Souverain de Kharezm et Historien Djaghataï, 1603–1644.* Reprint. Amsterdam: Philo Press, 1970.

Die Jagd bei den altaischen Völkern, Vorträge der VIII. Permanent International Altaistic Conference, 1965. Wiesbaden: Otto Harrassowitz, 1968.

Drouin, Edmond. "Notices sur les monnaies mongoles." *Journal asiatique* ser. 9; 7 (1896): 486–544.

Duda, Herbert. *Die Seltschukengeschichte des Ibn Bībī.* Copenhagen: Ejnar Munksgaard, A. S., 1959.

Dulaurier, E. "Les Mongols d'après les historiens arméniens." *Journal asiatique* ser. 5; 11 (1858): 192–255, 426–73, 481–508.

Dunlop, Douglas. "The Karaits of Eastern Asia." *Bulletin of the School of Oriental and African Studies, London University* 11 (1943–46): 276–89.

Ecke, Gustav, and Demiéville, Paul. *The Twin Pagodas of Zayton.* Cambridge: Cambridge University Press, 1935.

Eliade, Mircea. *Shamanism: Archaic Techniques of Ecstasy.* Trans. by Willard Trask. Princeton: Princeton University Press, 1964.

Elvin, Mark. *The Pattern of the Chinese Past.* Stanford: Stanford University Press, 1973.

Endicott-West, Elizabeth. "Aspects of Decision-Making and Personnel Management in the Early Yüan." Paper for American Council of Learned Societies Conference on the Evolution of Imperial Governance, Tenth to Fourteenth Centuries. Riesenberg, Germany. August–September 1982.

Esin, Emil. "A Pair of Miniatures from the Miscellany Collections of Topkapi." *Central Asiatic Journal* 21:1 (1977): 13–35.

Fairbank, John K. *Trade and Diplomacy on the China Coast: The Opening of the Treaty Ports, 1842–1854.* 2 vols. Cambridge: Harvard University Press, 1953.

Fairbank, John K., and Reischauer, Edwin O. *East Asia: The Great Tradition.* Boston: Houghton Mifflin Co., 1960.

Farmer, Edward L. *Early Ming Government: The Evolution of Dual Capitals.* Cambridge: East Asian Research Center, Harvard University, 1976.

Farquhar, David M. "The Official Seals and Ciphers of the Yüan Period." *Monumenta Serica* 25 (1966): 362–93.

———. "Emperors as Bodhisattvas in the Governance of the Ch'ing Empire." *Harvard Journal of Asiatic Studies* 38:1 (June 1978): 5–34.

Favier, A. *Pékin: Histoire et description.* Peking: Imprimerie des Lazaristes au Pé-tang, 1897.

Feuerwerker, Albert, ed. *History in Communist China.* Cambridge: M.I.T. Press, 1968.

FitzGerald, Charles Patrick. *Son of Heaven.* Cambridge: Cambridge University Press, 1933.

———. *The Southern Expansion of the Chinese People.* New York: Praeger Publishers, 1972.

Fletcher, Joseph F. "Turco-Mongolian Monarchic Tradition in the Ottoman Empire." *Harvard Ukrainian Studies* 3/4 (1979–80): 236–51.

Forke, Alfred. *Geschichte der neueren chinesischen Philosophie.* Hamburg: de

Gruyter, 1938.

Franke, Herbert. "Dschau Mong-fu: Das Leben eines chinesischen Staats-mannes, Gelehrten und Künstlers unter der Mongolenherrschaft." *Sinica* 15 (1940): 25–48.

――――. "Sen-ge: Das Leben eines uigurischen Staatsbeamten zur Zeit Chubilai's dargestellt nach Kapitel 205. der Yüan-Annalen." *Sinica* 17 (1942): 90–113.

――――. "Ahmed: Ein Beitrag zur Wirtschaftsgeschichte Chinas unter Qubilai." *Oriens* 1:2 (1948): 222–36.

――――. *Geld und Wirtschaft in China unter der Mongolenherrschaft.* Leipzig: Otto Harrassowitz, 1949.

――――. "Some Sinological Remarks on Rašîd Ad-Din's *History of China.*" *Oriens* 4:1 (1951): 21–26.

――――. "Could the Mongol Emperors Read and Write Chinese?" *Asia Major* n.s. 3:1 (1952): 28–41.

――――. "Die Agrarreformen des Chia Ssu-tao." *Saeculum* 9 (1958): 345–69.

――――. Review of E. P. J. Mullie, *De Mongoolse Prins Nayan. Asia Major* n.s. 12, pt. 1 (1966): 130–31.

――――. "Sino-Western Contacts under the Mongol Empire." *Journal of the Royal Asiatic Society, Hong Kong Branch* 6 (1966): 49–72.

――――. "Eine Mittelalterliche chinesischen Satire auf die Mohammedaner." In *Der Orient in der Forschung: Festschrift für Otto Spies zum 5 April 1966,* ed. Wilhelm Hoenerbach, pp. 202–8. Wiesbaden: Otto Harrassowitz, 1967.

――――. "Treaties between Sung and Chin." In *Études Song in memoriam Étienne Balázs* 1:1, ed. by Françoise Aubin pp. 55–84. Paris: Mouton & Co., 1970.

――――. "Chinese Texts on the Jurchen: A Translation of the Jurchen Monograph in the *San-ch'ao pei-meng hui-pien.*" *Zentralasiatische Studien* 9 (1975): 119–86.

――――. *From Tribal Chieftain to Universal Emperor and God: The Legitima-tion of the Yüan Dynasty.* Munich: Verlag der Bayerischen Akademie der Wissenschaften, 1978.

――――. "A Sino-Uighur Family Portrait: Notes on a Woodcut from Turfan." *Canada-Mongolia Review* 4:1 (April 1978): 33–40.

Franke, Herbert, ed. *Sung Biographies.* 4 vols. Wiesbaden: Franz Steiner Verlag, 1976.

Franke, Otto. "Kublai Khan und seine chinesischen Berater." *Forschungen und Fortschritte* 18:29–30 (20 October 1942): 283–85.

Fu Lo-shu. "Teng Mu: A Forgotten Chinese Philosopher." *T'oung Pao* 52 (1965–66): 35–96.

Fuchs, Walter. *The Mongol Atlas of China by Chu Ssu-pen.* Peiping: Monu-menta Serica Monographs, 1946.

――――. "Analecta zur mongolischen Übersetzungsliteratur der Yüan-Zeit." *Momumenta Serica* 11 (1946): 34–64.

Fung Yu-lan. *A History of Chinese Philosophy.* 2 vols. Trans. by Derk Bodde. Princeton: Princeton University Press, 1953.

Gabain, Annemarie von. *Das Leben im uigurischen Königreich von Qočo, 850–1250*. 2 vols. Wiesbaden: Otto Harrassowitz, 1973.

Gedalecia, David. "Wu Ch'eng: A Neo-Confucian of the Yüan." Ph.D. diss., Harvard University, 1971.

Gernet, Jacques. *Daily Life in China on the Eve of the Mongol Invasion, 1250–1276*. Trans. by H. M. Wright. New York: Macmillan Co., 1962.

Gibb, Hamilton A. R., trans. *Ibn Battúta: Travels in Asia and Africa, 1325–1354*. London: George Routledge & Sons, Ltd., 1929.

Gibb, Hamilton A. R., et al. *Encyclopedia of Islam*. Vol. 1. 2nd ed. Leiden: E. J. Brill, 1954.

Giles, Herbert A. *A Chinese Biographical Dictionary*. Reprint. Taipei: Ch'eng-wen Publishing Co., 1968.

Gompertz, G. M. *Korean Celadon and Other Wares of the Koryŏ Period*. London: Faber & Faber, 1968.

Goodrich, Luther Carrington. "Firearms among the Chinese: A Supplementary Note." *Isis* 39:1–2 (1948): 63–64.

————. "A Bronze Block for the Printing of Chinese Paper Currency." *The American Numismatic Society Museum Notes* 4 (1950): 127–30.

————. *A Short History of the Chinese People*. 3rd ed. New York: Harper & Bros., 1959.

Goodrich, Luther Carrington, and Fang Chaoying, eds. *A Dictionary of Ming Biography*. 2 vols. New York: Columbia University Press, 1976.

Goodrich, Luther Carrington, and Feng Chia-sheng. "The Early Development of Firearms in China." *Isis* 36:2 (1946): 114–23.

Gothein, Marie Luise. "Die Stadtanlage von Peking." *Wiener Jahrbuch für Kunstgeschichte* 7 (1930): 7–33.

Gray, Basil. "Art under the Mongol Dynasties of China and Persia." *Oriental Art* 1 (Winter 1955): 159–67.

Grekov, B., and Iakoubovski, A. *La Horde d'Or*. Trans. by François Thuret. Paris: Payot, 1939.

Griffing, Robert, Jr. *The Art of the Korean Potter*. New York: The Asia Society, 1968.

Groeneveldt, W. P. "The Expedition of the Mongols against Java in 1293 A.D." *China Review* 4 (1875–76): 246–54.

Grousset, René. *L'empire des steppes*. Paris: Payot, 1939. Trans. by Naomi Walford, under the title *The Empire of the Steppes: A History of Central Asia*. New Brunswick: Rutgers University Press, 1970.

————. *L'empire mongol (1ʳᵉ Phase)*. Paris: E. de Boccard, 1941.

————. *Conqueror of the World: The Life of Chingis Khan*. Trans. by Marian McKellar and Denis Sinor. New York: Viking Press, 1972.

Guzman, Gregory G. "Simon of Saint-Quentin and the Dominican Mission of the Mongol Baiju: A Reappraisal." *Speculum* 46:2 (April 1971): 232–49.

————. "Simon of Saint-Quentin as Historian of the Mongols and the Seljuk Turks." *Medievalia et Humanistica* n.s. 3 (1972): 155–78.

————. "The Encyclopedist Vincent of Beauvais and His Mongol Extracts from John of Plano Carpini." *Speculum* 49:2 (April 1974): 287–307.

Haeger, John W., ed. *Crisis and Prosperity in Sung China*. Tucson: University of Arizona Press, 1975.

―――. "Marco Polo in China: Problems with Internal Evidence." *Bulletin of Sung and Yüan Studies* 14 (1978): 22–30.

Haenisch, Erich. "Die letzten Feldzüge Čingis Khans und sein Tod: Nach der ostasiatischen Überlieferung." *Asia Major* o.s. 9 (1933): 503–51.

―――. "Steuergerechtsame der chinesischen Klöster unter der Mongolenherrschaft." In *Berichte über die Verhandlungen der Sächsischen Akademie der Wissenschaften zu Leipzig* (1940). 74 pp.

―――. *Die Geheime Geschichte der Mongolen.* Leipzig: Otto Harrassowitz, 1941.

―――. "Die Ehreninschrift für den Rebellengeneral Ts'ui Lih." *Abhandlungen der Preussischen Akademie Wissenschaften Phil.-Hist. Klasse* 4 (Berlin, 1944).

―――. "Zu den Briefen der mongolischen Il-Khane Arġun und Öljeitü an den König Philipp den Schönen von Frankreich (1289 und 1305)." *Oriens* 2 (1948): 216–35.

Hall, D. G. E. *A History of South-East Asia.* 2nd ed. London: Macmillan & Co., 1964.

Halperin, Charles. "Russia in the Mongol Empire in Historical Perspective." *Harvard Journal of Asiatic Studies* 43:1 (June 1983): 239–61.

Hambis, Louis. *Le chapitre cvii du Yüan che.* Leiden: E. J. Brill, 1945.

―――. *Le chapitre cviii du Yüan che.* Leiden: E. J. Brill, 1954.

―――. *Marco Polo: La description du monde.* Paris: Librairie C. Klincksieck, 1955.

―――. "Notes sur l'histoire de Corée a l'époque mongole." *T'oung Pao* 45 (1957): 151–218.

Hambly, Gavin. *Central Asia.* New York: Delacorte Press, 1969.

Hammer-Purgstall, Joseph. *Geschichte der Ilchane.* 2 vols. Darmstadt: Carl Wilhelm Leske, 1842–43.

Hammer-Purgstall, Joseph, trans. *Geschichte Wassaf's.* Vienna: Aus der Kaiserlich-Königlichen Hof-und-Staatsdruckerei, 1856.

Hana, Corinna. *Bericht über die Verteidigung der Stadt Te-an während der Periode K'ai-hsi, 1205–1208.* Wiesbaden: Franz Steiner Verlag, 1970.

Hangin, John, trans. *Köke Sudur (The Blue Chronicle): A Study of the First Mongolian Historical Novel by Injannasi.* Wiesbaden: Otto Harrassowitz, 1973.

Harada, Yoshito. *Shang-tu: The Summer Capital of the Yuan Dynasty in Dolon-Nor, Mongolia.* Tokyo: Toa-Koko Gakukai, 1941.

Harlez, Charles de. *Histoire de l'empire du Kin ou empire d'or.* Louvain: Charles Peeters, 1887.

Harrison, T. "Trade Porcelain and Stoneware in South-east Asia." *Sarawak Museum Journal* 10 (1961): 222–26.

Hart, Henry H. *Marco Polo: Venetian Adventurer.* Norman: University of Oklahoma Press, 1967.

Hartwell, Robert. "A Cycle of Economic Change in Imperial China: Coal and Iron in Northeast China, 750–1350." *Journal of the Economic and Social History of the Orient* 10:1 (1967): 102–59.

Harvard-Yenching Institute Sinological Index Series. *Combined Indices to Thirty Collections of Liao, Chin, and Yüan Biographies*. Reprint. San Francisco: Chinese Materials Center, Inc., 1974.

Hatada Takashi. *A History of Korea*. Trans. and ed. by Warren W. Smith and Benjamin Hazard. Santa Barbara: ABC-Clio Press, 1969.

Hayden, George A. "The Courtroom Plays of the Yüan and Early Ming Periods." *Harvard Journal of Asiatic Studies* 34 (1974): 192–220.

Hazard, Benjamin. "The Formative Years of the Wakō, 1223–63." *Monumenta Nipponica* 22 (1967): 260–77.

Hazard, Harry W., ed. *A History of the Crusades, Volume 3: The Fourteenth and Fifteenth Centuries*. Madison: University of Wisconsin Press, 1975.

Heissig, Walther. *The Religions of Mongolia*. Trans. by Geoffrey Samuel. Berkeley: University of California Press, 1980.

Heissig, Walther, ed. *Altaica Collecta*. Wiesbaden: Otto Harrassowitz, 1976.

Henderson, Gregory. "Koryŏ Ceramics: Problems and Sources of Information." *Far Eastern Ceramic Bulletin* 10 : 1–2 (March–June 1958): 5–28.

———. *Korean Ceramics: An Art's Variety*. Columbus: Ohio State University Exhibition Catalog, 1969.

Henthorn, William. *Korea: The Mongol Invasions*. Leiden: E. J. Brill, 1963.

———. *A History of Korea*. New York: The Free Press, 1971.

Herrmann, Albert. *An Historical Atlas of China*. 2nd ed. rev. by Norton Ginsburg. Chicago: Aldine Publishing Co., 1966.

Heyd, W. *Histoire du commerce du Levant au moyen-âge*. Reprint. Trans. by Furcy Raynaud. Amsterdam: Adolf M. Hakkert, 1967.

Hirth, Friedrich, and Rockhill, William W., trans. *Chau Ju-kua: His Work on the Chinese and Arab Trade in the Twelfth and Thirteenth Centuries Entitled Chu-fan-chi*. St. Petersburg: Printing Office of the Imperial Academy of Sciences, 1911.

History of the Mongolian People's Republic. Moscow: Nauka, 1973.

Ho Ping-ti. *Studies on the Population of China, 1368–1953*. Cambridge: Harvard University Press, 1959.

———. "An Estimate of the Total Population of Sung-Chin China." In *Études Song in memoriam Étienne Balázs*, ed. Françoise Aubin, pp. 3–53. Paris: Mouton & Co., 1970.

Ho Wai-kam. "Government Administration and Supervision of Crafts in the Yüan Dynasty." American Council of Learned Societies Conference on China under Mongol Rule. York, Maine. July 1976.

Hodgson, Marshall G. S. *The Order of Assassins: The Struggle of the Early Nizârî Ismâ'îlîs against the Islamic World*. The Hague: Mouton & Co., 1955.

Hoffman, Helmut. *The Religions of Tibet*. Trans. by Edward Fitzgerald. New York: Macmillan, 1961.

Holt, P. M., Lambton, Ann K. S., and Lewis, Bernard, eds. *The Cambridge History of Islam*. 2 vols. Cambridge: Cambridge University Press, 1970.

Hoog, Constance, trans. *Prince Jin-gim's Textbook of Tibetan Buddhism*. Leiden: E. J. Brill, 1983.

Hori Kyotsu. "The Mongol Invasions and the Kamakura Bakufu." Ph.D.

diss., Columbia University, 1967.

Houdas, O., trans. *Histoire du Sultan Djelal ed-din Mankobirti, prince du Kharezm*. Paris: Ernest Leroux, 1895.

Howorth, Henry H. *History of the Mongols from the Ninth to the Nineteenth Century*. 5 vols. London: Longmans, Green, & Co., 1876.

Hsia Chih-tsing. *The Classic Chinese Novel: A Critical Introduction*. New York: Columbia University Press, 1968.

Hsiao Ch'i-ch'ing. *The Military Establishment of the Yüan Dynasty*. Cambridge: Harvard University Press, 1978.

Hsiung, S. I. *The Romance of the Western Chamber*. New York: Columbia University Press, 1968.

Hucker, Charles O. *The Censorial System of Ming China*. Stanford: Stanford University Press, 1966.

―――. *China's Imperial Past*. Stanford: Stanford University Press, 1975.

Hucker, Charles O., ed. *Chinese Government in Ming Times: Seven Studies*. New York: Columbia University Press, 1969.

Humble, Richard. *Marco Polo*. New York: G. P. Putnam's Sons, 1975.

Hung Chin-fu. "China and the Nomads: Misconceptions in Western Historiography on Inner Asia." *Harvard Journal of Asiatic Studies* 41 : 2 (December 1981): 597–628.

Hung, William. "The Transmission of the Book Known as *The Secret History of the Mongols*." *Harvard Journal of Asiatic Studies* 14 (1951): 433–92.

Huntington, Ellsworth. *Mainsprings of Civilization*. New York: John Wiley & Sons, 1947.

Huth, George. *Geschichte des Buddhismus in der Mongolei*. Strassburg: Karl J. Trubner, 1896.

Hyer, Paul. "The Re-evaluation of Chinggis Khan: Its Role in the Sino-Soviet Dispute." *Asian Survey* 6 : 12 (December 1966): 696–705.

Hymes, Robert P. "Doctors in Sung and Yüan: A Local Case Study." Paper for Columbia University Seminar on Traditional China, 1982.

Idema, W. L. *Chinese Vernacular Fiction: The Formative Period*. Leiden: E. J. Brill, 1974.

Impey, Lawrence. "Shang-tu, Summer Capital of Khubilai Khan." *Geographical Review* 15 (October 1925): 584–604.

Inaba Shōju, trans. "The Lineage of the Sa skys pa: A Chapter of the Red Annals." *Memoirs of the Research Department of the Tōyō Bunko* 22 (1963): 107–23.

Inal, Sara Güner. "The Fourteenth-Century Miniatures of the Jāmi 'al-tavārīkh in the Topkapi Museum in Istanbul, Hazine Library No. 1653." Ph.D. diss., University of Michigan, 1965.

Ipşiroğlu, M. S. *Painting and Culture of the Mongols*. Trans. by E. D. Phillips. New York: Harry Abrams, Inc., n.d.

Iwamura Shinobu. "Mongol Invasion of Poland in the Thirteenth Century." *Memoirs of the Research Department of the Tōyō Bunko* 10 (1938): 103–57.

Jackson, Peter. "The Accession of Qubilai Qa'an: A Re-examination." *Journal of the Anglo-Mongolian Society* 2 : 1 (June 1975): 1–10.

―――. "The Dissolution of the Mongol Empire." *Central Asiatic Journal*

22:3–4 (1978): 186–244.

Jagchid, Sechin. "Chinese Buddhism and Taoism during the Mongolian Rule of China." *Mongolian Studies* 6 (1980): 61–98.

Jagchid, Sechin, and Bawden, Charles R. "Some Notes on the Horse Policy of the Yüan Dynasty." *Central Asiatic Journal* 10:3–4 (December 1965): 246–68.

Jagchid, Sechin, and Hyer, Paul. *Mongolia's Culture and Society*. Boulder: Westview Press, 1979.

Jahn, Karl. "A Note on Kashmīr and the Mongols." *Central Asiatic Journal* 2:3 (1957): 176–80.

———. "Wissenschaftliche Kontakte zwischen Iran und China in der Mongolenzeit." *Österreichischen Akademie der Wissenschaften* 106 (1969): 199–211.

———. *Die Chinageschichte des Rašīd ad-Dīn*. Vienna: Hermann Böhlaus Nachf., 1971.

Jenkins, Gareth. "A Note on Climatic Cycles and the Rise of Chinggis Khan." *Central Asiatic Journal* 18 (1974): 217–26.

Joinville, Jean Sire de. *Histoire de Saint Louis, Roi de France*. Paris: Imprimerie de Goetschy, 1822.

———. *Histoire de Saint Louis*. Paris: Librairie de la Société de l'Histoire de France, 1868.

Joinville, Jean Sire de, and Villehardouin. *Chronicles of the Crusades*. Trans. by Margaret R. B. Shaw. Baltimore: Penguin Books, 1963.

Juvaini, ʿAlā-ad-Dīn ʿAta-Malik. *The History of the World Conqueror*. 2 vols. Trans. by John Andrew Boyle. Manchester: Manchester University Press, 1958.

Kahle, Paul. "Chinese Porcelain in the Lands of Islam." *Transactions of the Oriental Ceramic Society* 18 (1940–41): 27–46.

Kains, Maurice. *Ginseng*. New York: Orange Judd, 1916.

Kates, George. "A New Date for the Origins of the Forbidden City." *Harvard Journal of Asiatic Studies* 7 (1942–43): 180–202.

Kelly, Amy. *Eleanor of Aquitaine and the Four Kings*. New York: Vintage Books, 1959.

Khetagurov, L. A., et al. *Rashīd ad-Dīn: Sbornik Letopisei* [Rashīd ad-Dīn: collection of chronicles]. 4 vols. Moscow: Nauka, 1946–60.

Kim Chewon. "Random Notes on Literary References to Koryŏ Ceramics." *Far Eastern Ceramic Bulletin* 9:3–4 (September–December 1957): 30–34.

Kirakos Gandzaketski. *Istoriia Armenii* [History of Armenia]. Trans. by L. A. Khanlarian. Moscow: Nauka, 1976.

Kiselev, S. V., ed. *Drevnemongol'skie goroda* [Ancient Mongolian cities]. Moscow: Nauka, 1965.

Klaproth, M. "Des enterprises des Mongols en Géorgie et en Arménie dans le xiiie siècle." *Journal asiatique* ser. 2, 12 (September 1833): 193–214.

Kolmas, Josef. *Tibet and Imperial China*. Canberra: Centre of Oriental Studies, Australian National University Occasional Paper No. 7. 1967.

Kotwicz, Wladyslaw. "En marge des lettres des Il-khans de Perse." *Collectanea Orientalia* (Lwow) 4 (1933).

————. "Quelques mots encore sur les lettres des Il-khans de Perse." *Collec-tanea Orientalia* (Wilno) 10 (1936).

Krueger, John R. "Chronology and Bibliography of the *Secret History of the Mongols.*" *Mongolia Society Bulletin* 5 (1966–67): 25–31.

Krueger, John R., trans. "Sagang Sechen, *History of the Eastern Mongols to 1662 (Erdeni-yin Tobči).*" *Mongolia Society Occasional Papers* 2. Bloomington: Mongolia Society, 1967.

Kubo Noritada. "Prolegomena on the Study of the Controversies between Buddhists and Taoists in the Yüan Period." *Memoirs of the Research Department of the Tōyō Bunko* 25 (1967): 39–61.

Kuczera, S. "The Influence of the Mongol Conquest on the Chinese System of Education and Selection of Officials." American Council of Learned Societies Conference on Mongol Rule in China. York, Maine. July 1976.

Kuwabara Jitsuzō. "On P'u Shou-keng." *Memoirs of the Research Department of the Tōyō Bunko* 2 (1928): 1–79; 7 (1935): 1–104.

Kwanten, Luc Herman M. "Tibetan-Mongol Relations during the Yüan Dynasty, 1207–1368." Ph.D. diss., University of South Carolina, 1972.

————. "Tibetan Names in the Yüan Imperial Family." *Mongolia Society Bulletin* 10:1 (Spring 1971): 64–66.

————. "The Career of Muqali: A Reassessment." *Bulletin of Sung and Yüan Studies* 14 (1978): 31–38.

————. *Imperial Nomads: A History of Central Asia, 500–1500.* Philadelphia: University of Pennsylvania Press, 1979.

Kychanov, E. I. *Ocherk istorii tangutskogo gosudartsva* [Selections from the history of Tangut government]. Moscow: Nauka, 1968.

Lach, Donald. *Asia in the Making of Europe I.* Chicago: University of Chicago Press, 1965.

Lamb, Harold. *Genghis Khan: Emperor of All Men.* New York: Robert McBride & Co., 1927.

Lanciotti, L., ed. *La Donna Nella Cina Imperiale e Nella Cina Repubblicana.* Florence: Leo S. Olschki, 1980.

Lane-Poole, Stanley. *Catalogue of Oriental Coins in the British Museum: Volume 10: Additions to the Oriental Collections, 1876–1888, Part 2: Additions to Volumes 5–8.* London: Trustees of the British Museum, 1890.

Langlois, John D. "Chin-hua Confucianism under the Mongols." Ph.D. diss., Princeton University, 1974.

Langlois, John D., ed. *China under Mongol Rule.* Princeton: Princeton University Press, 1981.

Lao Yan-shuan. "The *Chung-t'ang shih-chi* of Wang Yün: An Annotated Translation with an Introduction." Ph.D. diss., Harvard University, 1962.

————. "Notes on Non-Chinese Terms in the Yüan Imperial Dietary Compendium *Yin-shan Cheng-yao.*" *Bulletin of the Institute of History and Philology, Academia Sinica* 39 (October 1969): 399–416.

Lary, George. *The Medieval Alexander.* Ed. by D. J. A. Ross. Cambridge: Cambridge University Press, 1956.

Lattimore, Owen. *Inner Asian Frontiers of China.* New York: American Geographical Society, 1940.

————. *Studies in Frontier History*. London: Oxford University Press, 1962.

————. "Chingis Khan and the Mongol Conquests." *Scientific American* 209:2 (1963): 54–68.

Ledyard, Gari. "The Mongol Campaigns in Korea and the Dating of the *Secret History of the Mongols*." *Central Asiatic Journal* 9 (1964): 1–22.

Lee, Sherman, and Ho Wai-kam. *Chinese Art under the Mongols: The Yuan Dynasty (1279–1368)*. Cleveland: The Cleveland Museum of Art, 1968.

Lee, Thomas H. C. "A Report on the Recently Excavated Song Ship at Quanzhou and a Consideration of Its True Capacity." *Sung Studies Newsletter* 11–12 (1975–76): 4–9.

Legge, James. *The I Ching: The Book of Changes*. Reprint. New York: Dover Publications, Inc., 1963.

LeStrange, Guy. *Baghdad during the Abbasid Caliphate*. Oxford: Clarendon Press, 1900.

Lewicki, Marjan. "Les inscriptions mongoles inédites en écriture carrée." *Collectanea Orientalia* (Wilno) 12 (1937): 1–72.

Lewis, Bernard, and Holt, P. M., eds. *Historians of the Middle East*. London: Oxford University Press, 1962.

Li Chu-tsing. "Stages of Development in Yüan Landscape Painting." *National Palace Museum Bulletin* 4:2 (May–June 1969): 1–10; 4:3 (July–August 1969): 1–12.

————. "The Development of Painting in Soochow during the Yüan Dynasty." In *Proceedings of the International Symposium on Chinese Painting*, pp. 483–500. Taipei: National Palace Museum, 1972.

————. "The Uses of the Past in Yüan Landscape Painting." In *Artists and Traditions: Uses of the Past in Chinese Culture*, ed. Christian Murck. Princeton: The Art Museum, Princeton University, 1977.

Li Tieh-tseng. *Tibet: Today and Yesterday*. New York: Bookman Associates, 1960.

Ligeti, Louis, ed. *Mongolian Studies*. Amsterdam: Verlag B. R. Grüner, 1970.

————. *Monuments en écriture 'Phagspa: Pièces de chancellerie en transcription chinoise*. Budapest: Akademiai Kiado, 1972.

Lin Yutang. *Imperial Peking: Seven Centuries of China*. New York: Crown Publishers, 1961.

Liu, James T. C. *Reform in Sung China: Wang An-shih (1021–1086) and His New Policies*. Cambridge: Harvard University Press, 1959.

Liu Jung-en, trans. *Six Yüan Plays*. Middlesex: Penguin Books, 1972.

Liu Tsung-yuan. "The Three Teachings in the Mongol-Yüan Times." American Council of Learned Societies Conference on Yüan Thought. Issaquah, Washington. January 1978.

Lo Jung-pang. "The Emergence of China as a Sea Power during the Late Sung and Early Yüan Periods." *Far Eastern Quarterly* 14 (1954–55): 489–503.

————. "The Controversy over Grain Conveyance during the Reign of Qubilai Qaqan (1260–94)." *Far Eastern Quarterly* 13:3 (May 1954): 263–85.

————. "Maritime Commerce and Its Relation to the Sung Navy." *Journal of the Economic and Social History of the Orient* 12:1 (1969): 57–101.

Ma, Lawrence J. C. *Commercial Development and Urban Change in Sung China (960–1279)*. Ann Arbor: Department of Geography, University of Michigan, 1971.

Maejima Shinji. "The Muslims in Ch'üan-chou at the End of the Yüan Dynasty." *Memoirs of the Research Department of the Tōyō Bunko* 31 (1973): 27–51.

Makra, Mary Lelia, trans. *The Hsiao Ching*. New York: St. John's University Press, 1961.

Mangold, Gunther. *Das Militärwesen in China unter der Mongolenherrschaft*. Ph.D. diss., Munich University, 1971.

March, Andrew L. "An Appreciation of Chinese Geomancy." *Journal of Asian Studies* 27 : 2 (February 1968): 253–67.

Marek, J., and Knížková, H. *The Jenghiz Khan Miniatures from the Court of Akbar the Great*. Trans. by Olga Kuthanová. London: Spring Books, 1963.

Martin, Henry Desmond. *The Rise of Chingis Khan and His Conquest of North China*. Baltimore: Johns Hopkins University Press, 1950.

Maspero, Georges. *Le royaume de Champa*. Leiden, 1914.

Masterpieces of Chinese Figure Painting in the National Palace Museum. Taipei: National Palace Museum, 1976.

Masterpieces of Chinese Portrait Painting in the National Palace Museum. Taipei: National Palace Museum, 1971.

McNeill, William H. *Plagues and Peoples*. New York: Doubleday Anchor Books, 1977.

Medley, Margaret. *Yüan Porcelain and Stoneware*. New York: Pitman Publishing Co., 1974.

Mélanges offerts au R. P. Ferdinand Cavallera. Toulouse: Bibliothèque de l'Institut Catholique, 1948.

Meyer, Jeffrey F. *Peking as a Sacred City*. Taipei: The Orient Cultural Service, 1976.

Michell, Robert, and Forbes, Neville, trans. *The Chronicle of Novgorod, 1016–1471*. London: Camden Third Series, 25, 1914.

Mingana, Alphonse. *The Early Spread of Christianity in Central Asia and the Far East: A New Document*. Manchester: The University Press, 1925.

Minorsky, Vladimir. *Iranica: Twenty Articles*. Herford: Stephen Austin, 1964.

Mitamura Taisuke. *Chinese Eunuchs: The Structure of Intimate Politics*. Trans. by Charles Pomeroy. Rutland: Charles E. Tuttle, 1970.

Miyazaki Ichisada. *China's Examination Hell*. Trans. by Conrad Schirokauer. New Haven: Yale University Press, 1981.

Montgomery, James A. *The History of Yaballaha III, Nestorian Patriarch of His Vicar Bar Sauma*. New York: Columbia University Press, 1927.

Mostaert, Antoine. "À propos de quelques portraits d'empereurs mongols." *Asia Major* o.s. 4 : 1 (1927): 147–56.

————. *Sur quelques passages de l'Histoire secrète des Mongols*. Cambridge: Harvard-Yenching Institute, 1953.

Mote, Frederick W. "The Growth of Chinese Despotism: A Critique of Wittfogel's Theory of Oriental Despotism as Applied to China." *Oriens*

Extremus 8:1 (August 1961): 1–41.

Moule, A. C. *Christians in China before the Year 1550*. London: Society for Promoting Christian Knowledge, 1930.

――――. *Quinsai, with Other Notes on Marco Polo*. Cambridge: Cambridge University Press, 1957.

Moule, A. C., and Pelliot, Paul. *Marco Polo: The Description of the World*. 2 vols. London: George Routledge & Sons, Ltd., 1938.

Munkuev, N. Z., trans. *Men-da bei-lu*. Moscow: Nauka, 1975.

Murayama, S. "Sind die Naiman Türken oder Mongolen?" *Central Asiatic Journal* 4 (1959): 188–98.

Mydans, Shelley, and Mydans, Carl. "A Shrine City, Golden and White: The Seldom-Visited Pagan in Burma." *Smithsonian Magazine* (October 1974): 72–80.

Nagel's Encyclopedia-Guide: China. Geneva: Nagel Publishers, 1979.

Nakano Miyoko. *A Phonological Study on the 'Phags-pa Script and the Meng-ku Tzu-yün*. Canberra: Australian National University Press, 1971.

Needham, Joseph. *Science and Civilisation in China, vol. 3*. Cambridge: Cambridge University Press, 1959.

――――. *Clerks and Craftsmen in China and the West*. Cambridge: Cambridge University Press, 1970.

――――. *Science and Civilisation in China: Physics and Physical Technology, vol. 4, no. 3*. Cambridge: Cambridge University Press, 1971.

New Archaeological Finds in China: Discoveries during the Cultural Revolution. Peking: Foreign Languages Press, 1973.

Nowak, Margaret, and Durrant, Stephen. *The Tale of the Nišan Shamaness: A Manchu Folk Epic*. Seattle: University of Washington Press, 1977.

Ohsson, Constantin Mouradgea d'. *Histoire des Mongols, depuis Tchinguiz-Khan jusqu'à Timour-Bey ou Tamerlan*. 4 vols. The Hague-Amsterdam: Les Frères Van Cleef, 1834–35.

Olbricht, Peter. *Das Postwesen in China unter der Mongolenherrschaft im 13. und 14. Jahrhundert*. Wiesbaden: Otto Harrassowitz, 1954.

Olbricht, Peter, and Pinks, Elisabeth, trans. *Meng-ta Pei-lu und Hei-ta shih-lüeh*. Wiesbaden: Otto Harrassowitz, 1980.

Ollone, H. M. G. d'. *Recherches sur les Musulmans chinois*. Paris: Ernest Leroux, 1911.

Olschki, Leonardo. *Marco Polo's Precursors*. Baltimore: Johns Hopkins University Press, 1943.

――――. *Guillaume Boucher: A French Artist at the Court of the Khans*. Baltimore: Johns Hopkins University Press, 1946.

――――. *The Myth of Felt*. Berkeley: University of California Press, 1949.

――――. *Marco Polo's Asia*. Berkeley: University of California Press, 1960.

O'Neill, Eugene. *Nine Plays*. New York: Random House, 1954.

Oriente Poliano. Rome: Istituto Italiano per il Medio ed Estremo Oriente, 1957.

Ostrogorsky, George. *History of the Byzantine State*. Trans. by Joan Hussey. 2nd ed. Oxford: Basil Blackwell, 1968.

Overmyer, Daniel L. "The White Cloud Sect in Sung and Yüan China."

Harvard Journal of Asiatic Studies 42:2 (December 1982): 615–42.

Pelliot, Paul. "Les Mo-ni et le *Houa-hou king.*" *Bulletin de l'École Française d'Extrême-Orient* 3 (1903): 318–27.

―――. "Chrétiens de l'Asie centrale et d'Extrême-Orient." *T'oung Pao* 15 (1914): 623–44.

―――. *Les Mongols et la Papauté.* Paris: Librairie August Picard, 1923.

―――. "Les systèmes d'écriture en usage chez les anciens Mongols." *Asia Major* o.s. 2:2 (1925): 284–89.

―――. "Notes sur Karakorum." *Journal asiatique* 206 (1925): 372–75.

―――. "Une ville musulmane dans la chine du nord sous les mongols." *Journal asiatique* 211 (1927): 261–79.

―――. "Le vrai nom de 'Seroctan.'" *T'oung Pao* 29 (1932): 43–54.

―――. "Une tribu méconnu des Naiman: Les Bätäkin." *T'oung Pao* 37 (1944): 35–71.

―――. *Histoire secrète des Mongols.* Paris: Librairie d'Amérique et d'Orient, Adrien-Maisonneuve, 1949.

―――. *Notes sur l'histoire de la Horde d'Or.* Paris: Adrien-Maisonneuve, 1949.

―――. *Notes on Marco Polo.* 2 vols. Paris: Adrien-Maisonneuve, 1959–63.

―――. *Recherches sur les Chrétiens d'Asie centrale et d'Extrême-Orient.* Ed. by Jean Dauvillier and Louis Hambis. Paris: Imprimerie nationale, 1973.

Pelliot, Paul, trans. *Mémoires sur les coutumes du Cambodge de Tcheou Ta-kouan (version nouvelle).* Paris: Adrien-Maisonneuve, 1951.

Pelliot, Paul, and Hambis, Louis. *Histoire des campagnes de Gengis Khan: Cheng-wou ts'in-tcheng lou.* Leiden: E. J. Brill, 1951.

Perng Ching-hsi. *Double Jeopardy: A Critique of Seven Yüan Courtroom Dramas.* Ann Arbor: Center for Chinese Studies, University of Michigan, 1978.

Petech, Luciano. "Sang-ko, a Tibetan Statesman in Yüan China." *Acta Orientalia* 34:1–3 (1980): 193–208.

Pétis de la Crois. *Histoire du grand Genghizcan: Premier empereur des anciens Mongols et Tartares.* Paris, 1710.

Phillips, E. D. *The Mongols.* New York: Frederick A. Praeger, 1969.

Poliak, A. N. "The Influence of Chingiz-Khān's Yāsa upon the General Organization of the Mamlūk State." *Bulletin of the School of Oriental and African Studies, London University* 10 (1939–42): 862–76.

Pomet, M. *A Complete History of Drugs.* London: J. & J. Bonwicke, S. Birt, W. Parker, C. Hitch, & E. Wicksteed, 1748.

Pope, John Alexander. *Fourteenth-Century Blue-and-White: A Group of Chinese Porcelains in the Topkapu Sarayi Müzesi, Istanbul.* Washington, D.C.: Freer Gallery of Art, 1952.

―――. *Chinese Porcelains from the Ardebil Shrine.* Washington, D.C.: Smithsonian Institution, 1956.

Poppe, Nicholas. *The Mongolian Monuments in ḥP'ags-pa Script.* Trans. and ed. by John R. Krueger. Wiesbaden: Otto Harrassowitz, 1957.

―――. *Introduction to Altaic Linguistics.* Wiesbaden: Otto Harrassowitz, 1965.

————. *Grammar of Written Mongolian*. Wiesbaden: Otto Harrassowitz, 1974.

Poucha, Pavel. *Die geheime Geschichte der Mongolen als Geschichtsquelle und Literaturdenkmal*. Prague: Verlag der Tschechoslowakischen Akademie der Wissenschaften, 1956.

Prawdin, Michael. *The Mongol Empire: Its Rise and Legacy*. Trans. by Eden and Cedar Paul. London: George Allen & Unwin, Ltd., 1940.

Pritsak, Omeljan. "Āli-Burhān." *Der Islam* 30:1 (January 1952): 81–96.

Quatremère, Étienne, trans. *Raschid-Eldin: Histoire des Mongols de la Perse*. Paris: Collection Orientale, Manuscrits inédits de la Bibliothèque Royale, 1836.

————. *Histoire des sultans Mamlouks de l'Égypte*. Paris: Oriental Translation Fund, 1837.

Rachewiltz, Igor de. "The *Hsi-yu lu* by Yeh-lü Ch'u-ts'ai." *Monumenta Serica* 21 (1962): 1–128.

————. "Yeh-lü Ch'u-ts'ai (1189–1243): Buddhist Idealist and Confucian Statesman." In *Confucian Personalities*, ed. by Arthur Wright and Denis Twitchett, pp. 189–216. Stanford: Stanford University Press, 1962.

————. "Some Remarks on the Dating of the *Secret History of the Mongols*." *Monumenta Serica* 24 (1965): 185–205.

————. "Personnel and Personalities in North China in the Early Mongol Period." *Journal of the Economic and Social History of the Orient* 9:1–2 (1966): 88–144.

————. "Some Remarks on the Language Problem in Yüan China." *Journal of the Oriental Society of Australia* 5:1–2 (December 1967): 65–80.

————. *Papal Envoys to the Great Khans*. London: Faber & Faber, 1971.

————. "The Secret History of the Mongols." *Papers on Far Eastern History* 4 (September 1971): 115–63; 5 (March 1972): 149–75; 10 (September 1974): 55–82; 13 (March 1976): 41–75; 16 (September 1977): 27–65; 18 (September 1978): 43–80; 21 (March 1980): 17–57; 23 (March 1981): 111–46; 26 (September 1982): 39–84.

————. "Some Remarks on the Ideological Foundations of Chingis Khan's Empire." *Papers on Far Eastern History* 7 (March 1973): 21–36.

————. "Muqali, Bōl, Tas, and An-t'ung." *Papers on Far Eastern History* 15 (March 1977): 45–62.

Rachewiltz, Igor de, and Nakano Miyoko. *Index to Biographical Material in Chin and Yüan Literary Works, First Series*. Canberra: Australian National University Press, 1970.

Rachewiltz, lgor de, and Wang, May. *Index to Biographical Material in Chin and Yüan Literary Works, Second Series*. Canberra: Australian National University Press, 1972.

Rall, Jutta. "Zur persischen Übersetzung eines Mo-chüeh, einer chinesischen medizinischen Textes." *Oriens Extremus* 7 (1960): 150–57.

————. *Die vier grossen Medizinschulen der Mongolenzeit*. Wiesbaden: Franz Steiner Verlag, 1970.

Ratchnevsky, Paul. *Un code des Yuan*. Vol. 1. Paris: Ernest Leroux, 1937.

————. "Die mongolischen Grosskhane und die buddhistische Kirche." In

Asiatica: Festschrift Friedrich Weller zum 65. Geburtstag, ed. by Johannes Schubert, pp. 489–504. Leipzig: Otto Harrassowitz, 1954.

————. "Über den mongolischen Einfluss auf die Gesetzgebung der Yüan-Zeit." *Moscow, International Congress of Orientalists* (1960): 11–16.

————. "Zum Ausdruck 't'ouhsia' in der Mongolenzeit." In *Collectanea Mongolica: Festschrift für Professor Dr. Rintchen zum 60. Geburtstag*, pp. 173–91. Wiesbaden: Otto Harrassowitz, 1966.

————. "The Levirate in the Legislation of the Yüan Dynasty." *Tamura Hakushi shoju tōyōshi ronsō.* Kyoto, 1968.

————. "Rašīd al-Dīn über die Mohammedaner Verfolgungen in China unter Qubilai," *Central Asiatic Journal* 14 : 1–3 (1970): 163–80.

————. *Un code des Yuan.* Vol. 2. Paris: Presses Universitaires de France, 1972.

Raverty, H. G., trans. *Jūzjānī: Ṭabaḳāt-i-Nāṣirī: A General History of the Muhammadan Dynasties of Asia.* Reprint. New Delhi: Oriental Books Reprint Corporation, 1970.

Rawski, Evelyn Sakakida. *Education and Popular Literacy in Ch'ing China.* Ann Arbor: University of Michigan Press, 1979.

Read, Bernard E. *Chinese Materia Medica: 6, Avian Drugs.* Peiping: Peking Natural History Bulletin, 1932.

Recueil des historiens des croisades: Documents arméniens II. Paris: Imprimerie nationale, 1906.

Reischauer, Edwin O. *Ennin's Diary.* New York: Ronald Press, 1955.

————. *Ennin's Travels in T'ang China.* New York: Ronald Press, 1955.

Rerikh, Yú. N. "Mongol-Tibetan Relations in the 13th and 14th Centuries." Trans. by Janice Nattier. *Tibet Society Bulletin* 6 (1973): 40–55.

Riasanovsky, Valentin A. *Fundamental Principles of Mongol Law.* Reprint. Bloomington: Indiana University Uralic and Altaic Series, 1965.

Rice, David Talbot. *The Illustrations to the "World History" of Rashīd al-Dīn.* Ed. by Basil Gray. Edinburgh: Edinburgh University Press, 1976.

Richard, Jean. "La conversion de Berke et les débuts de l'islamisation de la Horde d'Or." *Revue des études islamiques* 35 (1967): 173–84.

————. "The Mongols and the Franks." *Journal of Asian History* 3 : 1 (1969): 45–57.

————. "Les causes des victoires mongoles d'après les historiens occidentaux du xiiie siècle." *Central Asiatic Journal* 23 : 1–2 (1979): 104–17.

Richards, D. S., ed. *Islam and the Trade of Asia.* Philadelphia: University of Pennsylvania Press, 1970.

Rideout, J. K. "The Rise of the Eunuchs during the T'ang Dynasty." *Asia Major* n.s. 1 (1949–50): 53–72; 3 (1952): 42–58.

Rock, Joseph F. *The Ancient Na-khi Kingdom of Southwest China.* 2 vols. Cambridge: Harvard University Press, 1947.

Rockhill, William W., trans. *The Journey of William of Rubruck to the Eastern Parts of the World.* London: The Hakluyt Society, 1900.

————. "Notes on the Relations and Trade of China with the Eastern Archipelago and the Coast of the Indian Ocean during the Fourteenth Century." *T'oung Pao* 15 (1914): 419–47.

Roerich, George N., trans. *The Blue Annals*. 2nd ed. Delhi: Motilal Banarsidass, 1976.

Rosner, Erhard. "Die 'Zehn schimpflichten Delikte' im chinesischen Recht der Yüan-Zeit." Ph. diss., Munich University, 1964.

Rossabi, Morris. "The Tea and Horse Trade with Inner Asia during the Ming." *Journal of Asian History* 4 : 2 (1970): 136–68.

————. "Ming China and Turfan, 1406–1517." *Central Asiatic Journal* 16 : 3 (1972): 206–25.

————. *China and Inner Asia from 1368 to the Present Day*. London: Thames & Hudson, 1975.

————. "Khubilai Khan and the Women in His Family." In *Studia Sino-Mongolica: Festschrift für Herbert Franke*, ed. by Wolfgang Bauer, pp. 153–80. Wiesbaden: Franz Steiner Verlag, 1979.

————. "The Muslims in the Early Yüan Dynasty." In *China under Mongol Rule*, ed. by John D. Langlois, pp. 258–99. Princeton: Princeton University Press, 1981.

————. "Kublai Khan." *Houston Chronicle* (18 May 1982), p. 2.

————. *The Jurchens in the Yüan and Ming*. Ithaca: China-Japan Program, Cornell University, 1982.

————. "Trade Routes in Inner Asia." Unpublished paper prepared for the *Cambridge History of Inner Asia*.

Rossabi, Morris, ed. *China among Equals: The Middle Kingdom and Its Neighbors, 10th–14th Centuries*. Berkeley: University of California Press, 1983.

Roux, Jean-Paul. "Tängri: Essai sur le Ciel-Dieu des peuples altaïques." *Revue de l'histoire des religions* 149 (1955): 49–82, 197–230; 150 (1956): 27–54, 173–212; 154 (1958): 32–66.

————. "Le chaman gengiskanide." *Anthropos* 54 : 3–4 (1959): 401–32.

————. *La mort chez les peuples altaïques anciens et médiévaux d'après les documents écrits*. Paris: Librairie d'Amérique et d'Orient, Adrien-Maisonneuve, 1963.

Rudolph, Richard C. "Medical Matters in an Early Fourteenth Century Chinese Diary." *Journal of the History of Medicine and Allied Sciences* 2 : 3 (Summer 1947): 299–306.

————. "Kuo Pi: A Yüan Artist and His Diary." *Ars Orientalis* 3 (1959): 175–88.

Runciman, Steven. *A History of the Crusades, vol. 3: The Kingdom of Acre*. Cambridge: Cambridge University Press, 1954.

Saar, John. "Japanese Divers Discover Wreckage of Mongol Fleet." *Smithsonian Magazine* (December 1981), pp. 118–29.

Saccheti, Maurizia Dinacci. "Sull'adozione del nome dinastico Yüan." *Annali, Istituto Orientale di Napoli* 31, n.s. 21 (1971): 553–58.

Sadeque, Syedah Fatima. *Baybars I of Egypt*. Dacca: Geoffrey Cumberlege, Oxford University Press, 1956.

Sagaster, Klaus. "Herrschaftsideologie und Friedensgedanke bei den Mongolen." *Central Asiatic Journal* 17 (1973): 223–42.

Sagaster, Klaus, trans. *Die weisse Geschichte*. Wiesbaden: Otto Harrassowitz, 1976.

Sandquist, A., and Powicke, M. R., eds. *Essays in Medieval History Presented to Bertie Wilkinson*. Toronto: University of Toronto Press, 1969.

Sansom, George. *A History of Japan to 1334*. Stanford: Stanford University Press, 1958.

Sarre, Friedrich. *Die Keramik von Samarra*. Berlin: D. Reimer, 1925.

Saunders, John Joseph. "Genghis Khan and the Communists." *History Today* 20 (1970): 390–96.

———. *The History of the Mongol Conquests*. New York: Barnes & Noble, 1971.

Schafer, Edward H. "The Camel in China Down to the Mongol Invasion." *Sinologica* 2 (1950): 165–94, 263–90.

———. "Falconry in T'ang Times." *T'oung Pao* 46 (1958): 293–338.

Schlegel, Dietlinde. *Hao Ching (1222–1275): Ein chinesischer Berater des Kaisers Kublai Khan*. Bamberg: Offsetdruckerei Kurt Urlaub, 1968.

Schlepp, Wayne. "Yeh-lü Ch'u-ts'ai in Samarkand." *Canada Mongolia Review* 1 : 2 (1975): 5–14.

Schlösser, Richard. "Die Münzen der beiden Epochen Chi Yüan." *Artibus Asiae* 5 (1935): 38–46.

Schmidt, Isaac Jacob, trans. *Geschichte der Ost-Mongolen und ihres Fürstenhauses verfasst von Ssanang Ssetsen Chungtaidschi*. St. Petersburg: N. Gretsch, 1829.

Schram, Louis M. J. "The Monguors of the Kansu-Tibetan Border." *Transactions of the American Philosophical Society* n.s. 47 : 1 (1957): 164 pp.; n.s. 44 : 1 (April 1954): 138 pp.

Schubert, Johannes, ed. *Asiatica: Festschrift Friedrich Weller zum 65. Geburtstag*. Leipzig: Otto Harrassowitz, 1954.

Schuh, Dieter. *Erlasse und Sendschreiben mongolischen Herrscher für tibetische Geistliche*. St. Augustin: VGH Wissenschaftsverlag, 1971.

Schurmann, Herbert Franz. *Economic Structure of the Yüan Dynasty: Translation of Chapters 93 and 94 of the Yüan shih*. Cambridge: Harvard University Press, 1956.

———. "Mongolian Tributary Practices of the 13th Century." *Harvard Journal of Asiatic Studies* 19 (1956): 304–89.

———. "Problems of Political Organization during the Yüan Dynasty." In *Trudi xxv mezdunarodnovo Kongressa Vostokovedov, Moskva*. Moscow: Nauka, 1963.

Schwarz, Henry. *Bibliotheca Mongolica, Part 1: Works in English, French, and German*. Bellingham: Western Washington University, 1978.

Schwarz-Schilling, C. *Der Friede von Shan-yüan (1005 n. Chr.)*. Wiesbaden: Otto Harrassowitz, 1959.

Serruys, Henry. "Remains of Mongol Customs in China during the Early Ming Period." *Monumenta Serica* 16 : 1–2 (1957): 137–90.

———. "Ta-tu, Tai-tu, Dayidu." *Chinese Culture* 2 : 4 (May 1960): 73–81.

———. *Kumiss Ceremonies and Horse Racing: Three Mongolian Texts*. Wiesbaden: Otto Harrassowitz, 1974.

———. "Mongol 'Qori': Reservation." *Mongolian Studies* 1 (1974): 76–91.

———. "Two Remarkable Women in Mongolia: The Third Lady Erketü

Qatun and Dayičing-Beyiǰi." *Asia Major* 19:2 (August 1975): 191–245.

Shakabpa, Tsepon W. D. *Tibet: A Political History*. New Haven: Yale University Press, 1967.

Shiba Yoshinobu. *Commerce and Society in Sung China*. Trans. by Mark Elvin. Ann Arbor: Center for Chinese Studies, University of Michigan, 1970.

Shih Chung-wen. *The Golden Age of Chinese Drama: Yüan Tsa-chü*. Princeton: Princeton University Press, 1966.

———. *Injustice to Tou O (Tou O Yüan)*. Cambridge: Cambridge University Press, 1972.

Shiratori Kurakichi. "The Queue among the Peoples of North Asia." *Memoirs of the Research Department of the Tōyō Bunko* 4 (1929): 1–69.

Simon de Saint Quentin. *Histoire des Tartares*. Ed. by Jean Richard. Paris: Paul Geuthner, 1965.

Sinor, Denis. "Un voyageur du treizième siècle: le Dominicain Julien de Hongrie." *Bulletin of the School of Oriental and African Studies, London University* 14:3 (1952): 589–602.

———. *History of Hungary*. London: George Allen & Unwin, Ltd., 1959.

———. *Introduction à l'étude de l'Eurasie centrale*. Wiesbaden: Otto Harrassowitz, 1963.

———. "Horse and Pasture in Inner Asian History." *Oriens Extremus* 19:1–2 (December 1972): 171–83.

Sinor, Denis, ed. *Aspects of Altaic Civilization*. Bloomington: Indiana University Press, 1963.

Siren, Osvald. *The Imperial Palaces of Peking*. 3 vols. Paris-Brussels: G. Van Oest, 1926.

Skinner, G. William, ed. *The City in Late Imperial China*. Stanford: Stanford University Press, 1977.

Slessarev, Vsevolod. *Prester John: The Letters and the Legend*. Minneapolis: University of Minnesota Press, 1959.

Smith, John Masson. "Mongol and Nomadic Taxation." *Harvard Journal of Asiatic Studies* 30 (1970): 46–85.

———. "Mongol Manpower and Persian Population." *Journal of the Economic and Social History of the Orient* 18:3 (October 1975): 271–99.

———. "ʿAyn Jālūt: Mamlūk Success or Mongol Failure." *Harvard Journal of Asiatic Studies* 44:2 (December 1984): 307–45.

Soedjatmoko, ed. *Introduction to Indonesian Historiography*. Ithaca: Cornell University Press, 1965.

Soothill, William Edward, and Hodous, Lewis, comps. *A Dictionary of Chinese Buddhist Terms*. Reprint. Taipei: Ch'eng-wen Publishing Co., 1975.

Spence, Jonathan D. *Emperor of China: Self Portrait of K'ang-hsi*. New York: Alfred Knopf, 1974.

Spuler, Bertold. *Die Goldene Horde: Die Mongolen in Russland, 1223–1502*. Wiesbaden: Otto Harrassowitz, 1965.

———. *Die Mongolen in Iran: Politik, Verwaltung, und Kultur der Ilchanzeit, 1220–1350*. Berlin: Akademie-Verlag, 1968.

———. *The Muslim World, a Historical Survey: Part 2, The Mongol Period*.

Trans. by F. R. C. Bagley. Leiden: E. J. Brill, 1969.

————. *History of the Mongols Based on Eastern and Western Accounts of the Thirteenth and Fourteenth Centuries*. Trans. by Helga and Stuart Drummond. Berkeley: University of California Press, 1972.

————. *Handbuch der Orientalistik, 5, 5: Geschichte Mittelasiens*. Leiden: E. J. Brill, 1966.

Stein, M. Aurel. *Innermost Asia*. Oxford: Clarendon Press, 1928.

Stein, R. A. *Tibetan Civilization*. Trans. by J. E. Stapleton Driver. Stanford: Stanford University Press, 1972.

Steinhardt, Nancy Schatzman. "Currency Issues of Yüan China." *Bulletin of Sung and Yüan Studies* 16 (1981): 59–81.

————. "Imperial Architecture under Mongolian Patronage: Khubilai's Imperial City of Da-du." Ph.D. diss., Harvard University, 1981.

————. "The Plan of Khubilai Khan's Imperial City." *Artibus Asiae* 44 : 2–3 (1983): 137–58.

Strakosch-Grassman, Gustav. *Der Einfall der Mongolen in Mitteleuropa in den Jahren 1241 und 1242*. Innsbruck: Verlag der Wagner'schen Universitäts-Buchhandlung, 1893.

Tao Jing-shen. "The Horse and the Rise of the Chin Dynasty." *Papers of the Michigan Academy of Science, Arts, and Letters* 53 (1968): 183–89.

————. "The Influence of Jurchen Rule on Chinese Political Institutions." *Journal of Asian Studies* 30 : 1 (1970): 121–30.

————. "Political Recruitment in the Chin Dynasty." *Journal of the American Oriental Society* 94 : 1 (1974): 24–34.

————. *The Jurchen in Twelfth-Century China: A Study of Sinicization*. Seattle: University of Washington Press, 1976.

Tekin, Şinasi. *Buddhistische Uigurica aus der Yüan-Zeit*. Wiesbaden: Otto Harrassowitz, 1980.

Thiel, Joseph. "Der Streit der Buddhisten und Taoisten zur Mongolenzeit." *Monumenta Serica* 20 (1961): 1–81.

Tikhvinskii, S. L., ed. *Tataro-mongoly v Azii i Evrope* [The Tartar Mongols in Asia and Europe]. Moscow: Nauka, 1970; 2nd ed., 1976.

Tisserant, E. "Une lettre de l'Ilkhan de Perse Abagha adressée en 1268 au pape Clement IV." *Muséon* 59 (1946): 547–56.

Togan, Isenbike. "The Chapter on Annual Grants in the *Yüan shih*." Ph.D. diss., Harvard University, 1973.

Tractata Altaica: Festschrift für Denis Sinor. Wiesbaden: Otto Harrassowitz, 1976.

Tregonning, K. G. "Kublai Khan and South-East Asia." *History Today* 12 : 3 (March 1957): 163–70.

Tsunoda Ryūsaku and Goodrich, L. C. *Japan in the Chinese Dynastic Histories*. South Pasadena: P. D. & Ione Perkins, 1951.

Tucci, Guiseppi. *Tibetan Painted Scrolls*. Rome: Libreria dello stato, 1949.

Tullock, Gordon. "Paper Money—A Cycle in Cathay." *Economic History Review* 2nd ser. 93 (April 1957): 393–407.

Vasiliev, A. A. *History of the Byzantine Empire, 324–1453*. Madison: University of Wisconsin Press, 1952.

Vernadsky, George. "The Scope and Contents of Chingis Khan's *Yasa*." *Harvard Journal of Asiatic Studies* 3 (1938): 337–60.

―――. *The Mongols and Russia*. New Haven: Yale University Press, 1953.

Vissière, A. *Études sino-mahométanes*. 2 vols. Paris: Ernest Leroux, 1911–13.

Vladimirtsov, Boris. *La régime sociale des Mongols: Le féodalisme nomade*. Trans. by Michel Carsow. Paris: Librairie d'Amérique et d'Orient, Adrien Maisonneuve, 1948.

―――. *The Life of Chingis Khan*. Trans. by D. S. Mirsky. Reprint. New York: Benjamin Blom, 1969.

Voegelin, Eric. "The Mongol Orders of Submission to European Powers, 1245–1255." *Byzantion* 15 (1940–41): 378–413.

Vreeland, Herbert Harold, III. *Mongol Community and Kinship Structure*. New Haven: Human Relations Area Files, 1953.

Waley, Arthur. *The Analects of Confucius*. New York: Vintage Books, n.d.

―――. *The Travels of an Alchemist*. London: Routledge & Kegan Paul, Ltd., 1931.

―――. *The Secret History of the Mongols and Other Pieces*. London: George Allen & Unwin, Ltd., 1963.

Watson, Burton, *Records of the Grand Historian of China*. 2 vols. New York: Columbia University Press, 1961.

Wegman, Konrad. *Kuo Pi: Ein Beamter und Literaten-Maler der Mongolenzeit*. Ph.D. diss., University of Munich, 1967.

Welch, Holmes. *Taoism: The Parting of the Way*. Boston: Beacon Press, 1966.

Wheatley, Paul. *The Pivot of the Four Quarters: A Preliminary Inquiry into the Origins and Character of the Ancient Chinese City*. Chicago: Aldine Publishing Co., 1971.

Wiet, Gaston. *Baghdad: Metropolis of the Abbasid Caliphate*. Trans. by Seymour Feiler. Norman: University of Oklahoma Press, 1971.

Wilhelm, Hellmut. *Eight Lectures on the I Ching*. Trans. by Cary F. Baynes. New York: Harper & Row, 1960.

Williams, Oscar. *F. T. Palgrave's The Golden Treasury*. New York: Mentor Books, 1961.

Wittfogel, Karl, and Feng Chia-sheng. *History of Chinese Society: Liao (907–1125)*. In *Transactions of the American Philosophical Society* n.s. 36 (1949).

Wright, Arthur. F. *Buddhism in Chinese History*. Stanford: Stanford University Press, 1959.

―――. "Symbolism and Function: Reflections on Changan and Other Great Cities." *Journal of Asian Studies* 24:4 (August 1965): 667–79.

Wright, Arthur F., ed. *The Confucian Persuasion*. Stanford: Stanford University Press, 1960.

Wright, Arthur F., and Twitchett, Denis, eds. *Confucian Personalities*. Stanford: Stanford University Press, 1962.

―――. *Perspectives on the T'ang*. New Haven: Yale University Press, 1973.

Wu, K. T. "Chinese Printing under Four Alien Dynasties." *Harvard Journal of Asiatic Studies* 13 (1950): 447–523.

Wylie, Alexander. *Chinese Researches*. Shanghai, 1897.

Wylie, Turrell V. "The First Mongol Conquest of Tibet Reinterpreted."

Harvard Journal of Asiatic Studies 37:1 (June 1977): 103–33.

Wyngaert, Anastasius van den. *Sinica Franciscana*. 5 vols. Quaracchi-Firenze: Collegio di S. Bonaventura, 1929–54.

Yamada Nabaka. *Ghenkō: The Mongol Invasion of Japan*. London: Smith, Elder, & Co., 1916.

Yamane Yukio and Ohshima Ritsuko. *A Classified Bibliography of Articles and Books Concerning the Yüan Period in Chinese and Japanese*. Tokyo, 1971.

Yang Lien-sheng. *Money and Credit in China: A Short History*. Cambridge: Harvard University Press, 1952.

————. *Studies in Chinese Institutional History*. Cambridge: Harvard University Press, 1963.

Yang, Richard F. S. "The Social Background of the Yüan Drama." *Monumenta Serica* 17 (1958): 331–52.

Yang, Gladys, and Yang Xianyi. *Selected Plays of Guan Hanqing*. Beijing: Foreign Languages Press, 1979.

Yule, Henry, trans. *The Book of Ser Marco Polo, the Venetian, Concerning the Kingdoms and Marvels of the East*. 2 vols. 3rd ed. rev. by Henri Cordier. London: John Murray, 1903.

————. *Cathay and the Way Thither*. Rev. ed. by Henri Cordier. Reprint, 4 vols. in 2. Taipei: Ch'eng-wen Publishing Co., 1966.

Žamcarano, C. Ž. *The Mongol Chronicles of the Seventeenth Century*. Trans. by Rudolf Loewenthal. Wiesbaden: Otto Harrassowitz, 1955.

Zürcher, Erik. *The Buddhist Conquest of China: The Spread and Adoption of Buddhism in Early and Medieval China*. 2 vols. Leiden: E. J. Brill, 1959.

Bibliography of Works in Oriental Languages

PRIMARY SOURCES

Chao Meng-fu 趙孟頫. *Sung-hsüeh-chai wen-chi* 松雪齋文集 [Collection of studies from the *Sung-hsüeh-chai*]. Reprint. Shanghai: Commercial Press, 1929.

Ch'en Pang-chan et al. 陳邦瞻. *Sung-shih chi-shih pen-mo* 宋史紀事本末 [Record of the history of the Sung from beginning to end]. Reprint. Peking: Chung-hua shu-chü 中華書局, 1977.

———. *Yüan-shih chi-shih pen-mo* 元史紀事本末 [Record of the history of the Yüan from beginning to end]. Reprint. Peking: Chung-hua shu-chü, 1979.

Chŏng In-ji 鄭麟趾 *Koryŏ-sa* 高麗史 [History of Koryŏ]. Tokyo, 1909.

Hsiang-mai 祥邁. *Pien-wei lu* 辯僞錄 [Record of debates over falsehoods]. Tokyo: Taishō shinshū daizōkyō 大正新修大藏經, 1924–30.

Hsü Tzu-chih t'ung-chien 續資治通鑑 [Supplement to the *Comprehensive Mirror for Aid in Government*]. Reprint. Shanghai, 1957.

Kao Wen-te et al. 高文德. *Meng-ku shih-hsi* 蒙古世系 [Genealogy of Mongolia]. Reprint. Peking: Chung-kuo she-hui k'o-hsüeh 中國社會科學, 1979.

K'o Shao-min 柯劭忞. *Hsin Yüan shih* 新元史 [New Yüan history]. In *Erh-shih-wu shih* 二十五史 [The twenty-five dynastic histories]. Reprint. Taipei: K'ai-ming shu-tien 開明書店, 1962–69.

Ma Wen-sheng 馬文升. *Fu-an tung-i chi* 撫安東夷記 [Record of pacifying the eastern barbarians]. Reprint. Shanghai: Commercial Press, 1937.

Nien-ch'ang 念常. *Fo-tsu li-tai t'ung-tsai* 佛祖歷代通載 [Record of successive generations of Buddha]. Tokyo: Taishō shinshū daizōkyō, 1924–32.

Shao Yüan-p'ing 邵遠平. *Yüan-shih lei-pien* 元史類編 [Compilation of Yüan history]. Reprint. Taipei: Kuang-wen shu-chü 廣文書局, 1968.

Sung Lien et al. 宋濂. *Yüan shih* 元史 [Yüan dynastic history]. Peking: Chung-hua shu-chü, 1976.

Ta Yüan hai-yün chi 大元海運記 [Record of the great Yüan's transportation by sea]. Reprint. Peiping: Kuo-hsüeh wen-k'u 國學文庫, 1936.

Ta Yüan ma-cheng chi 大元馬政記 [Record of the great Yüan's horse administration]. Reprint. Peiping: Kuo-hsüeh wen-k'u, 1937.

Ta Yüan ts'ang-k'u chi 大元倉庫記 [Record of the great Yüan's granaries and treasuries]. Reprint. Peiping: Kuo-hsüeh wen-k'u, 1936.

T'o T'o et al. 脫脫. *Chin shih* 金史 [Chin dynastic history]. Peking: Chung-hua shu-chü, 1975.

————. *Sung shih* 宋史 [Sung dynastic history]. Peking: Chung-hua shu-chü, 1977.

T'u Chi 屠寄. *Meng-wu-erh shih-chi* 蒙兀兒史記 [Historical records of the Mongols]. Reprint. Taipei: Shih-chieh shu-chü 世界書局, 1962.

Yang Shen 楊愼. *Nan-chao yeh-shih* 南詔野史 [Historical accounts of the Nan-chao]. Taipei: Hua-wen shu-chü 華文書局, 1969.

Yao Sui 姚燧. *Mu-an chi* 牧庵集 [Compilations from the shepherd's hut]. Ssu-pu ts'ung-k'an 四部叢刊 ed.

Yüan Kao-li chi-shih 元高麗紀事 [Record of Korea in Yüan times]. Reprint. Peiping: Wen-tien ko-yüan 文殿閣鉛, 1937.

Yüan shih. See Sung Lien et al.

Yüan tien-chang 元典章 [Regulations of the Yüan]. Reprint. Taipei: Wen-hai ch'u-pan-she 文海出版社, 1964.

SECONDARY SOURCES

Abe Takeo 安部健夫. "Gendai chishikijin to kakyo," 元代知識人と科舉 [Yüan dynasty scholars and the civil service examinations]. *Shirin* 史林 42:6 (November 1959): 136–45.

————. *Gendai shi no kenkyū* 元代史の研究 [Studies on the Yüan Period]. Tokyo, 1972.

An Shou-jen 安守仁. "Pa-ssu-pa ch'ao-chien Hu-pi-lieh pi-hua," 八思巴朝見忽必烈壁畫 [Painting of 'Phags-pa's audience with Khubilai]. *Wen-wu* 文物 7 (1959): 12–13.

Aoyama Sadao 青山定雄, ed. *Sōdai shi nenpyō* 宋代史年表 [Chronological tables of Sung period history]. Tokyo: Tōyō Bunko, 1974.

Aritaka Iwao 有高巖. "Gendai no nōmin seikatsu ni tsuite" 元代の農民生活に就いて [Concerning the livelihood of farmers in the Yüan period]. In *Kuwabara hakushi kanreki kinen tōyōshi ronsō* 桑原博士還曆記念東洋史論叢, pp. 945–97. Kyoto, 1935.

Chan Po-lien 詹焰煉. "Yüan-tai Hang-chou I-ssu-lan chiao ti yen-chiu" 元代杭州伊斯蘭教的研究 [Studies on Islam in Hang-chou in the Yüan period]. *Chung-hua wen-hua fu-hsing yüeh-k'an* 中華文化復興月刊 3:6 (1970): 53–54; 3:7 (1970): 44–46; 3:8 (1970): 31–34.

Chang Hsing-lang 張星烺. *Chung-hsi chiao-t'ung shih-liao hui-pien* 中西交通史料彙編 [Compilation of historical materials on communication between China and the West]. 6 vols. Taipei: Shih-chieh shu-chü 世界書局, 1962.

Chao Yi 趙翼. *Nien-erh shih cha-chi* 廿二史箚記 [Detailed records of the twenty histories]. Reprint. Taipei: Shih-chieh shu-chü, 1970.

Ch'en Yüan hsien-sheng chin nien-nien shih-hsüeh lun-chi 陳垣先生近廿年史學論集 [Compilation of historical essays of Mr. Ch'en Yüan in the past twenty years]. Hong Kong: Ch'ung-wen shu-tien, 1971.

Chin-shih jen-ming so-yin 金史人名索引 [Index of persons in the Chin dynastic history]. Peking: Chung-hua shu-chü, 1980.

Chou Liang-hsiao 周良霄. *Hu-pi-lieh* 忽必烈 [Khubilai]. Chi-lin: Chi-lin chiao-yü ch'u-pan-she 吉林教育出版社, 1986.

Chou Tsu-mo 周祖謨. "Sung-wang hou-shih Yüan chih ju-hsüeh chiao-shou" 宋亡後仕元之儒學教授 [Confucian teachings of those who served the Yüan after the fall of the Sung]. *Fu-jen hsüeh-chih* 輔仁學誌 14:12 (1946): 191–214.

Chu Hsieh 朱偰. *Yüan Ta-tu kung-tien t'u-k'ao* 元大都宮殿圖考 [Examination of the plans of the palaces of Ta-tu in Yüan times]. Shanghai: Shang-wu yin-shu-kuan 商務印書館, 1936.

Fang Hao 方豪. *Chung-hsi chiao-t'ung shih* 中西交通史 [History of the communication between China and the West]. Taipei: Chung-hua wen-hua ch'u-pan-she 中華文化出版社, 1952.

Fang Kuo-yü 方國瑜. "Kuan-yü Sai-tien-ch'ih fu-Tien kung-chi" 關於賽典赤撫滇功績 [Concerning Sai-tien-ch'ih's achievement in pacifying Yünnan]. *Jen-wen k'o-hsüeh tsa-chih* 人文科學雜誌 1 (1958): 47–50.

Feng Ch'eng-chün 馮承鈞. *Yüan-tai pai-hua pei* 元代白話碑 [Stelae in the colloquial language in the Yüan period]. Shanghai: Commercial Press, 1933.

Fu Shen 傅申. "Nü-ts'ang chia huang-tzu ta-chang kung-chu: Yüan-tai huang-shih shu-hua shou-ts'ang shih-lüeh" 女藏家皇姊大長公主—元代皇室書畫收藏史略 [Historical sketch of the collection of paintings of the Yüan emperors: the collection of Princess Sengge]. *Ku-kung chi-k'an* 故宮季刊 13:1 (Autumn 1978): 25–52.

"Gen no Sei So no kōgo" 元の世祖の皇后 [The empresses of Khubilai Khan of the Yüan]. *Rekishi kyōiku* 歷史教育 12:3 (1937): 680–83.

Haneda Tōru 羽田亨. *Genchō ekiden zakko* 元朝驛伝雜考 [The postal stations of the Yüan court]. Tokyo, 1930.

Hsia Kuang-nan 夏光南. *Yüan-tai Yün-nan shih-ti ts'ung-k'ao mu-lu* 元代雲南史地叢考目錄 [Catalog of historical places in Yünnan in Yüan times]. Shanghai: Chung-hua shu-chü, 1935.

Hsiao Ch'i-ch'ing 蕭啟慶. "Hu-pi-lieh shih-tai 'ch'ien-ti chiu-lü' k'ao" 忽必烈時代潛邸舊侶考 [Concerning Khubilai's group of advisers]. *Ta-lu tsa-chih* 大陸雜誌 25:1 (15 July 1962): 18–20.

———. *Hsi-yü-jen yü Yüan-ch'u cheng-chih* 西域人與元初政治 [Men from the West and early Yüan government]. Taipei: Kuo-li T'ai-wan Ta-hsüeh Wen-hsüeh-yüan 國立臺灣大學文學院, 1966.

Huang Ch'ing-lien 黃清連. *Yüan-tai hu-chi chih-tu yen-chiu* 元代戶計制度研究 [Studies on the system of population estimates of the Yüan period]. Taipei: Kuo-li T'ai-wan Ta-hsüeh wen-shih ts'ung-k'an 國立臺灣大學文史叢刊, 1977.

Huang Yung-ch'üan 黃湧泉. *Hang-chou Yüan-tai shih-k'u i-shu* 杭州元代石窟藝術 [The art of stone carving in Hang-chou in Yüan times]. Peking: Chung-kuo ku-tien i-shu ch'u-pan-she 中國古典藝術出版社, 1958.

Inosaki Takaoki 井崎隆興. "Gendai shasei no seijiteki kōsatsu" 元代社制の政治的考察 [Examination of the government of Yüan society]. *Tōyōshi kenkyū* 東洋史研究 15:1 (July 1956): 1–25.

———. "Gendai no take no senbai to sono shikō igi" 元代の竹の専売とその施行意義 [On the Yüan monopoly of bamboo and its significance]. *Tōyōshi kenkyū* 16:2 (September 1957): 29–47.

Ishida Mikinosuke 石田幹之助. "Gendai no kōgeika Nepāru no ōzoku 'A-ni-ko' no den ni tsuite" 元代の工芸家ネパールの王族阿尼哥の伝に就いて [On the life of the Nepalese craftsman A-ni-ko of Yüan times]. *Mōko gakuhō* 蒙古学報 2 (1941): 244–60.

———. "Gen no Jōto ni tsuite" 元の上都に就いて [On Shang-tu in Yüan times]. *Nihon Daigaku sōritsu shichijisshūnen kinen ronbunshū* 日本大学創立七十週年紀念論文集 1 (October 1960): 271–319.

Jagchid Sechin. "Shuo *Yüan shih* chung ti 'Pi-she-ch'ih' ping chien-lun Yüan-ch'u ti 'Chung-shu ling'" 說元史中的必闍赤並兼論元初的中書令 [On the secretaries of the *Yüan shih* and the "Chung-shu ling" of the early Yüan]. *Bulletin of the Institute of China Border Area Studies* 2 (July 1971): 19–113.

———. "Meng-ku ti-kuo shih-tai tui T'u-fan ti ching-lüeh" 蒙古帝國時代對土番的經略 [On the Mongol khans' campaigns in Tibet]. *Bulletin of the Institute of China Border Area Studies* 2 (July 1971): 115–54.

———. "Meng-ku yü Hsi-tsang li-shih shang ti hsiang-hu kuan-hsi ho t'a tui chung-yüan ti ying-hsiang" 蒙古與西藏歷史上的相互關係和它對中原的影響 [The historical relationship of Mongolia and Tibet and its influence on China]. *Bulletin of the Institute of China Border Area Studies* 6 (July 1975): 25–56.

———. *Meng-ku yü Hsi-tsang li-shih kuan-hsi chih yen-chiu* 蒙古與西藏歷史關係之研究 [Studies on the historical relationship of Tibet and Mongolia]. Taipei: Cheng-chung shu-chü 正中書局, 1978.

Kanda Kiichirō 神田喜一郎. "Gendai no Bunshū no fūryū ni tsuite" 元代の文宗の風流について [On the taste of the Yüan emperor Wen-tsung]. *Haneda Hakushi shōju kinen tōyōshi ronsō* 羽田博士頌寿記念東洋史論叢, pp. 477–88. Kyoto, 1950.

K'ao-ku 考古 1 (1972): 19–28; 4 (1972): 54–57; 6 (1972): 2–15, 25–34.

Katsufuji Takeshi 勝藤猛. *Fubirai Kan* 忽必烈汗 [Khubilai Khan]. Tokyo, 1966.

Kobayashi Shinzō 小林新三. "'Shih-tsu' to Jusha" 世祖と儒者 [Khubilai Khan and the Confucians]. *Shichō* 史潮 47 (1952): 45–50.

Komai Kazuchika 駒井和愛. "Gen no Jōto narabi ni Daito no heimen ni tsuite" 元の上都並びに大都の平面に就いて [On the ground plans of Ta-tu and Shang-tu of the Yüan]. *Tōa ronsō* 東亜論叢 3 (1940): 129–39.

Koyama Fujio 小山富士夫. "'Pa-ssu-pa' moji aru Shina kotōji," 八思巴文字ある支那古陶磁 [Chinese porcelains with 'Phags-pa writing]. *Gasetsu* 画記 1 (1937): 23–31.

Kunishita Hirosato 圀下大慧. "Gensho ni okeru teishitsu to Zensō to no kankei ni tsuite" 元初に於ける帝室と禅僧との関係に就いて [On the relationship of the early Yüan emperors and the Buddhist monks]. *Tōyō gakuhō* 東洋学報 11 (1921): 547–77; 12 (1922): 89–124, 245–49.

Kuwabara Jitsuzō 桑原騭藏. "Rōshi Kekokyō" 老子化胡経 [On Lao Tzu's *Hua-hu ching*]. *Geibun* 芸文 1:9 (1910): 1–14.

Lao Yen-hsüan 勞延煊. "Lun Yüan-tai ti Kao-li nu-li yü ying-ch'ieh" 論元代的高麗奴隸與媵妾 [On Korean female slaves and concubines in Yüan times]. *Ch'ing-chu Li Chi hsien-sheng ch'i-shih-sui lun wen-chi* 慶祝李濟先生七十歲論文集, pp. 1005–31. Taipei: Ch'ing-ke hsüeh-pao she-yin hang 清華學報社印行, 1967.

Li Chieh 黎傑. *Yüan shih* 元史 [History of the Yüan]. Hong Kong: Hai-ch'iao ch'u-pan-she 海僑出版社, 1962.

Li Fu-t'ung 李符桐. "Wei-wu-erh jen tui-yü Yüan-ch'ao chien-kuo chih kung-hsien" 畏兀兒人對於元朝建國之貢獻 [The contributions of the Uighurs to the establishment of the Yüan court]. In *Shih-hsüeh lun-chi* 史學論集. Taipei, 1976.

Li Ssu-shun 李思純. *Yüan-shih hsüeh* 元史學 [Studies on Yüan history]. Taipei: Hua-shih ch'u-pan-she 華世出版社, 1974.

Li T'ang 李唐. *Yüan Shih-tsu* 元世祖 [Khubilai Khan of the Yüan]. Taipei: Ho-lo t'u-shu ch'u-pan-she 河洛圖書出版社, 1978.

Liu Ming-shu 劉銘恕. "Yüan-tai An-nan chin-kung chih tai-shen chin-jen," 元代安南進貢之代身金人 [The substitute gold man sent as tribute by Annam during the Yüan]. *Bulletin of Chinese Studies* 8 (1948): 93–98.

———. "Yüan Hsi-yü ch'ü-chia A-li Yao-ch'ing fu-tzu" 元西域曲家阿里耀卿父子 [A-li Yao-ch'ing and his son, lyric poets of the Western Regions during the Yüan]. *Bulletin of Chinese Studies* 8 (1948): 105–09.

Lü Shih-p'eng 呂士朋. "Yüan-tai chih Chung-Yüeh kuan-hsi" 元代之中越關係 [The relations of China and Annam in Yüan times]. *Tung-hai hsüeh-pao* 東海學報 8:1 (January 1967): 11–49.

Maeda Naonori 前田直典. "Gendai no kahei tan-i" 元代の貨幣単位 [Monetary units in the Yüan]. *Shakai keizai shigaku* 社会経済史学 14:4 (1944): 1–22.

Maejima Shinji 前島信次. "Senshū no Perushiyajin to Ho Jukō" 泉州の波斯人と蒲寿庚 [The Persians of Ch'üan-chou and P'u Shou-keng]. *Shigaku* 史学 25:3 (1952): 256–321.

Matsumoto Yoshimi 松本善海. "Gendai ni okeru shasei no sōritsu" 元代における社制の倉立 [Foundations of the *she* system in the Yüan period]. *Tōhō gakuhō* 東方学報 (Tokyo) 11:1 (March 1940): 328–37.

Meng Ssu-ming 蒙思明. *Yüan-tai she-hui chieh-chi chih-tu* 元代社會階級制度 [The social class system in Yüan times]. Reprint. Hong Kong: Lung-men shu-tien 龍門書店, 1967.

Murakami Masatsugu 村上正二. "Genchō ni okeru senfushi to kandatsu" 元朝に於ける泉府司と斡脱 [The Ch'üan-fu ssu and the *Ortogh* during the Yüan]. *Tōhō gakuhō* 東方学報 13:1 (May 1942): 143–96.

Niwa Tomosaburō 丹羽友三郎. "Gen Sei So Jaba ensei zakkō—toku ni gunshi narabi ni kaisen sū ni tsuite" 元世祖ジャバ遠征雑考—特に軍士

なろびに海船数について [Notes on the numbers of the armed forces sent to Java by Khubilai Khan]. *Shigaku kenkyū* 史学研究 53 (1954): 57–63.

Nogami Shunjō 野上俊静. "Gendai Dō Butsu nikyō no kakushitsu" 元代道仏二教の確執 [The hostility between Taoism and Buddhism in Yüan times]. *Ōtani Daigaku kenkyū nenpō* 大谷大学研究年報 2 (1943): 213–65.

———. "Gen no senseiin ni tsuite" 元の宣政院について [On the *Hsüan-cheng yüan* of the Yüan]. In *Haneda hakushi shōju kinen tōyōshi ronsō* 羽田博士頌寿記念東洋史論叢, pp. 779–95. Kyoto, 1950.

Otagi Matsuo 愛宕松男. "Gendai shikimokujin ni kansuru ikkōsatsu" 元代色目人に関する一考察 [On the *Se-mu-jen* of the Yüan period]. *Mōko gakuhō* 蒙古学報 1 (1937): 33–67.

———. *Fubirai Kan* 忽必烈汗 [Khubilai Khan]. Tokyo, 1941.

———. "Ri Dan no hanran to sono seijiteki igi" 李璮の叛乱と其の政治的意義 [The rebellion of Li T'an and its political significance]. *Tōyōshi kenkyū* 東洋史研究 6:4 (August–September 1941): 253–78.

———. "Mōkojin seiken-chika no Kanchi ni okeru hanseki no mondai" 蒙古人政権治下の漢地に於ける版籍の問題 [The census of Northern China taken by the Mongol government]. *Haneda hakushi shōju kinen tōyōshi ronsō* 羽田博士頌寿記念東洋史論叢, pp. 383–429. Kyoto, 1950.

Saguchi Tōru 佐口透. "Mongoru-jin shihai jidai no Uiguristan" モンゴル人支配時代のウィグリスタン [Uighuristan at the time of Mongol rule]. *Shigaku zasshi* 史学雑誌 8 (August 1943): 788–855; 9 (September 1943): 988–1012.

Shao Hsün-cheng 邵循正. "*Yüan shih La-t'e-chi-shih Meng-ku ti-shih* shih-hsi so-chi Shih-tsu hou-fei k'ao" 元史拉特集史蒙古帝室世系所記世祖后妃考 [On the khatuns and concubines of Khubilai Khan as mentioned in *Yüan shih, Jami'-at Tawarikh,* and *Moezz-et-ansab*]. *Ch'ing-hua hsüeh-pao* 清華學報 11:4 (October 1936): 969–75.

Shimazaki Akira 島崎昌. "Gendai no kaikyōjin Saitenseki Tanshitei" 元代の回教人賽典赤瞻思丁 [On the Muslim Saiyid Ajall Shams al-Dīn of the Yüan]. *Kaikyō ken* 回教圈 (July 1939): 562–71.

Sun K'o-k'uan 孫克寛. *Yüan-ch'u ju-hsüeh* 元初儒學 [On the Confucian scholars of early Yüan]. Taipei: I-wen yin-shu kuan 藝文印書館, 1953.

———. "Yüan-ch'u Li T'an shih-pien ti fen-hsi" 元初李璮事變的分析 [An analysis of the Li T'an rebellion of the early Yüan]. *Ta-lu tsa-chih* 大陸雜誌 13:8 (1956): 7–15.

———. *Sung Yüan Tao-chiao chih fa-chan* 宋元道教之發展 [The development of Taoism in the Sung and Yüan]. Taichung: Tung-hai ta-hsüeh 東海大學, 1965.

———. *Yüan-tai Tao-chiao chih fa-chan* 元代道教之發展 [The development of Taoism in the Yüan period]. Taichung: Tung-hai ta-hsüeh, 1968.

———. *Meng-ku Han-chün yü Han-wen-hua yen-chiu* 蒙古漢軍與漢文化研究 [Researches on the Mongols' Chinese troops and Chinese culture]. Taichung: Tung-hai ta-hsüeh, 1970.

Ta-lu tsa-chih shih-hsüeh ts'ung-shu: Liao Chin Yüan shih yen-chiu lun-chi 大陸雜誌史學叢書：遼金元史研究論集 [Collection of articles on Liao,

Chin, and Yüan history in *Ta-lu tsa-chih*]. Taipei, 1967.

Taishō shinshū daizōkyō 大正新修大藏經 [Newly edited Tripitaka of the Taishō era]. Tokyo, 1924–32.

Tamura Jitsuzō 田村実造. "Ari Buka no ran ni tsuite" アリブカの乱について [On the rebellion of Arigh Böke]. *Tōyōshi kenkyū* 東洋史研究 14:3 (November 1955): 1–16.

Tamura Jitsuzō et al. *Ajia-shi kōza* アジア史講座 [Course on Asian history]. 6 vols. Tokyo: Iwasaki shoten 岩崎書店, 1955–57.

———. *Genshi goi shūsei* 元史語彙集成 [Glossary of the *Yüan shih*]. 3 vols. Kyoto, 1961–63.

T'ao Hsi-sheng 陶希聖. "Yüan-tai fo-ssu t'ien-yüan chi shang-tien" 元代佛寺田園及商店 [Lands and shops of the Buddhist temples in the Yüan period]. *Shih-huo* 食貨 1:3 (1935): 0108–14.

Tazaka Kōdō 田坂興道. *Chūgoku ni okeru kaikyō no denrai to sono kōtsū* 中国における回教の伝来とその弘通 [The transmittal and growth of Islam in China]. Tokyo: Tōyō Bunko ronsō 東洋文庫論叢 43:1–2, 1964.

Ts'ai Mei-piao 蔡美彪. *Yüan-tai pai-hua-pei chi-lu* 元代白話碑集錄 [Collection of stele in the colloquial language of the Yüan period]. Peking: K'o-hsüeh ch'u-pan-she 科學出版社, 1955.

Uematsu Tadashi 植松正. "Gensho kōnan ni okeru chōzei taisei ni tsuite" 元初江南における徴税体制について [On the system of tax collection south of the Yangtze in the early Yüan]. *Tōyōshi kenkyū* 東洋史研究 23:1 (June 1974): 27–62.

Umehara Kaoru 梅原郁. "Gendai saeki-hō shōron" 元代差役法小論 [On the forced labor system of the Yüan]. *Tōyōshi kenkyū* 東洋史研究 33:4 (March 1965): 329–427.

Umehara Kaoru and Kinugawa Tsuyoshi 衣川強, eds. *Ryō Kin Gen jin denki sakuin* 遼金元人伝記索引 [Index of biographies of men of Liao, Chin, and Yüan]. Kyoto, 1972.

Wada Sei 和田清. *Tōashi kenkyū: Manshū hen* 東亜史研究満洲編 [Studies on East Asian history: Manchuria]. Tokyo: Tōyō Bunko 東洋文庫, 1955.

Wang Te-i et al. 王德毅. *Sung-jen chuan-chi tzu-liao so-yin* 宋人傳記資料索引 [Index of biographical materials on men of Sung]. 6 vols. Taipei: Ting-wen shu-chü 鼎文書局, 1977.

———. *Yüan-jen chuan-chi tzu-liao so-yin* 元人傳記資料索引 [Index of biographical materials on men of Yüan]. 5 vols. Taipei: Hsin-wen feng ch'u-pan kung-ssu 新文豐出版公司, 1979–82.

Wang Wei-ch'eng 王維誠. "Lao-tzu hua-hu-shuo k'ao-cheng" 老子化胡說考證 [Examination of Lao-tzu's *Hua-hu*]. *Kuo-hsüeh chi-k'an* 國學季刊 4:2 (1934): 44–55.

Weng Tu-chien 翁獨健. "Wo-t'o tsa-k'ao" 斡脫雜考 [On the *Ortogh*]. *Yen-ching hsüeh-pao* 燕京學報 29 (June 1941): 201–18.

Wu Chung-han 吳重翰. "Yüan Ming Wo-tsei ju-k'ou yü Chung-kuo chiao-tsei ta-shih piao" 元明倭賊入寇與中國剿賊大事表 [Tables of Japanese pirates' attacks and China's defeat of these robbers in Yüan and Ming]. *Nan-feng* 南風 1 (1940): 12–19.

Yanai Wataru 箭內亘. *Mōkoshi kenkyū* 蒙古史研究 [Studies of Mongol

history]. Tokyo, 1930.

─────. *Yüan-tai ching-lüeh tung-pei k'ao* 元代經略東北考 [On the north-eastern campaigns of the Yüan period]. Trans. by Ch'en Chieh 陳捷 and Ch'en Ch'ing-ch'üan 陳清泉. Taipei: Commercial Press, 1963.

Yang Na 楊訥. "Yüan-tai nung-ts'un she-chih yen-chiu" 元代農村社制研究 [Studies on the agricultural *she* system of the Yüan period]. *Li-shih yen-chiu* 歷史研究 4 (1965): 117–34.

Yao Ta-li 姚大力. "Nai-yen chih luan-tsa k'ao" 乃顏之亂雜考 [On Nayan's rebellion]. In *Yüan-shih chi pei-fang min-tsu-shih yen-chiu chi-kan* (Nan-ching University) 元史及北方民族史研究集刊, pp. 74–82. 1983.

Yao Ts'ung-wu 姚從吾. "Hu-pi-lieh han tui-yü Han-hua t'ai-tu ti fen-hsi" 忽必烈汗對於漢化態度的分析 [An analysis of Khubilai Khan's attitude toward Chinese culture]. *Ta-lu tsa-chih* 11:1 (July 1955): 22–32.

─────. "Yüan Hsien-tsung (Meng-ko han) ti ta-chü cheng-Shu yü t'a tsai Ho-chou Tiao-yü Ch'eng ti chan-ssu" 元憲宗(蒙哥汗)的大舉征蜀與他在合州釣魚城的戰死 [The great expedition against Shu led by Emperor Hsien-tsung (Möngke Khan) of the Yüan and his death at the battle of Tiao-yü Cheng near Ho-chou]. *Wen-shih che hsüeh-pao* 文史哲學報 14 (October 1964): 61–85.

─────. "Hu-pi-lieh han yü Meng-ko han chih-li Han-ti ti ch'i-chien" 忽必烈汗與蒙哥汗治理漢地的岐見 [The differences of opinion of Khubilai Khan and Möngke Khan on ruling North China]. *Wen-shih che hsüeh-pao* 16 (1967): 223–36.

─────. "Ch'eng Chü-fu yü Hu-pi-lieh p'ing-Sung i-hou ti an-ting nan-jen wen t'i" 程鉅夫與忽必烈平宋以後的安定南人問題 [Ch'eng Chü-fu and Khubilai's policy of conciliation of the Chinese after the overthrow of the Sung]. *Wen-shih che hsüeh-pao* 17 (June 1968): 353–79.

Yen Chien-pi 閻簡弼. "Nan Sung liu-ling i-shih cheng-ming chi-chu ts'uan-kung fa-hui nien-tai k'ao" 南宋六陵遺事正名暨諸攢宮發毀年代攷 [The pillage of the imperial tombs of the Southern Sung dynasty]. *Yen-ching hsüeh-pao* 30 (1946): 27–50.

Yoshikawa Kōjirō 吉川幸次郎. "Gen no shotei no bungaku" 元の諸帝の文学 [The literary bent of the Yüan emperors]. *Tōyōshi kenkyū* 8:3 (May–June 1943): 27–38.

Yüan Chi 袁冀. *Yüan-shih yen-chiu lun-chi* 元史研究論集 [Collected essays of studies on Yüan history]. Taipei: Commercial Press, 1973.

Index

Compositor: Asco Trade Typesetting Ltd
Text: Apollo 11/13
Display: Apollo
Printer: Vail-Ballou Press
Binder: Vail-Ballou Press